Twentieth Century America

VOLUME 3 WORLD WAR II AND SINCE

BY DAVID A. SHANNON

UNIVERSITY OF VIRGINIA

MAPS BY WILLIS R. HEATH

RAND McNALLY & COMPANY / CHICAGO

RAND McNALLY HISTORY SERIES
Fred Harvey Harrington, *Advisory Editor*

SECOND EDITION 1969

To Molly and Sarah

Preface

TEXTBOOK PREFACES ARE AN ODD LITERARY GENRE. Many of them spin an elaborate intellectual justification for the study of their subject. This one shall not do that. I take it as self-evident and accepted that the recent history of the United States well merits serious study. Some textbook prefaces describe in detail what is in the book and the author's philosophical assumptions. For what is in this book, I refer the reader to the Table of Contents and to the chapters themselves. My philosophic assumptions will become apparent to the discerning reader.

But I do want to make clear that the historian, perhaps in recent history especially, necessarily makes judgments. What the historian brings to his subject from his background and values affects his product, even if only in what he decides should receive emphasis and what should be rejected. I am no exception. Some parts of this work have a strong point of view, but I have endeavored to be fair and judicious. Yet students should approach this book—indeed, all books—with an appraising and critical attitude as well as an open mind.

Prefaces frequently tell the story behind the volume. This textbook has no unusual background. It is intended primarily for students in college courses in recent American history. I have taught such courses for the past several years, and this book grew from that experience. Aimed primarily at the college classroom, it developed in a college classroom. Explanations, examples, emphases, and methods that I have found successful in my own teaching are employed here.

Finally, prefaces usually acknowledge the help that the author received. I shall be orthodox and do likewise because I want publicly to express my gratitude. Professors Arthur Dudden of Bryn Mawr College and Warren Susman of Rutgers University read the manuscript for the publisher, saved me from several errors of omission and commission, and offered many useful suggestions. Dr. Willis Heath of the University of Washington applied his fertile mind and skill to the maps. Mr. Paul Vanderbilt, curator of the Iconography Collection of the Wisconsin State Historical Society, was of great help to me in the selection of the illustrations. My wife Jane shared in the book's development from first to last. Lastly, my students in their responses sharpened and modified many of my ideas.

DAVID A. SHANNON

October, 1962

Preface to the Second Edition

FOR REASONS THAT ARE SOMETIMES OBSCURE TO THEIR PROFESSORS, students like to have their history courses "come down to the present." The updating of this work should help to satisfy that student desire since it now treats most of the 1960's, that era of assassination, strife in the streets, sharpened social conflict, accelerated social change, and the most unpopular foreign war since the Polk administration.

Looking over the preface to the first edition of *Twentieth Century America*, I see nothing from which I now dissent, but I wish to repeat my earlier admonition to read this book and others both critically and open-mindedly. Historical understanding, which is no easy task, comes to those who read history actively rather than passively, questioning rather than blindly accepting.

Despite the care I have put into this work and the help of its editors and of my wife, there may be slips and typographical errors. I will be pleased if readers will call these to my attention.

D. A. S.

November, 1968

Table of Contents

VOLUME 3 WORLD WAR II AND SINCE

CHAPTER TWENTY-ONE

Depression Diplomacy, 1929-1938

THE GREAT DEPRESSION ULTIMATELY HAD TO AFFECT AMERICA'S relations with other countries. The central fact of the depression was. in either the foreground or the background of developments in American foreign policy from 1930 until Pearl Harbor.

Economic conditions forced both Hoover and Roosevelt to make modifications in the nation's foreign economic policies, although neither departed seriously from traditional objectives. Hoover faced a direct effect of the depression in the crisis over European reparations and war-debt payments. The depression indirectly was a factor in the Japanese Manchurian crisis confronting Hoover since Japan had decided to take a militarist course partly because of economic disruption. Roosevelt faced the problem during his first months in office of whether to combat the depression through international cooperation or through national policies at odds with the desires of other nations. His reciprocal trade program was a frontal attack upon the depression, his recognition of the Soviet Union had economic motives, and his headaches over German and Italian militarism and expansion were due, ultimately, to the depression's effects in Europe.

America's Foreign Economic Policies

During the 1920's there had evolved an irrational but, in the short run, workable scheme of loans, reparations, and war debts. American investors, through Wall Street bankers, lent money to Germany which enabled that country to pay its reparations to the Allies and which in turn enabled the Allies to keep up payments on their war debts to the United States Treasury (see pp. 241–245). The Wall Street crash brought the circular financial complex to an abrupt halt. As the flow of American loans to Germany dried up, the stoppage of reparations and war debt payments was only a matter of time. If the American tariff wall had been lowered, thereby stimulating European imports and building up dollar exchange funds in Europe, payment of war debts might have continued. However, Congress raised the tariff with the Hawley-Smoot Act in June, 1930.

The international financial crisis came to a head in the spring of 1931. In March, Germany and Austria announced their intention to form a customs union. France denounced the proposal as the first step toward union of the two countries which the peace treaties forbade, and eventually the World Court ruled against such a customs arrangement. French bankers recalled millions in short-term loans to German and Austrian banks which were thereby placed on the brink of ruin. In May, the largest bank of Austria, the Kreditanstalt, announced its imminent failure, and it was saved only by the actions of the Austrian government. A large bank of North Germany did go under due to the strain. Far more was involved than the failure or saving of just a bank. If a major financial institution such as the Kreditanstalt closed its doors, foreign holders of assets in Kreditanstalt would have to compensate for their loss by calling back other funds, thereby jeopardizing the whole economic and political stability of Central Europe.

President Hoover made a startling proposal on June 20. Congress was not then in session, but after consulting with congressional leaders from both parties, Hoover proposed a one-year moratorium, or postponement, in the payment of international obligations. Subject to the approval of Congress, Hoover announced that the United States would not demand payments on war debts for a year beginning July 1, 1931, if other governments would do the same. Hoover's hope was that in a year free of reparations commitments Germany and Austria could overcome the financial crisis. The European nations agreed, although France resisted for three weeks and thereby worsened the German situation.

When Congress convened late in 1931, Hoover submitted the moratorium for approval and urged the re-establishment of the World War Foreign Debt Commission with authority to negotiate further on foreign debts. Congress approved the moratorium but balked at any step that might further reduce the war debts. So far as Congress was concerned, the United States would expect to receive full payment on the next due date after the end of the moratorium, December, 1932.

Hoping for a long-term settlement, Germany and her creditors met at Lausanne, Switzerland, in June and July, 1932, and reached an agreement by which about 90 per cent of the remaining German reparations bill would be cancelled if the former Allies could get corresponding relief from their creditors. In other words, since the United States was the creditor at the ultimate end of the line, ratification of the Lausanne agreement was contingent upon American cooperation. But Congress was in no mood to change its position. After the 1932 election, Hoover vainly pleaded with Roosevelt to use his influence with Congress. When he got no results, Hoover sent the debtor nations notices of payments due December 15, 1932. Most of the debtors met this payment, but except for some subsequent token payments these were the last payments on the war debt. (Finland was a special exception. She had an export surplus to the United States and was able to continue paying her small obligation.) In April, 1934, Congress passed a law sponsored by Senator Hiram Johnson of California designed to punish debtor governments in default. The Johnson Act made it illegal to sell within the United States the bonds or other securities of foreign governments, or their subdivisions, which were in default on debts owed to the American federal government. The measure did not stimulate any further payments from depressed Europe. The Attorney-General later ruled that token payments did not prevent a country's being considered in default under the terms of the Johnson Act; thereafter, even token payments stopped.

Despite Roosevelt's failure to act on Hoover's urging to persuade Congress to accept war debt reductions—motivated probably by political considerations—and despite his "bombshell message" to the World Economic Conference at London in June, 1933 (see pp. 327–328), Roosevelt clearly, at least from late 1933, considered the revival of foreign trade as a direct assault on the depression. In seeking to stimulate American exports and to find foreign markets for American goods as a means of getting the domestic economy on its feet again, Roosevelt was operating within a tradition at least as old as the depression of the 1890's. In 1895, a group of industrialists had organized the National Association of Manufacturers, and the original purpose of the NAM had been to stimulate exports and thereby ease the economic difficulties within the nation that came from the panic of 1893. The search for foreign markets and investments had played a major role in the American decision to embark upon a colonial imperialist role later in the decade. Exports of munitions to the Allies after the outbreak of war in Europe had lifted another depression, and the Webb-Pomerene Act had been designed to give American industrialists a competitive position in foreign markets by exempting their overseas operations from the antitrust laws. Oddly enough, one of the Roosevelt administration's first efforts to stimulate exports involved recognition of the Soviet Union, since 1917 a prize exhibit in American conservatives' chamber of horrors.

It was a painful fact in the early depression that the Soviet economy continued to grow while the western economy sagged. In the fall of 1932, about one hundred thousand Americans applied for jobs in Russia through Amtorg, the Russian foreign trading organization. Hoover was fully committed to continue the nonrecognition policy toward Russia, but he did yield a little when the Reconstruction Finance Corporation underwrote some cotton exports to the USSR. Roosevelt had not committed himself to nonrecognition, and businessmen from both parties put considerable pressure on the State Department to recognize the Soviet Union so that exports to that country would be facilitated. There were other considerations in Roosevelt's mind besides a foreign market (the logic of recognizing a government of sixteen years' standing, for example, and a hope that recognition might hamper Japan in Manchuria), and he began a correspondence with Soviet leaders looking toward formal recognition. The Soviet government agreed to refrain from spreading propaganda designed to overthrow the United States government, to grant religious freedom and protection in its courts to American nationals living in Russia, and to negotiate the question of unpaid prerevolutionary debts and claims. The United States recognized Russia on November 16, 1933; the Soviet Union's first ambassador to Washington was Maxim Litvinov, hardly a typical Russian leader of the 1930's in that he was Jewish and well acquainted with the western world. The negotiations on debts and claims came to nothing. Nor did Russian-inspired Communist propaganda cease, although technically the Russians could truthfully say that the American Communist party had its affiliation with the Third International, or Comintern, rather than directly with the Soviet government. Actually, the distinction was not real: the Comintern was a willing tool of the Russian government. Nor did the fond hopes of American businessmen to send large orders to the Soviet materialize in any significant way.

The Export-Import Bank, a government agency that later played an important role in American foreign economic policy, developed directly from the hope to sell to the newly recognized Soviet government. American business firms hoping to export or make investments abroad sometimes found that private bankers considered the risks too great to undertake the financing. Such was the case with many proposed deals with the Russians. Roosevelt established the first Export-Import Bank under National Industrial Recovery Act authority early in 1934 to finance exports to the USSR. Its original funds came from the Reconstruction Finance Corporation. When the negotiations with the Russians over the debt fell through, the first Export-Import Bank became inactive. Early in 1935, Congress set up "Ex-Im" on a two-year basis, renewing its life each biennium until it made the Bank a permanent independent agency in 1945. By 1938 the Bank began to make development loans to underdeveloped nations. A $5 million loan to Haiti in that year went for improved roads, agricultural experiment stations, and drainage facilities. A $25 million loan to China for the Burma Road, from Chungking to Burma, strategically important in World War II, strengthened China's position against the Japanese. Besides the obvious benefits to the countries involved—helping them to create the capital prerequisite for a more advanced economy—these loans helped to create new foreign markets for American products. Thus "Ex-Im" gradually changed from underwriting of exports to already existing markets to active creation of foreign markets in economically backward areas.

Secretary of State Cordell Hull's reciprocal trade agreement program was another facet of the New Deal's assault on the depression by stimulating foreign trade. Indeed, the purpose of the June, 1934, law as stated in its preamble was "expanding foreign markets for the products of the United States (as a means of assisting in the present emergency . . .)." The idea of reciprocity was an old one, and Hull, a traditional low-tariff southerner, pushed the idea vigorously when he took the State Department's direction. He had hoped that reciprocal trade agreements would come from the fruitless London Economic Conference in 1933. Hull saw reciprocity as a precondition to world peace. Commercial rivalry, as he viewed it, jeopardized peaceful international relations, and reciprocity would reduce commercial rivalry.

The Reciprocal Trade Agreements Act of 1934 empowered the executive branch for a period of three years to negotiate agreements with other countries to change by as much as one-half the existing American duties on imports in exchange for reciprocal concessions by the other nation on its duties on

American products. Such agreements did not need Senate ratification to become effective. The law further directed that such agreements contain a "most favored nation" clause. That is to say, if an agreement with Venezuela reduced United States duties on certain imports, the United States would be obligated to reduce its duties on those same commodities imported from any other country that did not discriminate against American trade. Venezuela would have the same obligation. Thus, for the commodities included in reciprocal trade agreements, there developed a wide tendency toward lower tariffs. Congress has extended executive authority to conclude such agreements by two- and three-year periods since 1934.

By the spring of 1939, the State Department had negotiated twenty-one reciprocal trade agreements, not only with Latin American nations and Canada, but with the more important non-Fascist West European nations as well. The precise effect of these agreements on trade and the business cycle was impossible to determine since there were several other variables affecting international trade, but it was clear that until the recession of late 1937 and 1938 American exports increased more rapidly than the total exports of all nations. The United States increased its relative share in world markets. This was because every trade agreement concluded affected America's important exports while few agreements affected the important exports of other countries. The share of American imports from agreement countries increased more rapidly than those from nonagreement countries, and the Latin American economies became more closely tied with the United States.

"Yanquis" as "Good Neighbors"

Roosevelt in his first inaugural address said, "In the field of world policy I would dedicate this Nation to the policy of the good neighbor—the neighbor who resolutely respects himself and, because he does so, respects the rights of others." From this vague, even meaningless, statement about foreign relations in general came the label used to describe the New Deal's extension of the better manners in Latin American matters instituted during the 1920's.

The Seventh International Conference of American States was to meet at Montevideo, Uruguay, in December, 1933. Latin American nations were eager to get through the conference a resolution condemning intervention by one country into the affairs of another, a proposal aimed particularly against the United States. In 1930, the State Department had published the Clark memorandum which denied that the Monroe Doctrine could be used as justification for American intervention, but at the last conference, in 1928, Charles Evans Hughes as head of the United States delegation had refused to allow a nonintervention resolution even to be discussed. The United States had by no means renounced intervention as a Latin American policy.

Secretary Hull, head of the American delegation to the Montevideo conference, surprised the Latin American delegations and fully accepted the nonintervention position. The conference went on to write a Convention on the Rights and Duties of States that included the statement, "No state has the right to intervene in the internal or external affairs of another." The United

States signed the convention. Two days later, the President in a speech at home said, ". . . the definite policy of the United States from now on is one opposed to armed intervention." In December, 1936, at a special Latin American conference at Buenos Aires, Argentina (a meeting initiated in Washington which the President himself attended), Hull signed a protocol which forbade intervention "directly or indirectly, and for whatever reason." The Senate approved the protocol without reservation and without even a record vote. Nonintervention was the essence of the Good Neighbor policy, but another aspect of it was increased trade between the northern Colossus and the Latin nations. Hull at Montevideo helped to prepare the way for the yet-to-be-authorized reciprocal trade agreements by getting a resolution through the convention calling for lower trade barriers.

Simultaneously with its renunciations of intervention, the administration moved to make the Monroe Doctrine multilateral. Enunciated by President James Monroe in 1823, the Doctrine had declared the United States opposed further European colonization in the New World and further European "interposition" into the affairs of American nations. The United States had invoked the Monroe Doctrine upon several occasions. But it had been a unilateral policy of Washington alone. Now, after 1935, when Mussolini's Italy and Hitler's Germany threatened the peace of the world, the United States sought to commit all of Latin America to the Monroe Doctrine's principles.

It was in pursuit of this intention that the administration initiated in 1935 the calling of the Buenos Aires conference. No conference was scheduled until 1938. At the conference the delegates signed documents that called upon Latin American nations to consult one another in situations that formerly would have brought the United States to invoke the Monroe Doctrine unilaterally. Consultation in the face of any threat from outside America to the peace and independence of an American state did not necessarily mean that action would follow, but the step was clearly in the direction of "continentalizing" the old Doctrine.

The Buenos Aires documents did not stipulate just how consultation should be done. At the next regularly scheduled international Conference of American States at Lima, Peru, in December, 1938, the delegates agreed that the foreign ministers of any of the twenty-one American states could call a meeting to consider methods of meeting any outside threat. The American states did in fact meet under this plan: at Panama just after the outbreak of war in Europe in the fall of 1939; at Havana, Cuba, in the summer of 1940 after the fall of France; and at Rio de Janeiro, Brazil, in January, 1942, after Pearl Harbor. All of the Latin American powers followed the United States into World War II, although some followed late and reluctantly. The Good Neighbor policy, in effect, paid off in a time of crisis.

The United States, with but one partial exception in the case of Cuba, observed well the nonintervention policy it had adopted. Most of the Cuban partial exception occurred before the Montevideo conference. Cuba's president, Gerardo Machado, led a tyrannical government over that politically unhappy island when Roosevelt took office. Machado had suppressed a rebellion in 1931 and was still using dictatorial powers in a futile effort to stamp out his opposition. Roosevelt's intervention was diplomatic rather than military, although parts of the fleet did go to Cuba for the announced purpose of being ready to evacuate United States citizens if necessary. The proximity of naval power unquestionably lent weight to the statements of Sumner Welles, the Foreign Service officer who had recently been appointed ambassador to Cuba and whose ostensible mission was to mediate between Machado and his opponents. Welles's real mission was to get Machado to resign. This Welles accomplished in the summer of 1933 with the support of some Cuban army officers. For the rest of the year, the United States helped select the next Cuban president by withholding recognition from those of whom it did not approve. In January, 1934, Carlos Mendieta became president of Cuba with the blessing of the United States, and thereafter intervention ceased. Four months later the United States and Cuba negotiated a new treaty which abrogated the Platt Amendment of 1903. In other words, the United States renounced its treaty right to intervene in Cuban affairs and to supervise Cuban finances. The Senate ratified the treaty without a dissenting vote only two days after it was signed. The American naval base at Guantanamo Bay was to remain until the right to maintain it was withdrawn by mutual action.

The United States pulled back elsewhere in the Caribbean during the Roosevelt years. FDR inherited a problem in Haiti from the Hoover administration. Hoover had sent an investigating commission to Haiti in 1930 when internal difficulties flared up there. The commission recommended new elections, and Haiti held its first elections since World War I. Americans relinquished control of Haitian public works to the islanders. A treaty in the fall of 1932 provided for withdrawing American marines and relinquishing control of the Haitian constabulary but for continuation of United States control of Haiti's finances until its American-held bonds were paid off. The Haitian legislature rejected the treaty, objecting to United States financial control. Roosevelt in the summer of 1933 reached an executive agreement with Haiti. The constabulary was to be controlled entirely by Haitians after October 1, 1934, and the marines were to be withdrawn within a month thereafter. Through an American-appointed "fiscal representative," United States control over the customs was to remain, although less obviously, until the bonds were satisfied. Roosevelt in fact withdrew the marines in the summer of 1934, the first time in decades that American marines were not stationed somewhere within the boundaries of a nominally sovereign Caribbean state. In 1941, the United States government withdrew the "fiscal representative." In 1940, a treaty with the Dominican Republic, at the other end of Santo Domingo, relinquished American control of Dominican customs but imposed a lien on the little state's general revenues until its bonds were discharged. An American remained as collector of the customs in Nicaragua until its American loans were repaid in 1944.

It was Mexico far more than any other Latin American nation that put the Good Neighbor policy to the test. More dollars were involved in the Mexican crisis than elsewhere in the Caribbean. The Mexican revolution progressed in a series of waves, each of them demanding foreign withdrawal from Mexican oil fields and other resources and then subsiding. A wave had subsided in 1927 and 1928 when the clever Dwight Morrow had been the American ambassador. Another wave began to build in 1934 with the election of Lázaro Cárdenas to the Mexican presidency. It came to a crest in early 1938.

Cárdenas accelerated the expropriation (taking national possession with compensation) of foreign-owned agricultural lands and led in the organization of a single large union of Mexican oil company employees. The oil workers' union presented the companies, both American and British, with extensive demands that infringed conventional management prerogatives. The oil companies rejected them. A Mexican arbitration board found the demands just and ordered the oil companies to accept them. Again the companies refused. On March 18, 1938, Cárdenas expropriated the property of foreign oil companies within Mexico. Simultaneously, the anticlericalism of the Mexican revolution aroused intense opposition to the Cárdenas government among Roman Catholics north of the border.

The British broke diplomatic relations with Mexico and did not reach a settlement on compensation of their oil companies' claims until after World War II. The United States, despite the touchy political situation created by American Catholic opposition, lived up to its good-neighbor declarations. Roosevelt's smooth politicking (he even arranged to have his letters in reply to outraged Catholic leaders written for him by a priest); the folksy shrewdness of the American ambassador in Mexico City, Roosevelt's old boss in the Navy Department, Josephus Daniels; and the administration's firmness with the American oil companies saved the Good Neighbor policy.

The American oil companies conducted their own negotiations with the Mexican government. They claimed $260 million in compensation. This the Mexican government rejected, although it did come to terms with the Sinclair Oil Company. The oil companies hoped that the next Mexican president, to be elected in 1940, would be less demanding and were disappointed with the election of Manuel Avila Camacho. Both Cárdenas and Camacho were vigorously anti-Nazi and eager to make some arrangement with the United States before the Western Hemisphere might become embroiled in war with Hitler, but neither would back down on expropriation.

Mexico and the United States signed an agreement on November 19, 1941. The United States agreed to continue purchasing Mexican silver at the world price, to extend Mexico credits through the Export-Import Bank, and to negotiate a reciprocal trade agreement. Mexico agreed to pay $40 million for all American claims exclusive of oil claims. The oil claims were referred to two commissioners, one from each country. The commissioners set the total of the claims at $24 million, payable over several years. Mexico completed the payments in 1949. The United States oil companies protested that they should receive more, but the administration refused to support them further.

Latin Americans had a special interest in United States treatment of its Spanish populations in its colonial empire, Puerto Rico and the Philippines. Under the New Deal, the Washington-appointed governors of Puerto Rico made an effort to diversify the economy, to make it less dependent upon sugar. Public works with Washington's financial support both relieved hardship on the island and provided some of the prerequisites for the development of industry. Illiteracy (over 77 per cent in 1898) also handicapped economic growth, and Puerto Ricans put a special emphasis upon elementary education. Their results were gratifying but less than fully satisfactory: illiteracy in 1940 was still 31.5 per cent. The governorship of Rexford Tugwell from 1941 to 1946 brought the island's difficulties to the attention of citizens of the mainland even more. In 1948, Puerto Rico for the first time was permitted to elect its own governor.

The progress of the Philippine Islands toward independence was a confusing one, complicated by Filipino hesitation to be outside American tariff barriers and by United States naval strategic considerations in the western Pacific. In 1932, Congress passed the Hawes-Cutting Act granting the Philippines independence in 1945 with a transitional period until then. Hoover vetoed the measure, and Congress overrode the veto. Manuel Quezon, leader of the Filipino Nationalists, opposed the law because it left American naval bases in the islands and put Filipino products outside the American tariff system. The Philippine legislature rejected the law. There matters stood when FDR became president. In 1934, Congress passed and Roosevelt signed the Tydings-McDuffie Independence Act, which provided for independence on July 4, 1946, and commonwealth status meanwhile. The Filipinos accepted the arrangement in a plebiscite and installed Quezon as their president.

Difficulties with Japan, 1931–1938

In 1931, Japanese militarists embarked upon an expansionist policy on the Asian mainland that eventually led to war with the United States and defeat in 1945. The late 1920's saw shifts in the relative strength of Asian national power and an increase in international tension. In 1924, Dr. Sun Yat-sen, leader of the Chinese revolutionary nationalists, accepted aid from the Russian Communist government and strengthened the Chinese nationalist movement. Upon his death in 1925, his successor as head of the Kuomintang party, Chiang Kai-shek, continued collaboration with the Russians. The central Chinese government extended its authority in the north and hoped to bring reunification with Manchuria. Two years after assuming leadership, Chiang broke with the Russians, and in 1929 and 1930 Sino-Russian relations were severely strained; there was even undeclared warfare before China backed down in the face of superior Soviet strength. But Chinese power in North China was growing. In the winter of 1929–1930, the warlord of Manchuria acknowledged Chinese suzerainty. Simultaneously, the Chinese organized a boycott of Japanese goods and began to skirt treaty obligations they had been forced to yield to the Japanese under duress. Japanese militarists, fearful of growing Chinese strength, were eager for action before China became too strong for them to handle.

Without the consent of the Premier or the Foreign Office, Japanese troops on the night of September 18–19, 1931, seized the Chinese garrison at Mukden, Manchuria, and several key points along the South Manchurian Railway. Their pretext was an explosion on the railroad, which was minor in any case and may have been altogether fictitious. The Kuomintang government of China protested Japan's action to the United States and to the League of Nations. Japan's action was inconsistent with her membership in the League, with the Kellogg-Briand Pact, and the Nine-Power Treaty of 1922, but the League's first action, after the Japanese government promised to withdraw as soon as practicable, was only to request China and Japan to do nothing to irritate the situation. Secretary of State Henry L. Stimson at first was cautious in the hope that American forbearance would strengthen the moderates in the Japanese civil government against the militarists and the army.

When the Japanese army continued its aggressions in Manchuria, President Hoover instructed Prentiss Gilbert, an official in the American consulate at Geneva, to sit with the League Council in discussions of Manchurian matters. Although the decision to cooperate this closely with the League raised eyebrows in the United States, the cooperation had little practical effect. The Japanese ignored the League's resolution calling for withdrawal of all Japanese troops to the area that they had occupied before the Mukden incident.

Stimson and Hoover did not see eye-to-eye on the proper course to be followed. After he recognized that moderation was having no effect, Stimson was for a policy of nonrecognition of Japanese conquests and was prepared to impose economic sanctions against Japan. Secretary of War Patrick Hurley wanted even to threaten military force, but Hoover was unwilling to go beyond nonrecognition and moral sanctions. Events moved swiftly at the turn of the year. On December 11, 1931, the Japanese cabinet resigned; the new one was more militaristic. On the following January 3, Japanese forces practically completed their conquest of Manchuria. On January 7, Stimson addressed identical notes to Japan and China setting forth what at the time was known as the Stimson Doctrine, since then more generally called the Hoover-Stimson Doctrine because it went no further than the nonrecognition policy upon which the two men agreed and did not threaten economic sanctions such as Stimson favored. The notes declared that the United States would not "admit the legality of any situation de facto nor . . . recognize any treaty or agreement . . . which may impair the treaty rights of the United States or its citizens in China . . . or the international policy relative to China, commonly known as the open-door policy. . . ." The Hoover-Stimson Doctrine was unilateral; Stimson had asked Britain and France to join in his declaration, but each declined.

Then the Japanese attacked the Shanghai area in an attempt to get the Chinese to repeal their boycott, and the British were moved to action for the first time. British naval units joined American ships in going to Shanghai to protect each nation's citizens. Both the United States and Britain stimulated negotiations between China and Japan which in time led to the end of hostilities in the Shanghai area. By the end of May, 1932, Japanese troops in the international city had been reduced to their normal number. But the Japanese did not retreat in Manchuria. Their method of fastening control over the area was to create a puppet state, called Manchukuo, which declared its independence from China on February 18, 1932.

The creation of Manchukuo was a direct challenge to the Hoover-Stimson Doctrine. Five days later Stimson released a public letter to William Borah, chairman of the Senate Foreign Relations Committee, that was intended for the eyes of the Japanese, the Chinese, the League, the British, and the American public more than it was for Senator Borah. Stimson had based his previous condemnations of Japanese aggression upon the Kellogg-Briand Pact. In the letter to Borah he urged that other nations join the United States in nonrecognition and shifted his basis for judging the Japanese to the Washington naval treaties of 1922. The Nine-Power and the Five-Power treaties,

Stimson pointed out, released all signatory nations from the treaty provisions if any one of the signatories violated the pacts. In other words, if Japan violated the integrity of China (one of the provisions of the Nine-Power Treaty) America would no longer be obligated to limit the size of her navy. The United States moved its fleet to the Pacific in 1932, but it did not build its navy beyond treaty strength limitations. In fact, until Roosevelt became president there was no effort to keep the navy up to the strength authorized by the Washington treaties.

If the Borah letter had no visible effect upon Japanese policy, it did bring the League around to nonrecognition. In March, 1932, the League Assembly declared League members should not recognize any situation achieved by means contrary to the League Covenant or to the Kellogg-Briand Pact. The League later received the report of its special commission to investigate the Manchurian problem headed by a British subject, the Earl of Lytton. The Lytton report was moderate, urging Chinese sovereignty in Manchuria but protection of Japanese economic interests. The Japanese were not content with its recommendations and on September 15, 1932, recognized Manchukuo as an independent power. When the League advised its members against recognition of Manchukuo, Japan served the necessary two-year notice of its withdrawal from the League.

Roosevelt assured Stimson between the election of 1932 and the inauguration that his administration would continue the Hoover-Stimson policies in East Asia. Roosevelt kept the fleet in the Pacific and announced that it would be built up to treaty strength, but during his first few years in office tensions with Japan became less serious. When the Japanese began expanding from Manchuria they encountered stiffer Chinese military resistance, and in late May, 1933, the Chinese and Japanese signed a truce. The truce was not altogether effective, but until 1937 there was no more large-scale military action in East Asia.

During these years, however, there were other matters of Japanese-American relations that form part of the background to war in 1941. The two main issues were Japanese efforts to close the open door in China and naval armaments. Over intermittent protests from the State Department, Japan used her control of the Manchukuo puppet government to slam the open door shut in that part of the Chinese mainland. Manchuria became a private preserve for Japanese trade and capital, and Japan consistently denied she had anything to do with Manchukuo policies that kept trade from other nations out of the area. Japan even proposed to Secretary Hull in 1934 that the United States, in effect, withdraw from the Far East, a "Japanese Monroe Doctrine" for Asia. Although America was at the time making preparations for ultimate withdrawal from territorial control of the Philippines, there was no intention of withdrawing from open-door imperialist policies in East Asia. Hull rejected the Japanese proposal. Continued American determination to retain the East Asian *status quo* and Japanese determination to make the area a special reservation for her commercial and military interests made an increase in international conflict inevitable. East Asia was an arena of conflict between empires: between American and British, on the one hand, primarily economic or informal in nature rather than colonial, and the Japanese, on the other hand, militaristic and colonial as well as economic.

The Japanese announcement in December, 1934, that they would not renew the naval limitations agreed upon at Washington and London when those agreements expired at the end of 1936 indicated that they meant business. Japan did send delegates to a naval conference at London in 1935–1936, but the delegates withdrew when the American and British delegations would admit no change in the traditional ratios. The American, British, and French delegations reached an agreement on the size of vessels but not on their number, and early in 1938 these three nations abandoned limitation of any kind by mutual consent. The naval race had begun. In January, 1938, while the economy was suffering from a serious recession, Roosevelt in a special message to Congress asked for the largest naval authorization in the nation's history. The measure passed a few months later.

The 1933 truce between China and Japan ended dramatically in a skirmish at the Marco Polo bridge near Peiping on July 7, 1937. (This city was known as Peking until 1928 when the Kuomintang moved the capital from there and renamed the city Peiping. The Japanese called the city by its old name, as have the Chinese Communists since 1949.) The incident at the bridge seems not to have been a staged one as the one at Mukden had been in 1931, but the Japanese army used it as an excuse to launch a full-scale offensive in the northern China provinces. The Kuomintang and the Chinese Communists under Mao Tse-tung had recently concluded a truce in their civil war and made a common front against Japan. Japan decided to move before China could become stronger.

Japan enjoyed quick military success. Her method was to bomb major cities and follow the raids with land expeditions. Japan had bombed civilians at Chinchow, Manchuria, in 1931, Italy had bombed defenseless Ethiopians in 1935, and Germany and Italy had used airplane bombardment against civilians in Spain in their aid to Franco, but most of the world was still repelled by the airplane's bringing war to noncombatants. A photograph widely published in America showed a terrorized Chinese infant crying amidst bomb rubble. Japanese troops took Nanking in December, 1937, and the Chinese moved their capital to Hankow, which fell in October, 1938, along with Canton. The Chinese retreated to the interior and set up their capital at Chunking. Japan controlled the coastal cities and the principal railroad lines by the end of 1938. But the Chinese armies had not been destroyed and they would not quit. As the Japanese learned, to defeat China in battle to gain control of the strategic positions was one thing, to win a war with all China and to control the whole country, with its vast distances and its enormous population accustomed to a low living standard, were something else.

Though disgusted by Japanese bombing of civilians, the American public was not ready to pursue policies with Japan that might lead to war. At an international conference at Brussels in November, 1937, convened to consider what Japan called the Chinese incident or the Chinese affair but never the Chinese war, the American delegation was instructed not to press for economic sanctions because the administration knew the position was more advanced than public opinion would support. On December 12, 1937, Japanese aircraft bombed and sank a United States navy gunboat, the *Panay*, in the Yangtze River although the American flag was painted on its decks and it was obviously an American ship. Japan apologized profusely and quickly made financial restitution for the loss of property and the lives of two crewmen. In 1898, the sinking of the *Maine* had brought a sharp demand for war with Spain. The *Panay* sinking provoked only fear of war. What business, many people asked, did a naval vessel have in convoying Standard Oil Company tankers in the Yangtze? The memory of the horrors of 1917–1918 were too strong for most Americans to consider risking war on the other side of the world. Within two weeks after the *Panay* sinking, the whole affair was a closed matter. The most that was done against the Japanese until the outbreak of war in Europe was to aid China (for example, the Export-Import Bank's credit to China for the Burma Road) and to request American airplane manufacturers in July, 1938, not to supply planes to Japan.

Yet the United States government did not retreat from its historic Far Eastern policies. Japan in November, 1938, announced a "new order" in East Asia based on "a tripartite relationship of mutual aid and coordination between Japan, Manchukuo and [Japanese-controlled] China." The State Department protested that such a "new order" could not legitimately annul previous treaty rights, meaning mostly the open-door safeguards in the 1922 Nine-Power Treaty. The United States never abandoned its open-door policy in East Asia; Japan would not abandon its position as the paramount power in the "new order." By the winter of 1938–1939, Japan and the United States were completely at loggerheads, but American public opinion was far more concerned with the situation in Europe than it was with Asian tensions.

Fascism in Europe: Hitler and Mussolini

When Benito Mussolini came to power in Italy in late 1922 and instituted his fascist order, majority opinion about him in the United States was not adverse. Many Americans commended Mussolini for driving beggars from the streets and praised him for "making the trains run on time."

Majority public opinion, however, was opposed to Adolf Hitler's National Socialist or Nazi rule in Germany almost from the time the Nazis came to power early in 1933, although Italian Fascism and German Nazism were only national variations of the same totalitarian idea. Hitler's blatant anti-Semitism alarmed many Americans, and millions, remembering the war, feared the resurgence of German militarism. When both Italy and Germany endangered the peace of the world with their expansionist policies, only a small proportion of the American population favored the two nations.

To summarize fascism (both Italian Fascism and German Nazism were generally known as fascism) in a few sentences is not simple. Fascist nations were vigorously anti-Communist. Both Hitler and Mussolini rode to power on middle-class fear of communism, and both their regimes essentially maintained the class systems that had existed earlier. To a degree, then, fascism was "capitalism by violence." But it was not conventional capitalism. The corporate state intervened extensively in the nation's economic life and regulated it. Industrial and landed capitalists accepted fascist regulation in preference to some form of Marxist control. Ironically, fascism had one major similarity to Stalinism: totalitarianism or the subordination of the individual and all social institutions to the needs of the national state. Hitler's Nazis, for example, urged children to inform on their parents to the authorities. Fascist nations were also extremely militaristic. They glorified the military life and praised war as a means of bringing out the best in a people. Fascists had nothing but contempt for democracy, either in the sense of shared decisions by a wide electorate or in the Bill of Rights' sense of protection of the individual from the state. In sum, fascism was antidemocratic nationalism run riot.

Fascism in Germany was extremely racist, although it was not in Italy and in some lesser fascist states. The Nazis exploited the latent anti-Semitism of the German people in their rise to power and used the Jews as a scapegoat to explain away all of the country's difficulties. At the same time, Nazis exalted the mythical racial purity, "Aryanism," of non-Jewish Germans. Beginning with mob action against Jews, the requirement that they wear identifying clothes, and boycotts of their businesses, German anti-Semitism ended with what the Nazis euphemistically called "the final solution of the Jewish question": killing all Jews and eradicating Jewish culture in all areas under German control. By the time Nazi Germany collapsed in 1945, the Nazis had killed six million Jews, most of them in efficient slaughterhouses, where their corpses were rendered into fats for soap manufacture and other uses.

For the first few months after Hitler came to power in Germany (January 30, 1933), he displayed an attitude toward other nations which, while not cooperative, would seem remarkably moderate in retrospect. Perhaps he was only waiting for consolidation of his power within Germany. In March, 1933, he was voted dictatorial powers for four years, and after Paul von Hindenburg's death in 1934 he combined the offices of the German presidency and chancellorship. He was, however, always known as Der Führer (the leader) rather than as president or chancellor. Hitler at first was even willing to talk about disarmament. A General Disarmament Conference had met first at Geneva in February, 1932. It met again in the spring of 1933. Hitler announced that he was willing to go along with disarmament and to postpone for five years his insistent demands for German arms equality, but he refused to sign any agreements or to consent to abide by majority votes of the Conference members. In October, 1933, Germany withdrew from both the Conference and the League of Nations. A few months later the Conference broke up altogether.

In March, 1935, Hitler declared the Treaty of Versailles limitations upon German armed strength no longer valid, instituted compulsory military service, and began to build the German army toward an announced five hundred thousand men. At the same time he said Germany would continue to respect the rest of the treaty, including keeping the Rhineland as a demilitarized zone. With such promises he managed to prevent France and Britain from presenting a solid front of opposition. Britain three months later even signed a treaty with Germany which allowed the Reich a navy 35 per cent as large as Britain's. In March, 1936, Hitler again took advantage of French-British discord, this time over what to do about Italy's undeclared war against Ethiopia, and he denounced the whole of the Treaty of Versailles, as well as the Locarno Treaty of 1925, and marched two hundred thousand soldiers into the Rhineland. The League of Nations failed to take any action.

Germany's and Italy's increased belligerence and disregard of international agreements caused grave concern in the United States, but the reaction was not so great as it would have been if the citizenry could have known what the end of German-Italian policies would be. In the mid-1930's the American population was far more concerned with domestic problems than with foreign affairs in either Europe or Asia and was undergoing a deep reaction against its involvement in the war of 1914–1918.

Neutrality and Anxiety, 1933–1938

In discussions of foreign policy with respect to expansionist Germany, Italy, and Japan in the 1930's, politicians and publicists used terms of opprobrium for their opponents that did little to clarify the actual situation. All too often, historians since that decade have trapped themselves by accepting these political catchwords without efforts to use them with precision. The most common loosely used term in the lexicon of commentators about foreign policy is *isolationist,* which has described those who opposed colonial imperialism in 1898 and after, who opposed American participation in World War I, who fought ratification of the Treaty of Versailles, who resisted entrance into World War II, and, in recent years, who criticized the United Nations and foreign aid programs. Actually, the term means one who advocates a policy of nonparticipation in international affairs, and very few Americans indeed have advocated such a position. In the context of the 1930's, "isolationism" embraced a wide range of positions. All they had in common was a fear of engagement in another world war. An insignificant number were partisans of fascism (for example, members of the German-American Bund) who, seeing that the United States would not become an ally of Germany or Italy, wanted the nation to stay clear of associations with antifascist governments. Another small group was composed of pacifists, many of them religiously motivated, who believed that violence and war were un-Christian and subversive of all decent values. Most "isolationists" were antifascist but fearful that vigorous opposition to expansionist foreign nations would involve the United States in an unwanted war. Some would have taken a few risks of war to hamper fascism; some would not. Some were for a strong military defense; some were not. To lump all of these positions into any single term is not precise, but some kind of general term is valid on occasion if one remembers that it is loose and general. The term *isolationist* will not be used here because it has become emotionally loaded. *Noninterventionist* is no more precise, but it avoids political passion.

Interventionist also is a loose term, but it is one that has somehow not acquired strong emotional overtones. Almost no one was an open, outright interventionist demanding a quick declaration of war against fascist nations until war began in Europe in September, 1939, and they were few even then. However, especially after the beginning of the European war, an increasing number of people advocated strong aid to the antifascist European nations and actions "short of war" that might result in armed conflict. As with the noninterventionists, the interventionists represented a considerable range of positions, from the quite bellicose to those who genuinely believed that only through cooperation with the western democracies could American belligerency be prevented.

Foreign policy cut across conventional political lines, whether party, regional, ethnic, or ideological. Both major parties, all regions of the nation, and all major nationality and racial groups divided on foreign policy issues. Frequently, debates between interventionists and noninterventionists made bedfellows of political leaders who vigorously opposed one another on domestic matters. Thus, on the interventionist side, the Roosevelt administration worked in harness with conservative eastern and southern congressional leaders of both parties, and the other side displayed the unusual spectacle of Colonel Robert R. McCormick, publisher of the extremely conservative *Chicago Daily Tribune*, agreeing with the leader of the Socialist party, Norman Thomas.

Clearly, in the early and middle 1930's American public opinion was overwhelmingly and vigorously antiwar. Given the depression-induced popular hostility to bankers and manufacturers and what was known about loans to the Allies from 1914 to 1917 and of profits in munitions, it was perhaps inevitable that antiwar sentiment would focus upon the role of business in American entrance into the war in 1917, widely felt to have been a disastrous mistake. In the spring of 1934, the Senate created a special committee, headed by Senator Gerald P. Nye, Republican of North Dakota, to conduct an inquiry into the adequacy of legislation on government control of munitions. For nearly three years the Nye Committee provided headlines and newspaper stories full of sordid details of greed and chicanery in the American munitions business during the war. It was easy for people to conclude that "merchants of death," a favorite phrase of the time, had been solely responsible for America's going to the aid of the Allies. Operating upon the assumption that legislation that presumably would have prevented participation in the war of 1914–1918 would prevent entrance into a future war, Congress moved to write a series of neutrality measures into the statutes.

At the end of his administration, Hoover, with a view to cooperation with the League in economic sanctions, requested Congress to pass a bill authorizing the chief executive to deny the export of arms from the United States to whatever countries the president might designate. The House passed such a bill, but the Senate amended it to make an arms embargo applicable to all parties in a war. Roosevelt succeeded Hoover before the Senate and House reached agreement, and the bill died.

In the summer of 1935, it seemed likely that Mussolini would soon begin a war to expand his colonial empire in North Africa. Roosevelt and Hull had a bill introduced which would have authorized the president to impose an arms embargo upon the nation he considered the aggressor. The bill was much like the one Hoover had desired in January, 1933. Instead, Congress passed the First Neutrality Act, which Roosevelt signed with misgivings on August 31, 1935. This law required the president to impose an embargo on arms to both nations engaged in conflict, created a government board whose special permission was necessary before munitions could be exported to any country, whether at war or not, and prohibited American ships from carrying munitions to or for a belligerent. The president's only discretionary power under the Act was whether or not to warn citizens that they traveled on ships of belligerent nations at their own risk.

Then, on October 3, 1935, well-equipped Italian troops invaded Ethiopia, whose soldiers were armed with the most primitive of weapons. Two days later FDR declared that a state of war existed and thereby invoked the Neutrality Act of 1935. Italy at no time made an official war declaration. In this case the prohibition of arms shipment to both sides probably did not harm Ethiopia, which had no seaport and probably would not have been able to get American arms anyway, although many people at the time thought it did. But, on the other hand, the arms embargo did not hurt Italy to any appreciable extent, particularly in a war against a foe as defenseless as Ethiopia. The Neutrality Act made no provision for an embargo on oil, and it was petroleum products that Italy needed most desperately for her motorized legions and air force. Hull applied a "moral embargo" on oil to Italy, requesting American oil companies to keep their shipments to Italy at normal levels. Hull thought the "moral embargo" was "reasonably successful," but how much American gasoline the Italians diverted from peaceful uses to tanks and army trucks is not known. Mussolini completed his conquest of Ethiopia in May, 1936.

Most of the provisions of the First Neutrality Act were due to expire at the end of February, 1936. Congress passed the Second Neutrality Act on the last day of February. The new measure extended the previous legislation until May 1, 1937, and added some new features. Under the old legislation, the president had been authorized but not directed to impose an arms embargo against any third power that might become involved in war with a nation already embargoed. The new legislation made such an embargo of a third nation mandatory. The new law also exempted from embargo any American nation that became a belligerent against any non-American nation and forbade loans by any person living in the United States to belligerent governments. This last provision was designed to prevent the repetition of such loans as the House of Morgan began to handle for the Allies in 1915.

None of this neutrality legislation mentioned civil wars and thus did not apply when the Spanish Civil War began in July, 1936. In 1931 the Spanish had overthrown their monarchy and established a republic; five years later General Francisco Franco led a revolt against the republican government. Franco and his followers were unmistakably Fascist, although not cut precisely from the German pattern. Franco's revolt was ostensibly directed against communists in the Spanish government, who at the beginning of the Civil War did not control the Spanish state. Fearful that the Spanish war would lead to a general European war, France persuaded other European governments to agree to a nonintervention policy. However, Germany and Italy soon violated the agreement, sent military units to aid Franco, and made Spain a testing ground for their new military techniques. Russia also violated the nonintervention agreement with direct aid to the Spanish government, or Loyalist cause, although her intervention was less extensive than was that of the Fascist powers.

When the European nations decided upon nonintervention, Roosevelt and Hull complied and declared another "moral embargo" upon shipments to either side of the Spanish conflict. No further action was possible under existing law. When Congress convened in January, 1937, Roosevelt asked Congress to extend the neutrality laws to civil as well as international wars. According to Hugh Thomas, a British author who has written the best single book on the Spanish Civil War, Ambassador to Great Britain Joseph P. Kennedy, a prominent Catholic layman, was influential in bringing about the administration's refusal to aid the Loyalists. Congress complied hastily. The decision to take a hands-off policy toward the Spanish war—in effect, to aid Franco because denying the Spanish government help made German and Italian intervention decisive—sharply divided the American population. The American Catholic hierarchy approved of the arms embargo to Spain because of the Spanish government's anticlericalism and the support the Spanish hierarchy gave Franco. The American political left, both Communist and non-Communist, vigorously condemned the embargo. The Communists organized the Abraham Lincoln Brigade, and almost three thousand young Americans, all of them anti-Fascist but not all of them Communist, enlisted in this military organization to fight Spanish fascism. Hundreds of thousands of others donated funds to Spanish war relief organizations.

The Third Neutrality Act of May 1, 1937, the date of the expiration of the second measure, extended the main provisions of earlier neutrality laws without a definite time limit. The Third Act also made two minor and one major change in the basic legislation. The new law gave the president discretionary power in invoking an embargo in the case of a foreign civil war and forbade United States citizens to travel on the ships of nations at war. An embargo against both sides of a civil war had been mandatory since January, 1937, and existing legislation had only authorized the president to warn citizens that they traveled on belligerent ships at their own risk. Potentially more important was the "cash and carry" provision of the Third Neutrality Act, which gave the president considerable discretionary power to wage economic war. As in earlier legislation, whenever the president declared that a state of war existed between two or more foreign powers an arms embargo would become mandatory. But the "cash and carry" provision empowered the president also, for a period of two years, to extend the embargo, if he so wished, to commodities that were not arms or munitions if the commodities were carried in American ships or title to them had not yet been transferred to a foreign buyer. No such situation arose during the two years this provision was in effect. (After war began in Europe in September, 1939, Congress enacted another "cash and carry" provision but one that was quite different in nature.) Interestingly, Roosevelt did not invoke the Third Neutrality Act until war broke out in Europe. He declined to take official recognition that a state of war existed between Japan and China after July, 1937. Apparently, Roosevelt concluded that to "find" the Asian war and thereby make neutrality legislation applicable would have the practical effect of strengthening Japan's hand. Instead, he relied upon appeals to other nations to reaffirm their treaty obligations and to pleas for international morality. Since American public opinion would not support strong measures, the American delegation to the Brussels Conference on the Asian situation was powerless to provide strong leadership.

Indeed, it became increasingly apparent in 1937 and 1938 that noninterventionist public opinion was a thorn in the President's side and that noninterventionists meant to keep the thorn sharp. This antagonism between the public and the President over foreign policy was illustrated by the reaction to Roosevelt's speech at Chicago, October 5, 1937, at the dedication of a new bridge on the Outer Drive. In this address, commonly called the "Quarantine the Aggressors Speech," Roosevelt said, "It seems to be unfortunately true that the epidemic of world lawlessness is spreading. And mark this well! When an epidemic of physical disease starts to spread, the community approves and joins in a quarantine of the patients in order to protect the health of the community against the spread of the disease." Such a medical methaphor was not precise language, and no one could say just what Roosevelt had in mind. But whatever he had in mind, the public did not approve of it. Press reaction to the speech was unfavorable. Later in the month a public opinion poll put this question to a supposedly scientifically calculated cross section of the population: "Which plan for keeping out of war do you have more faith in— having Congress pass stricter neutrality laws, or leaving the job up to the President?" Only 31 per cent preferred the latter alternative. The strength behind the Ludlow amendment to the Constitution was another indication of noninterventionist power and distrust of the President's foreign policies. An idea that went back at least as far as the period of American neutrality during World War I, the Ludlow amendment, named for Representative Louis Ludlow, Democrat of Indiana, proposed that a national referendum would be necessary to declare war except in the case of armed invasion of the United States or its territories. Roosevelt had to use great pressure to defeat the amendment in the House where it failed by only twenty-one votes in January, 1938.

Also in January, 1938, the State Department perceived that Hitler's next move would be to absorb Austria under German rule. With public opinion being what it was, Hull only impressed upon the German ambassador in Washington that the United States would not look favorably upon any such aggression. This did not deter Germany whose troops marched into Austria with the aid of Austrian Nazis in March.

In the summer of 1938 Hitler began a war of nerves over the question of the Sudetenland of Czechoslovakia, an area populated largely by German-speaking people. Hitler demanded the area, and the Czechs were willing to fight to keep it since it was vital to the defense of the rest of the country. But Britain, France, and the United States were by no means prepared to go to war to defend Czechoslovakia. Indeed, many British and French leaders regarded Hitler as less of a menace than the Russians. Prime Minister Neville Chamberlain and Premier Édouard Daladier were prepared to go to great lengths at Czechoslovakia's expense to prevent the outbreak of war. Matters came to a crisis in late September. Millions of Americans kept close to their radios to hear the frequent news bulletins. After European heads of state and foreign ministers had conferred both personally and by cable for days without a final settlement, Roosevelt, on September 26, sent messages to Hitler, Chamberlain, Daladier, and President Eduard Beneš of Czechoslovakia in which he asserted that war would only wreck every country involved and urged continued negotiations. Hitler's reply only repeated his previous demands for the Sudetenland. Three days later the State Department urged all other countries to support the American appeal for further negotiations, and Roosevelt personally appealed to Mussolini to use his influence with Hitler. At the last minute, Hitler issued invitations to Mussolini, Chamberlain, and Daladier for a conference at Munich. When Roosevelt heard that Chamberlain had accepted the invitation, he dispatched a cabled instruction to his ambassador at

London, Joseph P. Kennedy, to give Chamberlain this oral message: "Good man." On September 30, Chamberlain and Daladier signed a Four-Power Pact at Munich which gave the Sudetenland to Germany in exchange for only a promise from Hitler, who had already broken several promises, to refrain from further demands for European territory. When the gray Chamberlain returned to London, carrying the umbrella which came to be considered a symbol of appeasement, he announced, "I believe it is peace for our time." The same day the State Department in a press release announced that the Munich agreement had brought "a universal sense of relief," but it declared that the United States would not "pass upon the merits of the differences to which the Four-Power Pact . . . related."

War in Europe had been averted—for about eleven months.

Part IV

WAR AND BOOM AGAIN
1941–1968

CHAPTER TWENTY-TWO

And the War Came

IF PRESIDENT ROOSEVELT AT ANY TIME THOUGHT THE MUNICH PACT would avert war in Europe, he was disillusioned within a week after the crisis. The ambassador to France, William C. Bullitt, reported to him that French premier Édouard Daladier did not for a minute believe Hitler's assurances. Daladier's skepticism was well founded. Almost immediately after Munich, Hitler called for an increase in German armaments upon the pretext that Britain would not keep the peace if a man like Winston Churchill, who opposed the Munich settlement, should come to political power. At this point, Roosevelt announced a $300 million increase in the American arms program. While public-opinion polls continued to show overwhelming American opposition to war, the President enjoyed some support for rearmament because he couched his statements in national defense terms and because the Nazis, in November, 1938, intensified their oppression of the Jews. Nevertheless, Roosevelt could not move very far very fast. He was at the moment at about his weakest point in domestic political strength, and he remembered the difficulties President Wilson had when he allowed his political fences to rot while he concerned himself with foreign affairs.

On March 14, 1939, Germany gained control over the balance of Czechoslovakia. In early April, Mussolini's troops took Albania. A week after Italy's invasion of her neighbor across the Adriatic, Roosevelt, without consulting Paris or London, proposed in a message to Hitler and Mussolini that they should assure thirty-one European and Near Eastern countries that for at least ten years they would commit no aggression. In return, the United States would participate in disarmament discussions and in easing the way of all nations to obtain necessary raw materials. Mussolini in a speech of April 20 called the idea "absurd." In a speech to the Reichstag, Hitler said he had surveyed the governments Roosevelt had asked assurances for and found none of them felt any need for assurance. The whole idea collapsed on this cynical note.

As early as his annual message to Congress in January, 1939, Roosevelt had urged revision of neutrality legislation to give him a stronger hand to aid an invaded nation if war should begin. After Hitler began to press Poland in April, 1939, to grant Germany access across the Polish Corridor between the main part of Germany and East Prussia and for consent to annex the free city of Danzig, Roosevelt renewed his efforts to get amendment of the neutrality laws. The "cash and carry" provisions of the Third Neutrality Act (1937) expired on May 1; after that date, if war came, Britain and France would be forbidden to buy arms in America even if they carried them in their own ships. Despite great pressure from the administration, neither house would budge to amend the law. Senator Borah even, upon being informed by Secretary Hull that State Department cables indicated European war was imminent, said, "I have my own sources of information . . . and on several occasions I've found them more reliable than the State Department." Congress adjourned without yielding to the President.

In Europe tension mounted but events dragged from April, 1939, when Hitler began to torment Poland, until August. During those months, Russia, Britain, and France conferred, at Stalin's invitation, about forming a defensive alliance against Germany. The difficulty lay in the status of the small countries between Germany and Russia. Fearing Russian power almost as much as German, sometimes more, the Baltic countries (Lithuania, Latvia, and Estonia), Poland, and Rumania felt that acceptance of Russian protection would mean Russian occupation. Britain and France refused to enter an alliance with Russia against these countries' wishes, and the negotiations dragged on uselessly.

In May, Vyacheslav Molotov replaced Maxim Litvinov as the Russian foreign minister. Molotov soon began secret negotiations with Germany but made no commitments until he became convinced no agreement could be reached with the English and French. On August 20, 1939, Germany and Russia announced that they had signed a trade agreement. Three days later the two countries shocked the world by signing a nonaggression pact that assured Germany of Russian neutrality should the Nazis invade Poland. A secret part of the agreement split Poland between the two countries and arranged spheres of influence in the Baltic states.

On September 1, after a week of fruitless last-minute efforts by the United States, Britain, France, and Poland for a settlement, German troops crossed the Polish frontier. Two days later, acting on previous commitments, Britain and France declared war on Germany. World War II had begun, less than twenty-one years after the end of the first tragedy.

The "Phony War"

The winter of 1939–1940 saw no real war in western Europe. After Germany overran Poland with a Blitzkrieg, or lightning war, so quickly that Britain and France could not endanger the Third Reich from the west, the western front settled down to a Sitzkrieg, or sitting war. The main area of hostilities that winter was Finland, which Russia invaded November 30, 1939. American opinion strongly supported the Finns—"brave little Finland" that paid its war debts —and Herbert Hoover headed a Finnish war relief organization that collected $2 million in the United States. But neither Congress nor the administration would go beyond an effective "moral embargo" on war shipments to Russia, partly because of political caution, partly for fear of strengthening the unexpected German-Russian alliance with outside pressure. In March, 1940, the "Winter War" ended with Russia settling for its minimum demands. (By the end of the war, Finland had a peculiar record. When Germany invaded Russia in June, 1941, Finland cooperated and invaded Russia from the northwest. In the fall of 1944, after a successful Russian campaign, the Finns capitulated, but the German troops in North Finland refused to leave, and Finland fought a bitter campaign against her former comrades at arms.)

The night Britain and France declared war, September 3, 1939, Roosevelt spoke to the nation by radio.

> This nation will remain a neutral nation, but I cannot ask that every American remain neutral in thought as well. . . . Even a neutral cannot be asked to close his mind or his conscience. . . . I hope the United States will keep out of this war. I believe that it will. And I give you assurance and reassurance that every effort of your Government will be directed toward that end.

Two days later, the President invoked the existing neutrality law, thereby prohibiting exports of war material to the belligerents. But at the same time, the President continued his campaign to have the law amended.

After calling a special session of Congress, Roosevelt on September 21 addressed the assembled Senators and Representatives, telling them "that by the repeal of the embargo the United States will more probably remain at peace than if the law remains as it stands today." He urged new legislation to keep American ships and citizens out of combat areas and to prohibit credits by individual citizens to the belligerents, but to permit belligerents to take title to American products in American ports on a "cash and carry" basis. After sharp debates, Congress passed the Fourth Neutrality Act, or the Neutrality Act of 1939, by 243 to 172 in the House and 55 to 24 in the Senate. Roosevelt signed the bill November 4, 1939, and put it into effect immediately. The "cash and carry" provisions of the law applied to all commodities, arms or not. Roosevelt's executive order prohibited American ships to sail to belligerent ports or in the Baltic Sea, the North Sea, and the waters around Great Britain, including the English Channel.

A conference of the twenty-one American republics at Panama City— called by Panama as provided for by the conference at Lima in 1938—met only days after the war began and unanimously made the Americas neutral territory. The Panama conference created a neutral zone three hundred miles wide around the Americas (with the exception of belligerent Canada), in which the American states would admit no war action. In December, 1939, when British cruisers damaged the German battleship *Graf Spee* and it limped into port at Montevideo, the government of Uruguay ordered the German captain to leave the neutral zone within seventy-two hours. Rather than face the British again, the crew scuttled the ship and subsequently were interned in Uruguay.

The period of "phony war" afforded Americans an opportunity to clarify their thinking about neutrality, but they reached no consensus. The population was torn between a strong desire to remain apart from the horrors of war and sympathy for the Allies. Despite imperfections of British and French democracy and these nations' colonial imperialism, most people in the United States preferred an Allied victory to military success for the positively antidemocratic, militaristic, and expansionist German and Italian governments. For the United States to go to war, most citizens thought, would be a disaster; for Germany to win, practically all agreed, would also be a disaster. Which was the worse eventuality? In the absence of real war in the West, Americans hoped the dilemma would not come to a showdown, but they arrived at no firm conclusions about what to do if a choice had to be made. The American people never made a clear-cut decision through their regular representative processes, but they moved ever closer to full-scale belligerency. The war came eventually from outside, but by then the United States was practically a belligerent in everything but name.

Roosevelt's views about the war were of particularly great importance because he was the most effective individual molder of public opinion in the nation and because, as leader of the majority political party and as chief executive, he could create conditions which reduced the range of practical choice of the citizens and their elected representatives. But to describe his personal views on the war is difficult because he did not reveal his thoughts candidly to the people, and if he recorded them privately the record has not become available. We must infer his personal views from a less than perfect record.

Clearly, from the beginning of the war in September, 1939, Roosevelt's sympathies were strongly with the Allies. To Roosevelt, defeat of the Axis powers was paramount. (Germany and Italy were generally known as the Axis powers; Japan joined the Axis with the Berlin Pact of September 27, 1940, which created a German-Italian-Japanese military alliance.) His desire for Axis defeat became stronger after the German victories of the spring of 1940. Just as clearly, at least early in the European conflict, Roosevelt genuinely wanted the United States to stay out of the war as a full-scale belligerent. The question was which was the lesser evil, Axis victory or American participation? Gradually, Roosevelt came to believe that an Axis victory was more to be deplored, over the long run, than his nation's entrance into war, and at some time in mid-1941 he apparently became convinced that American participation was necessary to bring Axis defeat. He meanwhile led the nation away from neutrality to what came to be known as *nonbelligerence*—not at war but actively supporting one belligerent side through loans, armament aid, and, to a limited degree, military and naval cooperation. That Roosevelt was not candid with the public and that his executive actions brought the nation ever closer to active war participation are obvious. Also, his policies and actions raised serious constitutional questions about the power of the president in a democratic country. This is not to say that Roosevelt "tricked us" or "lied us" into World War II, as the more extreme "revisionist" critics of Roosevelt have written; it is to say that the President, without taking the people fully into his confidence, moved the United States into what amounted

440

to undeclared war in such a manner that causes serious concern to those who believe that the electorate, through its representatives in Congress, should make the basic and ultimate decisions about war and peace.

Majority public opinion lagged behind the President's position until Pearl Harbor, but it moved in the President's direction. According to public opinion polls, only a minority believed in September, 1939, that the declaration of war in 1917 had been a proper decision, but a majority came to that opinion during the fall. Until the collapse of France and the subsequent Battle of Britain in the skies over England, a minority thought aid to England more important than keeping the United States out of the war; thereafter, a majority would have risked war to help the British. In the early spring of 1941, for the first time, a majority came to think it wise to risk war with Japan rather than allow her to continue her expansion.

Although public opinion slowly came toward Roosevelt's position with each major change in the war in Europe, the heat of the arguments between interventionists and noninterventionists increased. Diametrically opposed to one another were two important nonpartisan propaganda groups, the interventionist Committee to Defend America by Aiding the Allies and the noninterventionist America First Committee. Just after war began in Europe, William Allen White, progressive Republican editor of the Emporia, Kansas, *Gazette* and a journalist of national reputation, organized the Non-Partisan Committee for Peace through Revision of the Neutrality Law. The Committee faded after the passage of the Fourth Neutrality Act, but came to life in May, 1940, after the Nazi invasion of France, under its new name. White again was its chairman, and it was widely known as the White Committee. By August, 1940, the White Committee had six hundred local chapters and sufficient money for national advertising and radio network time. It had considerable influence with the national leaders of both political parties. Among the prominent newspapers editorially supporting the Committee to Defend America were the New York *Times* and the New York *Herald-Tribune*, whose columnists were syndicated nationally.

The America First Committee organized in the summer of 1940. The prime mover in its establishment was R. Douglas Stuart of Chicago, then a student in the Yale Law School; its national chairman was General Robert E. Wood, who was Acting Quartermaster General in World War I and was then chairman of the board of Sears, Roebuck and Company. Like the White Committee, it tried to influence public opinion through print and radio. The most important papers supporting it were the *Chicago Daily Tribune* and the Hearst chain.

In each camp there was considerable diversity of opinion on domestic affairs. Within the White Committee the range was at least as far as from Lewis Douglas on the right to Paul H. Douglas and Reinhold Niebuhr on the left. The national committee of America First contained such diverse types as Hanford MacNider, Iowa manufacturer and former national commander of the American Legion, Oswald Garrison Villard, former editor of *The Nation*, and Chester Bowles. Both sides had military men: in the White group, Clark M. Eichelberger; in the America First, besides General Wood himself, Colonel Charles A. Lindbergh and "Eddie" Rickenbacker, the most celebrated American pilot of World War I. Nor was either camp unanimous in its foreign policy positions. Although the official position of America First was for strong continental defenses, many traditional pacifists and antimilitarists belonged to the organization. Differences within the White Committee became so intense that White himself resigned as chairman in January, 1941, and growled about a nucleus of "warmongers" in the organization.

From the Fall of France through the Elections

On April 9, 1940, Hitler unleashed his powerful war machine on Denmark and Norway. Militarily weak compared to the Germans and without natural geographic barriers, the Danes offered no more than token resistance. They were more than usually bitter, considering that only a year before, at Hitler's suggestion, they had signed a nonaggression pact with Germany and that some of the Nazi troopers who invaded their country had as children during World War I been taken in by Danish farmers so that they could get enough to eat. The Norwegians put up greater resistance and received some help from the British. But they were no match for the Nazis, and they were betrayed by native Nazis, "fifth columnists," led by Vidkun Quisling.

On May 10, the Nazis invaded the Netherlands, Belgium, and Luxembourg and the following day entered France. Although the Dutch declared Rotterdam an open city, the Luftwaffe bombed and utterly destroyed forty blocks in Rotterdam's central district to demonstrate its power to the world. The Nazi motorized battalions swept toward Paris and pinned the British army against the English Channel. In late May and early June, a motley collection of British boats managed to evacuate their army from Dunkirk in an heroic and miraculous operation. The Germans occupied Paris on June 14, and on June 22, 1940, Hitler received the French surrender in the same railroad car in the same Compiègne forest in which the Germans had agreed to armistice in November, 1918. On June 10, Mussolini's Fascist legions had attacked France from the southeast. In six weeks Hitler and Mussolini had conquered more than had the Central Powers in all of World War I.

The new turn in the war had a great impact upon American opinion and actions. An overwhelming majority of Americans, including those who were ardent noninterventionists, sympathized with France. The new British prime minister, Winston Churchill, who replaced Neville Chamberlain the day the Nazis began their sweep through the Low Countries and who installed a national government including Labor party leaders, captured the imagination of America with his pledge to fight on and on in his "blood, sweat, and tears" speech. Roosevelt's speech at the University of Virginia on the day Italy invaded France was well received. The President described his efforts to keep Mussolini out of the war and declared, "The hand that held the dagger has struck it into the back of its neighbor." With anxious interest, the nation followed the progress of the air battles between the Luftwaffe and the Royal Air Force for control of the skies and, after the Germans switched from the strategy of destroying RAF bases to a punishing bombardment of London, the "blitz" of the fall and winter of 1940–1941.

Even before the German conquest of France was complete, the United

States indirectly began sending some of its arms to Britain. The navy sent some of its planes back to the manufacturer on a "trade in" for new models to be delivered much later. The manufacturer then sent the planes on to belligerent Canada. The United States also permitted the Royal Canadian Air Force to send its personnel to Florida air fields for training. This kind of hemispheric cooperation for the Allies and against the Axis extended to Latin America. In July, 1940, the foreign ministers of the American nations met at Havana. Besides arranging for the United States, through the Export-Import Bank, to engage in economic warfare with Germany in the Latin American market, the Havana Conference created a system for American states to take over as trustees the American territory of European countries conquered by the Nazis. Eventually, the United States became the trustee for Greenland which had been Danish.

The Republican party met in national convention at Philadelphia on June 24, just two days after Hitler received France's surrender. Until soon before the convention the main contenders for the GOP presidential nomination were all noninterventionists: Senators Robert A. Taft of Ohio and Arthur H. Vandenberg of Michigan and Thomas E. Dewey, the thirty-eight year old district attorney of New York's Manhattan who had gained national attention as a "racket buster." Late in the preconvention campaign a group of eastern interventionist Republicans advanced the name of Wendell L. Willkie, president of the Commonwealth and Southern Corporation that had led the fight of the privately owned public utilities against TVA. Willkie, originally of Elwood, Indiana, a big rumpled man who had been a Democrat, even a delegate to the 1924 convention, and who had registered as a Republican for the first time earlier in the year, moved up fast. His initial support was from the eastern elements in the GOP, but he soon picked up popular backing in the Midwest. Willkie managers packed the convention galleries, and his claque there kept up the chant "We want Willkie." Dewey led on the first ballot, with Taft second and Willkie third, but Willkie gained thereafter and won a majority on the sixth ballot. Charles McNary of Oregon, Republican leader in the Senate and co-sponsor of the McNary-Haugen bills, received the vice-presidential nomination.

The Republican convention, sensing the general popularity of the New Deal, did not offer the electorate a platform sharply different from what was expected from the forthcoming Democratic convention. Its criticisms of the New Deal were restricted to its administration rather than its general outline. It promised retention and even extension of the Social Security Act. It demanded a constitutional amendment to restrict the president to two terms. On foreign policy, the platform straddled in the historic fashion of the major parties, which have to satisfy the major wings of their coalitions. The Republicans stated that they were unalterably opposed to American involvement in a foreign war but supported aid to countries under attack or the threat of attack. On the whole, the Republican convention produced another "Me Too" candidate and platform but had come up with the first candidate with flair and potential wide personal support since Theodore Roosevelt.

The President said nothing about a third term despite frantic efforts to get him to commit himself. He allowed his name to be entered in state primaries, and in each case he won handily. But several other Democratic politicians, notably Postmaster General Farley, Vice-President Garner, and former Governor of Indiana Paul V. McNutt, yearned for the nomination. They were at a considerable disadvantage. Roosevelt had a well-organized machine working at the Chicago convention—its leader Harry Hopkins had a direct telephone to the White House installed in his hotel bathroom, the only place he could be assured of privacy—but few in the machine knew the President's intentions for sure. Finally, Senator Alben Barkley in a rip-roaring convention speech declared that Roosevelt wished "in all earnestness and sincerity to make it clear that all the delegates . . . are free to vote for any candidate." This ambiguous statement started a huge Roosevelt demonstration. After all, Roosevelt too was "any candidate." Delegates placed other names in nomination—Farley, Garner, Senator Millard Tydings of Maryland, and Secretary of State Hull—but Roosevelt ran away with the nomination on the first ballot. He received 946 votes; all the others combined received only 147. The real fight at the convention was over the choice of FDR's running mate. The President wanted Secretary of Agriculture Henry Wallace, who was never popular with the professional party leaders. At the White House, Roosevelt threatened not to accept the nomination unless Wallace were nominated, but his threat was not known to the Chicago delegates. In a hard struggle, Wallace beat out McNutt and Speaker of the House William B. Bankhead of Alabama. The Democratic platform emphasized the New Deal accomplishments and straddled opposition to foreign war and aid to the allies on foreign matters.

Willkie began his campaign in a big way in mid-August before a huge crowd in his hometown, but Roosevelt restricted himself to well-publicized inspections of defense industries and avoided campaign speeches until almost time for balloting. Nevertheless, during the summer FDR took two actions relevant to the war-peace issue that were risky immediately preceding an election; he urged the passage of and signed the nation's first peacetime military conscription act and by administrative action alone negotiated the Destroyer-Bases Deal with Great Britain.

Although both sides had resorted to a draft during the Civil War and conscription had proved necessary to build an effective army during World War I, Americans had never liked the idea of military conscription. Conscription, especially during peacetime, evoked visions of European autocracy. However, in June, 1940, Senator Edward Burke, a Democratic conservative from Nebraska, and James W. Wadsworth, Jr., a conservative Republican Congressman from New York, jointly introduced a conscription bill. Roosevelt supported it. He urged the draft in his acceptance speech to the Chicago nominating convention. Congress passed the bill by almost two-to-one votes in each house, and on September 16, Roosevelt signed the Burke-Wadsworth or Selective Service Act of 1940. The measure called for the registration of all men between the ages of twenty-one and thirty-six. Those called to service by a lottery system, a maximum of nine hundred thousand in any year, were subject to a year's military training at a base pay of $21 a month. Draftees were not to be sent outside of the western hemisphere. In addition, in another measure, the president received authority to call National Guard units into federal service. The first Selective Service Administrator was Clarence Dykstra, former city manager of Cincinnati and then president of the University of Wisconsin. Potential draftees registered under the Act on October 16. On October

444

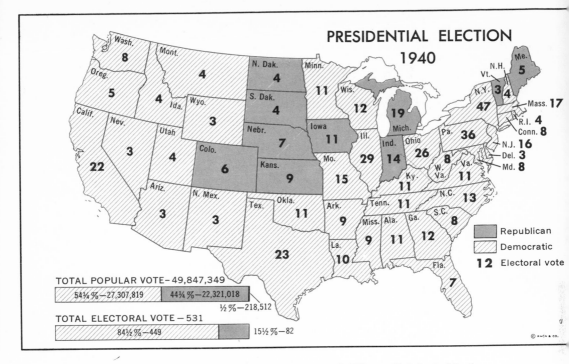

PRESIDENTIAL ELECTION
1940

Wash. 8
Oreg. 5
Calif. 22
Nev. 3
Ida. 4
Mont. 4
Wyo. 3
Utah 4
Ariz. 3
N. Mex. 3
Colo. 6
N. Dak. 4
S. Dak. 4
Nebr. 7
Kans. 9
Okla. 11
Tex. 23
Minn. 11
Iowa 11
Mo. 15
Ark. 9
La. 10
Wis. 12
Ill. 29
Miss. 9
Ala. 11
Ga. 12
Tenn. 11
Ky. 11
Ind. 14
Mich. 19
Ohio 26
W. Va. 8
Va. 11
N.C. 13
S.C. 8
Fla. 7
Pa. 36
N.Y. 47
Vt. 3
N.H. 4
Me. 5
Mass. 17
R.I. 4
Conn. 8
N.J. 16
Del. 3
Md. 8

Republican
Democratic
12 Electoral vote

TOTAL POPULAR VOTE— 49,847,349
54¾%—27,307,819   44¾%—22,321,018
½%—218,512
TOTAL ELECTORAL VOTE — 531
84½%—449   15½%—82

© RAND & CO.

29, just a week before election day, Department of War officials held the ceremony of drawing the draft lottery numbers. The first draftees began their training in November.

The Destroyer-Bases Deal arose from British need for more protection against submarines in the North Atlantic and from an anticipated German invasion of their island in the late summer. Attorney General Robert Jackson found a legal route through a maze of possibly prohibiting laws for the United States to turn fifty destroyers over to the British. These vessels constituted about two-sevenths of a reconditioned fleet from World War I storage. To turn over the destroyers, Jackson found, did not violate the neutrality laws because they had not been built specifically to be granted to a belligerent power. An amendment to a naval appropriations act in June, 1940, had forbidden transfer of such equipment to a foreign nation unless the Chief of Naval Operations and the Army Chief of Staff certified that the equipment was not necessary to the nation's defense. General George C. Marshall and Admiral Harold R. ("Dolly") Stark approved the transfer to Great Britain, calculating that bolstering English defenses strengthened American security. But there was no precedent for the Destroyer-Bases Deal and no express constitutional authority; FDR clearly altered the conventional, constitutional role of the president's power to conduct foreign affairs. Representatives of Great Britain and the United States signed an agreement at Washington, September 2, 1940. In return for the fifty reconditioned destroyers, Britain granted America ninety-nine year leases for naval and air bases in Jamaica, the Bahamas, St. Lucia, Antigua, Trinidad, and British Guiana. America received leases for bases on Newfoundland and Bermuda in addition as gifts, although it is doubt-

445

ful if the gifts would have been forthcoming if the destroyers had not been. The British also guaranteed that the destroyers would never be surrendered.

When Roosevelt announced the agreement to Congress on the following day, there was a storm of protest from some newspapers and politicians. The Destroyer-Bases Deal was clearly a major move away from neutrality. Churchill later wrote in his memoirs that by earlier standards of neutrality Hitler would have been justified in declaring war upon the United States. The ablest defenders of Roosevelt's prewar foreign policies have written, "After the Destroyer Deal American neutrality was hardly more than a technicality. . . ."[1] But Willkie had already gone on record as an advocate of a strong British fleet and confined his criticism to FDR's failure to consult Congress about the deal before he consummated it. Noninterventionists were partially disarmed by the bases given to the United States; they were for strong hemispheric defense, which would be improved with the new bases. In the absence of the Republican candidate's strong opposition, the Destroyer-Bases Deal passed by without most people being fully aware of the implications of the arrangement. Analyses of public opinion showed that a bare majority of the population favored the Roosevelt-Churchill agreement.

For most of the campaign Willkie was inhibited by his basic agreement with the Roosevelt policies. He confined his criticisms to the failure of the New Deal to solve unemployment and to charges that national defense was inadequate. He also hammered away at the idea of a third term, but none of these themes produced any marked response. Then in late September, taking the advice of Republican professionals, Willkie let go on the war-peace issue and charged that Roosevelt was a warmonger. "If his promise to keep our boys out of foreign wars is no better than his promise to balance the budget, they're already almost on the transports." The Republican campaign caught fire. Roosevelt saw that he would have to campaign. October public opinion polls showed Willkie gaining. Roosevelt announced in mid-October that he would make a series of five political addresses. In these addresses he not only proudly enumerated the New Deal reforms and stated that his Republican opponents had resisted them all, he reassured the nation about war. At Philadelphia: "There is no secret treaty, no secret obligation, no secret commitment, no secret understanding in any shape or form, direct or indirect, with any other Government, or any other nation in any part of the world, to involve this nation in any war or for any other purpose." At Boston: "I have said this before, but I shall say it again and again and again: Your boys are not going to be sent into any foreign wars."

Roosevelt's popular vote on November 5 was 27,243,466; Willkie's was 22,304,755. The popular plurality, while significant, was less than any since 1916. But Roosevelt had a huge majority in the electoral college, 449 to 82. Besides Maine and Vermont, Willkie carried Indiana, Michigan, and Iowa and five Great Plains states. Roosevelt carried the big cities. The Democrats gained six seats in the House and lost three in the Senate.

With little change in the congressional party line-up, the legislative branch remained under the control of the Republican-Dixie coalition. But by

---

[1] William L. Langer and S. Everett Gleason, *The Undeclared War, 1940–1941* (New York: Harper and Brothers, 1953), p. 2.

1940, the administration itself was something of a conservative coalition. In May, 1940, when Roosevelt created the Defense Advisory Commission, he appointed William S. Knudsen, a General Motors official who had been a heavy contributor to the Liberty League. Just before the Republican convention in June he had startled the nation by appointing two prominent Republicans to the cabinet: Henry L. Stimson, who had been Secretary of War under Taft and Secretary of State under Hoover, became Secretary of War again; Frank Knox, who had been Landon's running mate less than four years before, became Secretary of the Navy.

Moving toward "Shooting Nonbelligerence"

In early December, 1940, Roosevelt embarked on a vacation cruise on the U.S.S. *Tuscaloosa*. While on the cruise he received a long communication from Prime Minister Churchill. Great Britain was in a desperate situation, wrote Churchill, even if it had been able to prevent the Nazis from delivering a knockout blow. To prevent defeat in 1941 and to lay the groundwork for eventual victory over Germany, assistance from the United States would be vital. To hold out, Britain needed American goods transported on American merchant ships and protected by American naval vessels. For eventual victory, Britain needed all kinds of war supplies, including seven thousand combat planes by the spring of 1942 and a like number of training aircraft. Churchill wrote not as a suppliant but as a fellow opponent of fascism:

> If, as I believe, you are convinced, Mr. President, that the defeat of the Nazi and Fascist tyranny is a matter of high consequence to the people of the United States . . . you will regard this letter not as an appeal for aid, but as a statement of the minimum action necessary to the achievement of our common purpose.[2]

Roosevelt quickly went to work on the problem of how best to aid the British. The difficulty, as FDR saw it, was how to provide the material of war Britain needed without creating a festering sore of bad will through a war loan. Allied loans during World War I had created collection problems that plagued the 1920's and 1930's. Roosevelt's solution was to lend goods rather than money to be repaid after the war in goods and services. This idea became the essence of the Lend-Lease Act. In a press conference on December 17, 1940, FDR used the analogy of lending a neighbor one's garden hose to put out a fire in the neighbor's house. Roosevelt said that one would not say, "Neighbor, my garden hose cost me $15; you have to pay me $15 for it." One would just connect the hose and get it back after the fire was out. In a radio "fireside chat" on December 29, he took his argument for massive aid to the British directly to the people. "We must," he said, "be the great arsenal of democracy." His argument was that such a policy would lessen the chances of American belligerence: ". . . there is far less chance of the United States

---

[2] Winston S. Churchill, *Their Finest Hour* (Boston: Houghton Mifflin Company, 1949), p. 567.

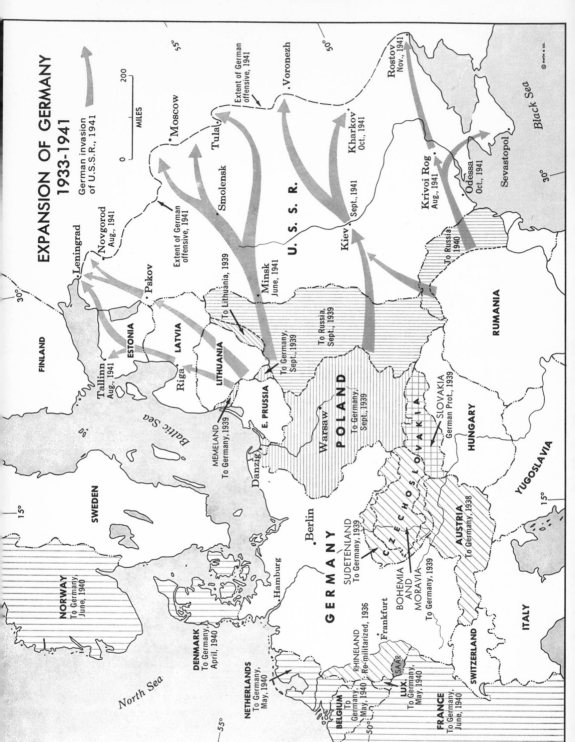

EXPANSION OF GERMANY
1933-1941

German invasion
of U.S.S.R., 1941

MILES
0   200

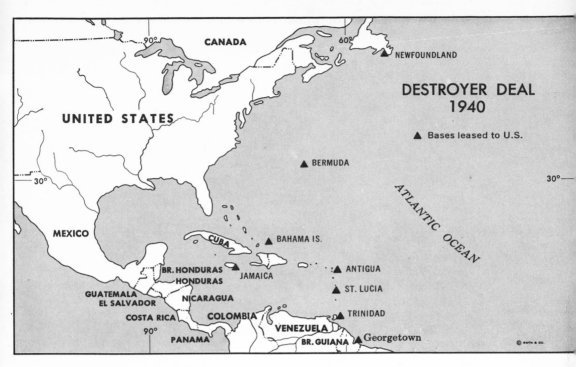

DESTROYER DEAL
1940

▲ Bases leased to U.S.

getting into the war, if we do all we can now to support the nations defending themselves against attack by the Axis than if we acquiesce in their defeat, submit tamely to an Axis victory, and wait our turn to be the object of attack in another war later on." Public response to the radio talk, somewhat to FDR's surprise, was heavily favorable.

Treasury Department officials drafted the Lend-Lease bill in the first week of January, 1941. On January 6, FDR helped prepare Congress and the people for the measure in his State of the Union message. In the speech he called upon America to pledge itself to give the victims of Axis aggression "the strength to regain and maintain a free world." The United States should send "in ever-increasing numbers, ships, planes, tanks, guns." He looked forward, he said, to a world "founded upon four essential human freedoms": freedom of speech and expression, freedom to worship as one chooses, freedom from want, and freedom from fear. He optimistically added, "That is no vision of a distant millennium. It is a definite basis for a kind of world attainable in our own time and generation."

The Lend-Lease bill, H.R. 1776, was introduced in the House on January 10. Despite hearings in each house of Congress and prolonged debate by the bill's opponents, the measure went through fairly quickly. Secretary Hull guided the administration witnesses in the congressional hearings. Its opponents were a mixed lot. Among those appearing against the bill were Colonel Charles A. Lindbergh, Colonel Robert R. McCormick of the *Chicago Daily Tribune*, General Robert E. Wood of the America First Committee, the constitutional lawyer John Bassett Moore, historian Charles A. Beard, and the editor of the *Christian Century*, Charles Clayton Morrison. Wendell Willkie publicly supported the bill. The House passed H.R. 1776 on February 8. The vote was 260 to 165; 236 Democrats and 24 Republicans voted for the bill; 25 Democrats, 135 Republicans, and one American Labor party member (Vito Marcantonio) voted against it. The bill passed the Senate on March 8 by a margin of 60 to 31; voting against it were 13 Democrats, 17 Republicans, and one Progressive (Robert M. LaFollette, Jr.). Roosevelt signed the bill into law three days later. Soon thereafter Congress appropriated $7 billion to put the measure into effect.

Clearly, the passage of Lend-Lease indicated that the United States was by no means a traditionally neutral power. Even before Lend-Lease, America had at times moved beyond the conventional bounds of neutrality to aid Great Britain. In March, 1941, the United States abandoned all pretense of neutrality and became a nonbelligerent, neither at war nor neutral. Before many months passed, the United States would even draw up with Great Britain a statement of general war aims and engage in naval warfare with the Axis, all the while without becoming a declared belligerent.

Lend-Lease pledged America's enormous economic power and resources to defeat the Axis. Now the problem was to produce the goods and deliver them to England. Production was under the general planning and coordination of the Office of Production Management created in December, 1940, with William S. Knudsen as director and labor leader Sidney Hillman as associate director. Production problems were many and intricate, but the economy's basic capacity to produce was never seriously in question. Economic indices climbed with the stimulation of enormous spending for defense and Lend-Lease. Delivery, however, was a serious problem. In the spring of 1941, German submarines stepped up their operations in the North Atlantic. On March 25, Germany extended the war zone westward to include all of Iceland and the strait between Iceland and Greenland. That month German action destroyed over five hundred thousand tons of merchant shipping, and bettered that mark in the succeeding two months.

In the spring and summer of 1941, Roosevelt took many actions calculated to increase the number of ships engaged in delivery to Britain and to protect them from German attack. At the end of March, he permitted a British battleship to be repaired in an American port; thereafter, British naval vessels frequently used United States repair facilities. At about the same time, the Coast Guard seized thirty Axis ships and thirty-five Danish ships that had been interned in American ports and soon thereafter FDR obtained from Congress authority to put the ships to general use. Roosevelt transferred ten Coast Guard cutters to the British navy for antisubmarine operations. Then on April 10, Roosevelt proclaimed that the neutral zone set by the Panama Conference in 1939 should be extended eastward to the twenty-fifth meridian. This was a line running roughly halfway between the Brazilian bulge of South America and the westernmost bulge of Africa north to the northeastern coast of Greenland. West of that line American ships and planes would patrol convoys, notifying them of the presence of enemy force. Also on April 10, Roosevelt removed the Red Sea region from the areas banned to American shipping since the British needed supplies for the defense of Egypt and the Middle East.

In another "fireside chat" on May 27 Roosevelt declared "an unlimited national emergency exists and requires the strengthening of our defense to the extreme limit of our national power and authority." Historians have sometimes cited the German sinking of the *Robin Moor*, an American merchant ship, on May 21 about seven hundred miles off the Brazilian coast as the stimulus to this emergency proclamation, but that could not have been the case because the sinking was not known in Washington until the crew was rescued from its lifeboats nearly three weeks after the sinking. Probably the reason was that Hitler was at the moment enjoying great successes in North Africa, the Mediterranean, and the Balkans.

In July, the United States navy began regular convoy escort duty as far east as Iceland. Iceland, then a Danish possession, had been occupied by British and Canadian troops after the fall of Denmark in April, 1940. On July 7, 1941, American marines replaced them. With American troops to support on Iceland, the navy began convoy escort service. Admiral Ernest J. King's order of July 19 directed a naval unit to "escort United States and Iceland flag shipping, including shipping of any nationality which may join such . . . convoys, between United States ports and bases, and Iceland." The British navy escorted the convoys on to British ports. So far as the western Atlantic was concerned, only one order remained to be made before undeclared naval war was a fact: an order to shoot the enemy on sight. Until then, American naval vessels could only track submarines, direct convoys in evasive action, and notify British destroyers of the location of the enemy.

The nature and scope of the war changed dramatically on Sunday, June 22, 1941, when the Nazis invaded the Soviet Union. Hitler betrayed Stalin, and, as Nikita Khrushchev revealed in his "secret" speech of February, 1956, Stalin was so stunned and unprepared for attack that at first he refused to believe it or take effective counter measures. The Nazi panzer divisions struck quick and deep blows, often being welcomed by subject Soviet peoples such as the Ukrainians. (The Nazis so mistreated these people that in time they turned against their new masters.) American military experts predicted that Germany would conquer Russia in three weeks. Now, American Communists, for the first time since the Nazi-Soviet pact, came out strongly for the defense effort and war. They suddenly ended a strike they had fomented in the aircraft industry in California. In mid-July Harry Hopkins, Lend-Lease administrator and by then FDR's closest adviser, went to London to arrange for a meeting between Roosevelt and Churchill. Churchill suggested he go on to Moscow and discuss affairs with Stalin. Stalin and his lieutenants told Hopkins that they would be able to stop the Nazi advance and launch a counterattack in the winter, which proved to be true. He also said Russia wanted Lend-Lease supplies and hoped the United States would enter the war. He offered to allow American military units to fight under their own command on the Russian front. In October, Britain and the United States promised to give Russia $1 billion worth of aid by mid-1942; Congress also increased Lend-Lease appropriations by another $6 billion and defeated an amendment to deny the Soviets Lend-Lease equipment. In early November, FDR officially declared Russia eligible to receive Lend-Lease. The Soviets eventually received over $11 billion worth of aid.

The meeting between Churchill and Roosevelt that Hopkins arranged for in London took place aboard the American battleship *Augusta*, Admiral

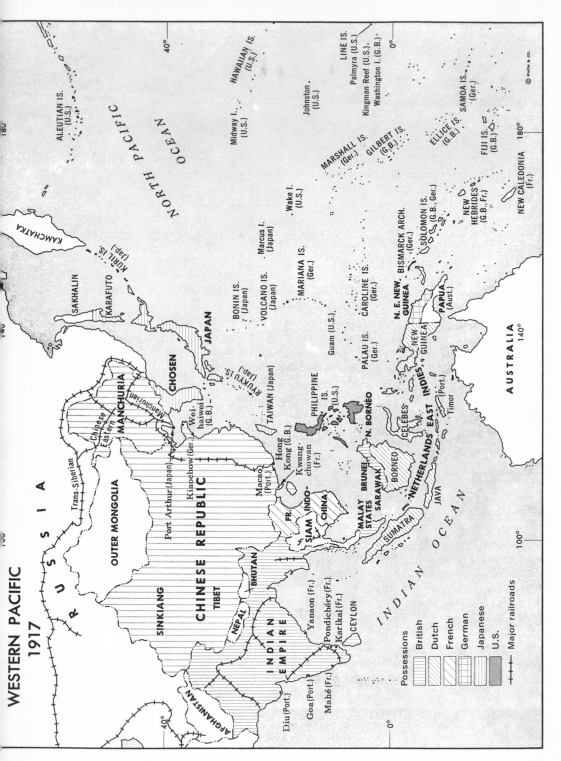

WESTERN PACIFIC
1917

Possessions
British
Dutch
French
German
Japanese
U.S.
Major railroads

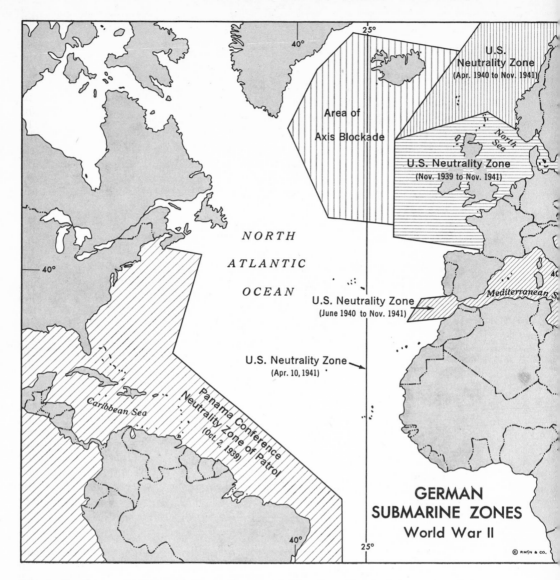

GERMAN
SUBMARINE ZONES
World War II

King's flagship, off the coast from Argentia, Newfoundland, August 9 to 12, 1941. Never before had an American president during a time of official peace had such a conference with a prime minister of a belligerent power. Roosevelt and Churchill discussed technical matters such as long-range purchasing policies, general strategy, and postwar aims. Churchill tried but failed to get a commitment from Roosevelt that the United States would come to Britain's aid if the Japanese attacked British possessions or dominions in the Pacific. Roosevelt agreed only to warn Japan against such a course and did not accept the British draft of the warning. The most publicized result of the meeting was the Atlantic Charter, which was released to the world's press on August 14, the first public announcement of the Argentia Conference. The President and the Prime Minister "deem it right to make known certain common principles in the national policies of their respective countries on which they base their hopes for a better future for the world." There followed a set of eight points similar to Wilson's Fourteen Points of World War I: no aggrandizement of any nation of any kind; no territorial changes not in accord with the expressed wishes of the people concerned; the right of all people to choose the form of government under which they live and self-government restored to those people forcibly deprived of it; equal access for all nations to world trade and raw materials; economic collaboration of all nations to improve the material status of all; freedom from fear and want; freedom of the seas; and disarmament after the war. The American noninterventionist press replied to the announcement of the Atlantic Charter with outraged editorials, but the high-sounding principles enunciated in the document had an appeal to the electorate. Public opinion polls indicated no great change of opinion about war and peace one way or another.

The public was more loath to accept the new amendment to the Selective Service Act of 1940 than to accept the Argentia Conference. In June, 1941, the administration began a campaign to extend the terms of service of the draftees who had been inducted. Roosevelt originally wanted the term of service extended to the end of the emergency and wanted to lift the ban on sending draftees overseas. Congressional leaders informed the White House that this would not pass. Many argued that to extend the term of service beyond the original twelve months amounted to a breach of faith with the soldier. Roosevelt dropped the request for lifting the overseas ban and had to settle for an eighteen-month extension. The Senate passed the amendment on August 7; on August 12, the House passed the bill by one vote, 203 to 202. The House Democrats divided in favor of the bill, 182 to 65; the Republicans lined up against it, 133 to 21.

The German-proclaimed war zone and the American-proclaimed neutral zone overlapped in the waters west and south of Iceland. With both German U-boats and American naval vessels engaged in convoy escort in these waters, it was only a matter of time before a serious incident occurred. On September 4, a British patrol plane notified the American destroyer *Greer*, on its way to Iceland with passengers and mail, that a German submarine was submerged about ten miles ahead of it. The *Greer* then located the submarine and trailed it for several hours, meanwhile broadcasting the submarine's position to the British. Finally, the submarine fired two torpedoes at the *Greer*. Both of them missed the target. The *Greer* answered with depth charges. Their effect, if any, was not known.

The *Greer* affair provided the President the kind of incident he wanted. In a worldwide radio broadcast on September 11 he declared, ". . . our patrolling vessels and planes will protect all merchant ships—not only American ships but ships of any flag—engaged in commerce in our defensive waters." His speech ended, "From now on, if German or Italian vessels of war enter the waters the protection of which is necessary for American defense, they do so at their own peril." Two days later official naval orders implemented the new policy: the fleet in the Atlantic was to provide "protection against hostile attack of United States and foreign flag shipping (other than German and Italian shipping) by escorting, convoying and patrolling as circumstances may require, or by destroying German and Italian naval, land, and air forces encountered." Without a declaration of war, a shooting war in the North Atlantic had begun.

The undeclared Atlantic war proceeded. In mid-October a Nazi torpedo hit the destroyer *Kearny*, and eleven of the crew were killed. On October 31, a German submarine sank another destroyer, the *Reuben James*, with the loss of 115 lives.

With shooting war and Lend-Lease, the neutrality law still in effect became an anachronism. On October 9, 1941, Roosevelt asked Congress to repeal the critical parts of the Neutrality Act of 1939. He asked specifically for repeal of Section VI, which forbade the arming of merchant ships, but expressed the additional hope that Congress would repeal the sections preventing American ships from traveling in combat zones the President designated and from visiting belligerent ports. Since naval vessels were already authorized to shoot on sight, there seemed little point in denying merchant ships authority to arm themselves. The House passed a bill repealing Section VI of the Neutrality Act on October 17 by a vote of 259 to 138. With such a wide margin, the President was emboldened to ask the Senate to include his other repeal requests. The Senate complied on November 7, but the vote, fifty to thirty-seven, was the narrowest administration victory in the Senate on any foreign policy issue since the beginning of the war in Europe. Back went the bill to the House, as the Senate had repealed more of the Neutrality Act than had the House in its October vote. Again, Roosevelt's proposal had a narrow majority, 212 to 194. Democrats supported the measure, 189 to 53; Republicans opposed it, 137 to 22. Representatives from the South generally supported the repeal, those from the Midwest generally opposed, and those from the Far West and the large industrial states of the East divided about evenly.

By November 13, 1941, when the Neutrality Act was finally repealed and armed American ships were free to go even to British ports and when American naval convoy escorts had standing orders to shoot German and Italian craft on sight and had exchanged blows with Axis vessels, it may fairly be said that the United States through its elected constitutional officers had decided to accept war with Germany and Italy. Still, such was the strength of the belief that the United States should not declare war without extreme provocation that, as late as December 6, it is almost certain that Congress would not have passed a war resolution if Roosevelt had asked. A public opinion poll in November indicated that less than 35 per cent of the people would have voted for war if a national referendum had been held. "All aid short of war" remained the motto of the majority until the war came. And it came not at the focus of primary attention in the Atlantic, but in the Pacific.

The Long Negotiations with Japan

In February, 1939, the Japanese seized the Chinese island of Hainan in the South China Sea. While actually fighting only China, Japan was moving south

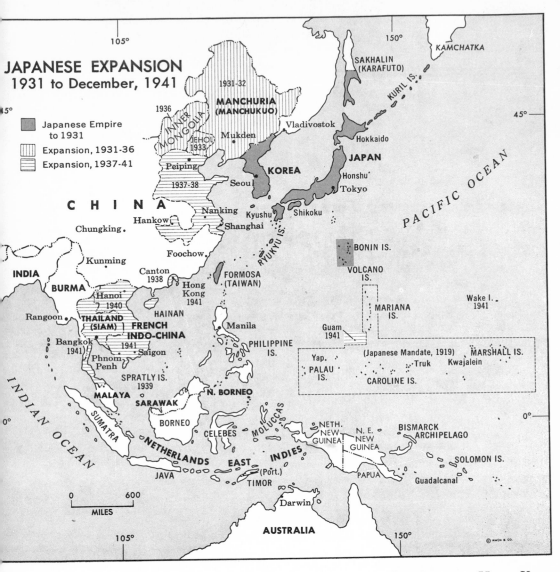

JAPANESE EXPANSION
1931 to December, 1941

Japanese Empire to 1931
Expansion, 1931-36
Expansion, 1937-41

and threatening French Indochina, British shipping between Hong Kong and Singapore, and even the Philippines. The United States replied with a threat of economic warfare. On July 26, 1939, the United States gave Japan the six months' notice necessary to abrogate the Japanese-American commercial treaty of 1911. After late January, 1940, no treaty obligation prevented the United States from withholding such strategic materials as oil and scrap iron from Japan. Deficient in many natural resources, Japan had relied upon America to fulfill over half the raw materials for its military and naval needs.

The "phony war" in Europe, September, 1939, to April, 1940, brought no change in Japanese ambitions. In January, 1940, a moderate government headed by Mitsumasa Yonai came to power. But Hitler's spectacular successes in the spring of 1940 encouraged Japanese militarists to press for a more aggressive policy. The defeat of France and Holland left French Indochina and the Dutch East Indies ripe for Japanese plucking, and hard-pressed Great Britain was hardly in a position to resist strongly. Japanese militarists' dream of a Greater East Asia Co-Prosperity Sphere seemed impelled toward realization by European events. The militarists successfully applied pressure on the Yonai government to begin negotiations for a military alliance with Germany, and on July 16 the army high command succeeded in toppling the regime altogether. The new government, headed by the moderate Prince Fumimaro Konoye, had at least two ardently expansionist and militaristic officials in key positions: the Minister for Foreign Affairs, Yosuke Matsuoka, and the Minister of War, General Hideki Tojo. The new government lost no time in pressing expansionist policies and forming an alliance with Germany and Italy.

The Konoye government sought from the Vichy government, the accommodating French government in the south of France that Germany allowed to exist after the conquest, the right to station Japanese troops in northern Indochina. It sought from the Churchill government in London an order closing the Burma road, one of the main lifelines to the Nationalist Chinese capital at Chungking. Neither was in a strong position to resist, and both granted Japanese demands quickly. The British reopened the road in October, 1940. The Dutch stalled the Japanese and managed to prevent them from getting all the East Indian oil they wanted until war began and the Japanese took the islands by force.

Then, on September 27, 1940, the Japanese concluded the Tripartite, or Berlin, Pact with Germany and Italy. Japan recognized German and Italian leadership in a new European order, and the European powers reciprocated. The critical clause was Article Three, in which the three powers agreed "to assist one another with all political, economic and military means when one of the three contracting powers is attacked by a power at present not involved in the European war or in the Chinese-Japanese conflict." Since another part of the agreement specifically excluded Russia, the treaty obviously was aimed at the United States. The alliance was defensive in its wording. There was no guarantee, for example, that Germany would or would not declare war on the United States if Japan should attack America. Japan completed its treaty arrangements with European powers on April 13, 1941, when it made a neutrality agreement with Russia. The Japanese and the Soviets agreed to remain neutral if either were attacked by another power or powers. This left Japan free to develop her plans for Asia, but it also allowed Russia to put its main attention upon Europe. The agreement proved much to Russia's advantage when Germany attacked in June.

Washington responded to these Japanese developments with a policy of economic pressure and diplomatic warnings. When the Japanese made their demands upon the French and British, Roosevelt replied with an order requiring a federal license for permission to export petroleum or its products and high-grade scrap metal. Soon thereafter, he completely embargoed shipments of aviation gasoline out of the Western Hemisphere. When it became apparent that the Tripartite Pact was in the offing, he also embargoed all scrap iron and steel, making an exception only for Great Britain. At the same time he announced an additional Export-Import Bank loan to China of $25 million. The diplomatic notes were equally strong. In February, 1941, the State Department notified Japan that threats to its sources of "essential primary commodities" in Southeast Asia—oil, rubber, and tin—"would not be tolerated." These actions, as well as publicized discussions of American naval officers with their counterparts from Britain, the Netherlands, and Australia, induced Japan to adopt a more conciliatory position at least temporarily. Roosevelt thus was able to forestall an all-out Japanese drive while the anti-fascist powers of Europe suffered their heaviest reverses in 1940 and most of 1941.

Important Japanese political groups and figures were sharply divided about how adventurous Japan should be in its expansionist ambitions. Some moderates, including important naval officers, were fearful of a war with the United States; others, particularly the army high command, itched for war. Few Japanese moderates, however, were willing to concede Washington's intractable position on China: that Japan should withdraw and grant Chinese political integrity. Failure to reach any agreement on the central Chinese question strengthened Japanese extremists and increased the likelihood of war, perhaps making it inevitable.

Division in Japanese political circles was apparent from the tangled story of negotiations, official and unofficial, between Tokyo and Washington in the first half of 1941. Two American Roman Catholic clergymen, Bishop James E. Walsh and Father James M. Drought, in Japan on business for their order, discussed Japanese-American problems unofficially with moderate Japanese officials. Eventually, the two were asked to carry some generous proposals to President Roosevelt that they understood came from Prince Konoye himself. The proposals they carried conceded a great deal on China; in return, Japan wanted the United States to let up on its anti-Japanese economic policies. Secretary Hull, dubious that any Japanese government could actually and officially deliver on such generous offers in the face of Japanese militarist strength, suggested that nothing be done until the arrival in Washington of the new Japanese ambassador, Admiral Kichisaburo Nomura, who had attended the United States Naval Academy as a youth. Discussions with Admiral Nomura proceeded promisingly but inconclusively until Foreign Minister Matsuoka returned to Tokyo from Moscow, where he had been negotiating the Russo-Japanese neutrality agreement. Angry about the discussions in Washington conducted during his absence from Tokyo, Matsuoka insisted upon very hard terms. The discussions thereupon deadlocked with no results.

In late July, 1941, after Germany had moved deeply into Russia and thereby changed the Asian picture despite the Russo-Japanese neutrality agreement, Japan completed its military domination of French Indochina. In the summer of 1940, Japan had moved troops into northern Indochina; now it moved them into the South as well, all with the consent of the Vichy government. The suspicion that the real purpose of this maneuver was to put the Japanese in position to attack the Dutch East Indies and British Malaya was confirmed by "Magic," the United States Navy Intelligence code-breaking operation, which had recently succeeded in solving one of the important Japanese codes. Roosevelt retaliated on July 25 by freezing Japanese funds in the United States, thus seriously crippling Japan's power either to buy or sell in America. The Netherlands government in exile and Great Britain soon followed suit. Roosevelt also closed the Panama Canal to Japanese shipping and called the Philippine militia to active duty. American public opinion seemed more strongly behind FDR's Japanese policy, at least in the summer of 1941, than it was behind his European policies. When FDR left for the Atlantic Conference with Churchill in early August, Japanese-American relations were more strained than they had ever been.

At the Argentia meeting, Churchill urged Roosevelt to take an even stronger position with Japan. Roosevelt agreed that upon his return to Washington he would inform Ambassador Nomura that "any further encroachment by Japan in the Southwestern Pacific would produce a situation in which the United States Government would be compelled to take countermeasures even though these might lead to war between the United States and Japan." The very day FDR returned to the White House, August 17, he and Hull had a conference with Nomura. Nomura, however, had come to the conference with a conciliatory proposal about which he had already informed Hull. Hull, fearful that the strong statement agreed to at the Atlantic Conference might even cause the Konoye cabinet to fall and be replaced by a less moderate one, persuaded FDR to water down the American warning.

Nomura's proposal was no less than a suggestion that Roosevelt meet with Konoye in a Pacific conference to attempt to resolve the difficulties between their nations. Konoye had decided that in the face of the economic stranglehold America had on his country only two alternatives remained: either some kind of Japanese-American agreement or war. Afraid that war would bring Japanese defeat, probably quickly, Konoye decided to make a major effort to bring about an agreement despite the considerable pressure for war that came from the military. If an agreement were possible, Konoye calculated, only he and Roosevelt could do it. If an agreement still proved impossible, the world at least would know that the greatest efforts had been expended to prevent war. Joseph C. Grew, the United States ambassador in Tokyo, was optimistic about such a Pacific conference and strongly supported it.

Roosevelt at first was inclined to view a meeting with Konoye favorably. He especially was impressed with Japanese notes in late August and early September that indicated that Japan was "prepared to withdraw its troops from Indo-China as soon as the China Incident is settled or a just peace is established in East Asia" and that it could be induced to loosen its ties with the Axis. But Hull urged caution. Before Roosevelt agreed to a meeting, Hull argued, the Japanese must be specific about what they would concede, and unless they were prepared to make concessions about China there should be no bargain. Roosevelt took Hull's advice. Konoye made no more specific concessions in writing, perhaps because politics within Japan dictated that he should avoid a stance that looked like appeasement. On October 16, the Konoye government had to resign when it could not produce anything solid as the fruit of its moderation. Two days later, General Tojo himself became premier.

Because Roosevelt declined to "go to the summit" with Konoye, to use a journalistic phrase not coined until years later, and because war did come between Japan and the United States, Roosevelt has been severely criticized. No one, of course, knows what would have happened if there had been a Pacific conference. Both Roosevelt's critics who say that a conference with Konoye could have prevented war or postponed it until after Germany and Italy were defeated and his defenders who say that a conference would have been useless argue from assumption rather than evidence.

Pearl Harbor

Even the elevation of General Tojo to the premiership did not mean an immediate Japanese decision for war. Emperor Hirohito himself, with the support of the navy, urged restraint upon the militarists. At a conference of Japanese leaders with the emperor on November 5, the various factions made an agreement. The Japanese government would make one major effort for peace with the United States. The conference spelled out what Japan would concede under certain conditions and sent a second ambassador, Saburo Kurusu, to Washington to help Nomura. But, it was agreed, if some kind of agreement were not made with the United States by late November, Japan would go to war. The Japanese negotiators at Washington knew, therefore, that time was running out, that peace depended upon the success of the negotiations.

The Roosevelt administration also realized the crucial importance of the November negotiations because "Magic" had picked up and decoded important messages to the Japanese embassy in Washington. American negotiators knew that Japan had two plans, the second to be presented if the United States rejected the first. The second plan made more concessions than the first but was to be only a temporary arrangement, not so much a permanent agreement as a stopgap truce to allow still more time for negotiations. Japan conceded nothing on China in either plan. Then on November 22 "Magic" intercepted a message from Tokyo to the Japanese embassy which extended the deadline for negotiations from November 25 to November 29 but which stated if there were no results by then "things are automatically going to happen." Precisely what things and where were unknown, but the implication of war was clear.

Ambassadors Nomura and Kurusu presented the second Japanese plan on November 20. Between then and November 26, when Hull replied, activity within the Roosevelt administration was feverish; yet the activity brought relatively few results. After receipt of the "things are automatically going to happen" message, Washington warned military and naval commanders in the Pacific that surprise attacks on Guam and the Philippines were possible. Rather quickly the administration decided to reject the second Japanese plan and to concentrate on preparing a counterproposal. Discussion centered upon the provisions of a *modus vivendi* of three months to be proposed to the Japanese. During a three-month truce, Japan and the United States would continue to search for a solution to peace and the United States would build up its force of B-17 bombers in the Philippines. Secretary of War Stimson believed that a strong bomber force there could prevent a Japanese movement to the south. Since a comparable build-up of fighter support for these B-17's was out of the question, such faith in unprotected bombers was naive. Again, the Chinese question proved to be the stumbling block. One draft of the *modus vivendi* had a vague statement to the effect that the United States "would not look with disfavor" upon conversations between China and Japan looking toward a peaceful settlement of their differences. When the State Department showed this draft to the Chinese, British, and Dutch embassies, the Chinese protested and the Dutch and British expressed no enthusiasm. In any case, it is dubious that Japan would have been attracted by the proposal about China, vague as it was.

By November 26, the administration was so pessimistic about any real solution that it proposed no *modus vivendi* at all but rather put forward a ten-point program for a long-range settlement that encompassed all the American demands. The statement Hull read to Nomura and Kurusu on November 26, demanding as it did complete Japanese withdrawal from China and Indochina and abandonment of the puppet Japanese government in China, was obviously unacceptable to Tokyo. Hull knew that the Japanese would not accept the United States demand. On the day after he replied to the Japanese ambassadors, he told Stimson that the situation was in the hands of the military rather than the diplomats. Actually, both sides had by late November taken a "take it or leave it" attitude and accepted the probability of war, even though reluctantly.

In the discussions within the American government, November 20 to 26, one of the main subjects was what the United States would do if the Japanese launched a major attack in Southeast Asia. A large Japanese convoy was moving south along the China coast. The United States anticipated an attack, possibly a surprise attack, on Malaya, Thailand, the Dutch East Indies, or the Philippines, maybe against all of them. The focus clearly was on the western Pacific and the perimeter of Asia rather than the middle Pacific and Hawaii. The administration believed that if Japan attacked toward the south then the United States should enter the conflict. To the administration, the main question was how to persuade the American people that a Japanese attack upon a non-American territory was sufficient grounds for war. Roosevelt's speech writers worked on a message to Congress designed to persuade Congress and the public that Japanese advance southward jeopardized the United States and constituted justifiable cause for a war declaration. At a meeting of the so-called war cabinet—Roosevelt, Hull, Stimson, Secretary of the Navy Knox, Chief of Staff George C. Marshall, and Chief of Naval Operations Harold R. Stark—on November 25, according to Stimson's diary, the group discussed "the question of how we should maneuver them into the position of firing the first shot without allowing too much danger to ourselves." After World War II, this selection from Stimson's diary was a major arrow in the quiver of Roosevelt critics who charged that FDR tricked the American people into the war by maneuvering the Japanese into attack. FDR's purpose, according to these critics, was to get into a war with Hitler that the public would accept. The soundest interpretation of the "maneuver" sentence is that "we" meant the Americans, British, and Dutch and that the first shot was expected in the western Pacific or Southeast Asia, not that the quotation indicates a Roosevelt scheme to bait Japan with Pearl Harbor in order to get into war with Europe.[3] In fact, it is not certain, despite Roosevelt's predilection and the advice of his cabinet and military subordinates, that the United States would have gone to war over a Japanese movement south. Indeed, when on December 6 Washington received word that Japanese troops were moving on Malaya, Roosevelt dispatched a final desperate plea for peace to Emperor Hirohito. The message did not arrive before the shooting actually began.

On November 25, a Japanese naval force set out from the Kurile Islands north of Japan proper with orders to attack the American naval base at Pearl Harbor and airfields elsewhere in Hawaii at dawn on Sunday, December 7. The task force was prepared to turn back without attacking upon word from Tokyo. No word ever came. At 7:55 A.M. on December 7, planes from Japanese carriers attacked Hawaiian airfields and the American fleet at Pearl Harbor. The attack was an utter surprise. A second wave of planes attacked fifty minutes later. So thorough and devastating was the first attack that only a few American planes from a base the Japanese had negligently overlooked were able to get into the air for the second attack. Only a few antiaircraft batteries were able to respond. Some destroyers went into action against attacking Japanese submarines. The Japanese attack, on the whole, was one of the best planned and executed major raids in the history of warfare. In less than two hours the American military and naval establishment in Hawaii, one of the biggest in the world, was reduced to impotence. Japanese losses consisted of six submarines and twenty-nine planes. Over half of the American planes in Hawaii were destroyed or disabled, five battleships were sunk or seriously damaged, and over three thousand soldiers, sailors, and marines were killed or missing. So serious were American losses that the government refrained from making their extent public for fear of damage to national morale. The Japanese launched almost simultaneous attacks upon Thailand, Malaya, and the Philippines.

Japan timed its reply to the American counterproposal of November 26 to be delivered in Washington early on Sunday afternoon, December 7, a few minutes before the first bombs were to fall on Hawaii. In one of the few hitches in the whole Japanese operation, the Japanese embassy had difficulty deciphering the message and delayed its delivery until just after the American government received word of the Pearl Harbor attack. When Nomura and Kurusu saw Hull, all three parties knew their meeting was a diplomatic mockery.

Who was responsible for the American debacle? This has been a major question of partisan politics and historical bickering ever since the war's end. Obviously, someone was negligent. Was it the commanders in Hawaii, General Walter C. Short and Admiral Husband E. Kimmel, their military and civilian superior officers in Washington, or both? Despite the reams that have been written and the weeks of congressional investigations, the whole story is not yet clear. No major American figure was blameless, nor was any solely responsible. A bigger and more important question is why had American foreign relations deteriorated to such an extent that a surprise attack was

---

[3] For the best account and interpretation of the Stimson diary entry see, Richard Nelson Current, "How Stimson Meant to 'Maneuver' the Japanese," *Mississippi Valley Historical Review*, XL (June, 1953), 67–74, and the same author's *Secretary Stimson: A Study in Statecraft* (New Brunswick, 1954).

possible. There is no simple answer. Quite obviously, the answer will not be reached by debates, professional or political, between those who, on the one hand, want to prove Roosevelt a devilish conspirator who tricked the nation into war by the back door or those who, on the other hand, argue that FDR was entirely blameless and candid.

Japan officially declared war upon the United States about two hours after the Pearl Harbor attack. On December 8, Congress voted a declaration of war against Japan, unanimously in the Senate and with one dissenting vote in the House. The lone dissenter was Jeannette Rankin, Republican of Montana. A former suffragette, the first woman to sit in Congress, and a congressional opponent of war in 1917, she tearfully explained that Christian principles dictated that at least one vote should be cast against war and that it was appropriate that a woman should cast it. Great Britain had declared war upon Japan only hours before the American declaration. The day of the American declaration, Japan asked Germany to declare war upon America. On November 29, Germany had notified Japan she would join her if Japan went to war with America. On December 11, Germany and Italy declared war upon the United States. The same day the United States declared war upon the Axis, this time without a dissenting vote.

Such unanimity for a declaration of war would have been an impossibility before the Japanese attack at Pearl Harbor. Indeed, never before had the United States ever entered a war with such unanimity. In the long run, the Japanese attack was a psychological mistake because it unified America without knocking it out of contention. Grimly, almost fatalistically, with little of the evangelical spirit that characterized America in 1917 and 1918, the American people as a nation set about finishing up the distasteful and ugly business they felt had been forced upon them.

CHAPTER TWENTY-THREE

Mobilizing for Victory

TOTAL WARS ARE FOUGHT AT HOME AS MUCH AS THEY ARE AT THE front. Modern war is a contest between competing industrial complexes as well as combat between military units. As great as the achievements of America's fighting men were in World War II, the United States and its allies could not have won the ultimate victory without the efforts of those who stayed home.

The magnitude of America's wartime economic problem was perhaps as great as its depression problem, although it was considerably different. The task for all productive and distributive facilities and workers was to get sufficient numbers of trained fighting men wherever they were needed in the world and to supply them and allied forces with more and better arms and other material than the enemy's. This meant the economy had to function at forced draft and at well-oiled efficiency. To get the job done, it was necessary, intelligently and forcefully, to allocate and coordinate man-power resources, raw materials, fuel and other energy sources, industrial and agricultural products, and transportation facilities. It followed that the volume of the economy had to be increased and many more goods and services had to be made available and distributed systematically. To insure the ultimate success of these efforts required central planning and direction of the whole complex operation—some kind of national economic planning.

America did the job, but did not do it perfectly; poor decisions, in-justices, raids of organized greed, big and small inefficiencies there were in plenty, but still America did the job. The farmer, the worker, the manager, the bureaucrat, and the investor succeeded in enlarging the relative trickle of war production of 1941 to a huge and steady flow by 1945. Indeed, pro-tected as it was from enemy action, America's power to produce grew mighti-

464

ly during the war. No other major nation emerged from the war industrially stronger than it had entered it.

Politics, Almost as Usual

A supposed advantage of a totalitarian state over a democracy is that it eliminates the indecision, disunity, and distraction of democratic politics. Yet, if World War II was fought to protect democracy in an increasingly totalitarian world, it was necessary to preserve conventional democratic politics. Although there were some who strongly urged the creation of a national economic czar and many who voiced a hope that partisanship would be submerged in national unity, few were ready to give up political advantage or hope for advantage. Political conflict among organized groups, Democrats and Republicans, labor and capital and agriculture, inevitably continued; for the most part, it continued within the traditional democratic ground rules.

The trend was toward increasing power of the political and economic conservatives. Ever since the congressional elections of 1938, the Congress had in fact been governed by a cautious, orthodox coalition of Democratic and Republican conservatives who controlled the chairmanships, through the seniority principle, of most of the important committees. The White House, eager to have the cooperation of Congress, compromised in its requests and found usually that Congress compromised them further. Although many Democrats and a few unusual Republicans hoped the war could be used to extend the social welfare principles of the second New Deal, the President explicitly said that "Dr. Win-the-War" had been substituted for "Dr. New Deal." The President's opponents succeeded in keeping "Dr. New Deal" permanently on the sidelines.

The voters seemed to endorse this rightward drift in the 1942 congressional elections. The party out of the White House usually gains in congressional elections in nonpresidential years, but the Republicans in 1942 went beyond the usual by gaining forty-seven seats in the House of Representatives and ten in the Senate. Senate Democrats lost still another vote on most issues when Nebraska Republicans in their primary elected Kenneth Wherry, who bowed to no man in his conservatism, to replace George Norris, the man who had curbed the power of Speaker Cannon in 1910 and become known as "the father of TVA." Probably part of the anti-Democratic vote reflected concern over the poor way the war was going (the landing in North Africa came just after the election) and with the quite obvious confusion in Washington over industrial mobilization.

Heartened by the off-year elections and strife between the President and conservative congressional Democrats, especially in the Senate and in particular over tax matters, Republicans dared to hope for victory in 1944. The main contenders for the GOP presidential nomination were Wendell Willkie, Governor John W. Bricker of Ohio, and Governor Thomas E. Dewey of New York. Willkie did not stand high with most Republican leaders because of his defeat in 1940 and because of his rather close identification with FDR's policies after the election. Bricker did not have a great deal to command national attention, but, being the chief executive of an important mid-western state, he had good support in that part of the nation. Dewey, who had received national headlines as a "racket-busting" district attorney in New York City before he became governor, was not only attractive and vigorous but had the support of the financially strong eastern wing of the GOP. Willkie withdrew from consideration after his defeat in the Wisconsin presidential primary. (He died before the end of the year.)

The Republican convention in Chicago in late June nominated Dewey on the first ballot and went on to name Bricker as his running mate. Perhaps the most interesting aspect of the convention was the platform it advocated. First, it adopted a strongly internationalist declaration that party leaders had written the previous year at a special conference at Mackinac Island, Michigan. Second, although it was critical of the way Democrats had administered the laws, it endorsed such New Deal measures as social security and aid to farmers. One could fairly conclude that, no matter what political groups actually thought, it was good politics in 1944 to appear to be for the measures that had gained Roosevelt such electoral success.

Roosevelt, as in 1940, played coy and cool. Not until eight days before the Democratic convention did he publicly announce that he was available. The real Democratic battle was over the nomination for the vice-presidency. The incumbent, Henry A. Wallace, was anathema to conservatives in the party as well as to others for a variety of reasons of which the most important probably was that he was the darling of the farthest left elements in the party. However, if one considered what Wallace had done rather than what he had said or what his critics said of him, the intensity of the conservative opposition was puzzling. At any rate, most of the party leaders were bent upon unseating the Iowan. Since FDR did not appear to be in good health—he had lost weight upon doctor's recommendations after a bout of bronchitis—interest in the vice-presidency had a special urgency. The main opposition to Wallace came from former Supreme Court Justice and then "Assistant President" for war mobilization, James F. Byrnes of South Carolina. FDR publicly supported Wallace but said the nomination was the convention's responsibility. Just before the convention Byrnes thought he had FDR's nod. But others in the party vigorously opposed Byrnes. Edward Flynn of the Bronx, as a Roman Catholic, informed Roosevelt that Catholics were uneasy about Byrnes because he had left the church; Sidney Hillman, the main spokesman for labor in the Democratic fold, flatly and firmly told Roosevelt that Byrnes would not do because labor and Negroes would not support the conservative South Carolinian. Roosevelt thereupon informed Party Chairman Robert E. Hannegan that Senator Harry S. Truman of Missouri or Justice William O. Douglas were acceptable to him but that in any case he should "clear it with Sidney." Sidney, of course, would not clear Byrnes.

The convention, as was to be expected, nominated Roosevelt on its first ballot. His opponents mustered eighty-nine votes for Senator Harry F. Byrd of Virginia, and one die-hard delegate cast a vote for former Postmaster General Jim Farley. The convention went through the motions of a contest for the second spot, but Truman's nomination was foreordained. Wallace led on the first two ballots but Truman, who had only recently come to national

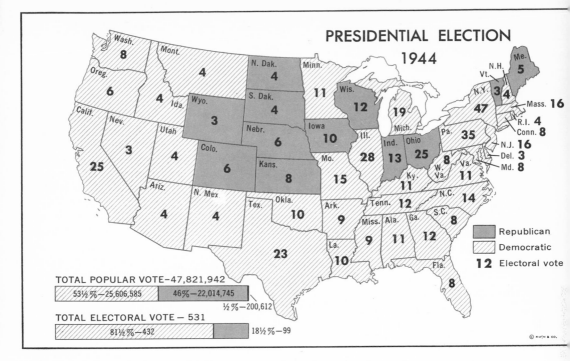

PRESIDENTIAL ELECTION 1944

TOTAL POPULAR VOTE—47,821,942
53½%—25,606,585 | 46%—22,014,745
½%—200,612

TOTAL ELECTORAL VOTE—531
81½%—432 | 18½%—99

Republican
Democratic
12 Electoral vote

notice as chairman of a special Senate committee investigating mismanagement in war industries, won on the third. For a platform, the Democratic party cited its record.

The newly formed Political Action Committee of the CIO, generally called the CIO-PAC, provided about all that was novel in the campaign. The PAC spent a lot of money for the Democratic cause, conducted many a mass rally, and bought radio time. When Republicans attacked hard on the "clear it with Sidney" theme, first reported by an admirer of Byrnes, Arthur Krock of the New York *Times*, they apparently only consolidated the big city vote behind FDR. Roosevelt, extremely busy with the duties of commander in chief, restricted his campaign to well-publicized visits of war installations until late in the race when it appeared that Dewey was gaining rapidly. In a speech aboard a ship at Bremerton, Washington, FDR had appeared overtired, uncertain, and old. Rumors circulated that the President had suffered a stroke. Then the old campaigner went to work. He demonstrated his champion deft touch in a speech to the Teamsters' Union convention in Washington on September 23 that lives as a masterpiece of light but effective campaign oratory. His later campaigning in eastern cities, including a day-long drive in an open car in a hard rain at New York, seemed to dispel fears about his health.

The voters again overwhelmingly elected FDR. He received 25,602,505 popular votes and 432 in the electoral college to Dewey's 22,006,278 and 99. Roosevelt lost only Maine, Vermont, Ohio, Indiana, Wisconsin, Iowa, Kansas, Colorado, Nebraska, Wyoming, and North and South Dakota. The new Senate had the same balance as the old: 57 Democrats, 38 Republicans, and 1 independent. Democrats gained 20 House seats, to give them 242 to the Republicans' 190 and 2 independents.

Mobilizing Manpower

The nation's first task after Pearl Harbor was to expand its armed services enormously. Accordingly, Congress quickly amended the Selective Service Act of 1940 so as to extend the service of men already in the armed forces to the duration of the war plus six months and to require draft registration of all men between the ages of twenty and forty-four for possible military service and of all men over military age up to sixty-five for possible labor service. None were ever drafted for labor service, however. In November, 1942, another amendment lowered the draft age to eighteen. Only a few men past thirty-eight were ever drafted, and in 1944 the services began to release enlisted men in noncritical positions who were over forty-one.

The key administrative unit in Selective Service, which was under the general administration of General Lewis B. Hershey, was the local draft board, of which there were almost 6,500 over the country. Congress and Hershey set general policy, and the draft boards administered it. The citizens who served as draft board members, without pay, had a thankless, time-consuming, and heart-breaking task. The plan was to draft unmarried men without dependents first, then married men without children, and fathers last of all. Some boards, however, exhausted their registration of men without dependents and began to induct fathers while other boards still had a supply of young unattached men.

About 31,000,000 men registered for selective service, of whom 9,867,707 were inducted. Still others volunteered. A total of over 15,000,000 men and women were in uniform at one time or another, although the services never had that many at any one time. The army, which then included the air corps, gave the oath to almost 10,500,000, the navy to about 4,500,000 including almost 600,000 marines, and the coast guard to about 250,000. About 200,000 women volunteered for the various women's branches: the Women's Army Corps (WAC), the largest with about 100,000 of whom one-sixth served overseas; the navy's Women Accepted for Volunteer Emergency Service (WAVES), who numbered about 85,000; the marine corps' Women's Reserve; and the coast guard SPARs.

Industry's immense task required a startling growth of the civilian labor force, which increased from 46,500,000 in 1940 to over 53,000,000 at the same time as the armed forces took millions off the labor market. About 7,000,000 came from the unemployed. Almost 4,000,000 came from young people growing into the labor force, including altogether too many youngsters who quit high school to take jobs. About 1,000,000 elderly people left retirement to go back to work. The rest of the difference came from women, hundreds of thousands of whom took jobs that had once been considered only for men. The lure of the dollar was probably a greater incentive for women working than the image of Rosie the Riveter, the propaganda symbol of the wartime woman industrial worker who managed in the ads to look glamorously attractive even in coveralls, but Rosie undoubtedly stimulated social acceptance of women workers.

In the hope of getting the right skilled worker at the right job at the right time and of minimizing "job hopping," Roosevelt in April, 1942, established the War Manpower Commission with Paul V. McNutt, former governor of Indiana, as its head. At first practically without real powers, the WMC later made it mandatory for defense workers who wanted to change jobs to get permission from the United States Employment Service. Actual enforcement, however, was next to impossible when both the employee and his prospective employer wanted a change. To meet this situation, the suggestion came of a total national service system to mobilize all·labor power more effectively, such as Great Britain had adopted. Objections were vigorous. Opponents of the scheme argued that national labor service was at least not yet necessary and that it would be too easily misadministered at the worker's expense. Trade unions feared such a plan would become an antilabor device. Roosevelt delayed taking action for concern about the possible political consequences, but in his annual message to Congress in January, 1944, he requested such legislation. For nearly a year Congress let the proposal lie fallow. In December, in the wave of near hysteria over the Nazi counteroffensive in the "Battle of the Bulge," the House passed a labor draft bill. The Senate delayed, and as American forces soon began once again to force the Germans back, pressure for the measure decreased. The Senate never acted.

Mobilizing Industry

Government direction of the extremely difficult task of coordinating and stimulating production got off to a bad start long before Pearl Harbor, went through a painful and involved series of reorganizations, and eventually became adequate for the task in the winter of 1942–1943. In August, 1939, the War Resources Board under the War and Navy Departments, composed mostly of executives from big corporations, came into being to advise upon industrial mobilization. The Board, in effect, made political recommendations when it urged that businessmen should administer mobilization through agencies apart from the regular executive offices and that labor laws should be shunted aside for the duration of the defense emergency. The Board further recommended that in the event of war an economic czar should direct the whole operation, a suggestion that would have taken power from regular constitutional officers. Roosevelt dissolved the Board. Bernard Baruch, who had been chairman of Wilson's War Industries Board, suggested another plan, which FDR sat on promptly. Finally, after the fall of France in the spring of 1940, FDR, drawing upon a World War I congressional authorization, appointed an Advisory Commission of the Council of National Defense. The Advisory Commission represented a broader cross-section of economic interests, and it was clearly under Roosevelt's authority. The Commission, however, abdicated authority to allocate supplies and raw materials to the military, and Roosevelt quite properly objected because American civilian and allied military interests also were involved.

In January, 1941, FDR established the Office of Production Management with William S. Knudsen, formerly of General Motors, and Sidney Hillman in command. OPM began to direct a gradual transformation to a war economy but got bogged down on the central and critical issue of allocating supplies, such as steel, building materials, and aluminum, which were too few for industrial demands even before the United States was officially at war. In August, FDR made still another but on the whole inadequate reshuffle when he created a special Supplies Priorities and Allocation Board with Sears, Roebuck executive Donald M. Nelson as its head. Allocation improved, but still confusion and working at cross purposes were prevalent. When one considers that almost until Pearl Harbor the task was essentially one of putting depression-idle men and machinery to work, the prewar defense mobilization must be termed a failure.

Still, confused and inefficient though it was, American production in December, 1941, was greater than that of any other nation, including Germany. Further, the building of an expanded industrial plant was well under way. Some of the expansion had come directly from government, through the Reconstruction Finance Corporation, which in June, 1940, had been authorized to finance construction of new facilities or expansion of old ones and lease them to private enterprises. In many cases, the task of persuading corporations to expand their productive capacity was difficult. Continuing to think in terms of the restricted markets of the depression and of an economy of scarcity, many corporation officials were dubious about expanding their potential for a relatively short term and ending up with excess productive capacity. One way out of this was for government to go far toward underwriting expansion's cost and toward practically guaranteeing profits. Congress, in the Revenue Act of October, 1940, allowed fast tax write-offs for capital put into expanded defense capacity. Instead of the usual 5 per cent a year depreciation, businesses were allowed to take a 20 per cent annual depreciation on the cost of new defense plants. Generous ordinary contracts or "cost plus" arrangements, under which the contracting corporation received the cost of production plus an agreed upon percentage of profit, sweetened the pot and attracted industry to defense production. The trouble with "cost plus" was that it was an invitation to squander on production costs. Senator Truman's committee, acting as a watchdog on defense and war contracts, inhibited corporate raids on government funds.

Roosevelt juggled industrial mobilization machinery again soon after the declaration of war when he created the War Production Board under Nelson. WPB was given the powers that Baruch had urged be granted such an organization in his report in 1940. Nelson, however, fell short of success. Under his administration the military continued to dictate supply priorities, and he let expansion develop unevenly. For example, facilities for ship construction, an industry that had grown very quickly, got far ahead of steel and engine production and had to be cut back. Nelson also was under a great deal of fire, much of it from the Truman Committee, for allowing a disproportionate share of defense contracts to go to the biggest industrial corporations. In October, 1942, FDR appointed Justice Byrnes to a new agency set up above WPB, the Office of Economic Stabilization. Byrnes got results, but the job became too big for any one man to administer. In May, 1943, Roosevelt made the last reorganization. He created still another agency, the Office of War Mobilization, with Byrnes in charge. Many of the details continued to be handled by OES, headed then by a former Congressman from Kentucky, Judge Fred M. Vinson. Thereafter, government's direction of war production went reasonably smoothly.

Indeed, production and transportation performed what to depression-conditioned eyes seemed an industrial miracle. The war economy was, in one way of looking at it, an economy of abundance. Total production nearly doubled between 1939 and 1945. By early 1944, American industry was producing twice as much each month as all of the Axis powers combined. Whole industrial centers came into being where nothing had been before the war, and small centers evolved under pressure into vast industrial complexes. Aluminum production, necessary for aircraft, almost tripled. The totals in some categories were astronomically impressive: nearly 300,000 airplanes, almost 12,000 ships (both merchant and naval), 64,000 landing craft, 86,000 tanks, and millions of machine guns, rifles, carbines, and side arms. These items were not useful to a society in normal times, but they nevertheless represented economic abundance of a sort. In 1944, the government was able to relax production restrictions on some civilian articles so successful had war production become.

The new economy of abundance had come primarily through a special kind of government economic pump priming. Federal spending during the depression, undertaken to revive the economy, was minor compared to what it became during the war. A glance at the statistics reveals the point. In 1939 the GNP (gross national product) stood at about $88.6 billion, of which federal expenditures contributed about 9 per cent. In 1944, the peak wartime year, GNP was $199.2 billion, of which federal spending contributed about 45 per cent. Incidentally, government controls of the economy of all kinds increased tremendously along with its increased spending. Much of the grousing about "Dr. New Deal's" governmental "meddling" would be more accurate if attributed to "Dr. Win-the-War."

Yet, in another sense, the wartime economy was quite the reverse of an economy of abundance because many of the goods and services which Americans considered necessary to a good life were in exceedingly short supply. Japanese conquest of Southeast Asia cut America off from its main source of rubber, and the government stockpile was insufficient to last a year of normal demand. Roosevelt delegated Baruch to make a study of the problem in mid-1942. FDR took his suggestions and ordered construction of synthetic rubber plants, stepped up production of rubber in other parts of the world, and instituted a national speed limit of thirty-five miles per hour to save tires. The government imposed gasoline rationing to save rubber as well as petroleum. Before the end of the war, the synthetic rubber industry was producing well over the normal peacetime rubber demand. The government found it necessary also to ration shoes when leather ran short and shoe manufacturers were occupied with making footwear for the armed forces. Housewives had to have rationing stamps to buy meat, fats, coffee, and sugar. Government control of these items was partly to combat inflation, partly to assure more equitable distribution of scarce items. Although never rationed, cigarettes became difficult to purchase in the winter of 1944–1945. Soldiers in the European theater were short of smokes, and at home long lines appeared at drug stores fortunate enough to have a supply. Nylon stockings, which had come onto the market only soon before the war, became almost impossible to purchase. Some services became difficult to obtain. As the armed forces inducted more and more physicians and dentists, their colleagues at home, at least in some communities, were unable to treat adequately all patients.

Mobilizing Money

War is expensive. For the five years, 1941 through 1945, the federal government spent $320,189,941,396, most of it on military purposes. This sum was about twice as large as the government had spent in its entire history since 1789. How to raise and spend such a vast figure without wrecking the economy by wild inflation was the primary fiscal problem of World War II. Roughly two-fifths of the funds came from taxes. The balance came from borrowing (the sale of government bonds and other securities) which increased the national debt from $49 billion in 1941 to $259 billion in 1945.

The first part of 1942, during which American armed forces were suffering reverses, saw a considerable debate over taxation and fiscal policy concerned, essentially, with who should pay for the war. The business community, speaking through the National Association of Manufacturers and the United States Chamber of Commerce, was concerned about the growth of the national debt and wanted the war to be paid by taxation to as great a degree as possible, but by a national sales tax and an excess profits tax. The President at one time talked about limiting incomes so as to prevent anyone from receiving over $25,000 net income a year, but he did not pursue the suggestion. The Revenue Act of 1942, not passed until October, which FDR called "the greatest tax bill in American history," increased tax revenues by more than $7 billion. It set the ordinary corporate tax at a maximum of 40 per cent and excess profits taxes at a flat 90 per cent, 10 per cent of which could be rebated to corporations for reconversion to peacetime activity after the war. It also set rather steep excise taxes on communication, transportation, amusements, and luxuries, most of which were not repealed after the war. But most important for the immediate interests of many people was an increase in revenue to be collected through personal income taxes. The new tax rate went up to as high as a maximum of 94 per cent, but most of the new revenues came from lowering personal exemptions, thereby increasing the number of people under the tax net. In 1939, only about 4,000,000 Americans paid any income tax whatsoever. This number increased to about 12,000,000 in 1941, and the 1942 Revenue Act brought enough new taxpayers into being to make the total over 50,000,-000. Since most people were inexperienced at filling out income tax reports, the filing system had to be simplified. Most people were also inexperienced at putting money aside to pay their income tax in one lump sum. Congress in 1943 began a withholding system ("pay as you go" it was popularly called) which considerably improved the collection of taxes from people with relatively low incomes.

Roosevelt, in his budget message of January, 1943, asked for a tax in-

TABLE 8

PUBLIC DEBT OF THE FEDERAL GOVERNMENT, 1940-1946.

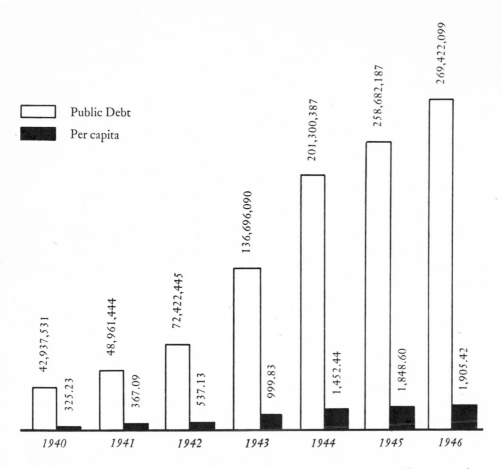

Public Debt

Per capita

	1940	1941	1942	1943	1944	1945	1946
Public Debt	42,937,531	48,961,444	72,422,445	136,696,090	201,300,387	258,682,187	269,422,099
Per capita	325.23	367.09	537.13	999.83	1,452.44	1,848.60	1,905.42

crease of $16 billion. Response was overwhelmingly negative. The executive branch trimmed its requests to $10.5 billion, but Congress still refused to go along. Not until February, 1944, did Congress pass a new revenue measure at all, and it increased tax yields by only an estimated $2.2 billion. Roosevelt vetoed the new revenue act with a message so sharp that it brought a congressional rebellion. Senate Majority Leader Alben W. Barkley of Kentucky, normally the manager of the President's measures, resigned his office rather than support the veto. The Democratic caucus in the Senate quickly reappointed Barkley by unanimous vote and went on to override Roosevelt's veto, as did the House.

So far as taxes were concerned, the answer to the debated question about who should pay for the war was that practically everyone paid for it. The bulk of tax revenues came from the personal income taxes of people with modest incomes, yet, due to improved wartime earnings, most of these people were economically better off during the war than they had been before it. The wealthiest recipients of income did not suffer despite the increased tax rates. It is true that the share of disposable income received by the top 1 per cent declined from 11.5 per cent in 1940 to 6.7 per cent in 1944, but this was a relative decline, not an absolute one. The disposable income of lesser income groups and the total disposable income increased sufficiently to reduce the share, but not the amount, of the richest. To the degree that there was income leveling during World War II, the leveling was upward rather than downward.

Roughly three-fifths of the war's expenses came from funds gained by the sale of Series "E" bonds, the type purchased by individuals. This kind of bond buying was anti-inflationary since it took money that probably otherwise would have gone to purchase scarce consumer articles. The government, therefore, pushed series "E" sales vigorously through a payroll deduction scheme, but it refrained from the coercive techniques used in World War I. Nonbanking institutions took $60 billion in bonds of other series, and banks bought $87 billion worth. Bank bond purchases were inflationary since they increased bank credits and, thereby, the amount of money in circulation.

Series "E" bonds and taxes helped to combat inflation, but the most publicized agency to keep prices at a reasonable level was the Office of Price Administration, created by executive order in April, 1941. Without effective power, its first head, the New Deal economist Leon Henderson, was unable to prevent a steady price rise during the defense period that reached 2 per cent a month by the end of 1941. Roosevelt demanded greater power for OPA, and in January, 1942, Congress responded with the Emergency Price Control Act. In April, an OPA directive froze prices of consumer goods and rents in defense areas at their March level. However, the law prevented fixing prices of farm products until they reached 110 per cent of parity, a legislative work of the farm bloc. Consequently, the cost of living continued to rise. FDR notified Congress that unless it rectified this situation that he would act himself, basing his action on presidential war powers. Congress in October passed the Anti-Inflation Act. Immediately, Roosevelt froze prices, including agricultural prices, wages, salaries, and rents throughout the country. People, thwarted by this order, took it out on Henderson, who in December, 1942, resigned his job. Former Senator Prentiss S. Brown of Michigan held the job for a half-year and was succeeded by a former advertising firm official, Chester Bowles of Connecticut. The farm bloc twice got bills through Congress designed to permit a rise in farm prices, but FDR vetoed them. In May, 1943, Roosevelt even ordered a 10 per cent reduction in the retail prices of coffee, meat, and butter.

People complained about rationing, there was a black market in some items, and families that moved frequently were often the victims of devious ways to avoid rent control. Still, the government managed to win the battle against a runaway cost of living. Living costs increased less than 2 per cent in the last two years of the war. The cost of living increased only 29 per cent from 1939 to the end of the war, most of it in 1941 and the first three quarters of 1942. Considering that living costs increased by almost two-thirds from 1914 to the end of World War I, the record in World War II was good indeed.

Workers, Farmers, and Living Standards

Soon after Pearl Harbor, both the AFL and the CIO adopted a no-strike pledge for the duration of the war. With a few exceptions, organized labor honored the pledge. But the exceptions were well publicized, antilabor sentiment increased, and, although trade union membership and general strength grew, organized labor faced a more hostile public opinion at the end of the war than it had in 1941.

During the whole war, labor went out on strike 14,371 times, resulting in the loss of an estimated 36,301,000 man-days. Most of the strikes were short, and most of them were "wildcat," called by locals against the policy of the national organization. Although the strike statistics seem big, actual time lost due to strikes was only an estimated one-ninth of 1 per cent of total working time.

Labor's two main problems during the war were to maintain its position in industry and to keep workers' incomes in line with rising living costs. The first problem was solved by the adoption by the War Labor Board, composed of management, labor, and public representatives and established in January, 1942, for the purpose of being responsible for the settlement of labor disputes which the Secretary of Labor deemed dangerous to the war effort, of the compromise called "maintenance of membership." Some managements hoped to break the power of unions with the flood of new industrial employees; unions wanted to require all new employees to join in shops that were already organized. The "membership of maintenance" compromise provided that workers who were union members and those who might join would remain members during the life of the labor contract and that failure of a worker to maintain his membership would make him liable to discharge from his job. The union would remain as the bargaining agent. On the other hand, new employees were under no obligation to join. The solution prevented management from using the no-strike pledge to destroy unionism; it did not allow unions to use their power automatically to improve their position. Total union membership grew during the war from about 10,500,000 to about 14,000,000; about 3,000,000 workers chose not to join a union under the "maintenance of membership" scheme.

The problem of keeping wages in line with living costs proved far more difficult. The fairly sharp rise in prices in early 1942 brought the first crisis. Labor in Little Steel demanded a raise of a dollar a day to offset higher prices. The WLB recognized a hardship existed, granted a pay increase of forty-four cents a day, and made this Little Steel formula of a 15 per cent increase the pattern for industry generally. Prices were said to have increased a similar amount. The Little Steel formula of July, 1942, became the norm. Thereafter, the administration made it the basis of both wage and price stabilization. In 1944, however, labor began to complain that the Little Steel pattern was preventing it from participating in wartime prosperity to the degree that other economic groups did. The WLB that year yielded "fringe benefits," such as health insurance, pay for vacations and holidays, and bonuses for night work, but it retained the 1942 formula.

The history of labor in the war's last two years can largely be told by an account of John L. Lewis of the United Mine Workers, still labor's best-known leader and certainly its stormiest and most controversial major figure. Lewis, who had resigned as CIO president over its support of Roosevelt in 1940, quarrelled with his old friend and colleague, Philip Murray, the CIO's new chief. In October, 1942, Lewis pulled the UMW out of the CIO and a year later took it into the AFL. While this little war within labor's larger civil war was in progress, Lewis in April, 1942, demanded a $2.00 a day raise for miners when the contract expired at the end of the month. The WLB reminded Lewis of his no-strike pledge, and he replied that he would not call a strike but that he doubted if the miners would want to "trespass" upon mine property when the contract expired. The miners went out on May 1. FDR quickly seized the mines and urged the miners to return under the old contract until a new settlement could be made. Lewis announced a thirty-day truce. FDR put the mines under the jurisdiction of the Department of the Interior, and for six months two of the most pugnacious public figures in the country, Secretary Ickes and Lewis, bargained with one another in an attempt to reach an arrangement the WLB would accept. During the bargaining, the miners struck briefly three more times. The ultimate agreement was complicated. It provided for an hourly wage increase within the Little Steel formula, but it gave the UMW additional benefits, vacation pay, and payment for all time spent underground—"portal to portal" pay.

Lewis' actions were largely responsible for a considerable growth of antilabor sentiment which resulted in restrictive labor legislation. Five states prohibited the closed shop. Congressional hoppers received many antilabor proposals. One of these, sponsored by Representative Howard Smith of Virginia and Senator Tom Connally of Texas, passed through Congress with large majorities only to run into a veto. However, Congress overrode the veto and the War Labor Disputes Act, more often called the Smith-Connally Act, became law in June, 1943. The new law forbade union contributions to political campaigns, provided for government seizure of strike-bound plants engaged in war production, permitted strikes only after an election during a thirty-day "cooling off" period, and sanctioned criminal prosecution of persons who instigated strikes.

World War II brought the agricultural sector of the economy to a degree of health such as it had not enjoyed since the last war. Yet the major benefits went to the most efficient farms, usually the large ones, and hundreds of thousands of submarginal farms went out of production altogether. Although farmers were frequently plagued with labor shortages and found new equipment difficult to obtain, they expanded their production from an index of 108 to 123. The increase in food production alone was even greater. Favorable weather and heavier use of hybrid seed and fertilizer brought about these increases despite a 17 per cent decline in the farm population. When one considers that farm prices more than doubled and net cash incomes climbed fourfold, the prosperity of the more favorably situated farmers becomes apparent.

Indeed, it was the war, far more than federal depression agricultural policies, that brought prosperity back to the farm. Farmers not only cut their mortgages by a national total of $2 billion, they saved an estimated $11 billion. At the same time, the war hastened the process of "factoryizing" most farm production, of specialized production by big, efficient, and at least partly scientific farm units. The small, family farm with diversified production faded into limbo faster than ever.

In fact, during the war years most Americans lived better than they had for years. In 1943, ten million families received less than $1,675, the figure then deemed a minimum to provide a decent standard of living, but the others, while by no means rolling in luxury, were better off than they had been since at least the 1920's. Better family incomes came not so much from higher wage rates as from working wives, steadier employment, and more overtime pay. Over considerable management protest, the administration stuck to the time-and-one-half for over forty hours standard, and labor gave up double time for Sundays and holidays. In 1941, the average work week was 40.6 hours; in 1944 it was 45.2. The average of gross weekly wages increased from $25.20 in 1940 to $43.39 in 1945, a greater increase than there was in the cost of living. No small factor in prosperity was the serviceman's family allotment. In 1942, Congress amended pay legislation to provide a $50 allotment to the wives of servicemen in return for a deduction of $22 in the man's pay. The soldier's first child brought an additional allotment of $12, and each additional child brought $10. These figures were later changed to $30 and $20. One family complained bitterly in December, 1945, when its husband and father was discharged; this family of thirteen children had to give up an allotment of $320 monthly.

Two aspects of wartime prosperity were to have postwar significance. First, only in the United States did the people live better than they had before the war, a fact that had worldwide repercussions. Second, unable to spend their incomes on new houses, new household appliances, or new cars (none were produced after a few in 1942), and urged to put their excess income into war bonds, more Americans saved more money than ever before. This fact contributed to postwar prosperity brought about by a buying spree and to postwar inflation.

Mobilizing Science and Technology

With the fall of France in the spring of 1940, Roosevelt appointed the National Defense Research Committee with Vannevar Bush, head of the Carnegie Institution, as its head. A year later the President reorganized the governmental research program by establishing the Office of Scientific Research and Development, again under Bush's direction. OSRD proved a highly effective organization, and the work of its scientists and technicians shortened the war.

The most spectacular scientific achievement, of course, was the development of the atom bomb. In 1939, Albert Einstein and Enrico Fermi, each of them refugees from fascism, informed the President indirectly that German scientists had accomplished atomic fission in uranium. Physicists realized the destructive possibilities of this achievement, although to most laymen the whole concept was a mystery, and urged the administration to support a huge research program. Research groups at Columbia University, the University of Chicago, and the University of California at Berkeley advanced the solution, and in December, 1942, physicists brought about the first controlled chain reaction in an atomic pile constructed under the stands of Stagg Field at the University of Chicago. Huge problems remained: how to produce fissionable material in usable quantities and how to build a nuclear bomb.

The Army Engineer Corps created a special project, the Manhattan District, under the command of General Leslie R. Groves, to work on plutonium production. The government secretly spent nearly $2 billion in the huge Manhattan District installations at Oak Ridge, Tennessee, and Hanford, Washington, and in the scientists' bomb-building project, headed by J. Robert Oppenheimer, at Los Alamos, New Mexico. The security problem of such a huge undertaking was extremely complicated, and, as it turned out, security was not perfect. Finally, on July 16, 1945, near Alamogordo, New Mexico, the scientists hopefully and yet apprehensively detonated the world's first nuclear fission bomb. An eerie mushroom cloud, to become the midcentury symbol of nightmarish destruction, floated up from the detonation site. The atomic age was born.

Not so dramatic but important nevertheless were such scientific and technological achievements as proximity fuses, radar, and rockets. The proximity fuse, developed by ORSD alone, was a tiny radio set in the head of an artillery shell which detonated the shell as it neared its target. Near misses thereby became hits. At first used only above oceans and against German rockets aimed at English cities to prevent an unexploded shell from falling into enemy hands and being copied, the proximity fuse proved a potent destroyer when first used by ground forces late in the war against Germany. Radar, first developed crudely by the navy in the 1920's, was developed into an effective device in Great Britain. Radar detection of German aircraft in the Battle of Britain provided Britain's narrow margin of victory, and it was an invaluable aid in navigation and detection of submarines. Rocket research was not as advanced as Germany's, but small rockets on airplanes and the bazooka, an infantry weapon with which two men could launch a small rocket capable of knocking out a tank, were highly effective.

Fortunately for the modern conscience, not all research was directed toward destructive devices and some of the principles discovered in working for destructive ends had wholesome and peaceful possible applications. Medical researchers developed penicillin and other antibiotics until they were available for mass treatment of disease. DDT provided a better weapon for man's war with the insect world than he had ever had. Routine DDT dusting of wartime refugees and prisoners of war prevented the outbreak of any serious epidemics which had previously been a grisly companion of major wars. Blood plasma, a kind of "instant blood," had enormous advantages over the old direct blood transfusion and saved an untold number of lives both during the war and later. Regardless of all the positive wartime scientific achievements, however, the development of nuclear fission with its fantastic power presented mankind with a problem it never before had had to face so clearly.

Civil Liberties and Minorities in Wartime

Americans in World War II were far less hysterical about disloyalty than they had been in 1917-1918, probably because after Pearl Harbor opposition to the war was only negligible. The United States won its greatest war while maintaining a toleration at home of which, with one glaring exception, it could well be proud.

Censorship worked fewer injustices than it had in World War I. The Office of Censorship, established in December, 1941, under Byron Price, an Associated Press executive, was at times overcautious in what it allowed newspapers to publish, but the war was still the best reported one the nation had ever fought. A large staff of censors cut information that might be useful to the enemy from mail destined for overseas delivery, but civilian censors abused their power much less than officers in the armed forces overseas who sometimes went beyond the limits of reason when they censored letters written by their enlisted men. The Office of War Information, headed by Elmer Davis, drew the ire of many Republicans who accused the OWI of pro-Roosevelt domestic propaganda, but it certainly never approached the earlier Creel Committee's irresponsibility. The OWI all but ceased aiming at American minds after 1943 and concentrated on shaping opinion abroad. Religiously motivated conscientious objectors, if they would register for the draft, fared far better than their World War I counterparts. They went to Civilian Public Service camps rather than to prison; many entered the military medical services.

Pacifists were rarely seriously harmed, and enemy sympathizers, mostly ideological pro-Fascists, suffered far less than war opponents in the Wilson administration. The Supreme Court in 1944 ruled that in cases under the Espionage Act the prosecution had to prove the accused had specifically intended to hamper the war effort, and intent is extremely difficult to prove in law. The biggest wartime dissent trial was a Smith Act case against twenty-eight defendants, of whom one was Mrs. Elizabeth Dilling, author of *The Red Network*, indicted for attempting to establish a Nazi system in the United States and for inciting disloyalty in the armed forces. A wild mass trial in 1944 went on for several months, only to end in mistrial when the presiding judge died. A second indictment in 1945 ended with an appellate court's dismissal.

The government recognized that the presence of thousands of aliens who were citizens of enemy countries constituted a potential menace. Enemy aliens were required to register with the government, denied access to defense areas, and required to deposit with the government their cameras, firearms, and short wave radios. Federal Bureau of Investigation agents rounded up 1,700 enemy aliens suspected as potential saboteurs within a week after Pearl Harbor, thereby successfully preventing German sabotage plans. Germany later landed saboteurs by submarine on the beaches of Long Island and Florida, but the FBI apprehended them quickly. There was no known act of sabotage committed in the United States during the war.

Of popular hostility to Italian-Americans there was practically none, and German-Americans were the objects of only a little overt discrimination. But Japanese-Americans suffered badly. Their treatment was by far the blackest mark on the World War II record. The government and the army surrendered to regional prejudice. The West Coast, where most Japanese-Americans lived, became highly panicky in the weeks following the Japanese attack. Although the roundup of potentially dangerous enemy aliens had included Japanese, many people on the coast demanded that something be done about the Japanese-Americans, who had long been victims of discrimination there. Roosevelt caved in. On February 19, 1942, he authorized military commanders to remove "any or all persons" from any area the Secretary of War or other military commanders might designate. Soon thereafter the commanding general of the Pacific Coast army district, John L. De Witt, ordered the removal of all Japanese-Americans from the western parts of Washington, Oregon, and California, even though he did not declare martial law. About 112,000 people were forced into barbed wire stockades and then moved out to ten permanent camps in the interior, euphemistically called "relocation centers." Two-thirds of those removed were American citizens. All but about eighteen thousand Japanese-Americans were released in time. Only a few returned to the coast when the evacuation order was rescinded. Forced sales and abandonment of property cost the removed people heavily. The whole affair was the result of panic and prejudice; this was indicated by the contrast of the Japanese-Americans in Hawaii, where much less prejudice existed. There these people lived as they had for years without serious incident.

The Supreme Court in Hirabayashi v. United States (1943) and Korematsu v. United States (1944) upheld the removal order on grounds of national security in a time of crisis. It did not reverse itself when in the Endo case it granted a writ of habeus corpus to a loyal Japanese-American; it only ruled that a person against whom no charge had been made and whose loyalty was not questioned could not be interned after being removed from an excluded zone. Constitutional scholars agree upon the seriousness of the whole Japanese removal episode. One of them, E. S. Corwin, has called the affair "the most drastic invasion of the rights of citizens . . . by their own government that has thus far occurred in the history of our nation."

The Jehovah's Witnesses flag salute cases, however, illustrated that the federal government could maintain traditions of civil liberty during wartime. In mid-1940, the Supreme Court in the Gobitus case had held that public school children could be compelled, upon pain of expulsion, to salute the flag in school ceremonies even though such action violated the students' religious principles. After the outbreak of war, the Witnesses were frequent victims of persecution. Nine states had requirements that school children salute the flag. In mid-1942 the Department of Justice began to intervene to prevent flagrant persecution, and a West Virginia Witness family went to court rather than obey the flag salute requirement of the state board of education. In June, 1943, the Supreme Court in the Barnette case held in a six-to-three decision that no civilian could constitutionally be required to salute the flag or to take part in a pledge of allegiance.

Despite a great deal of prejudice directed against them, Negroes in general improved their position in American society during the war years. Although the army never permitted any more than token integration during the war, and that only at the front in the German war when manpower of any color was badly needed; although the Red Cross yielded to demands that Negro blood plasma be segregated; although Detroit in June, 1943, indulged itself in a race riot; and although many southern whites so resented the loss of cheap Negro labor to better paying war jobs that some southern communities became tension-ridden tinder-boxes, the Negro in general was better off by V-J Day than he had been at Pearl Harbor.

The main improvement in Negro relations was economic. A. Philip Randolph's wresting the FEPC order in 1941 made discrimination in war industries illegal, and a handful of state fair employment practice laws forbade employment discrimination in all kinds of work. But it was mainly the availability of cash-paying jobs of any description that put Negroes on the move. From the farms they moved into southern towns and cities, and from there they moved on to northern and western industrial centers. Negro migration in the first war was minor compared to the 1941–1945 conflict, and Negroes jammed into New York City, Philadelphia, Cleveland, Chicago, Los Angeles, and other major cities.

The long-term effects of migration and relative prosperity were many. For one thing, the Negro in the North and the West could vote, and he increasingly constituted a voting bloc with which candidates had to deal. For another, his newly achieved degree of economic independence stimulated militant demands for the exercise of equal rights. For still another, millions of Negro youngsters gained access to schools far better than their parents had attended. Negroes' postwar surge forward thus derived largely from wartime experiences.

CHAPTER TWENTY-FOUR

Fighting for Victory

UNTIL DECEMBER, 1941, THE WAR THAT HAD BEGUN IN SEPTEMBER, 1939, had been almost altogether a European war. With Pearl Harbor the conflict became a truly global war, the first one in the world's history. Asia, Europe, Africa, and the seas and oceans, including those around the Americas, were the scene of warfare between Axis powers and the United Nations.

The role of Americans in this global war was more important than they ever before had performed. Although they had participated in other "world wars"—the three colonial wars, the War of 1812, and World War I—Americans had never before played so decisive or central a part in the final outcome. From 1941 to 1945, Americans produced the war supplies, delivered them, planned the strategy, and did the actual fighting as full senior partners.

In 1917–1918, the United States had insisted that it was no more than an "associated power" and refused to be considered as one of the Allies. In World War II, the United States took the lead in uniting into a loose alliance the various nations at war with one or more of the Axis powers. On January 1, 1942, at the White House, Roosevelt, Churchill, Ambassador Litvinov from Russia, and representatives of twenty-three other nations signed the Declaration by the United Nations. Subsequently, twenty other countries signed the document which restated the "four freedoms" enunciated in the Atlantic Charter and pledged each signatory nation to "employ its full resources" in the war effort, to cooperate with other signatory powers, and not to make a separate armistice or peace.

More important in the actual conduct of the war, however, was the close cooperation that developed between Great Britain and the United States and, to a lesser extent, between them and Russia, China, and, later, France. The Grand Alliance, as it came to be called, had actually begun before the

United States declared war when Roosevelt and Churchill met and corresponded freely. Churchill arrived in Washington for a series of conferences only two weeks after the United States war declaration. From then until the end of the war, the Prime Minister and the President were in almost daily communication. At this first wartime conference, Roosevelt and Churchill agreed to war production goals for the next two years, to the establishment of a Combined Chiefs of Staff in the American capital, to the creation of a joint Munitions Assignment Board, to a joint command in the Pacific which included the Dutch, and to some future military strategy, notably an invasion of North Africa sometime in 1942.

The most basic decision at the Washington conference in December, 1941, was to put a higher priority for the immediate future on the European war than on the Asian theater. The strategy was to fight a holding action in the Pacific and concentrate on the defeat of Germany and Italy. Then, when victory seemed assured in Europe, the allies would concentrate their efforts against Japan. Actually, the United States began to carry the war against the Japanese long before Hitler's downfall was assured, but the military emphasis remained in Europe. To make this decision in the first weeks of the war involved a degree of risk since Japan's first thrusts were devastating. Japan's strategy was to make a series of lightning blows at the beginning of the war and stake everything upon them. Japan's high tide came before the middle of 1942. But in the war's first half-year it looked as if the flag of the rising sun were really rising.

The Japanese blow at Pearl Harbor had been only a relatively minor part of a general Japanese attack. As the United States government had expected, the Japanese moved south. The list of Japanese victories was impressive. Japanese armies had no difficulty landing in Thailand and quickly controlling it. They moved on into the Malay peninsula, routed the British, and moved south to capture the big British naval base at Singapore on February 15, 1942. During the campaign, incidentally, Japanese planes sank two British battleships off the Malayan coast, the *Prince of Wales* and *Repulse*, the first time unassisted airplanes had sunk modern battleships equipped for combat. The British had lost their base at Hong Kong on Christmas Day, 1941. Allied defeat in the Battle of the Java Sea, February 27 and 28, 1942 (a defeat so disastrous that only four American destroyers escaped) sealed the fate of the Dutch East Indies. The Dutch surrendered to the Japanese on March 9. The Japanese also took control of the Celebes, Borneo, New Britain, the Solomons, and part of New Guinea. These Japanese acquisitions were of tremendous strategic importance; they afforded Japan a major source of oil and denied their opponents the world's major source of rubber.

Less important in terms of resources but of major importance to American pride were the losses of two small islands, Guam on December 10, 1941, and Wake on December 23. The marines' defense at Wake Island was heroic but hopeless; for sixteen days they held off a numerically superior foe. More important strategically was the loss of the Philippines. General Douglas MacArthur, the former chief of staff, commanded about one-hundred twenty thousand men, not counting army air corps personnel. The Japanese quickly gained control of the air after their initial landings on December 10 and soon had the Philippine and American forces in retreat. Overwhelming numbers of

Japanese pushed MacArthur's forces toward the Bataan Peninsula, one of the arms of land forming Manila Bay. In March, 1942, Roosevelt ordered Mac-Arthur to leave in order to save his military talents for a happier day; the thankless task of fighting the hopeless fight fell upon Lieutenant General Jonathan M. Wainwright. After being on half rations or less for three months, the last forces on Bataan surrendered April 9; those holed up on the small island fortress of Corregidor succumbed on May 6. Isolated from help and supplies, doomed almost from the start, the defenders of the Philippines, American and Filipino alike, fought gallantly and delayed the inevitable far longer than the Japanese had reasonably expected.

The War Against Germany and Italy: First Phase

No two allied nations in the history of warfare ever better coordinated their efforts than did the United States and Great Britain in World War II. Their leaders also, with but few exceptions, saw eye to eye on general objectives. Coordination with the other major Allied military power, the Soviet Union, was another matter. Russian, American, and British leaders meshed their supply and shipping schedules with one another, and late in the war the Russians and Americans even brought about a degree of tactical cooperation with the flight of a few B-17 American bombers from their English bases, over the German targets, and on to Russian air bases. Yet, on the whole, Russian-Western tactical coordination was infrequent. Their troops fought mostly in different theaters. Neither was there consistent agreement on strategy between Russia on the one hand and Britain and America on the other, because strategy inevitably involved postwar international politics. Although Roosevelt's more ardent defenders would dispute the generalization, Churchill and Stalin were usually more acute than FDR in perceiving the postwar implications of wartime decisions.

Churchill and Roosevelt had their first difficulty with Stalin soon after Pearl Harbor. Stalin asked British Foreign Minister Anthony Eden in December, 1941, for an Anglo-Russian treaty of alliance in which Britain would agree to Russia's extending her boundaries to include the Baltic countries (Latvia, Lithuania, and Estonia) and parts of Finland and Poland. Russian foreign minister Vyacheslav Molotov repeated the proposal to Churchill in London the following May. But Churchill refused, and Russia and Britain agreed to a twenty-year treaty of alliance that ignored the question of Russia's postwar boundaries. That Russian leaders dared to present such a request when the German armies had the Russians deep in their own territory and still on the defensive indicated a strong appetite for territory.

Molotov went on to Washington where he strongly urged Roosevelt to open a second front in western Europe, presumably in an amphibious operation across the English Channel so as to take Nazi pressure off the Russians. He wanted the invasion of the European continent as soon as possible, certainly no later than the end of 1942. He said it was possible, unless diverted from the west, that Hitler's Wehrmacht might be able to knock out Russia, thus leaving Britain and America to face Germany alone. Roosevelt told

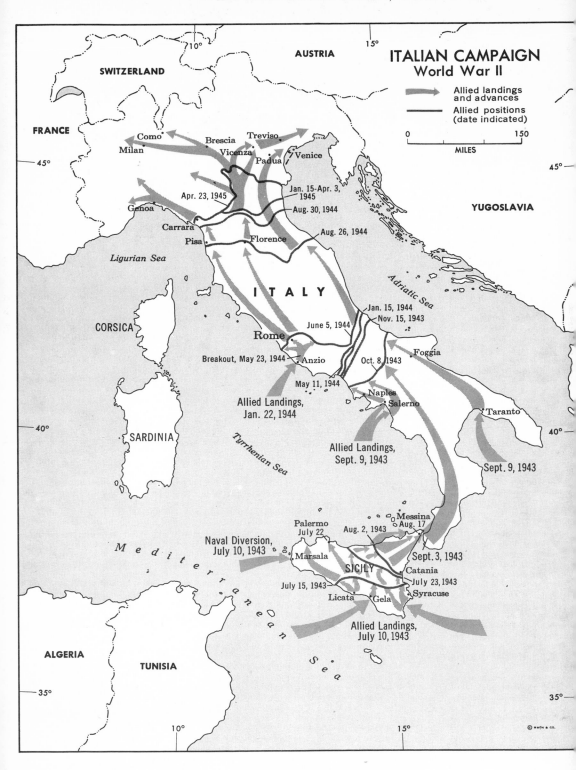

ITALIAN CAMPAIGN
World War II

Allied landings
and advances
Allied positions
(date indicated)

0   150
MILES

AUSTRIA

SWITZERLAND

FRANCE

Como
Brescia   Treviso
Milan   Vicenza
Padua   Venice

Apr. 23, 1945   Jan. 15–Apr. 3, 1945

Aug. 30, 1944

Genoa   Aug. 26, 1944

Carrara

Pisa   Florence

Ligurian Sea

YUGOSLAVIA

I T A L Y

Adriatic Sea

Rome   Jan. 15, 1944
June 5, 1944   Nov. 15, 1943

Breakout, May 23, 1944   Anzio   Oct. 8, 1943   Foggia

May 11, 1944

CORSICA   Naples   Taranto
Salerno

SARDINIA

Allied Landings,
Jan. 22, 1944

Tyrrhenian Sea   Allied Landings,
Sept. 9, 1943   Sept. 9, 1943

Messina
Aug. 17
Palermo   Aug. 2, 1943
July 22
Sept. 3, 1943
Naval Diversion,   Marsala   Catania
July 10, 1943   SICILY   July 23, 1943
July 15, 1943   Syracuse
Licata   Gela

M e d i t e r r a n e a n   S e a

ALGERIA

TUNISIA

Allied Landings,
July 10, 1943

485

Molotov he would do whatever possible to start a continental invasion in the next few months.

Soon after Molotov's departure from Washington, Churchill arrived for his second face-to-face meeting with Roosevelt within six months. Churchill and his military advisers vigorously opposed a cross-Channel operation in the immediate future, arguing that Allied strength did not yet permit such an invasion and that they should use what power they had to drive the Germans and Italians from North Africa. The breakthrough at about that moment of German General Erwin Rommel's Afrika Korps, forcing the British Eighth Army back into Egypt and thereby threatening the Suez Canal, helped to decide the issue. After the chief of staff, General George C. Marshall, and his commander in the European theater, General Dwight D. Eisenhower, had failed to bring the British around to agreement on an invasion of Europe, Roosevelt agreed in July to a North Africa campaign provided it be launched by the end of October.

The Allied operation in North Africa was a giant pincers movement. On October 24, the British Eighth Army, under the command of General Sir Bernard L. Montgomery, opened an attack from the east. On November 8, three American task forces, to which were attached some British units, landed by sea at Casablanca, Oran, and Algiers. The three-pronged attack was a surprise to the enemy, an amazing lapse of German intelligence. General Eisenhower commanded this operation. Then Eisenhower's force drove to meet Montgomery's advancing army, trapping the Axis forces in Tunisia. General Rommel fought shrewdly, taking advantage of every opportunity, and succeeded in inflicting a serious but not fatal defeat at the Battle of Kasserine Pass in February, 1943. By the middle of May, German resistance had ended in Africa. Germany's loss of fifteen divisions and over two thousand airplanes hurt her seriously, but perhaps equally important was the fact that Britain and America had turned the tide against the Nazis. They had begun to "tighten the ring."

A political-diplomatic tangle relating to the American operations in North Africa will be debated for a long time. The proud but weak and hopelessly divided-against-themselves French created a sticky problem in that their pro-Nazi Vichy government had at least nominal control of the area where the United States planned its landings. The Vichy French in Africa resisted the American landings. On November 11, 1942, three days after the North African landings, Germany took over the unoccupied part of France, until then controlled by the Vichy government, whereupon the Vichy commander in Africa, Admiral Jean Darlan, reached an armistice with General Eisenhower. Darlan agreed to a cease-fire; Eisenhower agreed to recognize Darlan's control of the French forces in Africa. The outcry at home against cooperating with a Vichy officer was considerable. Darlan was assassinated on December 24. Then the question for the United States was whether to recognize the vigorously anti-Vichy General Charles De Gaulle, with whom the British were working, or General Henri Giraud, who had escaped from the Germans but whose supporters had served the Vichy government. In January, 1943, Roosevelt personally got De Gaulle and Giraud to meet and ostensibly compromise their differences. De Gaulle soon eased Giraud aside, and in time Roosevelt recognized De Gaulle as the French leader.

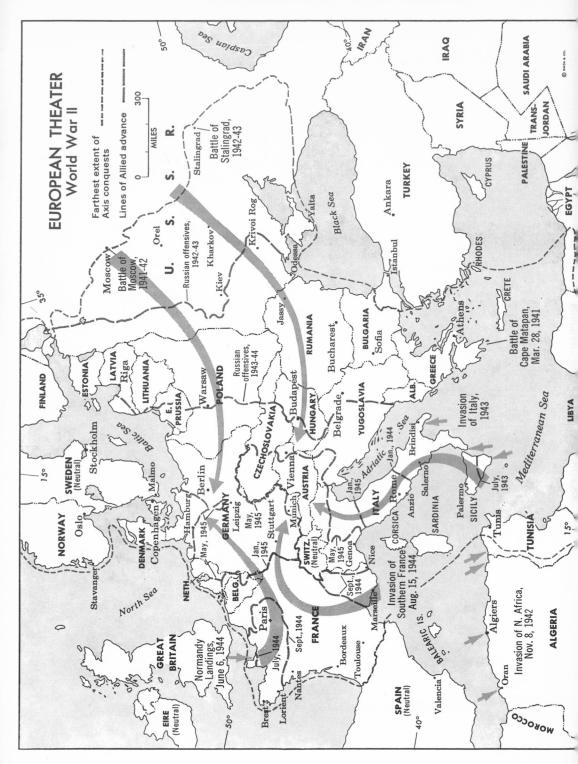

EUROPEAN THEATER
World War II

Farthest extent of
Axis conquests
Lines of Allied advance

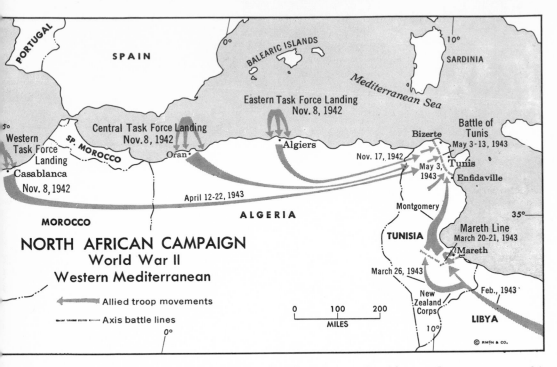

PORTUGAL

SPAIN

BALEARIC ISLANDS

0°

10°

SARDINIA

Mediterranean Sea

Eastern Task Force Landing
Nov. 8, 1942

Central Task Force Landing
Nov. 8, 1942

5°

Western
Task Force
Landing
Casablanca
Nov. 8, 1942

SP. MOROCCO

Oran

Algiers

Bizerte

Battle of
Tunis
May 3-13, 1943

Nov. 17, 1942

May 3,
1943

Tunis

Enfidaville

April 12-22, 1943

MOROCCO

ALGERIA

Montgomery

35°

NORTH AFRICAN CAMPAIGN
World War II
Western Mediterranean

TUNISIA

Mareth Line
March 20-21, 1943

Mareth

March 26, 1943

New
Zealand
Corps

Feb., 1943

LIBYA

0   100   200

MILES

Allied troop movements

Axis battle lines

0°

10°

© RMcN & CO.

The Churchill-Roosevelt conference at Casablanca, January 14 to 24, 1943, during which Roosevelt brought about the surface solution of the De Gaulle-Giraud impasse, was notable for two decisions: to demand "unconditional surrender" of the Axis powers and to invade Sicily and Italy. The unconditional surrender demand, like the Vichy episode, will long be a subject for debate. Roosevelt's critics have argued—with the advantage of hindsight—that unconditional surrender caused Germany to fight on until destroyed, thereby prolonging the war and creating a power vacuum in central Europe which the Russians filled. The other side of the argument is that Roosevelt explicitly said that unconditional surrender did not mean the destruction of the German population but the end of fascism and that a compromise with Nazism would have been immoral. But, clearly, the unconditional surrender policy did stiffen Axis resistance and narrowed America's range of alternatives in its dealings with its allies.

The fighting for North Africa was by no means over when Roosevelt and Churchill ordered Eisenhower to invade Sicily in July. Landing craft and paratroopers hit Sicily on July 10. With bold tank tactics by General George S. Patton's troops, American forces were able to complete the whole Sicilian operation in only thirty-eight days. The loss of Sicily brought about Mussolini's downfall. The Italian people, including the soldiers, had long shown a lack of enthusiasm for the war and for the Germans. On July 25, 1943, a group of Mussolini's opponents got the consent of King Victor Emmanuel III to form a new government under Marshal Pietro Badoglio, who ordered Mussolini's arrest and began secret negotiations to surrender. (Early the next month a daring operation by German paratroopers rescued Mussolini

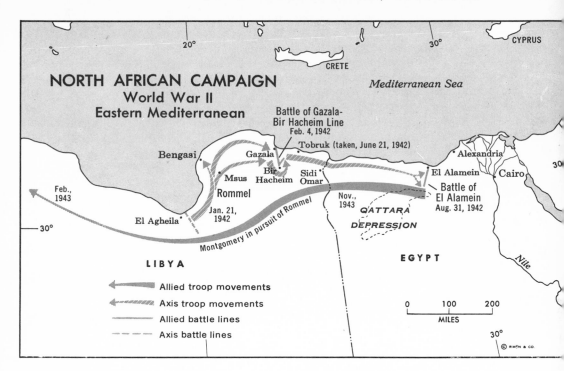

and took him to the north of Italy.) The Germans suspected the Italians and moved additional troops into Italy in an attempt, if possible, to prevent Italian surrender and in any case to secure the territory against the Allies. Badoglio surrendered unconditionally on September 3. By that time, German forces in Italy were strong enough that the surrender made little actual military difference.

The Allies began their invasion of Italy the very day of Badoglio's surrender. At the Roosevelt-Churchill meeting in Washington in May, 1943, known by the code name TRIDENT, it had been agreed the Allies would move on into Italy as soon as possible. General Montgomery's forces landed at Reggio Calabria, at the toe of the Italian boot, on September 3. On September 10, the American Fifth Army under General Mark Clark landed near Salerno, down the coast from Naples. The Allies advanced well at first, and by early October had taken Naples on the west coast and Foggia near the Adriatic and moved on north. However, the Germans dug in on a line south of Cassino in November. Taking advantage of the geography, the Germans held out all winter. A daring amphibious "end run" in January, 1944, established an American beachhead behind the German lines at Anzio, south of Rome, but the Germans soon nailed the attack down there. Not until spring did the Allies begin to roll again, taking Rome on June 4, 1944, and grinding on toward the Alps.

During the year 1943 the Grand Alliance began to function with more harmony and clearly turned the tide against Germany. Russia began to push back the Nazis during the winter of 1942–1943. The turning point came at Stalingrad, where on February 2, 1943, the Nazis surrendered about ninety

TABLE 9

INTERNATIONAL CONFERENCES OF WORLD WAR II

Place	Name	Date	Participants
Argentia, Newfoundland		August, 1941	Roosevelt, Churchill
Washington	ARCADIA	December, 1941-January, 1942	Roosevelt, Churchill
London		April, 1942	Churchill, Eden, Hull
Washington		June, 1942	Roosevelt, Churchill
Casablanca		January, 1943	Roosevelt, Churchill, De Gaulle
Washington	TRIDENT	May, 1943	Roosevelt, Churchill
Quebec	QUADRANT	August, 1943	Roosevelt, Churchill
Moscow		October, 1943	Hull, Eden, Molotov
Cairo-Teheran	SEXTANT EUREKA	November-December, 1943	Roosevelt, Churchill, Chiang Kai-shek, Stalin
Washington	DUMBARTON OAKS	August-September, 1944	Stettinius, Cadogan, Gromyko
Quebec	OCTAGON	September, 1944	Roosevelt, Churchill
Moscow		October, 1944	Churchill, Stalin
Yalta	ARGONAUT	February, 1945	Roosevelt, Churchill, Stalin
San Francisco		April-June, 1945	Representatives of all UN members
Potsdam	TERMINAL	July-August, 1945	Truman, Stalin, Churchill, Atlee

thousand men. German losses in the Stalingrad campaign were so terrible that never again was Hitler able to unleash a major, sustained offensive operation. By the end of the year, with great loss of life on each side, the Russians had steadily moved the Germans back until they had lost control of much of the Ukraine. The British and Americans had cleared Africa of the Nazis, Italy had given up, and the Allies controlled Sicily and the foot and ankle of the Italian peninsula. The war in the Atlantic had turned in the Allies' favor. The foremost historian of American naval operations in World War II, Samuel Eliot Morison, who was both an admiral and a Harvard professor, placed the turning point in the Battle of the North Atlantic in the spring of 1943. Germany lost 41 submarines to enemy action in May, 1943, alone and 237 for the year.

In 1943, the question of the shape of the postwar world came increasingly into public consideration, but even in the face of this potentially explosive matter, relations between Anglo-America and Russia improved. One matter, clearly, was the Roosevelt-Churchill decision at the TRIDENT conference in May, 1943, to launch a cross-Channel invasion of France, called OVER-LORD, by May 1, 1944. They reaffirmed this decision at the Quebec Conference in August, 1943, and they also heartened Russia at that conference by acceptance of the Morgenthau plan. Secretary of the Treasury Henry Morgenthau, Jr., had proposed that defeated Germany be entirely stripped of its industrial power and reduced to a permanently agricultural economy. Churchill never really liked the idea and FDR quietly abandoned it before the end of the year, but Nazi propagandists skillfully got full mileage out of the Morgenthau plan in their efforts to stiffen German resistance.

Roosevelt determined in 1943 to create a postwar international organization designed to mediate conflicts between national states and to keep the peace. In the fall of 1943, Congress, at the administration's urgings, passed the Connally and Fulbright Resolutions, which declared the nation "through its constitutional processes" should participate in a postwar international body. At a meeting of the Big Three foreign ministers in Moscow in October, Russia, Britain, and the United States committed themselves to a postwar substitute for the old League of Nations. At this conference and at the Roosevelt-Churchill-Stalin conference at Teheran in November (to which the American and British leaders had flown after conferring with Chiang Kai-shek in Cairo), Roosevelt and Churchill reassured Stalin about the second front, and Stalin agreed to go to war with Japan once Germany was defeated. The three leaders at Teheran and their foreign ministers at Moscow had been unable to come to important explicit agreements about postwar boundaries or about which rival Polish government should be recognized, but they agreed in principle on a harsh postwar policy toward Germany, an anti-Fascist Italy, and an independent Austria. From these Roosevelt-Churchill-Stalin conferences would come a whole bagful of problems to be faced when the war finally ended, but at the time all seemed harmonious and optimistic. The Grand Alliance was ready to deal Nazism its death blow.

Triumph in Europe

The Allies had carried the war directly to the German homeland through air bombardment since early in the conflict. When the German Luftwaffe in the fall of 1940 shifted its objective from destroying the Royal Air Force to punishment of London and other English cities, it permitted the survival of an Allied weapon that would in time seriously hurt Germany and soften it for invasion. The RAF conducted occasional attacks upon German-held Europe even in late 1940 and 1941, but not until 1942 did Allied bombing of Germany begin to be significant. On August 17 of that year, B-17's of the American Eighth Air Force in England first dropped their bomb loads on Germany. By the end of 1943, planes from the Ninth Air Force, transferred to England from the Mediterranean theater, and the Fifteenth Air Force in Italy were likewise hitting German targets.

The usual pattern was for the R.A.F. bombers to fly their missions at night and for the more heavily armed American bombers to operate during daylight. Although danger was greater during daylight, the accuracy of the bombing was much better when the bombardier could actually sight his target. Radar bombsights were not available at all for most of the war and were never fully satisfactory. After suffering heavy losses in B-17 missions deep into Germany—particularly during a disastrous raid against ball bearing plants at Schweinfurt in October, 1943—American officers decided to postpone further missions deep into Germany until long-range fighters capable of escorting bombers all the way to the target were available. Such a fighter plane, the P-51, became available in sufficient numbers early in 1944. In February, 1944, the Luftwaffe's fighters made one last desperate attempt to eliminate Allied daytime bombing. So many German planes went down in the week-long engagement that Germany never again was able to offer effective fighter opposition to bombers or to control the air over her ground forces. Jet fighters, the Germans' best hope, became operational late in 1944 but only in small numbers, due largely to lack of fuel. The German jets more than matched any Allied aircraft; had they been more numerous the final months of the war would undoubtedly have been quite different. With almost the only opposition being antiaircraft batteries, which frequently were quite effective, Allied bombers stepped up their work. From April through June, 1944, the Allies dropped over 50 per cent more tons of bombs on Europe than they had in all of 1943. A United States Strategic Bombing Survey conducted just after the war indicated that bombardment had shattered civilian morale, had destroyed or seriously disrupted German war production, and had almost ended efficient functioning of transportation throughout Germany and German-controlled west Europe. Others maintained, however, that strategic bombing had not been nearly as effective as its proponents claimed. But, clearly, Allied bombing harassed the enemy and helped prepare the way for the cross-Channel invasion.

OVERLORD, the code name of the Allied invasion of Normandy, was the biggest and most carefully planned major military offensive ever launched. General Eisenhower had directly under his command 2,876,000 officers and men in the American, British, and French land, sea, and air units. Orginally promised by May 1, 1944, D-Day had to be postponed until June 5 because of a shortage of landing craft. Then the giant operation had to be postponed another twenty-four hours because of bad weather. Three divisions of paratroopers dropped behind German lines soon after midnight on June 6. At 6:30 A.M., after both aerial and naval bombardment, the first troops hit the beaches. To disguise or hide an operation as large as D-Day was impossible, but nevertheless the plan contained an element of deception. Eisenhower and his advisers chose to make the landing on the Cotentin, or Cherbourg, peninsula, roughly one hundred miles from England, rather than in the Calais area, only about twenty-five miles from England, where the Germans expected the assault. The Germans were so convinced that the Normandy landings were a feint that six weeks later they still had nineteen divisions in reserve waiting for the main blow near Calais.

The second phase of the invasion, after securing the beachhead, was to capture the port at Cherbourg and build up forces and supplies for a breakthrough out of Normandy. Cherbourg fell after bitter fighting on June 27. The breakthrough began on July 25. General Patton's Third Army encircled the Germans, who were caught in a pocket near Falaise. The Germans then decided to retreat to the Westwall, or Siegfried Line. French troops led the march into Paris on August 25. By mid-September, Allied forces controlled Dieppe, Brest, Le Havre, Antwerp, and Brussels. Meanwhile, another invasion of France, this one from the south, had begun on August 15, and American forces were moving up the Rhone valley.

On July 20, just before the Normandy breakthrough, a loose alliance of German officers, Social Democrats, churchmen, and intellectuals unsuccessfully attempted to assassinate Hitler. A time bomb in a brief case left under Hitler's chair unaccountably only injured the German dictator while killing four of his companions. About five thousand people died in the resulting purge, and thereafter Hitler's control of the armed forces was absolute.

Western military operations in the fall and winter of 1944–1945 were concentrated in northwestern France, Luxembourg, western Belgium, Holland, and adjacent parts of Germany. The most dramatic military event of the winter was Germany's desperate counterattack in an effort to split the Allied forces and regain the port at Antwerp. This Ardennes campaign, often called the Battle of the Bulge, began December 16 when Field Marshal Gerd von Rundstedt attacked with twenty-four divisions, of which ten were armored. Heavy fog helped the surprise. After the German breakthrough, capture of the American-held Belgian towns of St. Vith and Bastogne was necessary to make the whole operation a success. St. Vith held out long enough to upset the Nazi schedule; Bastogne never capitulated. The first ten days of the battle settled its eventual outcome, but not until the end of January was the bulge the Germans had made in the American lines completely eliminated. The temporary setback caused widespread alarm in Britain and the United States, but the German counteroffensive's eventual failure so seriously depleted Nazi strength that Germany was never able again even briefly to reverse the tide. She had gambled her last crack troops in the Ardennes and lost them.

Germany's high hopes for her terror weapons, the V-bombs, proved unfounded. A week after D-Day, the Germans sent the first V-1 "buzz bombs" against England. In the next three months the Germans aimed about eight thousand of these low-flying, jet-propelled, pilotless flying bombs at London; about 2,400 got through the defenses. Then the Nazis switched to the V-2, a rocket against which there was no defense at the time. About five hundred of these hit London. Altogether the V-bombs caused about 35,000 casualties, a serious matter indeed but not sufficient to reverse the direction of the war.

The Russians had extraordinary military success in 1944. They decisively defeated the Germans on the central part of their front, and by July 1 were on the Vistula River, within sight of Warsaw. Rather than push on through Poland toward Germany, however, Russia concentrated upon conquering the Balkan peninsula and the Danube basin from the Nazis. The move had the effect of bringing the area into the Russian zone of influence after the war. While the Russians were stopped at the Vistula, the Poles fought the Warsaw Uprising. Russian troops stayed on the other side of the river, refused Polish pleas for help, let the Germans put down the rebellion and eliminate the most nationalistic elements of Poland, and then, after the whole affair was over, took Warsaw without difficulty in mid-January, 1945. On their northern sector, the Russians knocked Finland out of the war in September.

The last meeting between Roosevelt, Churchill, and Stalin, at Yalta in the Russian Crimea, February 3–11, 1945, was the subject of much political

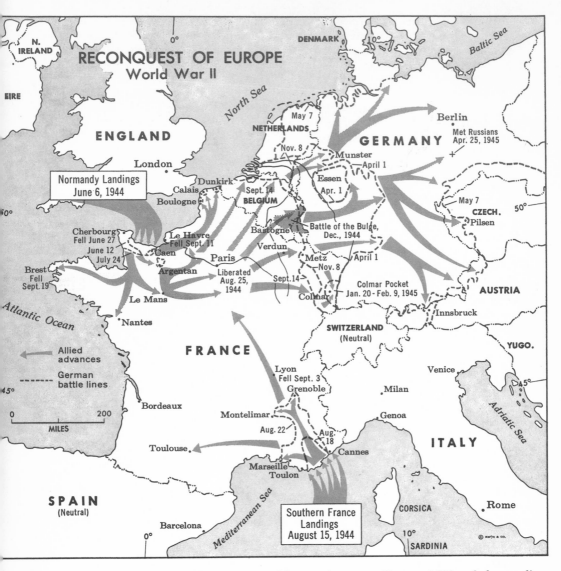

RECONQUEST OF EUROPE
World War II

Normandy Landings
June 6, 1944

Southern France
Landings
August 15, 1944

Allied
advances

German
battle lines

0   200
MILES

heat in the years after the war. Matters between East and West left standing from the Teheran conference remained to be settled as well as new problems. It was obvious that this would be the last Big Three conference before Germany was defeated, and settlement of differences within the Grand Alliance was imperative. Churchill and Eden met Roosevelt and his new Secretary of State, Edward R. Stettinius, Jr., former chairman of the board of United States Steel Company, for a preliminary meeting at Malta in order to decide upon certain matters before seeing Stalin and Molotov. (Cordell Hull had resigned in November, 1944, because of poor health.)

Four main subjects occupied the Yalta meeting: details of the proposed United Nations, postwar Germany, government of East Europe, and terms of Russia's entry into the war against Japan. Russia conceded practically all its positions on the UN. At the Dumbarton Oaks conference in Washington the previous September, Russia had been balky about a UN veto power and had demanded sixteen seats in the UN General Assembly, one for each of her constituent republics. At Yalta, Stalin agreed to three General Assembly seats and agreed not to oppose an American demand for three seats. The United States never asked. The veto question was met by a complicated formula, the essence of which was that any permanent member of the UN Security Council could veto sanctions against itself although it could not veto consideration of a dispute in which it was a party. The veto has since been severely criticized, but it is clear that in 1945 the Senate of the United States would not have ratified any UN charter that did not provide an American veto. Russia agreed to make France a permanent member of the Security Council and consented to allow any nation at war with Germany by March 1 to become a UN member. Apparently, Stalin saw that the UN, at least in its early years, was to be dominated by the Anglo-American bloc and resigned himself to that situation after he was guaranteed Soviet veto power on matters that directly affected Russia.

The conference hedged considerably on Germany's future but it did take some actions. The three leaders agreed that their governments were to be the "supreme authority" in Germany, although the French might be brought into the occupation. These governments could disarm, demilitarize, and dismember Germany as they thought necessary to bring about "future peace and security." Roosevelt and Churchill came to no final reparations settlement with Stalin, but they agreed to the establishment of a reparations commission at Moscow, they accepted the Russian figure of reparations of $20 billion (one-half of which was to go to the U.S.S.R.) as "a basis for discussion," and they went along with Stalin in declaring that reparations should be paid in kind from German capital goods, from the product of current German production, and from German labor. The three foreign secretaries were to decide among themselves the question of punishment of German war criminals.

The East European questions, particularly the thorny Polish problem, had special relevance for American politics and its ethnic voting blocs. Churchill and Roosevelt agreed to the Russian-Polish border being drawn roughly along the old Curzon Line. Because this border was somewhat to the west of the 1939 Polish-Russian border, Stalin proposed that the Polish-German border also be moved west to the Oder-Neisse Line, but the English and American leaders would do no more than consent to Poland's receiving "substantial accessions of territory in the north and west." East and West came to loggerheads over the Polish government question and finally reached only a surface and unenforceable compromise. Russia insisted upon a Polish government friendly to Russia and demanded western approval of the Russian-sponsored government at Lublin. Roosevelt and Churchill refused and argued for the Polish government in exile at London. The settlement was for the Lublin government to bring into it "democratic leaders from Poland itself and from Poles abroad" and for the Lublin government to pledge itself "to the holding of free and unfettered elections as soon as possible on the basis of universal suffrage and secret ballot." Such elections were never held. Poland's government remained Communist and, until 1956, altogether under Russian domination. For elsewhere in East Europe the three powers promised governments chosen in free elections.

Although Stalin had earlier agreed to enter the war against Japan once Germany was defeated, he began to get tough on that issue as European victory came into view. In December, 1944, Stalin demanded a *quid pro quo* from the American ambassador, Averell Harriman. At Yalta he received what he demanded. In exchange for war against Japan "in two or three months" after Germany's defeat, Russia received: (1) assurance of the continuation of Russian dominance in Outer Mongolia, which China claimed; (2) transfer of the Kurile Islands from Japan; (3) restoration to Russia of what Japan had won from her in the war of 1904–1905, which was (a) the south half of Sakhalin, (b) the lease of Port Arthur for a naval base, (c) the internationalization of the port of Dairen, and (d) joint control with China of the Chinese Eastern and Southern Manchurian railroads. Stalin also agreed to recognize Chinese sovereignty in Manchuria and to sign an alliance with the Chinese Nationalists. Neither Chiang Kai-shek nor anyone else knew of the Yalta decisions on Asia until later, but when Chiang heard of the agreements he was satisfied because he thought it meant Russian support of his government against the Chinese Communists.

These, in brief, were the Yalta agreements about which there has been much debate. There is much to be said both in defense and criticism. The outstanding fact to be remembered about the East European settlement is that the Red armies in February, 1945, already controlled that part of the world completely or had it within their ready grasp. The West had little bargaining power there. As for Germany as well as East Europe, no one could really foresee Russian postwar intransigence and aggressiveness in February, 1945. The mood at the moment was almost universally one of toughness with Germany, which was Russia's and America's common enemy, not toughness with Russia. The least defensible parts of the agreements had to do with the Far East. Roosevelt and his military advisers wanted Russian help against Japan badly. Such help was considered necessary to save hundreds of thousands of American servicemen's lives. The atom bomb, it should be remembered, was not yet developed. On the other hand, intelligence reports which for some inexplicable reason had not reached the White House or the Joint Chiefs of Staff indicated that Japan was much weaker as a result of conventional warfare than generally assumed. Further, it was naive to assume that Russia had to be baited to be active in East Asia. Her desire to be an Asian power was obvious, and it was unlikely that she would have passively watched America defeat Japan and become the area's sole major power. The Yalta agreement's inadequacies, however, were the result of honest error, of human frailty, of inability to penetrate the future. There is no evidence for the charge of subversion at Yalta despite the presence there in a relatively minor capacity of Alger Hiss, who later was convicted of perjury for denying complicity in Soviet espionage. Nor is there foundation for the belief that Roosevelt was so sick and feeble he was unfit properly to perform his duties. Stettinius in his memoirs described FDR at Yalta as "mentally alert" and in better health than he had been.

In late March, the Anglo-American armies crossed the Rhine in force, and events began to move with bewildering speed. An American offensive in northern Italy, begun April 2, ended in German surrender on April 29. On April 29, deep in his air-raid bunker under the Reichschancellery, Hitler turned over the reins of government to Admiral Karl Doenitz. The next day Hitler committed suicide. On May 2, the German troops in Berlin surrendered turned south to prevent the Germans from carrying out their threat of holing up in a supposed National Redoubt in the southern mountains for a bitter and bloody Wagnerian fight to the death. The National Redoubt proved to be a myth. On April 12, Roosevelt died at Warm Springs, Georgia, from a cerebral hemorrhage, and Vice-President Harry S. Truman succeeded to the chief executive responsibilities. On April 25, American and Russian troops met at the Elbe near Torgau, south and slightly west of Berlin. By late April, the Russians had surrounded Berlin and were pounding the suburbs. On April 29, deep in his air-raid bunker under the Reichschancellery, Hitler turned over the reins of government to Admiral Karl Donitz. The next day Hitler committed suicide. On May 2, the German troops in Berlin surrendered to the Russians, and the armies in northwest Germany, Denmark, and Holland capitulated two days later. Very early in the morning of May 7, at Eisenhower's headquarters at Rheims, the Germans unconditionally surrendered all their forces that remained. V-E Day—victory in Europe—saw vigorous celebration of the end of the war that had been going on for almost six years. Only the war with Japan remained.

In later years there was considerable criticism of the American failure to accept Churchill's advice and press on for the capture of Berlin and Prague before the Russians could get there. Churchill argued that the West should get as much of a foothold in Central and Eastern Europe as possible in order to be able to require the Russians to live up to their Yalta promises about that part of the world. In his memoirs Churchill even professed to have had an "aching heart" on V-E Day because of the Russian situation. Most people today would agree that, in the long run, it was a political mistake to turn south and not proceed east when the Elbe was reached. Although at the time of the Yalta Conference the Russians were much closer to Berlin and Prague than were the western armies, by early April the West had the better chance of reaching those cities first. The decision to turn south was prompted by military rather than political considerations, although perhaps the real weakness was the general American failure to see clearly the relationship between the two.

The War in the Pacific Theater

During the first several months of war in the Pacific, the Allies were steadily forced back, unable to make more than occasional counterblows to show the enemy they still had fight. The most spectacular counterpunch was the raid by sixteen B-25 bombers, led by then Colonel James Doolittle, against Tokyo itself on April 18, 1942. The planes took off from the carrier *Hornet*, completely surprised the Japanese, and created considerable confusion. The daring operation, however, had no real strategic importance other than helping American morale.

The American forces first stopped a Japanese offensive in the naval Battle of the Coral Sea, May 7–8, 1942. General MacArthur had decided to reinforce Port Moresby in southern New Guinea and build a major air base there. The Japanese determined to take the area. Fortunately, the American command knew about the Japanese decision through intercepted and decoded messages. An invasion force led by two carriers and eleven cruisers met the American force, likewise led by two carriers, the *Lexington* and *Yorktown*. Carrier-based planes decided the whole issue; surface craft did not exchange a single shot. Each force heavily damaged the other. The battle itself could be called a draw, but the Japanese were compelled to withdraw and thereby suffered a strategic loss. The engagement made less likely Japanese conquest of Australia.

The Japanese decided next to extend their operations to the east and north, toward Hawaii and the Aleutians, by a small diversionary attack in the Aleutians to be followed by a major one on Midway Island, roughly 1,300 statute miles from Hawaii. Again, American commanders learned of the plan through broken radio messages. Both sides moved naval units to the Midway area from hundreds, even thousands, of miles away. The Japanese force had four carriers with 250 planes; the United States had three carriers, *Enterprise, Yorktown,* and *Hornet,* with 225 operating aircraft and additional land-based air power. In the Battle of Midway, June 3–6, 1942, again planes rather than surface craft were decisive. The Japanese lost all four carriers; the Americans lost only the *Yorktown.* Having lost air superiority, the Japanese withdrew in their first major defeat of the war. The Coral Sea and Midway engagements reversed the direction of the war in the Pacific. The Japanese attack on the Aleutian chain, stretching from Alaska to Siberia, won them Attu and Kiska islands, where they established bases. Americans the next year, however, reseized each island.

At this point the Japanese shifted their operations back to the south. This was done with a land operation on Port Moresby from Gona, across the Owen Stanley Mountains on the other side of the island, and the beginning of construction of a large air base on Guadalcanal in the Solomon Islands that would afford them air superiority in the Southwest Pacific.

The Guadalcanal campaign developed into one of the bloodiest of the war after initial spectacular success. Within two days after the assault on August 7, 1942, the marines captured the partly completed air base. But then the Japanese counterattacked from other island strongholds. They sent in replacement troops regularly from Rabaul in New Britain via an efficient troop transport system that American forces nicknamed "the Tokyo Express." The First Marine Division, reinforced by one army regiment, held out gallantly while the navy went to work to gain control of the surrounding waters. A whole series of naval encounters, culminating in the fierce naval Battle of Guadalcanal, November 13–14, 1942, finally afforded the United States control of the approaches to Guadalcanal. It took until the following February, however, to eliminate the Japanese on the island.

Meanwhile, MacArthur was handling the Japanese attack back at New

Guinea. Australian and American units drove the Japanese back to the other side of the mountains, but then they became literally bogged down in the incredibly slimy mud and fell victim to fever. The Australians took Gona on December 9. The Americans took Buna Mission, the last Japanese stronghold in the area, on January 2, 1943. The whole campaign was over by the end of the month. Having defeated the Japanese offensive in the Solomons and New Guinea decisively—it turned out to be the last major offensive the Japanese would take—MacArthur was now in position to begin the huge counteroffensive "island-hopping" operation that slowly tightened the noose around Japan.

The strategy followed by MacArthur and Admiral Chester Nimitz was to attack in two areas in 1943–1944. In the Southwest Pacific MacArthur's forces proceeded with their task of clearing New Guinea of Japanese forces, a huge action not completed until February, 1944. Marine and army units pushed north from the Solomons to isolate the Japanese base at Rabaul, which was accomplished with the taking of the Admiralty Islands in the spring of 1944. Simultaneous with this huge mopping-up operation in the southwest, naval and amphibious forces under Nimitz cracked into Japanese defenses in the Central Pacific, first in the Gilbert Islands.

In November, 1943, marines landed on Tarawa and Makin Islands in the Gilberts. Makin fell easily, but Tarawa, while it fell in three days, was a much tougher problem of a kind American troops were to face time and again in Pacific islands. The Japanese on Tarawa holed up in strongly fortified and protected pill boxes that heavy bombardment before the landing had hardly affected. Then when the marines hit the beach the Japanese opened up with a deadly fire. The only way to clear out such defenses was to subject them to unusually heavy bombardment and to follow up with hand-to-hand combat. Moving north from the Gilberts, marines took control of the Marshall Islands with the successful conquest of Kwajalein and Eniwetok Atolls in February, 1944, and then moved on to Saipan and Guam in the summer. Both were under American control by August, although fighting continued in parts of Saipan for months afterward. This series of island hops into the center of the Japanese circle of armed strength, besides encircling Japanese centers of power such as Truk in the Carolines, afforded American forces a shot at the Philippines reconquest and gave them a base from which to conduct air raids against the Japanese home islands themselves. The bomber used for these raids against Japan, the first of which was executed on November 24, 1944, was the B-29, the biggest bomber yet developed.

The great American naval victory in the Battle of the Philippine Sea, June 19–20, 1944, also helped in the reconquest of the Philippines. Since her naval defeat in the Solomons, Japan had been rebuilding her carrier and naval air strength. This new strength disappeared in the Battle of the Philippine Sea in which Japan had one carrier sunk and four severely damaged.

Upon the suggestion of Admiral William F. Halsey, the high command moved forward the date for the invasion of Leyte, one of the Philippine Islands, from December to October 20, 1944. The Japanese spotted the huge invasion armada and decided to risk roughly half their total naval strength in an attack. A successful American invasion of the Philippines would cut the communications between Japan and Southeast Asia, which Japanese armies

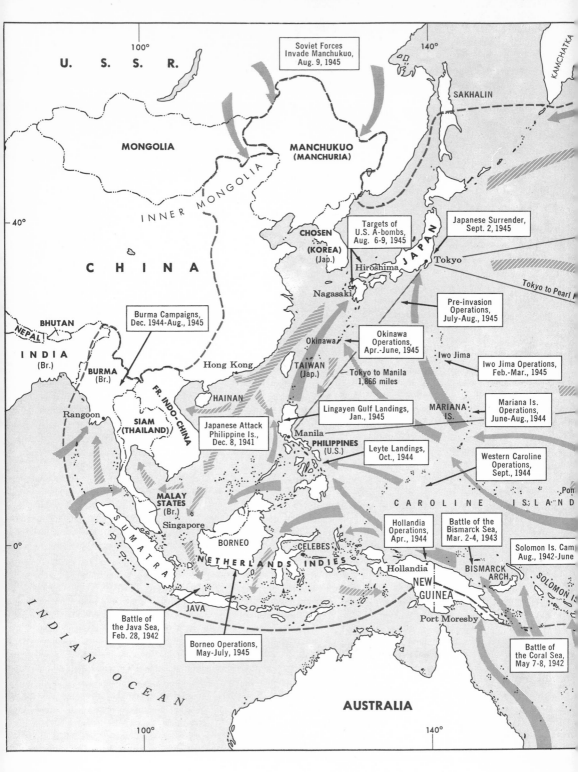

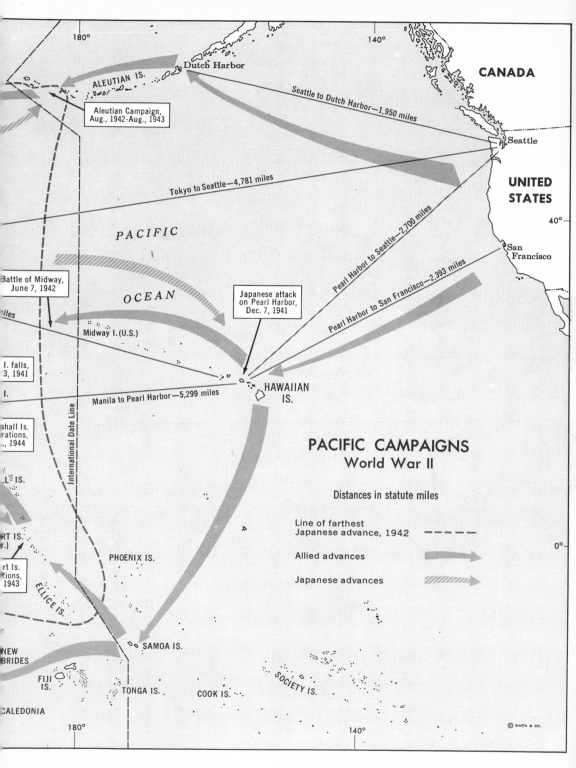

CANADA

Dutch Harbor

ALEUTIAN IS.

Seattle to Dutch Harbor—1,950 miles

Seattle

Aleutian Campaign,
Aug., 1942–Aug., 1943

UNITED
STATES

40°

Tokyo to Seattle—4,781 miles

PACIFIC

San
Francisco

Battle of Midway,
June 7, 1942

OCEAN

Midway I. (U.S.)

Japanese attack
on Pearl Harbor,
Dec. 7, 1941

Pearl Harbor to Seattle—2,700 miles

Pearl Harbor to San Francisco—2,393 miles

I. falls,
3, 1941

I.

Manila to Pearl Harbor—5,299 miles

HAWAIIAN
IS.

shall Is.
ations,
1944

International Date Line

PACIFIC CAMPAIGNS
World War II

Distances in statute miles

L IS.

RT IS.
r.)

Line of farthest
Japanese advance, 1942 — — — —

rt Is.
tions,
1943

PHOENIX IS.

Allied advances

0°

ELLICE IS.

Japanese advances

NEW
BRIDES

SAMOA IS.

FIJI
IS.

TONGA IS.

COOK IS.

SOCIETY IS.

CALEDONIA

180°

140°

© RM₅N & CO.

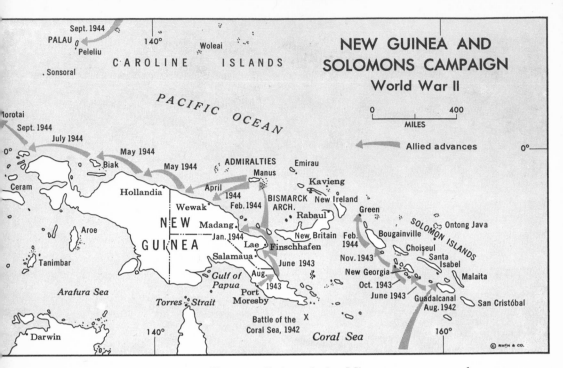

NEW GUINEA AND SOLOMONS CAMPAIGN
World War II

0 — 400 MILES

⟵ Allied advances

for the most part still controlled, and the Nipponese commanders were prepared to take great risks to keep the islands. The troops went ashore as scheduled. On October 24–25, the Japanese and American fleets engaged one another in a series of battles known collectively as the Battle of Leyte Gulf although parts of the battle occurred miles away. The greatest navy battle in history, it left the Japanese without the naval power to resist seriously. Japan lost all four of the carriers it had in the battle, three of its nine battleships, nine cruisers, and nine destroyers; the United States lost one light carrier and two escort carriers, two destroyers, and one destroyer escort. Both sides had extensive repairs to make, but the American navy was in a better position to make them. At the battle's end the Japanese first used the kamikaze or suicide bomber.

In the 1941–1942 Philippines campaign the Americans had the disadvantages of air inferiority and isolation from replacements and supplies. But in 1944–1945, Japan had these disadvantages, plus the opposition of Filipino guerillas. In December, while the fighting for Leyte was still intense, MacArthur was able to land forces on Mindoro, the southernmost big Philippine island, and in January he invaded Luzon, the largest of the islands and the one upon which Manila is located. By March, American ships were unloading in Manila Bay. By June, the Japanese had been defeated in the Philippines. Some Japanese soldiers hid in the remote and inaccessible highlands, there to remain until Japan's final defeat. Indeed, some of these troops, isolated from the news, remained in hiding until months and even years after the war had ended.

American forces invaded more island stepping stones on the difficult

502

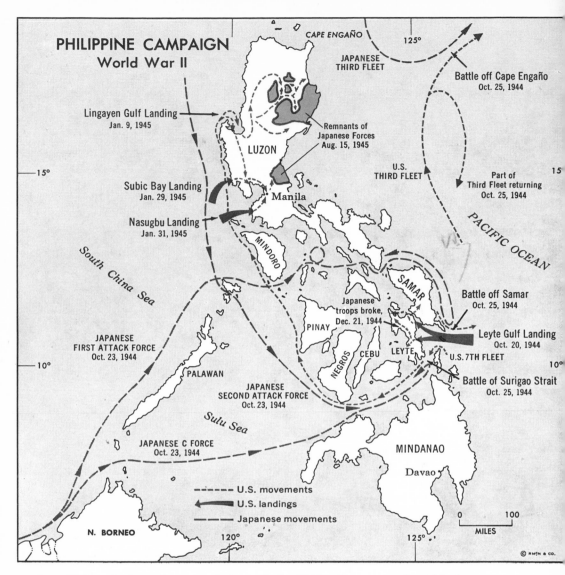

PHILIPPINE CAMPAIGN
World War II

Lingayen Gulf Landing
Jan. 9, 1945

LUZON

Remnants of
Japanese Forces
Aug. 15, 1945

Subic Bay Landing
Jan. 29, 1945

Manila

Nasugbu Landing
Jan. 31, 1945

MINDORO

JAPANESE
FIRST ATTACK FORCE
Oct. 23, 1944

PALAWAN

PINAY

NEGROS

CEBU

JAPANESE
SECOND ATTACK FORCE
Oct. 23, 1944

Sulu Sea

JAPANESE C FORCE
Oct. 23, 1944

N. BORNEO

South China Sea

CAPE ENGAÑO

JAPANESE
THIRD FLEET

Battle off Cape Engaño
Oct. 25, 1944

U.S.
THIRD FLEET

Part of
Third Fleet returning
Oct. 25, 1944

PACIFIC OCEAN

SAMAR

Battle off Samar
Oct. 25, 1944

Japanese
troops broke,
Dec. 21, 1944

LEYTE

Leyte Gulf Landing
Oct. 20, 1944

U.S. 7TH FLEET

Battle of Surigao Strait
Oct. 25, 1944

MINDANAO

Davao

- - - - U.S. movements
◄──── U.S. landings
── ── Japanese movements

MILES
0   100

Davao

road to Tokyo before the completion of the Philippines campaign. Marines invaded Iwo Jima on February 19, 1945, and had the eight-square-mile island under control within a month, but the action was one of the most difficult of the Pacific war. The Japanese had fortified Iwo Jima so cleverly that its camouflaged guns could cover every yard of the island and so deeply that seventy-two consecutive days of aerial bombing and three days of intense fire from naval vessels did little damage. The tiny volcanic island, only 775 miles from the main Japanese island of Honshu, was important as an air base. If the Japanese held it, they endangered the American air base at Saipan; if the Americans held it, they could use it as a base for fighters to escort the big B-29's on their Japanese attacks.

The successful American invasion and conquest of Okinawa, April 1 to June 20, were notable for several reasons. The largest amphibious operation of the whole Pacific war, the Japanese offered the landing almost no opposition. Their plan was to knock out the supporting naval force with an all-out attack by air and naval forces. About seven hundred planes, half of them kamikazes, struck incessantly on April 6 and 7. American guns destroyed about half of the attackers, but the Japanese aircraft, particularly the kamikazes, sank or put out of action thirty-six American ships. Never before had the American fleet suffered such losses so quickly. The next day, American carrier planes spotted a fleet of nine Japanese ships moving in for a hit-and-run attack, among them Japan's last superbattleship, *Yamato*. A concentrated attack sank five of the nine, including *Yamato*, and Japanese surface naval strength was all but wiped out. A wicked typhoon at this point seriously endangered the American fleet. Actually part of the same archipelago as Japan and only 350 miles from the southernmost Japanese island of Kyushu, Okinawa fitted into American plans as a base of operations for the invasion of Japan. The Okinawa campaign was the first one in the Pacific theater in an area fairly heavily populated by hostile people. Also, in this campaign Japanese soldiers surrendered in mass numbers for the first time. Some Japanese soldiers, at least, had become aware that the war was in its last stages and that Japan's cause was almost hopeless.

In the spring and summer of 1945, American naval and air forces brought the war home to Japan with a vengeance. Land-based bombers and fighters and carrier-based planes hit Japanese industrial centers with such overwhelming power that the nation's war potential was devastated. Raids on Japanese cities were terrible in their effects. Napalm incendiary bombs caused more havoc and death in flimsily built Japanese cities in a few months than did the far heavier bombing of Germany. Roughly 330,000 Japanese civilians died from American bombings; another 500,000 were injured. A single fire raid against Tokyo in March, 1945, destroyed sixteen square miles of the city. Planes and submarines destroyed what was left of the Japanese navy and systematically cut off shipping. With her industry strangled for lack of raw materials and many of her interisland railroad ferries destroyed, Japan was well softened up for the American invasion. The plan was to invade Kyushu in November, 1945, and Honshu the following March. American casualties were expected to run to about one million. The atom bomb, however, hastened the end of the war and made the invasion of Japan unnecessary.

The decision to drop the atom bomb on Japan was not taken lightly, although perhaps not with the recognition of the ramifications that hindsight would indicate as proper. The idea of warning Japan of the existence of the new weapon and urging Japan to surrender before the weapon was used was rejected as unworkable. The plan of demonstrating to Japan the power of the new weapon over some uninhabited island and then demanding surrender was rejected on grounds that the bomb might not detonate, and indeed there was no assurance that it would. Desire to finish off Japan with as little help from Russia as possible, so as to keep Russian influence in Asia to a minimum, was another consideration. Japanese reaction to the Potsdam Declaration also figured in the decision to drop the bomb. Some background to this declaration and its reception is necessary.

Japan's military successes in 1941 and 1942 submerged the political moderates' opposition to the most rabidly militaristic and imperialistic army leadership. But as Japan's military fortunes turned, the moderates again began to exert themselves, and in July, 1944, a group of navy moderates brought about the downfall of the Tojo government. The new government headed by General Kuniaki Koiso had moderates within it who were eager to bring the war to an end, saving whatever of Japan's territorial conquests her enemies would allow. In February, 1945, Emperor Hirohito gave his support to the moderates. In early April, he appointed still another premier, Admiral Kantaro Suzuki, and delegated him to sue for peace. Suzuki opened secret discussions with the Russians, whom he wanted to serve as mediators between Japan and America and Great Britain, but Suzuki's powers were severely restricted since he had no control over the army. The Japanese army leadership threatened revolt and assassination, its old weapons, if the government made peace. Just before the Potsdam Conference, Hirohito directed the Japanese ambassador in Moscow to urge the Russians to bring about peace.

One of the difficulties within the Japanese government was what was meant by "unconditional surrender." If that meant abandonment of the imperial monarchy, surely surrender would have more opponents within Japan than it would have if the Japanese could keep their traditional government. President Truman in a statement on V-E Day said nothing explicit about the government of Japan when he again called for Japanese unconditional surrender. He only pointed out that "unconditional surrender does not mean the extermination or enslavement of the Japanese people," which seemed rather obvious. The participants in the last wartime conference at Potsdam, July 17 to August 2, 1945, were preoccupied with European problems and were new as representatives in the Grand Alliance. Truman and his new Secretary of State, James F. Byrnes, spoke for the United States. Churchill and Eden opened the conference as the British delegates, but the British people had already voted in a new Labor party government and on July 28, Clement Atlee, the new prime minister, and Ernest Bevin, the new foreign minister, took over from their more conservative fellow countrymen. Stalin and Molotov, of course, had no voters to threaten their tenure.

The Potsdam Declaration of July 26 called upon Japan to surrender unconditionally or suffer "the utter devastation of the Japanese homeland." The Declaration said nothing to indicate such devastation would be by other than conventional weapons. With surrender, the Declaration went on, Allied forces would occupy Japan until militarism was utterly eliminated, war criminals punished, peace and security established, and a government installed that was consistent with the wishes of the Japanese people. Although much of this Declaration was vague to the point that different Japanese leaders could interpret it quite differently, Japanese moderates at least could take heart from it. The Suzuki government had still to mollify the army diehards and was still hopeful of negotiating peace through the Russians. A government statement on July 28, intended for home consumption, called the Declaration "unworthy of public notice." The top American leaders at Potsdam, now aware that a test of the atom bomb in New Mexico had been successful, understood this statement to be the Japanese reply, considered it inadequate, and ordered the dropping of the bomb on any of four Japanese industrial cities any time after August 3.

Early in the morning of August 6, 1945, a B-29 dropped an atom bomb on Hiroshima equal in power to twenty thousand tons of TNT. The bomb killed an estimated eighty thousand people and maimed thousands more. The blast and subsequent fire utterly destroyed the city. The Japanese army still balked at surrender. On August 8, Russia entered the war as agreed, charging quickly into Manchuria and Korea. On August 9, an American plane dropped a more powerful atom bomb on Nagasaki. The next day, Emperor Hirohito overruled the army and notified the United States that Japan accepted the terms of the Potsdam Declaration if the status of the Emperor were not altered. America replied that during the occupation the Emperor's authority would be secondary to that of the Supreme Commander of the Allied Powers and that the ultimate government of Japan would be decided by the Japanese people. Despite the disasters of Hiroshima and Nagasaki, the army still wanted to refuse these terms. Hirohito again overruled the army. On August 14, the Suzuki government accepted the Potsdam terms and President Truman announced Japan's surrender. On September 2, the Japanese formally surrendered aboard the American battleship *Missouri* in Tokyo Bay.

The destruction and death was over at last. The total costs could never accurately be assessed. Of American peak strength of 12,300,000 men in the armed forces, 291,557 were killed by enemy action. American monetary costs were about $330 billion, if we can say that the costs ended when the fighting stopped. Great Britain had fewer men killed in action, 244,723, but this was a higher proportion of her men under arms. China lost an estimated 2,200,000 men. Russia lost far more men than any other country in the war on either side: an estimated 7,500,000 killed by enemy action. Russia lost a similar number of civilians. The Axis powers lost heavily, too. Germany, which at one time had 10,200,000 men under arms, suffered 3,500,000 battle deaths; Japan had 1,219,000 battle deaths out of a little over 6,000,000 servicemen.

CHAPTER TWENTY-FIVE

The Truman Era: Foreign and Domestic Cold War

FEW AMERICANS DURING THE WAR HAD THE WISDOM TO SEE THAT Axis defeat would not solve most of the nation's problems. The hardships and horrors of war were such that their end, it seemed to most people in their innocent optimism, would mean automatically an era of peace and internal harmony. The most widespread anxiety about postwar America was that cessation of war spending would bring about the depression's return.

Fear of depression proved unfounded. The United States after World War II enjoyed the greatest and most sustained period of economic prosperity in its history. But optimistic expectation of a "brave new world" proved equally unfounded. On the domestic scene the nation faced inflation and shortages, labor unrest, irresponsible political battling, and deep, frustrating social problems arising from a rapidly increasing population and a general heightening of individual and family social aspirations. Nor was the world situation reassuring. On the world scene the nation faced a sharp and continual conflict between its desires and those of the communist parts of the world, upheaval and imbalances that arose with the revolt of dark-skinned peoples against colonial imperialism, and the constant dreadful knowledge that man's new weapons could, if used to their capacity in an all-out war, destroy civilization and perhaps life itself. Perhaps most confusing and frustrating was the increasing realization that the nation's problems, both foreign and domestic, were wondrously complex and subtle. Even relatively unsophisticated minds perceived that America's foreign, political, economic, social, and cultural problems had no simple solution, that to see them in sharp black and white or good and evil terms was naive, and that all alternatives for their solution contained the seeds of new predicaments.

A nation must have wise and efficient leadership to cope with situations of such nature. It must be said that America had no leadership adequate to the task. No party, no organized group, no individual was up to the mark. Perhaps the mark was too high for mortal men to reach.

Truman's Ordeal

Harry S. Truman took the oath of office as president the evening of April 12, 1945, a few hours after Roosevelt's death. The next day he told reporters, "I don't know whether you fellows ever had a load of hay or a bull fall on you. But last night the moon, the stars and all the planets fell on me." Truman had been born in May, 1884, in Jackson County, Missouri, and had spent nearly all of his life in that vicinity. He graduated from high school in Independence in the spring of 1901, just before Theodore Roosevelt became president. Denied admission to West Point because of poor eyesight, he became a bank clerk and then a farmer. He was an officer in a state guard artillery unit, and when his regiment went into federal service during the war he served overseas. After the Armistice, Captain Truman and his sergeant opened a retail men's clothing store in Kansas City; the business failed in 1922 in the postwar depression. Thirty-eight years old and broke, Truman accepted the offer of the Tom Pendergast Democratic machine of Kansas City to be nominated a county commissioner, called a judge in Missouri. Except for the election of 1924, when he opposed the Ku Klux Klan and went down to defeat, he kept getting re-elected and served efficiently and honestly despite the corruption of the machine that supported him. With Pendergast's help he won election to the United States Senate in 1934. There he had a consistent New Deal voting record, was too quiet and colorless to make a national reputation, and fitted in well in the Senate's clubby atmosphere. He won re-election in 1940 despite FDR's lack of support and Pendergast's 1939 conviction for income tax fraud. From a border state, a loyal party man, unidentified strongly with any ideology, Truman was an ideal compromise vice-presidential nominee in 1944. On the whole, his career had not educated him well for the presidency, and FDR had almost ignored him while he waited in the wings as a standby performer. At least the superficial contrast with Roosevelt was striking: the one urbane, tactful, articulate, confident; the other provincial, blunt, not clever with words, unprepossessing.

Truman never became a Roosevelt, but he grew in the White House as few other presidents had. Although his administration never solved the basic problems confronting the country (at best they attained only short-term satisfactory arrangements while waiting for a happier and more propitious time), Truman by the time he left the White House had shown his enemies he was a far stronger man than they had estimated and demonstrated to his friends that their misgivings had been exaggerated. He displayed courage, toughness, and a willingness to make hard decisions.

Within a week after Japan's surrender, Truman submitted to Congress a long domestic program, reminiscent of the political mood of the mid-1930's, that he in time came to call the Fair Deal. Truman wanted Congress to raise the minimum wage from forty to sixty-five cents an hour; to extend social security; to establish a permanent Fair Employment Practices Commission; and to enact a full employment program, an extensive slum clearance and public housing plan, and a series of regional flood control and hydroelectric projects. Before the end of the year, he asked Congress for legislation to provide nationalization of atomic energy, the St. Lawrence seaway, national health insurance, and federal aid to education. Some of these requests eventually became law, most of them were compromised, some were defeated.

It is easy to overlook some of the Truman administration's positive accomplishments in the era's political furor. Some of Truman's requests became law even early in his administration. "Full employment" after the war had been a Democratic pledge in 1944; Henry Wallace had written confidently of a postwar economy with "sixty million jobs" and been attacked as a wild visionary. (Employment reached sixty million in August, 1946.) The administration's Full Employment bill stated it was the federal government's responsibility to maintain the nation's economic health and contained a plan for compensatory deficit spending during economic slumps. The law that emerged from the congressional compromise mill was called the Maximum Employment Act. Becoming law in early 1946, it established a three-man Council of Economic Advisers and required the president to make an annual report on the nation's economy. It contained no guarantee of government action against recession, although in fact both Democratic and Republican administrations have since used federal power to compensate for and correct downswings in the business cycle. The Atomic Energy Act of 1946 vested all policy decisions about nuclear power in the hands of the civilian-controlled Atomic Energy Commission, as the manager of the legislation in Congress, Democratic Senator Brian McMahon of Connecticut wished, and over the opposition of Senator Arthur H. Vandenberg, Republican of Michigan. The Act provided for a Military Liaison Committee to work with the AEC, but the Committee had no statutory policy power and only the commander in chief was authorized to order the use of nuclear weapons.

Another measure affecting the military establishment was the National Security Act of July 26, 1947, adopted after nearly two years of backbiting and wrangling between the army and navy. Nearly everyone accepted in principle the idea of unification of the armed forces, but the admirals were fearful that their service would be subordinated to land-based air power, and marine officers, then under the Navy Department, were apprehensive that the corps might be abolished. The new law created a separate air force and maintained the marines, thereby creating four branches rather than three (five branches if one counts the coast guard which remained under the Department of the Treasury), but the old Departments of War and Navy disappeared to be replaced by the Department of Defense. Under the Secretary of Defense (the first was James V. Forrestal) were secretaries of army, navy, and air force with subcabinet rank. A Joint Chiefs of Staff with a rotating chairman was supposed to provide further coordination among the services, and three other new agencies, the National Security Council, the National Security Resource Board, and the Central Intelligence Agency, had the task of advising Congress and the president on national security. The new law by no means ended interservice rivalry, which extended to public propaganda and lobbying in Congress. Indeed, the fight over long-range bombers versus super aircraft carriers, which went on for years while attention to missiles lagged, was if anything more intense than interservice bickering before unification.

The vast and complicated civilian side of the executive branch also was the subject of reorganization. In 1947, Truman asked Congress to create a study group to study how best to straighten out the maze of bureaus and agencies. Congress consented, and Truman appointed former President Hoover to head the investigation. The Hoover Commission reported in 1949, suggesting the merger of sixty-five units into twenty-three and the creation of a new federal department to handle education, public health, and welfare. The Reorganization Act of June, 1949, authorized Truman to submit reorganization plans to Congress which would become effective unless Congress disapproved. Of Truman's many reorganization plans, Congress disapproved of only his proposed Department of Welfare.

The most spectacular aspect of the Truman era's political history, however, was the fierce, fluid, shifting partisan brawling, both between the parties and within them. Despite the Missourian's Fair Deal requests, he frequently appeared to be far removed from any New Deal sympathies. Those who had been enthusiastic FDR supporters found Truman extremely disappointing in his first two to three years. At the same time, division within the old New Deal coalition over foreign policy questions further reduced Truman's political base. The flight of Roosevelt aides from the new administration revealed disillusion in high places. After he had been in office only a few months, Truman nominated Edwin W. Pauley as Undersecretary of the Navy. Interior Secretary Ickes charged publicly that the nomination had a smell of oil about it reminiscent of Teapot Dome. Ickes said that Pauley had asserted when he was treasurer of the Democratic national committee that he could raise $300,000 for the party from oil interests if the administration would drop its test suit claiming title to California's offshore oil fields. In February, 1946, Ickes resigned in a well-publicized huff. Truman continued to support Pauley, but in August he vetoed a bill that would have yielded control of tidelands oil to the states. In September, 1946, Truman asked Secretary of Commerce Henry A. Wallace for his resignation after Wallace had given a speech in New York which appeared at the time to have had Truman's prior approval and in which Wallace had attacked the "get-tough-with-Russia" policy being conducted by Secretary of State James F. Byrnes. Byrnes had replaced Stettinius in that office in mid-1945.

Other Truman policies in 1945, 1946, and early 1947 contributed to conflict within the coalition Roosevelt had so skillfully put together. Needless to say, the Republicans, hungry for office after failing to win every congressional election since 1930 and every presidential election since 1932, were delighted with the fissures in the Democratic camp and pressed their attacks on Truman with uncommon vigor. The liberal-labor bloc in the Democratic fold became positively alarmed by Truman's vacillation over high prices and his labor policy.

Pressures building under prices were tremendous, more than the administration showed itself able to handle. Wartime controls disappeared quickly after V-J Day; OPA stopped rationing but was able to hold the cost of living index to only a 3 per cent increase between the war's end and mid-1946. Some goods were in genuine short supply, but businessmen and farmers held some commodities back from market in the expectation of higher prices and, they hoped, the elimination of price controls altogether. Clothes, cars, soaps and other fat products, and beef were the scarcest items. At the same time, consumers had billions to spend from their more or less enforced wartime savings. Black market operations and devious methods of circumventing price regulation became far more common than they had been during the war. Organized labor went on strike for higher wage rates to maintain at forty hours a week the incomes workers had received for overtime, aggravated by their long pent-up frustrations that grew under the no-strike pledge and anxiety about an antiunion drive such as followed World War I. Higher labor costs further built pressure for higher prices.

Yet millions of people saw clearly that significantly higher prices would seriously lower their standards of living. Retired people on relatively fixed incomes were exceedingly vulnerable, as were teachers and others who received their livelihood from public funds since government payrolls usually catch up with increased prices more slowly than private ones. Veterans of the armed forces living on the "GI Bill of Rights" were in no position to pay higher prices for basic necessities. (Congress in 1944 had passed the Servicemen's Readjustment Act which granted unemployment compensation of $20 a week for up to fifty-two weeks to unemployed veterans and provided free tuition and books and a subsistence cash allowance for veterans who went to school, either trade school or college.) The political pressures of consumers and the counterpressures of business put congressmen in an unenviable position.

Congress debated long and hard throughout the spring of 1946 about the extension of price controls due to expire under existing legislation at the end of June. Truman, on the one hand, urged Congress to extend price controls and on the other told a press conference that peacetime government controls were "police state methods." Three days before the deadline, Congress passed a weak bill that extended OPA for a year but eliminated most of its power and ordered it to cease price controls as soon as possible. To most people's surprise, Truman vetoed the bill thus ending controls altogether.

On July 1, the first "free-market" day, beef prices at the Chicago stockyards went up 22 per cent. Farmers flooded the livestock markets, yet prices continued to rise. Faced with vigorous protests, Congress quickly went to work on another price control bill. It produced a bill only slightly more effective than the one Truman had vetoed. This time, on July 25, Truman signed the measure but apologized for doing so. In August, OPA moved meat prices down again, and again livestock raisers kept their animals off the market. The administration slowly yielded. In October Truman announced the end of controls on meat. The butcher shops quickly had meat aplenty, but at prices that angered housewives. In November, Truman announced the lifting of all controls except for rent, rice, and sugar. Truman's popularity was low indeed. He had resisted inflation just enough to anger those who wanted higher prices for their products and had yielded enough to alienate large sections of the Democratic coalition that wanted strict controls.

Nor did Truman's labor policy in 1946 endear him to a big bloc in his party. His reputation grew not a bit in the wave of strikes of late 1945 and early 1946. The administration, which still had wartime powers and agencies, brought about compromises which granted labor slightly more than two-thirds

TABLE 10

BUREAU OF LABOR STATISTICS CONSUMER PRICE INDEX, 1926-1960.

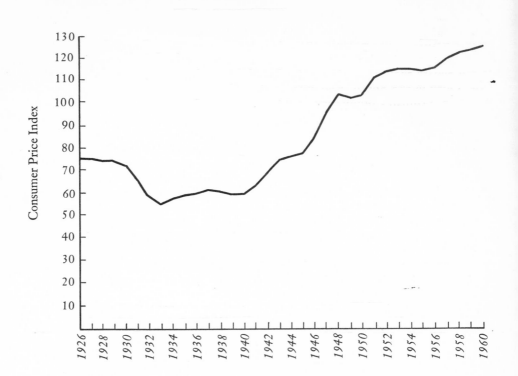

of the pay increases it demanded and granted employers price increases to compensate for the additional production costs. Many asserted, with considerable justification, that the price increases more than compensated for the higher wages. But the President's conduct in the May, 1946, railroad strike thoroughly displeased labor. The railroad brotherhoods and railroad management had negotiated for months over wages and working rules but had come to no agreement. When the brotherhoods threatened to strike, Truman on May 17 invoked the Smith-Connally Act and seized the railroads. He worked out a compromise which all the brotherhoods but the Engineers and the Trainmen accepted. They walked out on May 23, and rail transportation stopped utterly. Truman prepared an appeal to Congress to grant him extreme powers to deal with strikes that imperiled the public. Although he received a note informing him that the Engineers and Trainmen had surrendered just as he began his address to Congress, he went ahead and presented his request: power to draft strikers into the armed services in government-seized industries, loss of strikers' seniority benefits, and stiff fines for union leaders who continued strike activities. The House passed his measure; the Senate did not act.

Not since Wilson in 1918 or Hoover in 1930 had a president been so unpopular as he prepared to lead his party in congressional elections. Scenting victory, the Republicans capitalized on the administration's ineptitude with the slogan "Had Enough? Vote Republican." But perhaps more important, Democrats of most varieties were thoroughly disgusted with the administration. Southern Democrats disliked Truman's plea for a permanent FEPC and had defeated it. Northern and western urban Democrats, still divided among themselves over Truman's Russian policies, were mostly in agreement in condemnation of his price control and labor record. On November 5, the GOP won its first national victory since 1928. And it was a sweeping Republican electoral triumph. Elected to the House were 246 Republicans to the Democrats' 188; in the Senate there were 51 on the Republican side and 45 on the Democrats' aisle. Outside the South, Republicans elected governors in 25 states. The only direction Truman's popularity could go was up after this election.

The manner in which Truman restored his personal popularity and his party's strength in 1947 and 1948 was one of the most dramatic political comebacks in American history. His own foreign policies and developments of Soviet policy brought about a substantial healing of the divisions within the Democratic party on foreign affairs. The Truman Doctrine, enunciated in March, 1947, did not evoke popular response at first, but the Marshall Plan later that year proved a very popular proposal (see pp. 523–525). At the same time, the Soviets pursued a "get-tough" policy that dissolved most of the Democratic criticism of the kind Wallace had made in his September, 1946, speech.

The greatest percentage decline in Democratic votes in 1946 had been in the cities. For Truman, then, the task was to pursue domestic policies that would attract that part of the voting population in which labor and minority groups were important. In May, 1947, speaking from his hometown where he had gone to visit his sick and aged mother, he urged Congress to pass a long-range public health program, including provisions for worker disability insurance. He made a series of appointments that were popular with the liberal-labor bloc: Gordon Clapp to the TVA, David Lilienthal to the AEC. In 1948, he systematically began a program to eliminate segregation of and discrimination against Negroes in both the armed forces and civil federal employment that attracted large groups of voters in northern and western cities. His prompt recognition of Israel as an independent nation on May 14, 1948, within only minutes after the British mandate in Palestine ended also appealed to this voting group.

The Republicans seemed determined to help Truman in his effort to drape himself in Roosevelt's domestic mantle. Senate Republicans consistently challenged Truman's more liberal appointments, frequently impugning the loyalty of the nominees. Farmers, who had expected an agricultural depression momentarily since the end of the war, began to rally behind Truman when he beat down Republican demands for "flexible" price supports to maintain farm prices at from 65 to 90 per cent of parity. In June, 1948, Congress enacted a measure to continue supports at 90 per cent of parity for another year and a half. Republican Congressmen opposed Truman on rent controls and other anti-inflationary proposals, and prices continued to rise. And when Truman objected to tax reduction on grounds of inflationary pressures, he at least partly undermined whatever political advantage lower taxes gave the GOP. In both 1947 and 1948, Congress enacted tax bills over the President's veto.

But it was the Taft-Hartley Act of July, 1947, the first major overhaul of federal labor legislation since 1935, that provided the most political dynamite (see p. 581). Proposals to curb the power of organized labor had been gaining strength during the postwar strike wave, particularly when John L. Lewis and the UMW defied the government and public opinion. In 1946, Truman had successfully vetoed the quite restrictive Case bill. In the spring of 1947, Congress passed a labor bill sponsored by Senator Robert A. Taft of Ohio and Representative Fred Hartley of New Jersey, both Republicans. Organized labor called the measure a "slave labor act" and roundly condemned the Republicans for passing it, although it had actually been passed with a combination of Republican and conservative Democratic, mostly southern, votes. On June 20, 1947, Truman vetoed the measure with a strong message. Congress quickly overrode the veto, again with near unanimity on the Republican side.

Truman had allowed the old Roosevelt coalition to begin to fall apart before he began to rebuild it after the 1946 elections. Ironically, the Republican party, by playing the role of conservative bogey-man, helped Truman to paste the coalition back together.

Truman's Triumph—and Further Troubles

Yet in mid-summer of 1948, the old coalition appeared to be a long way from rehabilitation. At the end of December, 1947, Henry A. Wallace had announced his independent presidential candidacy on a program of negotiation with Russia and a kind of domestic reform he called "progressive capitalism." Hardly any important Democrats threw in their lot with Wallace, but a great many normally Democratic voters were sympathetic to him at first. In early 1948, in a special House of Representatives election in the Bronx, New York City, the Wallace-backed candidate won in a three-cornered race. Although much of Wallace's organization came from the Communists and those who cooperated with the Communists—Wallace, clearly, was not a Communist—early in the year political observers were granting Wallace from five to ten million votes in November, enough probably to insure Truman's defeat. Democratic Senator Glen Taylor of Idaho, a singing cowboy entertainer, became Wallace's running mate at the July, 1948, Progressive party convention.

In and around Americans for Democratic Action (ADA), an anti-Communist and anti-Wallace but left of center group founded in early 1947 by Democratic intellectuals, labor leaders, and urban political professionals, were many Democrats who wanted to dump Truman. They looked around desperately for another presidential candidate. When Justice William O. Douglas declined consideration, some of them wanted General Dwight D. Eisenhower, who had recently become president of Columbia University. Some Democratic city bosses—Jacob Arvey of Chicago, Frank Hague of Jersey City, and Edward Flynn of New York—joined them in this venture, which was to prove ironic in just a few years. Eisenhower was not interested.

With such apparent division in Democratic ranks, Republican hopefuls were more than usually eager for the nomination. The main contenders were Governor Dewey, former Governor of Minnesota Harold E. Stassen, and

514

Senator Taft. General Douglas MacArthur had some support. After the primaries, the fight settled down to Dewey versus Taft. Although perhaps even a majority of the Republican convention delegates—at Philadelphia in June—respected and loved Taft more than Dewey, they thought that Taft "could not win." Taft had remarkable talents and commanded wide respect, but he lacked the personal traits that denoted political magnetism. Further, as a professed conservative, although a flexible one, many GOP professionals feared that he could not attract the independent vote. On the third ballot the nomination went to Dewey; Governor Earl Warren of California received the vice-presidential nomination. The GOP platform was even more of a "me too" document than its 1944 declaration. Apparently, Republican party leaders were not confident that a conservative statement would attract enough votes to win. Republicans promised to do everything Democrats had done or promised to do but to do them more efficiently.

Frustrated because they really had no choice but to nominate Truman, the ADA faction at the Democratic national convention, also at Philadelphia, fought through a progressive platform over the southern delegations' opposition. When Senator Hubert Humphrey of Minnesota insisted upon and got a strong civil rights plank that called for a permanent FEPC, a federal antilynching law, and a law to eliminate poll taxes, many of the Alabama and Mississippi delegates walked out of the convention. With Wallace going off in one direction and the strong possibility of Dixie delegations going off in the other, the convention was indeed dismal in spirit. It nominated Truman and Senator Alben W. Barkley of Kentucky, president pro tempore of the upper house.

Within a week after the Democratic convention adjourned the Democratic bolters and other southerners met at Birmingham to form the States' Rights Democratic party and to nominate Governor J. Strom Thurmond of South Carolina and Governor Fielding Wright of Mississippi for the national executive positions. These so-called Dixiecrats controlled what had been the Democratic parties in South Carolina, Alabama, Mississippi, and Louisiana.

About the only person who thought Truman would win was Truman himself. He began a fighting campaign with his acceptance speech in which he announced that he was calling Congress into special session on July 26 so that the Republican majority could enact the "anything-you-can-do-I-can-do-better" platform the GOP had adopted at its convention. Congress met for almost two weeks and, as Truman expected, did practically nothing. Truman shrewdly aimed his campaign against the Republican Congress—the "do-nothing" Congress and "that awful Eightieth Congress" he called it—rather than against Dewey. The President undertook personal speaking tours that took him more than the distance around the world, speaking at "whistle stops" and wherever he could get a crowd. He seldom spoke from a prepared text; his extemporaneous stump speeches were much more effective. Truman had told his running mate, "I'm going to give them hell"; before long, people in the crowds gathered at the rear of the campaign train began to shout, "Give 'em hell, Harry," and Truman poured it on. As the campaign wore on, Truman's crowds became bigger and increasingly enthusiastic. Political commentators said that the voters liked Truman because he was the underdog and a battler but that they would not vote for him.

Since the polls and the experts declared that Dewey's victory was all

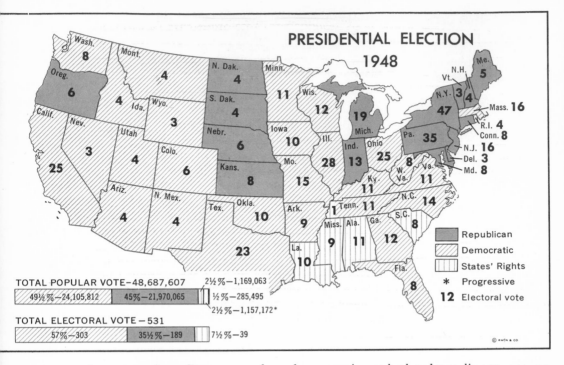

PRESIDENTIAL ELECTION
1948

Republican
Democratic
States' Rights
* Progressive
12 Electoral vote

TOTAL POPULAR VOTE—48,687,607
2½%—1,169,063
49½%—24,105,812   45%—21,970,065   ½%—285,495
2½%—1,157,172*

TOTAL ELECTORAL VOTE—531
57%—303   35½%—189   7½%—39

Dewey victory certain

but a certainty, Dewey conducted a campaign calculated to alienate no one, similar to Roosevelt's in 1932 when his election was as predictable as the tide. Dewey, of course, had no way of knowing that his basic premise was unfounded. Republicans other than Dewey frequently spoke as if they were still running against FDR, which played well into Truman's hands because he was doing his utmost to persuade the voters that he was Roosevelt incarnate.

So certain were the pollsters of Republican victory that they ceased their operations well before election day. So certain were editors and radio commentators of Truman's defeat that even when the early returns showed Truman leading they refused to believe the evidence and said to wait until the rural precincts reported. The *Chicago Daily Tribune* carried a banner headline proclaiming Dewey's victory. But Truman defeated Dewey by a rather large margin. Truman received 24,105,695 popular votes to earn him 304 votes in the electoral college to Dewey's 21,969,170 and 189. Democratic candidates also won a majority of congressional seats. The new Congress would have Democratic margins of ninety-three in the House and twelve in the Senate. Wallace received only 1,157,172 popular votes and none in the electoral college; the Dixiecrat candidate received 1,169,021 popular and 39 electoral votes. Dewey won in sixteen states: Oregon, Kansas north to Canada, Indiana, Michigan, and Maryland and Delaware north to the border with the exceptions of Massachusetts and Rhode Island. Thurmond carried the four states where the Dixiecrats pulled out of the Democratic party and picked up one additional electoral vote when a Tennessee elector refused to honor the Truman popular vote. In three of the states Truman lost, New York, Maryland, and Michigan, he would have won if all the Wallace vote had gone Democratic.

Why did Truman win? Politicians debated the subject strenuously. Conservative Republicans whose heart belonged to Taft argued that Dewey had lost the election rather than that Truman had won it. However, the record showed that Dewey did not fail to get any significant number of normally Republican votes. The hard fact for the Republican party was that the Roosevelt political revolution had tipped the scales until those who considered themselves Democrats outnumbered those who considered themselves Republicans, although "independents" or "swing voters" were numerous enough to throw a presidential election either way. The Wallace and Thurmond candidacies probably worked to Truman's benefit. Because Communist support of Wallace was so obvious—even to the stupid tactic of selling the *Daily Worker* at Wallace rallies in Texas—the red issue was largely irrelevant in the Truman-Dewey struggle. Thurmond's white supremacy movement only gained for Truman votes in the North and West, not only among Negroes but among ethnic groups that fearfully identified the Dixiecrats with the spirit of the Ku Klux Klan. Truman capitalized on this reaction outside of the South and stumped hard for civil rights carrying his campaign into Harlem, the first presidential candidate ever to do so. A final factor: Truman cut into the expected Republican farm vote with his strong support for continued high agricultural subsidies at a time when farm prices were falling and Republicans were talking about "flexible," meaning lower, federal price supports.

Election day of 1948 was the high tide of Truman's strength. His Fair Deal got only slightly off the ground, due mostly to the conservative Democrat-Republican coalition in Congress, partly to Truman's less than wholehearted support of proposed new departures, and partly to the press of foreign affairs and their consequences for domestic politics. On the whole, the Fair Deal only extended social welfare legislation a bit farther down already well-marked roads. It failed to enact laws that blazed new domestic trails.

Among the extensions of old programs by the Eighty-first Congress was a 1949 amendment to the Fair Labor Standards Act of 1938 that increased the hourly minimum wage to seventy-five cents an hour but added to the exemption list; a 1950 change in the Social Security Act of 1935 that brought an additional ten million people under the coverage of the Old Age and Survivors' Insurance plan and increased retirement benefits by slightly more than 75 per cent; and the National Housing Act of 1949, which provided for the building of eight hundred and ten thousand new housing units over the next six years, subsidies to builders of low-rent apartment buildings, and grants to aid in the clearance of slums, both urban and rural. Senator Taft, incidentally, supported federally financed public housing. Public housing administrators and builders rarely used great imagination, and many of the public housing apartment buildings erected on the sites of razed tenement slums actually housed more people per acre than the old housing. Despite its great wealth, the United States still had slums in all its major cities that shocked visitors from some less affluent nations.

Organized labor supported such legislation, but repeal of the Taft-Hartley Act was its primary goal. Truman, at trade union urging, argued in 1949 for full repeal and got nothing; probably Congress would have passed amendments altering some of the law's features—Taft was willing to make some concessions—but the administration refused a compromise. Indeed, at one point the House came close to making the law even more restrictive. A 1951 amendment, however, permitted union-shop clauses in labor contracts without a special vote of affected employees.

The northward migration of Negroes in the 1940's intensified the Democratic party's regional differences. Negro populations—voting populations, it should be noted—nearly doubled in northern industrial cities. In 1947, Truman's special Committee on Civil Rights, composed of distinguished people of both races from both the North and South, had recommended substantially what became the 1948 Democratic civil rights plank plus prohibition of segregation on public interstate transportation. But practically the entire Dixie delegation in Congress was dead set against any federal legislation to advance the Negro's status. Southern Congressmen who personally viewed changed racial relations in the South as inevitable knew that it was almost sure political suicide to vote for the Truman program. Southern Democrats had an almost foolproof defense against civil rights legislation in the Senate rule that granted unlimited debate. A two-thirds majority was necessary to invoke the cloture rule and shut off a filibuster. Civil rights advocates, therefore, concentrated on changing the Senate rule. A civil rights bipartisan group in March, 1949, sought to make it easier to stop a filibuster by changing the two-thirds rule to two-thirds of the Senators present and voting rather than two-thirds of the whole body. The Senate defeated the change sixty-three to twenty-three, twenty-nine Democrats voting for the amended procedure and fifteen against, eight Republicans for and thirty-four against. In other words, more Republicans voted to retain the stricter rule than did Democrats, despite the Republican 1948 civil rights plank. In May and July, 1950, Senate civil rights advocates brought motions to invoke cloture to a vote under the old rule; they failed by twelve votes on the first test and by nine votes on the second. FEPC was dead.

Unable to gain any civil rights legislation, Truman concentrated on executive actions. By the end of his term, segregation in the army and air force had practically disappeared; some southern white recruits took drill from Negro sergeants. He also appointed Negroes to higher positions than they had held heretofore and strengthened the Civil Rights Section of the Department of Justice.

Truman was more successful with Congress in getting it to admit displaced persons from Europe, those who had been set on the march by Nazi or Communist oppression or made homeless by the war. The Eightieth Congress had, near the end of its tenure, passed a measure admitting 205,000 "DP's" as they were commonly called. Truman signed the bill but criticized it on the grounds that it discriminated against Jews and Roman Catholics. Truman asked the next Congress for further DP legislation, and in June, 1950, Congress voted to admit a total of 415,000 without discrimination. But even the second act was filled with such qualifications for admission to the United States that thousands of aspiring refugees were unable to take advantage of the enlarged quota.

Two of Truman's proposals ran into such opposition that Congress never even brought them up for vote. Truman in 1949 proposed a national health insurance plan for prepaid medical, dental, and hospital care to be financed with employee and employer contributions through a payroll tax and government subsidy. The American Medical Association, which had opposed almost every public health proposal ever considered in Congress, vigorously opposed the scheme, both in Capitol lobbies and in mass communication media. It raised a $3 million fund to fight what it called "socialized medicine" by a special assessment on each AMA member. AMA propaganda easily carried the day. Congress would do no more than vote increased appropriations for medical research and education and for hospitals. The administration presented a plan also for federal aid to public education. This proposal triggered a Protestant-Catholic conflict over whether federal aid should go also to parochial schools. The Democratic party was particularly vulnerable to this kind of religious division, and the bill died in Congress without action.

social medicine

Perhaps the most original administration proposal was a new plan for agricultural subsidies put forward by Secretary of Agriculture Charles F. Brannan. Brannan argued that the consumer paid twice for agricultural subsidies, once in taxes and once in high food prices at the store. The Brannan Plan, announced in April, 1949, would have kept the existing system of purchasing imperishable farm commodities and storing them but revised it somewhat: the main innovation was an arrangement whereby prices of perishable products would seek their natural levels, presumably lower, and the farmer would be reimbursed sufficiently to give him an estimated fair price. For each farmer, government subsidy would be granted only for enough production to bring a payment not to exceed $20,000 at 1949 prices. It was probably this feature that brought the Brannan Plan the opposition of the American Farm Bureau Federation and the Grange, but the public argument of these organizations was that Congress would be less likely to maintain direct subsidies to farmers than it would through the existing commodity surplus purchase scheme. The Brannan Plan excited considerable interest among consumers, but it got nowhere at all in Congress, many of whose members were sensitive to the wishes of the major farm organizations. Instead, Congress in 1949 passed a law that provided for 90 per cent of parity prices through 1950 on imperishables, at least 80 per cent through 1951, and 75 per cent to 90 per cent thereafter. Producers of perishable products, primarily milk and eggs, would be subsidized by "flexible" supports. How the adopted plan furthered "free enterprise" more than the Brannan Plan, as the Farm Bureau asserted, was a mystery to amateur agricultural economists.

agr. subsidies

The Cold War to 1950

Antagonism between the Communist parts of the world, especially the Soviet Union and later China, and the nations of the West has been a fundamental condition of the postwar world that has affected in greater or lesser degree almost all aspects of public life, foreign and domestic. Some things about the conflict need to be understood at the outset to see this aspect of recent history clearly and dispassionately. First, the issue has not been purely between democracy and totalitarianism, for some of the governments within the western camp—Spain and South Korea, for example—have not been democratic by a reasonable definition. Nor has the issue been purely between capitalism and opposition to it, for some of the anticommunist nations have been socialist or semisocialist—Great Britain and Norway, for example. Both camps have had within them both underdeveloped and industrial nations, both Christian and non-Christian peoples, both Caucasians and non-Caucasians. Each side has committed acts which fall short of international moral conduct when measured by their own standards: Great Britain and France in the Suez affair, the United States in Guatemala, the Soviet Union in Hungary, to cite some examples, although it is not fair to equate the Central Intelligence Agency's 1954 ousting of the Guatemalan regime with the Russian armed suppression of the Budapest rebellion. The mutual distrust and suspicion has been complicated, deep-rooted in history, and pervasive as well as nearly universal in its effects.

We have already considered deteriorating relations between the Russians on the one hand and the United States and Great Britain on the other in the last months of the war. Their relations disintegrated even further in 1946 over Germany, the Middle East, and atomic energy. Our consideration of the German question will await treatment of the Berlin crisis of 1948.

Late in 1941, British and Russian troops invaded Iran to establish a supply route from the West to Russia, and in early 1942 Russia and Britain signed a treaty with Iran guaranteeing withdrawal of their troops at the end of the war. The British and few American troops there withdrew soon after the war. Russia not only left her troops but sent in more and applied pressure on the Iranian government through a Communist-controlled party. In early March, 1946, Washington and London sent notes to Moscow that only thinly veiled a threat to use force to defend Iran if that became necessary. Russia agreed to withdraw later in the month. In August, 1946, Russia demanded from Turkey leases for naval bases in the Dardanelles and notified London and Washington of its intention of "joint defense" of the area with Turkey. The United States sent a naval task force to the Mediterranean and rejected the whole idea of Turkish-Russian "joint defense."

At the time of these Russian-Iranian-Turkish developments American public opinion was by no means unified in belief that an era of Russian-American discord lay ahead. Only few Americans ever really approved of the Bolshevik regime (although many, perhaps most, considered that peculiarly Russia's affair), but during the war two sentiments had grown in the United States that delayed acceptance of cold war: the notion of "One World," the title of a best-selling wartime book by Wendell Willkie, so firmly and widely held that the "two worlds" actually developing were slow to be recognized; and respect and admiration for the Soviets' truly great and extremely sacrificing war against the Nazis. Furthermore, Americans were war-weary. Servicemen wanted to go home, and their families wanted them to. In early 1946, most Americans were far more interested in healing the wounds of the last war than in pursuing policies that might lead to another. Popular reception of Winston Churchill's "Iron Curtain" speech at Westminster College, Fulton, Missouri, in March, 1946, was indicative. Truman had arranged for Churchill to speak, and the President sat on the platform. Churchill, a master of language, said that although he did not think the Russians wanted war they wanted the fruits of war and that only military strength against them would prevent their getting the fruits of war. Americans adopted his "iron curtain" metaphor, which, incidentally, was somewhat of an exaggeration, but they only slowly came to agree with Churchill's general position.

The Russian leaders revealed a measure of their distrust of the United States in their reaction to the Baruch atom plan of 1946. The United States had a world monopoly of atom bombs from 1945 until September, 1949, when the Russians detonated their first one. Instead of using the terrible weapon against Russia, as a few "preventive war" proponents advocated, the United States offered, under certain conditions, to lay the weapon aside. In June, 1946, before the first meeting of the Atomic Energy Commission, Bernard Baruch presented a plan that State Department officials had formulated. Baruch called for an International Atomic Development Authority to own and operate all installations pertaining to atomic power and to conduct research. The atom bomb would be outlawed, and the international authority would have the power, without veto, to punish any violator of the agreement and to inspect throughout the world with an eye cocked for violations. The United States proposed the plan in the United Nations and promised, when the plan was accepted and the international authority was functioning, to tell the world what American scientists already knew of atomic energy, to stop manufacturing atom bombs, and to destroy its A-bomb stockpile. The Russians said "nyet." At first they rejected the idea of the international authority and inspection, demanding instead that the United States unilaterally divest itself of the atomic weapon. (The Soviets, of course, continued to work on their own atom bomb.) Later they yielded to the principle of inspection by an international authority but insisted that violators could be punished only by the United Nations Security Council where, of course, the Soviet Union had a veto. Russian leaders apparently decided that it was better for them to gamble on the success of their own development of an atomic bomb than to enter an international authority which of course would be dominated by the United States and powers friendly to it without a veto power. The United States rejected the Soviet atomic recommendations, and international nuclear disarmament became practically a dead issue until the mid-1950's.

Until 1947, the Truman administration, although it had been at loggerheads with Russia on several points and although it had practiced a "tough" policy, had no long-term policy toward the Soviet Union. In that year it adopted the "containment" policy, and its first application was with the Truman Doctrine in the Greek crisis. George F. Kennan, then of the State Department's policy-planning staff, prepared the classic statement of containment in an anonymous article (X was the only identity of the author when it first appeared) in the semi-scholarly, semi-official journal *Foreign Affairs* in July, 1947, months after the policy had been adopted. The article warrants examination.

Kennan concluded, " . . . United States policy toward the Soviet Union must be that of a long-term, patient but firm and vigilant containment of Russian expansive tendencies." Washington should not indulge in "threats or blustering or superfluous gestures of outward 'toughness' " and should at all times keep its wits and put forward its demands on the Soviets "in such a manner as to leave the way open for a compliance not too detrimental to Russian prestige." But containment would protect the West if applied intelligently, "by the adroit and vigilant application of counter-force at a series of constantly shifting geographical and political points. . . ." Although primarily defensive, offense was involved too: "It would be an exaggeration to say that American behavior unassisted and alone could exercise a power of life and death over the Communist movement and bring about the early fall of Soviet power in Russia. But the United States has it in its power to increase enormously the strains under which Soviet policy must operate, to force . . . a far greater degree of moderation and circumspection . . . and in this way to promote tendencies which must eventually find their outlet in either the breakup or the gradual mellowing of Soviet power. . . ."

The administration first applied the containment policy in Greece in March, 1947. At the end of the war Greece had been badly divided between left and right. Great Britain backed the royalist right, and in the March, 1946, elections, which the left boycotted, the right won. Thereafter, Communist guerillas in Greece, who had the support of Communist governments at the borders, became embroiled in a civil war with the government. Britain backed the Greek government as best she could, as well as the Turks against the Russians. But Britain was in poor economic condition as a result of the war, and in February, 1947, London notified Truman that it could no longer afford its Greek and Turkish aid. On March 12, 1947, Truman went to Congress and asked for an appropriation of $400 million for support of Greece and Turkey and for authority to send a team of military advisers. Truman declared, "I believe that it must be the policy of the United States to support free peoples who are resisting attempted subjugation by armed minorities or by outside pressures." This was the Truman Doctrine. In May, Congress granted the President the power he asked and appropriated the money. By 1950, the United States had spent $659 million for Greek aid, and a lesser amount in the less troublesome Turkish situation.

Stabilizing Greece proved no easy matter. Communist guerillas continued to achieve success until Tito's Jugoslavia broke with Stalin in mid-1948 and closed the border to the guerillas. Even then Greek unrest was widespread because the government was reactionary, inefficient, and adamant against any proposal to better the economic and social conditions against which Greeks revolted. Reluctant to intervene politically into domestic politics between non-Communist groups, the United States seemed to the Greeks actually to support the government a majority of them disliked. Finally, the Greek parliament, in the face of what it thought was American disapproval, voted no confidence in the government, which then resigned. The new regime, far more efficient, finished up the guerilla war in six months.

There were significant things to be noted in the Greek affair. First, for the United States to undertake the Greek commitment and for the President to declare himself for similar actions in other areas was a radical departure from traditional American foreign policy. Never had the United States done anything comparable in peacetime, although aid to Britain, 1939–1941, had some similarities. Second, in its support of an unpopular Greek government, the United States appeared to be a pillar of reaction. The American assumption that all anti-Communists were equally deserving of help was frequently embarrassing. Third, the United States learned that when it became involved in another country's internal affairs it was difficult, if not impossible, to get only its feet wet. Intervention of one kind led to intervention of another, because aid to the government that ruled a nation implied approval of that government.

Although the Greek-Turkish aid bill passed Congress with safe margins, the Truman Doctrine was not nearly as popular with the public at large as the Marshall Plan, first enunciated clearly by Secretary of State George C. Marshall at the Harvard University commencement in June, 1947. Going beyond a speech Undersecretary Dean Acheson had given at Cleveland, Mississippi, the previous month, Marshall proposed that the nation undertake a vast reconstruction of the still weak European economies. Healthy economies would produce a more stable political and social order less vulnerable to Communism; the Marshall Plan was containment plus humanitarianism. Secretary Marshall made it clear that he did not exempt Communist East European governments or even Russia itself, although he must have been confident that the Russians would reject the idea and refuse to allow other Communist regimes to participate and thereby put the blame for exclusion upon themselves rather than upon the United States.

Before the end of June, European foreign ministers met at Paris to consider the proposal. Ernest Bevin, Labor foreign minister of Britain, and Georges Bidault of France were enthusiastic; Molotov not only disapproved but tried unsuccessfully to disrupt the conference. During the summer, representatives of Britain, France, Italy, Turkey, and other non-Communist European nations planned how aid best could be used and asked the United States for a total of $22.4 billion in aid. The political situation in France and Italy was tense; Communists, who were numerous in each nation, made an all-out effort both in parliament and in street riots to block the Marshall Plan.

Opposition to the Marshall Plan in the United States was remarkably small. The major pressure groups in labor, industry, and agriculture supported it. One reason for popular support, other than the humanitarian and anti-Communist aspects, was that Marshall Plan aid would have a beneficial effect upon the American economy as well as the European. The United States did not give the European nations dollars with which they could go elsewhere in the world to purchase machine tools, generators, and tractors; it granted the European nations credits to be spent primarily in the United States. Thus, Marshall Plan government spending stimulated the domestic economy in much the same way government spending had during the war. Furthermore, some special interest groups within the United States assured themselves of a share of the spending; shipping companies and the National Maritime Union, for example, got Congress to require that half of Marshall Plan equipment be shipped in American ships. The proposal went through Congress without major difficulty or serious amendment. Truman signed it on April 3, 1948.

Inevitably, a confusing set of initial agencies conducted the program, which became known as the European Recovery Program (ERP). The American agency, the Economic Cooperation Administration (ECA), worked with the Committee of European Economic Cooperation (CEEC). Over the next three years, ECA spent $12 billion, and the scheme accomplished what it had been planned to do. Industrial production in the Marshall Plan countries of Europe increased 64 per cent. Their gross national products increased by about one-fourth. In many respects, by 1951 the European economy was stronger

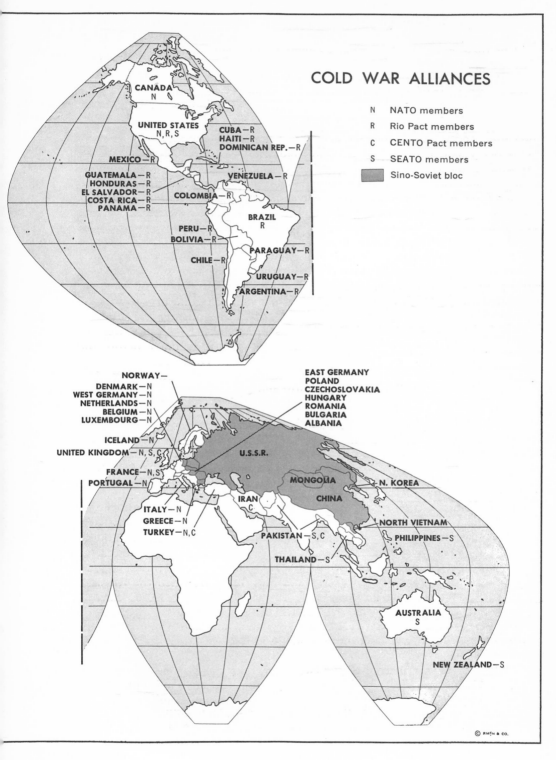

COLD WAR ALLIANCES

N   NATO members
R   Rio Pact members
C   CENTO Pact members
S   SEATO members
▓   Sino-Soviet bloc

CANADA
N

UNITED STATES
N, R, S

CUBA—R
HAITI—R
DOMINICAN REP.—R

MEXICO—R

GUATEMALA—R
HONDURAS—R
EL SALVADOR—R
COSTA RICA—R
PANAMA—R

VENEZUELA—R

COLOMBIA—R

BRAZIL
R

PERU—R
BOLIVIA—R
PARAGUAY—R

CHILE—R

URUGUAY—R

ARGENTINA—R

NORWAY—
DENMARK—N
WEST GERMANY—N
NETHERLANDS—N
BELGIUM—N
LUXEMBOURG—N

ICELAND—N
UNITED KINGDOM—N, S, C

FRANCE—N, S
PORTUGAL—N

ITALY—N
GREECE—N
TURKEY—N, C

EAST GERMANY
POLAND
CZECHOSLOVAKIA
HUNGARY
ROMANIA
BULGARIA
ALBANIA

U.S.S.R.

MONGOLIA

N. KOREA

IRAN
C

CHINA

NORTH VIETNAM

PAKISTAN—S, C

PHILIPPINES—S

THAILAND—S

AUSTRALIA
S

NEW ZEALAND—S

© RMN & CO.

than it had been in 1939. Furthermore, while the Communist parties of western Europe did not disappear, their strength declined significantly and the likelihood of these countries becoming Communist through internal pressures became small.

The German question, unsuccessfully solved since V-E Day, brought about a crisis in 1948. In early 1946, Russia declined to join the United States in an alliance to prevent resurgence of German military might. In September, 1946, Russia blocked an American proposal for the political and economic unification of the various military occupation zones in Germany. At that time, the Soviet Union was busy dismantling factories within its occupation zone and sending the equipment home and making its eastern zone a Communist satellite similar to the others. Through 1947, western policy continued to be neutralization and unification of Germany, but the Russian leaders demanded terms that would have given them influence in Germany's industrial western area. Although the western powers at no time explicitly embraced the idea of two Germanies, they began to move in that direction when in February, 1948, they consolidated the British, French, and American zones and created a German government with limited powers. In June, they adopted currency reforms in the consolidated zone and brought western Germany into the Marshall Plan. In October, the Germans in the western zone organized state governments, adopted a federal constitution the following spring, and formally launched the German Federal Republic in September, 1949. The western powers made West Germany a constitutional entity only slightly before the Russians transformed East Germany into the German Democratic Republic, another constitutional entity. The two Germanies had come into being. The sticky problem was Berlin, occupied jointly and deep within the Russian zone of East Germany.

On April 1, 1948, the Russians began to interrupt traffic from the western zone entering the Russian zone destined for West Berlin. On June 23, they stopped all traffic to West Berlin from the western zone. Their purpose was to get the West either to abandon its Berlin position or to back down on its program for western Germany. West Berlin, unable to feed itself, became an international pawn.

Rejecting the idea of sending armed convoys across the line of the Russian zone in an effort to shoot their way to West Berlin for fear of bringing on war, Truman decided to supply the city by a vast airlift and to impose a counterblockade. If the Russians began a war by shooting down the planes, the onus would be on them. The American and British air forces did an enormous job. Between late June, 1948, and May 12, 1949, when the Russians lifted the blockade, planes delivered to West Berlin almost 2,500,000 tons of supplies, largely food and coal. Within three months after starting the airlift, the RAF and the USAF were flying four thousand tons a day. The airlift, of course, could not have been a long-term solution, but it solved the immediate crisis.

Not only did Germany become two Germanies, but Europe became two Europes. The Soviets directed the essential political and economic integration of East Europe, and the West European nations increasingly cooperated with one another. In January, 1948, Bevin announced Britain's willingness to join some kind of West European organization. A year later, all the countries of

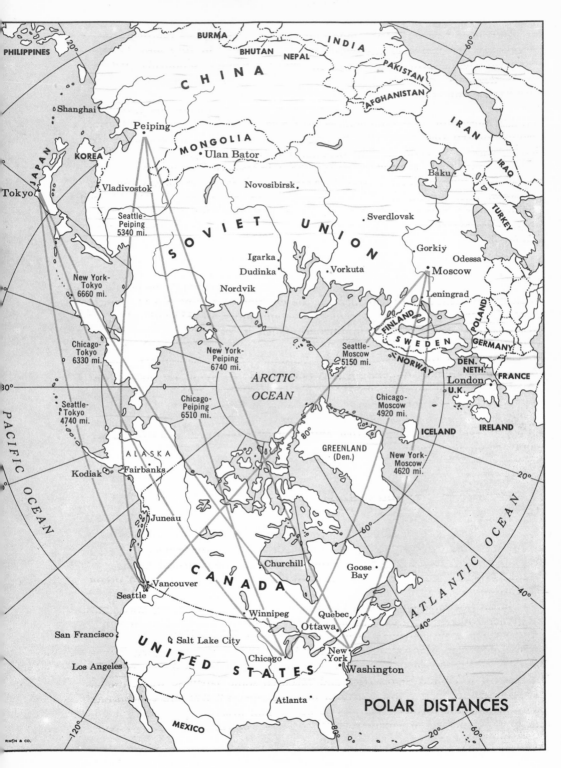

POLAR DISTANCES

West Europe, including West Germany but not Spain and Portugal, instituted the Council of Europe. More importantly, France and West Germany began negotiations for coal-steel integration which developed in 1951 into the Schuman Plan (named for French foreign minister Robert Schuman). Belgium, the Netherlands, and Luxembourg (the Benelux powers) and Italy joined with France and West Germany to erect an international authority, the European Coal and Steel Community, to govern and coordinate the production and distribution of those commodities. ECCS so interwove French and German heavy industry that these two historic enemies, within a decade after their biggest war, were economically dependent upon one another.

In June, 1948, the Senate passed the Vandenberg Resolution promising cooperation with a West European Alliance, and the next month the West European powers and the United States began discussions in Washington which resulted in the North Atlantic Treaty Alliance (NATO). On April 4, 1949, representatives of the United States, Canada, Iceland, France, Great Britain, Italy, Portugal, the Netherlands, Belgium, Luxembourg, Denmark, and Norway signed the treaty, which the Senate ratified by overwhelming vote in July. Greece and Turkey subsequently joined NATO. The treaty declared that an attack upon any of the signatory nations would be considered an attack on them all and provided for the creation of a joint NATO military force. General Eisenhower became the commander of SHAPE (Supreme Headquarters, Allied Powers in Europe) when it set itself up near Paris in early 1951. Much of its financial support came from the United States; Congress had passed the Mutual Defense Assistance Act in September, 1949, to appropriate a billion dollars for NATO armies. A West European–North American military alliance, inconceivable in 1939, was reality by 1949. Although NATO did not have as many divisions in Europe as the Russians had, it had enough to make a fight of it if it should come to that; more importantly, the Russians knew that any military adventures toward the west would result in a fight.

American Troubles in Asia

As America and Britain slowly proceeded toward alliance with their former common enemy, Germany, against their former ally, the Soviet Union, so did Japan and the United States slowly come together against China. The world's experience since 1940 should give pause to those who try to predict the future.

Japan's occupation, demilitarization, and eventual rebuilding was almost altogether America's project. Stalin demanded Russian occupation of half of the northern main Japanese island, but Truman rejected the idea firmly. General Douglas MacArthur, Supreme Commander of the Allied Powers (SCAP) in the Japanese occupation, encountered little resistance from the Japanese. The United States tried and executed some Japanese war criminals, but soon the occupation lost whatever punitive aspects it had and concentrated on reforming the former enemy. The occupation insisted upon and got considerable democracy in Japanese society, drastic reform of the land system, a

527

restriction on the power of the monopolistic industrial class, a great growth of labor unions, woman suffrage, and vast expansion and reform of the educational system. In 1947, the administration began economic policies designed to rebuild the Japanese economy. In 1950, Truman appointed John Foster Dulles, a Republican Wall Street lawyer, prominent Presbyterian layman, and student of foreign relations, to begin negotiations with Japan for a peace treaty and an alliance. The clear fact was that Japan was becoming America's friend as Chinese-American relationships changed from amity to hostility.

During the war, when the Russians said they would not aid the Chinese Communists, American policy was to urge the Chinese Nationalists, or Kuomintang, headed by Chiang Kai-shek, to form a coalition with the Chinese Communists. Chiang consistently refused. At the end of the war, the United States quickly transported Nationalist troops to formerly Japanese occupied areas so as to prevent their occupation by Chinese Communists or Russians, and the Kuomintang controlled the major ports and cities outside Manchuria. But the Communist armies, headed by Mao Tse-tung, controlled much of the countryside. Full-scale civil war seemed imminent when Truman dispatched General Marshall to China in December, 1945. The United States did not want a Communist China—later charges that important people in the administration regarded the Communists only as agrarian reformers were gross exaggerations —and quite correctly perceived that the Kuomintang government was inept, corrupt, and somewhat unpopular. But it quite strongly wanted to avoid becoming involved in a civil war on the other side of the earth. Marshall, therefore, tried to prevent the outbreak of such a conflict. He succeeded in bringing about a cease-fire, but months of work at finding some basis for agreement between the Communists and the Kuomintang came to nothing. Their differences were irreconcilable. In early 1947, Marshall abandoned the effort with a parting shot that damned both sides.

The civil war resumed. Chiang's troops were more numerous and had good equipment, both captured Japanese and American arms. But Mao's troops won most of the battles. Truman sent General Albert C. Wedemeyer, who had served with Chiang during the war, to investigate and suggest policy. Wedemeyer reported that indeed the Kuomintang was all its critics said it was but that the Communist alternative was worse. Further, if the United States intervened in a major way in behalf of the Nationalists, it might be able to bring about necessary reform. The general urged Truman to seek United Nations support for a five-nation UN trusteeship of Manchuria to prevent that province from becoming a Soviet-Communist Chinese satellite and to send ten thousand American military officers and other advisers to bring about reform and efficiency. Massive material assistance would be necessary, Wedemeyer added.

Truman neither accepted nor made the Wedemeyer recommendations public, for which he later suffered severe castigation including charges of disloyalty. Chiang's cause was not popular with the American people if it involved American intervention, and Truman held that the defense of western Europe was more important. In addition it was by no means guaranteed that the adoption of Wedemeyer's report would save the Nationalists from Communist defeat. Truman did request Congress to appropriate $570 million for aid to China; Congress cut the appropriation to $400 million, the same amount as the original Greek-Turkish grant of which just $125 million was for military supplies.

In October, 1948, Chinese Communist troops took Mukden, Manchuria. Thereafter, the Nationalists faded fast, more from poor morale and continued inefficiency than from lack of arms. Some Kuomintang units defected to the Communists en masse. The Communists took the important cities and ports of central and south China during 1949. In October, Chiang retreated to Chungking, his capital during the war with Japan, roughly a thousand miles into the interior. In December, he moved what was left of his government and army by air to Formosa, called Taiwan by the Chinese. Nationalists continued to hold, besides Formosa, some tiny offshore islands in the Formosa Strait.

The United States refused to recognize the new Communist regime in China, officially the People's Republic of China, although some of its European allies did. Nor would America countenance Red China's admission into the United Nations. To the United States government, the country of China was officially the Chiang government on Formosa and the offshore islands. On the mainland, the Communists quickly stamped out American influence. American citizens of all kinds (missionaries, government officials, businessmen) fled. Far harder, more anti-American, and less flexible than their Russian comrades, the Chinese Communists made their territory the headquarters for a campaign to eliminate American influence in Asia. On the whole, the Chinese Communist anti-American efforts failed. Japan moved ever closer to the United States. The two other major powers of Asia, India, which became independent from Great Britain in 1947, and Pakistan, which divided from India at the time of independence, likewise moved closer to the United States, in no small part because of their giant and aggressive Communist neighbor to the north. South Korea, too, remained in the American camp, but thereby hangs a tragic and painful tale.

The Korean War

Russian forces invaded Korea from the north on August 10, 1945. Nearly a month later and after V-J Day, American troops occupied the southern part of the peninsula. Russia and the United States agreed to divide their zones at the thirty-eighth parallel. Korea, which Japan had occupied for a generation, soon became two Koreas. The Russians introduced their system of government and economy in North Korea and raised and equipped an army. The United Nations Temporary Commission on Korea, created by the General Assembly upon American instigation, in early 1948 visited Seoul, the old capital, was denied permission to go north of the dividing line, and conducted elections for a national assembly in southern Korea. In July, 1948, the assembly adopted a constitution, calling the country the Republic of Korea (ROK), and elected Syngman Rhee, who had spent much of his life as an exile in the United States, as president. Rhee would have been pleased to have the whole peninsula under his government's jurisdiction, and the North Koreans were just as eager to have the South in their realm. Fearful of what Rhee might do and not wanting to get involved in a conflict over territory it did not deem militarily significant, the United States did not provide the South Korean government sufficient arms to engage in northern adventures. It did, however, furnish it considerable economic assistance, a factor of importance since the thirty-eighth parallel dividing line badly disrupted the Korean economy. By mid-1949, both Russian and American occupation troops had left. The United States maintained a five-hundred-man military advisory group to train the ROK army; the Russians furnished military advisers to the North Korean government. Few people in the United States, in fact few people in the western world, were more than dimly aware that Korea existed. Remote, economically unimportant, far from the main focus of existing international tensions, Korea seemed the last place in the world that anyone would fight over.

With the Chinese mainland under the Communists, the administration re-examined its policy for that part of the world in the winter of 1949–1950. Hoping that eventually Russia and China would become engaged in conflict as Russia and Jugoslavia had—"Mao Tse-tito" was the wisecrack—and thinking only in terms of total war rather than a limited war, the State Department, headed since January, 1949, by Dean Acheson, for all practical purposes wrote off the Chinese Nationalists on Formosa as an instrument of containment because they had been ineffective. In January, 1950, Acheson made public what the United States regarded as its "defense perimeter," a line that ran through the Aleutians, Japan, the Ryukyus (Okinawa the main island), and the Philippines. Formosa and Korea were not within the perimeter. When the implication became clear that the administration did not plan to defend Formosa if the Chinese Communists attacked, a group of Republican Senators, notably Taft, Wherry, and William Knowland of California, attacked Truman and Acheson mercilessly. Actually, a more propitious time for great pressure on the administration would have been before Chiang was run off the mainland. By early 1950, only massive American participation could have re-established the Nationalists, and that probably would have meant full-scale war.

After months of small skirmishes between the North and South Koreans, the North Koreans launched an all-out invasion across the thirty-eighth parallel at 4:00 A.M., Sunday, June 25, 1950, Korean time. Who made the decision for invasion (North Koreans, Chinese, or Russians) and why has never become known in the West. Neither is it known whether or not the invaders expected resistance from any country except the Republic of Korea, although they may well have interpreted Acheson's "defense perimeter" statement to mean the United States would not defend South Korea. Acheson's statement had hedged; if areas outside the perimeter were attacked, he had said, the invaded people would have to count upon their own power to resist "and then upon the commitments of the entire civilized world." One thing only is certain: North Korean troops invaded South Korea. Communists the world over asserted that the South Koreans had attacked first and that the North Koreans had only counterattacked, but no military operation of the magnitude of the invasion could have been begun without long and extensive preparation. The decision to invade had obviously been made long before the invasion.

News of the invasion reached Washington when it was still Saturday night there. Truman was visiting his home in Missouri. Acheson summoned his aides in the State Department. At about midnight Acheson telephoned Truman who agreed that the invasion should come before the Security Council of the United Nations immediately. For several months the Russians had been boycotting Security Council meetings because the other council members had refused a seat to the Communist Chinese. At a Sunday afternoon emergency session, the Security Council voted nine to zero to accept a resolution calling upon North Korea to withdraw north of the thirty-eighth parallel. The absent Russian delegate missed his opportunity to veto. Two days later, the Council by a vote of seven to one (Jugoslavia opposing, India and Egypt abstaining) called upon UN member nations to send a UN force to repel the attack. On June 29 and 30, after having returned to Washington and conferred with the Joint Chiefs of staff and congressional leaders of both parties, Truman ordered two divisions of MacArthur's ground troops in Japan to Korea and ordered the air force to bomb North Korean targets. At the time all concerned assumed that this American force would be sufficient to drive the North Koreans back. Simultaneously, Truman ordered the United States Seventh Fleet to neutralize Formosa. Fearing the conflict might spread to full-scale war, Truman wanted neither the Red Chinese to invade Formosa nor the Nationalists to try a mainland invasion. His Formosan order received more Republican criticism than the decisions on Korea.

At first the war went very badly for the UN forces. In the whole war, never more technically than "a police action by the United Nations," American troops fought under UN auspices; when UN forces were at their greatest strength, 48 per cent of them were from America, 43 per cent from South Korea, and the remaining 9 per cent from seventeen other nations, mainly Britain, the Philippines, Australia, and Turkey. By early September, 1950, the North Koreans had pushed UN forces south until they held only the port of Pusan in extreme southeastern Korea and a little area around it. Upon receiving reinforcements, MacArthur, the chief UN commander, first pushed back from Pusan and then executed a daring and brilliant end run with a landing at Inchon on the west coast not far from Seoul and the thirty-eighth parallel. His troops took Seoul on September 27. The North Korean units fled north of the border.

Now the war entered a new political phase: whether or not UN troops should cross the thirty-eighth parallel. As early as October 1, some ROK units crossed the border, but MacArthur held back to await a clear mandate. On October 1, Communist China announced that she would be displeased if the war crossed the border; soon thereafter she informed India, which relayed the message to the UN, that she would send troops to North Korea if UN troops crossed the boundary. But on October 7 the UN Assembly approved forty-seven to five, with eight nations abstaining, a resolution recommending that "all appropriate steps be taken to ensure conditions of stability throughout Korea." On October 23, MacArthur's troops moved across the border in force. In a special conference at Wake Island on October 14, Truman had questioned MacArthur about the possibility of Russian or Chinese intervention and MacArthur had replied that the chance was, "Very little." MacArthur estimated that the Chinese would not be able to get more than fifty or sixty thousand men across the Yalu River, the northern boundary between Manchuria and North Korea, and that these men would be slaughtered.

These Korean events shared the front pages with news of the congressional election campaigns. On November 7, the voters handed the Democrats a defeat. Each house of Congress remained in Democratic hands but by such a narrow margin as to strengthen the bipartisan conservative coalition. The most significant aspect of the campaign was the extent that accusations of Communism and of being "soft on Communism" were part of Republican activity. Senator Joseph R. McCarthy, Republican of Wisconsin, was out to get rid of Senator Millard Tydings of Maryland whom he called an "appeaser" and smeared with a fake photograph that purported to show the Maryland Senator in a friendly pose with a Communist official. Representative Richard Nixon made Communism the main issue in his defeat of Helen Gahagan Douglas for a California Senate seat.

Back in Korea, the Chinese Communists were playing havoc with MacArthur's predictions. Late in October, UN troops captured a few Chinese "volunteers"; soon thereafter the air force reported encountering Russian-made MIG fighter planes. The UN invited China to explain its actions, which the Chinese Communists declined to do; but they did send a delegation to UN headquarters where they charged that the United States had been guilty of aggression against Formosa. On November 24, 1950, the day the Red Chinese delegation arrived at the UN, MacArthur launched a full-scale offensive, announcing that the drive would go to the Yalu. He intimated American troops might be home by Christmas.

Perhaps military intelligence was never faultier. MacArthur marched his men into an enormous trap. Red Chinese units counterattacked on November 26 and split the center of the UN line. The United States Eighth Army under General Matthew B. Ridgway retreated on the eastern part of the line back toward and then beyond the thirty-eighth parallel. The First Marine Division, two army infantry divisions, and ROK units fought desperately in bitter cold to get to the port of Hungnam, far north on the east coast, where the navy evacuated them and returned them to the main UN force in South Korea. Chinese troops crossed south to the thirty-eighth parallel, and now India cautioned the Chinese to stop. In January, 1951, the UN forces began to hold; in March they counterattacked and took Seoul for the second time. Soon thereafter they moved across the thirty-eighth parallel for the second and last time. The conflict stabilized along a line slightly north of that famous mark on the globe.

Partisan politics over military policy came to a head when, on April 11, 1951, President Truman relieved General MacArthur of his command. The news stunned the nation. The General, who had not come home after World War II, returned to an enthusiastic reception. Congress invited him to address a joint session on April 19, and millions watched the scene on their television sets. It was a dramatic speech whether one supported Truman or MacArthur. The General defended his position and ended by quoting from an old barracks song: "Old soldiers never die; they just fade away."

The Truman-MacArthur controversy involved more than a personal conflict. Throughout the Korean War, MacArthur had, upon several occasions, gone beyond his stated orders from Washington and had publicly disagreed

532

with civilian superior officers. In July, 1950, without authority from Washington, he had gone to Formosa to confer with Chiang Kai-shek. The next month he had sent a message to the national convention of the Veterans of Foreign Wars that was extremely critical of the administration's Formosa policy. Truman heard of the message before the convention and ordered MacArthur to withdraw it. MacArthur did so, but the message became public knowledge. In it MacArthur described Truman's position as "the threadbare argument by those who advocate appeasement and defeatism in the Pacific." At the Wake Island conference in October, the President informed his general that he must make no further provocative public statements. After the Red Chinese intervention in November, MacArthur publicly and frequently criticized Washington for refusing him authority to bomb supply bases in Chinese territory north of the Yalu. Wanting the war to remain limited, fearing that a full-scale war in Asia would make western Europe vulnerable to Soviet attack, Truman refused to allow action north of the Yalu other than that of fighter planes in "hot pursuit" of the enemy. On December 6, Truman forbade all civil and military officers to make public statements on foreign policy without prior clearance with the State Department. MacArthur continued to recommend to the Joint Chiefs of Staff that the United States blockade China, use the navy and air force to bombard China, and support a Kuomintang invasion of the mainland. The Joint Chiefs of Staff rejected the suggestions. On March 20, 1951, the Joint Chiefs of Staff informed MacArthur that a new statement on Korean policy would soon be forthcoming. Instead of waiting for it, MacArthur issued one of his own in which he said he was willing to meet with the Chinese commander and try to arrange a truce, but that if proper terms could not be arranged there should be raids on the Chinese coast and bombings of interior Chinese bases. Truman at that point was looking for a way to bring about a truce and negotiate a Korean settlement, the front having by then been stabilized. Truman also again warned MacArthur about making public policy statements without clearing them with Washington.

MacArthur's reply to this warning was to send a letter to Joseph W. Martin, Jr., of Massachusetts, Republican minority leader in the House of Representatives, in which he strongly disagreed with the administration's limited war policy: ". . . we must win. There is no substitute for victory." It was this point precisely that caused so much of the frustration of the Korean War. The American people were not accustomed to fighting for less than total victory, but total victory against North Korea and China was likely to erupt in World War III, and hardly anyone wanted that. After Representative Martin read MacArthur's letter in the House on April 5, Truman went to the Joint Chiefs of Staff and received their endorsement of his proposal to dismiss MacArthur. The die was cast.

Perhaps Truman wished at first that he had not started such action against MacArthur for Americans were initially strongly for MacArthur. Public opinion polls showed it; the General's reception showed it. Senator McCarthy's hammering at the Truman administration had helped to build support for MacArthur's point of view. But during the congressional hearings from May 3 to June 25, public opinion began to shift. More and more people came to agree with the statement of General Omar Bradley, chairman of the Joint

Chiefs of Staff, that the kinds of policies MacArthur recommended would lead to a war which would be "the wrong war at the wrong place, at the wrong time and with the wrong enemy." Many did not accept the implication that war with Russia in Europe was right, but they agreed that a war with China in Asia was undesirable. More and more people, too, saw that the Truman-MacArthur controversy involved the traditional authority of the civil government over the military establishment. The crowds at "total victory" rallies began to dwindle. The old soldier, probably to his distress, did fade away. When he gave the keynote address at the 1952 Republican convention he seemed a figure from the remote past.

On June 22, 1951, the Russians suggested an armistice. On July 10, General Ridgway, who had replaced MacArthur, began armistice negotiations with Chinese and North Korean officers at Kaesong. The negotiations later moved to Panmunjom, an unlikely name that was in the news for two years while the negotiations went on fruitlessly. Thereafter, the fighting in Korea was only sporadic, and the battle line remained relatively stationary slightly north of the thirty-eighth parallel.

During the Panmunjom armistice negotiations, the Truman administration concluded treaties with European powers to strengthen the United States position in Asia. On September 8, 1951, the United States and Japan signed the peace treaty that Dulles had negotiated. The treaty took Okinawa away from Japan, but otherwise it was generous; no reparations plus recognition of Japan's right to rearm. Since then Japan has shown no enthusiasm for rearmament. At the same time, the United States and Japan signed a Security Treaty that gave the United States the right to maintain bases in Japan. On August 30, 1951, the United States and the Republic of the Philippines signed a mutual defense treaty. On September 1, New Zealand, Australia, and the United States formed the "Anzus" mutual defense pact.

Disloyalty and Politics

American society has periodically indulged itself in waves of intolerance. In the 1840's and 1850's and again in the 1880's, large numbers of people were irrationally anti-Catholic. Alarm about anarchists became hysterical after McKinley's assassination in 1901. During World War I, anxiety about pro-Germans led many to attitudes and actions that went beyond ordinary reason, as did fear of Bolshevism in the years immediately after the war. From the late 1940's to the mid-1950's, the United States went on another such binge, this time over the question of national loyalty. Irrational intolerance has never completely disappeared; but it has risen to periodic high tides. The post-World War II Red scare was one of the highest tides.

Anti-Communism was by no means altogether irrational. Many anti-Communists maintained their sense of perspective and balance. Although by far the greatest danger to the United States from Communism came from outside the country, there was a basis for concern about it internally. Early in the postwar period some "liberals" were inclined to be sympathetic to the Soviet Union, to regard the Soviet Union as a great and noble experiment, a fulfillment of workers' aspirations the world over, perhaps not be copied in the United States because America had special advantages for the common man but not to be the object of hostility. This attitude waned to insignificance. As early as 1947, when the anti-Communist ADA came into existence, the Soviets were quickly losing American sympathizers by their foreign policy. Just after the war, almost one-third of the votes on the executive board of the CIO could be counted upon to support the position of the Communist party. Revolts by the membership against Communist leadership and a housecleaning by the CIO itself in 1949 and 1950 ended that situation. The Communist party had roughly eighty thousand dues-paying members in 1946. It shrank steadily; by 1953, according to FBI Director J. Edgar Hoover, its membership was a little under twenty-five thousand. It continued to shrink thereafter. But espionage cases probably did more than anything else to arouse public opinion.

Early in 1945, the FBI apprehended two of the editors of *Amerasia*, a Communist-connected magazine, collecting classified documents from government offices. In 1946, a Canadian royal commission revealed that at least twenty-three Canadians in "positions of trust" were involved in espionage for the Soviets and had sent classified information, some of it about atomic fission, to Russia. In early 1950, Klaus Fuchs, a British scientist of German origin who had worked on the atomic bomb project, confessed in London that he had been part of an espionage ring. His confession implicated four American citizens, Julius Rosenberg and his wife Ethel, David Greenglass, and Morton Sobell. A jury convicted them, and after several appeals, which went as high as the Supreme Court, the Rosenbergs died in the electric chair in mid-1953. Greenglass and Sobell went to prison.

But by far the most celebrated case was that of Alger Hiss. In 1948, a former Communist named Whittaker Chambers testified before the House Committee on Un-American Activities that Hiss, head of the Carnegie Endowment for International Peace and a former official in the State Department, had passed him classified documents in 1937 and 1938. Hiss denied the charge before the Committee. When Hiss sued Chambers for slander, Chambers produced microfilm from a pumpkin on his Maryland farm that he said proved his charge. The statute of limitations prevented an indictment for espionage, but Hiss stood trial for perjury. He asked some prominent people to serve as character witnesses, among them Justice Felix Frankfurter and Illinois Governor Adlai E. Stevenson, who said that to the best of their knowledge Hiss was a man of good character. The trial ended with a hung jury. A second trial ended in January, 1950, with Hiss's conviction. Hiss continued to profess innocence, served his prison sentence, and emerged to go into obscurity. But the superficial facts of the case reveal little of its political implications. In the popular mind, Hiss was the personification of the bright, young New Deal administrator. If Hiss was guilty, who else might be a disguised Communist? Were Roosevelt's braintrusters a pack of disloyal spies, as some of FDR's more violent critics had charged?

It was fears such as these that Senator Joseph R. McCarthy, Republican from Wisconsin, exploited for his and his party's—or a wing of his party's— political advantage. In a speech at Wheeling, West Virginia, on February 9, 1950, McCarthy charged that he had "here in my hand" a list of 205 (some said McCarthy claimed only 57) names of Communists and fellow-travelers then employed by the State Department. A Senate Foreign Relations Committee unit investigated the charge and found not one, but McCarthy's allegation had created the kind of sensation the freshman Senator wanted and needed. Although McCarthy never turned up a single proved Communist in government employ, he went on with sensational charge after sensational charge so quickly that, by the time the accused could deny, the front pages were already spread with a new accusation.

McCarthy was neither the first political figure to be concerned with Communism within the United States nor the first to use the issue for political advantage. President Truman had shown his concern when, in 1947, he instituted a "loyalty check" on government employees. In 1950, he authorized the firing of those whose present loyalty was not at issue but who were found to be "bad security risks." The investigation was remarkably thorough. It found and fired some who were suspicious indeed, but as Truman later admitted, it fired some people on flimsy evidence. Truman's Republican successors were unsuccessful in their attempts to find disloyal government employees who had slipped through the Truman administration comb. The Truman administration brought indictment after indictment of Communist party leaders under the Smith Act, and nearly all indicted were convicted and imprisoned. In the Republican party, the respected Senator Taft as early as January, 1946, had found it difficult to avoid the temptation to use the Red issue against a political opponent; he called Truman's legislative program in part "communist" and "left-wing." But no political leader developed anti-Communism as an instrument for political advantage to the degree that Senator McCarthy did. The fact that "McCarthyism" became the accepted term for politically motivated exploitation of fear about domestic Communism was recognition of his mastery of the technique.

With the outbreak of the Korean War, McCarthyism became so powerful that even many politicians who deplored what they considered its un-American means to protect America knuckled under its pressure. Various anti-Communist bills had been introduced in Congress since the war, and in 1950 Congress lumped many of these proposals together into the McCarran Internal Security bill, named for Democratic Senator Pat McCarran of Nevada. The bill provided for the establishment of a bipartisan Subversive Activities Control Board which, after hearing evidence, could declare an organization subversive and require it to register and submit membership lists and financial reports. The bill expressly stated that to be a member or even an officer of a Communist organization did not of itself constitute a criminal act, but made it illegal to perform "any act" that would "substantially" contribute to totalitarian overthrow of the government. It also banned Communists from defense industries, provided for the arrest of Communists in the event of war, required that printed matter distributed by organizations found by the SACB to be Communist must be labelled Communist propaganda, made Communists ineligible to receive passports, and forbade the entry into the country of any person who had ever been a member of a totalitarian organization. Truman, upon the advice of the Department of Defense and the Central Intelligence Agency, vetoed the bill. Among other things, Truman said that its registration feature was "about as practical as requiring thieves to register with the sheriff." Con-

536

gress passed it over his veto. In 1952, Congress passed, again over Truman's veto, the McCarran-Walter Immigration and Nationality Bill which eased the deportation of aliens found to be subversive and provided for denaturalization in some cases. The measure did broaden immigration and naturalization in one respect: Asians went under the quota system for the first time (two thousand a year), and they became eligible for citizenship.

McCarthyism certainly was not restricted to either party, but it reacted far more to the Republicans' electoral advantage than to the Democrats'. How many voters who otherwise would have voted Democratic decided to vote Republican in 1950 and 1952 because of the fog of distrust of New Deal Democrats created by McCarthy and the McCarthyites can never be known—there were other issues, of course—but undoubtedly McCarthy substantially aided the Republican cause. However, Republicans were soon to learn that McCarthyism could divide and disrupt their own party as well as their opponents'.

CHAPTER TWENTY-SIX

The Eisenhower Era: Moderation and Brinkmanship

EVEN WITH ONLY THE LITTLE TIME PERSPECTIVE AVAILABLE TO US, we can see that fundamentally there were no important or basic differences between the policies of the Truman and Eisenhower administrations. Political partisanship on both sides tended to magnify actual differences. Truman's administrations were more different from Roosevelt's, and Eisenhower's were more different from Harding's, Coolidge's, and Hoover's than they were different from one another. Their greatest difference was in their political rhetoric. Truman's style was that of an orator at a labor convention, and he endeavored mightily to appear to wear Roosevelt's cloak. Eisenhower strived above all to give the impression of moderation—"the middle of the road." He once even described his policies as "liberal conservatism." Although a strong wing of Truman's party wanted to extend the New Deal, his administration and Congress extended it only slightly; although a strong wing of Eisenhower's party wanted to repeal the New Deal, his administration and Congress not only did not rescind it but even extended it slightly. Truman and Eisenhower certainly were no Tweedledee and Tweedledum, but in actual results—new laws and new policies—there was little to distinguish them on domestic affairs.

There were other similarities. Both used the power of the federal government to even out fluctuations in the business cycle. Both were anti-Communist and both were plagued by "radical right" anti-Communists. Both resisted Communism abroad and both avoided World War III. In the fifteen years after World War II, both major parties controlled the White House, but the era had no real political watersheds. Under both parties the domestic political mood was one of moderation, prosperous complacency, and notable lack of enthusiasm for new departures.

The Election of 1952

Confident that it would defeat the Democratic ticket in 1952, the Republican party indulged itself in one of its sharpest internal battles for the nomination. The early front runner was Senator Robert A. Taft of Ohio, who had three times been passed over for a nominee that large parts of the GOP considered not quite such a "true blue." Announcing his candidacy in October, 1951, Taft had the support of a majority on the party's national committee.

GOP leaders in the East, notably Governor Dewey, Senator Henry Cabot Lodge, Jr., of Massachusetts, and Senator James H. Duff of Pennsylvania, vigorously opposed Taft's nomination. They thought he would be unable to attract independent voters and distrusted his tendency to put American interests in Asia ahead of concern for Europe. Their problem was to find a candidate. Dewey, as a two-time loser, was unacceptable. They wanted General Dwight David Eisenhower, then on leave as president of Columbia University while serving as the head of NATO. Well known because of his military leadership, Eisenhower seemed to millions of Americans the kind of man they conceived of as typical of their nationality: guileless, frank, friendly, quick to smile, able to get discordant subordinates to work together harmoniously. The trouble was that in 1951 no one knew for sure whether Eisenhower was a Republican. It was an open secret that Truman wanted him to be his party's champion in 1952. In January, 1952, Eisenhower, upon the urging of Senator Lodge, announced he would accept the Republican nomination, but that he would not battle for it. He won the Republican presidential primary in New Hampshire, and Minnesota Republicans advanced his nomination by a huge write-in vote in their primary. But the Taft forces, controlling most of the party machinery, continued to get convention delegates into their camp. Eisenhower could not win the nomination without working for it. Rallies that chanted "I like Ike" could not go on forever unless their hero seemed determined to win. Eisenhower resigned his command and returned from France on June 1. His first halting, undistinguished speeches did little to attract delegates, but the fact that he had decided actively to seek the nomination was enough to stimulate his wing of the party.

Many political commentators noted the similarity between the 1952 Republican convention at Chicago in early July and the 1912 convention which had nominated Taft's father and passed over Theodore Roosevelt. Both Tafts had the more numerous delegates and control of the national committee but both Roosevelt and Eisenhower had broad popular support and rank-and-file following. Senator Taft went to Chicago with 469 pledged delegates; only 392 had pledged themselves firmly to Eisenhower. The 1912 and 1952 similarity continued when the national committee granted seats temporarily to the Taft-pledged delegations from Georgia, Louisiana, and Texas, each of which faced opposition from an Eisenhower delegation claiming that it was the duly elected representative. But the similarity ended when the convention, by a narrow vote, changed its rules. Under the new rule, temporarily seated delegations could not vote on the seating of other contested delegations if the contestants had the support of one-sixth or more of the national committee. Seating the Georgia delegation provided the test. With the Taft-pledged delegates from Texas and Louisiana unable to vote under the new rule, the convention voted by another narrow margin to seat the Eisenhower-pledged delegation from Georgia. Seating of the other contested Eisenhower delegations followed.

On the first ballot the General received 595 votes to Taft's 500. Enough delegations switched their votes to Eisenhower after the roll call of the states to make a second ballot unnecessary. The nominee selected Senator Richard M. Nixon as his running mate, a move calculated to allay the bitterness of Taft supporters. The Republican platform was vague enough to prevent any wing of the party from rebelling. In a bid for southern votes, the GOP diluted its 1948 civil rights demands and promised to transfer control of tidelands oil from the federal government to the states.

The Democratic nomination was nearly as confusing. Although the Twenty-second Amendment to the Constitution (submitted to the states in March, 1947, and ratified February, 1951, forbidding a president more than two terms or, in the case of a president's coming to the office by his predecessor's death, more than ten years' tenure) specifically exempted Truman, he announced late in March, 1952, that he would not be a candidate. Governor Adlai E. Stevenson of Illinois, who had run well ahead of his ticket in 1948, declined to seek delegates but left the impression he would consent to a party draft. The hardest running contender was Senator Estes Kefauver of Tennessee, who had achieved a national reputation as chairman of a televised Senate investigation of organized crime. Vice-President Barkley's hat was in the ring, but his chances disappeared when the CIO announced that the popular "Veep," as he liked to be called, was too old—they meant too conservative—for their approval. Senator Richard B. Russell of Georgia was the favorite of the South, and Averell Harriman of New York and Senator Robert Kerr of Oklahoma had some support.

Kefauver, never popular with his party's leaders, led on the first ballot, but on the third the Stevenson draft blew hard. Stevenson came within two and one-half votes of a majority. Then Senator Kefauver moved that Stevenson be nominated unanimously, and the contest ended. In an effort—unsuccessful as it turned out—to keep southern Democrats happy, the party nominated one of the more liberal southern Senators, John Sparkman of Alabama, for the vice-presidency. The civil rights plank was not as strong as it had been in 1948, and northern and western Democrats were unsuccessful in their attempt to extract a "loyalty pledge" from the southern delegates and thereby head off another Dixiecrat revolt. There was no independent Dixiecrat ticket in 1952, but James F. Byrnes, then governor of South Carolina, came out for Eisenhower, as did Democratic Governor Allan F. Shivers of Texas when Stevenson refused to support state control of tidelands oil and Eisenhower consented to. In other southern states there were "Eisenhower Democrat" slates.

The urban and highly literate Stevenson aroused great enthusiasm among those who thought of themselves as liberal intellectuals, but his campaign to "talk sense to the American people," as he put it, fell far short in popular appeal of the more platitudinous Eisenhower speeches. (The New York *Times*

540

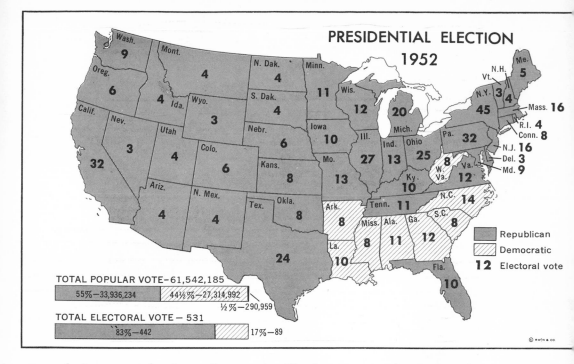

PRESIDENTIAL ELECTION
1952

Wash. 9
Oreg. 6
Calif. 32
Nev. 3
Ida. 4
Mont. 4
Wyo. 3
Utah 4
Ariz. 4
Colo. 6
N. Mex. 4
N. Dak. 4
S. Dak. 4
Nebr. 6
Kans. 8
Okla. 8
Tex. 24
Minn. 11
Iowa 10
Mo. 13
Ark. 8
La. 10
Wis. 12
Ill. 27
Ind. 13
Ky. 10
Tenn. 11
Miss. 8
Ala. 11
Ga. 12
Mich. 20
Ohio 25
W. Va. 8
Va. 12
N.C. 14
S.C. 8
Fla. 10
Pa. 32
N.Y. 45
Vt. 3
N.H. 4
Me. 5
Mass. 16
R.I. 4
Conn. 8
N.J. 16
Del. 3
Md. 9

■ Republican
▨ Democratic
12 Electoral vote

TOTAL POPULAR VOTE–61,542,185
| 55%–33,936,234 | 44½%–27,314,992 |
½%–290,959

TOTAL ELECTORAL VOTE – 531
| 83%–442 | 17%–89 |

© rand & co

reported the story of a journalist on the Eisenhower campaign train who awakened from a nap while Eisenhower was giving a speech from the rear of the train. He asked, "Where are we?" "Crossing the 38th platitude," another reporter told him.) First, Eisenhower healed the wounds his nomination had caused by effecting a compromise with Senator Taft. In a well-publicized conference, the General promised the Senator to make "creeping socialism" the main issue of his campaign and to grant some patronage to the Taft camp. Actually, the Republican battle cry was "Korea, Communism, and Corruption," a slogan that requires further explanation.

At the time of the political coventions the truce talks in Korea had been dragging on for a year, the main dividing issue being whether or not North Korean and Chinese prisoners who did not want to be repatriated should be forced to return. When Communist prisoners of war rioted, American leaders became convinced the enemy was using the truce talks only for propaganda purposes. In October, 1952, the armistice talks ended temporarily, and the UN forces started a limited offensive. Later in the month, Eisenhower promised to bring the war to an end, and his promise struck a responsive chord with the frustrated American people. Just before election day, Eisenhower's further promise to go to Korea—for precisely what purpose he did not make clear—undoubtedly attracted more votes for him.

The "Communism" part of the slogan was a sop to the McCarthyite wing of the Republican party. Highly effective as an anti-Democratic device in 1950, labeling the Democrats "soft on Communism" did not become part of Eisenhower's personal campaign but he did not disavow Republicans, including Senator McCarthy himself, who used the red brush. Indeed, by eliminating a favorable comment about General Marshall, a long-time friend of Eisenhower's but an object of one of McCarthy's attacks, from a speech in Milwaukee, Eisenhower seemed to accede to the McCarthyites.

The "corruption" part of the slogan hit the Democrats where they were vulnerable. Republicans had uncovered clear cases of corruption in the administration, and Truman's reactions had been inept. It was clear that Bureau of Internal Revenue officials had been bribed to sidetrack investigations of tax evaders, as it was that Reconstruction Finance Corporation officials had yielded to the blandishments of "five percenters," who arranged RFC loans for clients for a 5 per cent commission. Republicans tried to make it appear that honest Democrats were as scarce as Venezuelan snowballs, and mink coats and deep freeze units, used in two highly publicized bribes, became symbols of corruption. Truman reorganized the Internal Revenue Service by putting district collectorships under civil service, and he appointed Newbold Morris, an independent Republican from New York, to investigate the whole tax collection administration. But Attorney General J. Howard McGrath obstructed Morris. In the end, Truman fired both McGrath and Morris. Republican talk of "the mess in Washington" had such strong voter response that Stevenson quite obviously tried to disassociate himself from the Truman administration.

The most dramatic moment in the campaign, however, came with the disclosure that Nixon had received $18,000 while in the Senate from southern California businessmen to help him cover his Washington expenses. Eisenhower, who had announced that his administration would be "clean as a hound's tooth," was on a spot. Many powerful Republicans urged him to dump Nixon, and he briefly considered doing so. But the vice-presidential nominee staged a sentimental defense of his actions on a national television program, and Eisenhower accepted him once again. Republican efforts to pin a similar scandal on Stevenson by pointing out that the Illinois governor had used surplus Democratic campaign funds to supplement the salaries of some of his appointees who suffered income loses when they went into state service did not create the furors of the Nixon disclosure.

Two aspects of the campaign that aroused comment and concern were the tremendous costs to the parties that television entailed and the increased role of professional advertisers and public relations counselors in shaping the candidates' appeals. Candidates could be sold like detergents, according to Madison Avenue opinion-molders who specialized in creating an "image" of their political clients. Just before election day the Republicans' advertising agency ran dozens of television spot commercials in which professional actors, taking the roles of taxi drivers, nurses, and other ordinary people, delivered Eisenhower testimonials. These spot commercials were thought to be effective. Whether a Lincoln could ever have been elected in an era of calculated and synthetic "image" manipulation was a question that troubled serious citizens.

Eisenhower won by an overwhelming victory on election day. He received 33,824,351 popular votes and 442 electoral votes; Stevenson finished with 27,314,987 popular and 89 electoral votes. Stevenson carried only West Virginia, Kentucky, and seven former Confederate states even though he polled more popular votes than had any previous Democratic presidential candidate with the exception of Roosevelt in 1936. Eisenhower made inroads into the South, carrying Texas, Oklahoma, Virginia, Tennessee, and Florida. Yet the Republicans had only an eight-seat majority in the House of Representatives and a tie in the Senate. (Vice-President Nixon's vote enabled the GOP to organize the new Senate.) Quite obviously, despite "Korea, Communism, and Corruption," Eisenhower was far more popular than his party.

"Modern Republicanism"

The new President's background and experience determined the nature of his administration. Born in Denison, Texas, in 1890, "Ike" Eisenhower, as he was called all of his adult life, grew up in Abilene, Kansas. Despite his mother's membership in a pacifist Protestant sect, he accepted an appointment to West Point and graduated in 1915. During World War I, the new second lieutenant served as an instructor in the tank corps. Between the wars he gradually worked up in rank and responsibility. During the Hoover administration he was an assistant executive in the War Department. After he made an unusually good record in the 1941 Louisiana army maneuvers, he rose quickly, becoming first the army's chief of operations and then, in June, 1942, commander of American forces in the European theater.

Given the nature of modern warfare and the huge bureaucracy of recent military organization, no commander in World War II could be a Napoleon or Alexander or Washington. Strategy came from committees in the Pentagon, not from commanders in the field. Eisenhower's greatness as a military leader during the war had its roots in his personality; he had the patience, amiability, and flexibility to get generals from different nations and branches of service, some of whom were notorious prima donnas, to work together harmoniously. As a general, Eisenhower was primarily an administrator—and an excellent one. His simplicity and forthrightness helped to give him a highly favorable press.

As President, Eisenhower again was primarily an administrator, the head of a team or staff. He relied heavily on his cabinet and other assistants and avoided routine matters. He wanted reports to him condensed to no more than one typewritten page. He depended on staff briefings for information; indeed, normally he did not read newspapers except on Sunday. Just as he did not play the role of a strong president within the executive department, he did not attempt vigorously to lead Congress. After twenty years of Roosevelt and Truman, Eisenhower's administrative and leadership methods were a distinct change of style.

In this kind of administration, cabinet members played more important roles than they traditionally had. In Eisenhower's first term the most important members of the administration were Sherman Adams, former governor of New Hampshire, a close-mouthed Yankee who served as the President's principal assistant; Secretary of State John Foster Dulles; Secretary of the Treasury George Humphrey of Ohio, who had been head of the coal and steel firm named for Mark Hanna; and Secretary of Defense Charles E. Wilson, former president of General Motors. The new Attorney General, Herbert Brownell, had been closely associated with Thomas E. Dewey. Sinclair Weeks, a successful New England manufacturer, became Secretary of Commerce, and two automobile dealers, Arthur Summerfield and Douglas McKay, became the heads of the Post Office and Interior departments. Mrs. Oveta Culp Hobby became the head of the new Department of Health, Education, and Welfare when that department came into being in April, 1953. Mrs. Hobby, commander of the WAC's during the war, was the wife of a wealthy Houston newspaper publisher. Ezra Taft Benson, a remarkably conservative elder of the Mormon church, became Secretary of Agriculture. The most out-of-place member of the assemblage was the Secretary of Labor, Martin Durkin, president of the plumbers' union, who had supported Stevenson in the campaign. Durkin resigned before a year was completed. The snide remark that the Eisenhower cabinet was composed of "eight millionaires and a plumber" was not far from accurate, but more important was the fact that in the cabinet there were few politicians and many businessmen. They provided a businessman's administration.

Immediately, many people announced their misgivings about these men with a business background in the nation's highest offices. Among those who were dubious was Senator Taft. Secretary Wilson, who was to suffer an acute case of "foot in mouth" disease during his whole tenure, alarmed many with a statement before the Senate committee conducting hearings on his appointment. In a discussion of whether or not he should be required to sell his General Motors stock before his Senate confirmation, Wilson told the committee that he had always assumed that "what was good for our country was good for General Motors, and vice versa." If one substituted the term "business community" for General Motors in Secretary Wilson's famous quotation, one would have an expression of the whole Eisenhower administration's view.

Soon after taking office the new administration adopted fiscal policies similar to what business had been advocating for years. Although the Korean conflict was not yet at an end, the new administration dropped almost all wartime controls. In their place as anti-inflation devices, the government changed Federal Reserve Board policies and reduced government spending. The Federal Reserve Board stopped its practice of pegging the price of government bonds, and bond prices fell. One effect of this was to increase the government's debt-management charges; another was to increase private banker demand for Federal Reserve Bank loans. Rather than sell their government bonds in a falling market, bankers naturally preferred to borrow to meet their customers' loan requirements. The Federal Reserve then raised its discount rate—the interest rate it charged member banks—and thereby drove up the interest rates on loans by member banks. Credit became tighter and more expensive. Democrats claimed this tight money policy brought on the recession of 1953–1954, and it probably was a factor; but lessened military spending after the end of the Korean War was probably more important.

The Eisenhower administration began by promising a balanced budget and reduced federal spending. The administration soon came to realize, however, that most items in the budget just could not be cut very much for either national security or political reasons. The administration let about one hundred thousand government jobs remain unfilled when their occupants resigned, but the money saved was relatively insignificant. Military spending could not be cut back much. Particularly, before the Korean armistice, the State Department would not countenance a cut in foreign aid to nations it

"Cut backs"

feared would go Communist, and fixed obligations such as veterans' pensions could not be importantly reduced. When Secretary Benson proposed that the administration reduce agricultural price supports where the law permitted, Congressmen in both parties quickly brought overwhelming pressure to bear.

The downswing in the business cycle which began in the fall of 1953 changed the problem from one of combatting inflation to trying to prevent severe deflation. The administration, understandably reluctant to admit that a recession was a real possibility, referred to the downswing as a "rolling readjustment" and condemned Democratic Senator Paul Douglas of Illinois, a former professor of economics, as a "prophet of gloom and doom" when he asserted that unless the government soon adopted antirecession measures the results would be unhappy. Nevertheless, the administration did quietly and mildly pursue the kind of policies that Douglas and other Keynesian economists held were proper under the circumstances. It relaxed its tight money policy, reduced taxes by $3 billion, and incurred a federal deficit. The last quarter of 1954 saw a sharp rise in the business cycle, and 1955 became the nation's most prosperous year.

The tax bill of 1954 was one that Andrew Mellon, whose portrait Secretary Humphrey kept in his office, would have approved. Beating down demands by a group of Democrats for an across-the-board increase in personal exemptions, which would have increased mass purchasing power, the Congress granted significant tax favors for low-income groups only by a reduction on the income taxes of retired workers. The new tax law lowered the wartime excises on transportation and luxuries such as jewelry, perfume, and furs. It excluded from income taxation the first $70 that a taxpayer received from stock dividends, a provision that proved a boon to few workingmen. And, perhaps most important, it granted faster depreciation allowances to businesses.

The oil and electric power industries received special treatment from the Republican administration. True to his campaign pledge, Eisenhower secured the passage of the Submerged Lands Act of 1953. This measure passed control of tidelands oil to the states, which then received royalties from the companies it allowed to work the off-shore fields and which were more generous with the companies than the federal government. Congress decided that the states could control up to three leagues into the sea (10.3 land miles) if the states had such boundaries at the time the states entered the Union. From this confusing provision there arose a curious series of court cases which the Supreme Court did not decide until June, 1960. The Court ruled that Louisiana, Alabama, and Mississippi had never claimed more than three nautical miles (3.45 land miles) off shore and were, therefore, entitled to jurisdiction only to that point. Texas and Florida, on the other hand, had made bolder claims, and their boundaries, therefore, extended three leagues seaward.

Democrats gleefully hoped the Eisenhower policies on electric policy would provide them with a hot election issue. The Dixon-Yates affair and the Hell's Canyon dispute probably did help the Democratic cause, but the results were nothing spectacular. The Dixon-Yates fracas grew from the Atomic Energy Commission's unusual demands for electric power. TVA had supplied most of the AEC's needs, and it proposed to meet the increased demands by constructing a steam generating plant. A syndicate headed by two southern utility executives, Edgar H. Dixon and Eugene A. Yates, proposed instead to organize a private company to supply the city of Memphis with power and make TVA expansion for AEC needs unnecessary. Eisenhower, who in 1953 had referred to TVA as an example of "creeping socialism," supported Dixon and Yates. In mid-1954, he ordered the AEC to sign the agreement. Public power supporters, notably Republican maverick Senator William L. Langer of North Dakota, declared war with an investigation. The Dixon-Yates proposal fell through when, in July, 1955, the city of Memphis, calculating it could produce its own power cheaper than it could buy it from Dixon-Yates, announced it would build its own generator. The President thereupon cancelled the Dixon-Yates contract. But there was still more to come. The congressional committee revealed that Adolphe Wenzell, a vice-president of the First Boston Corporation, had been employed by the Bureau of the Budget to help negotiate the Dixon-Yates contract and that his corporation had later become Dixon-Yates's financial agent. The AEC held that Wenzell had been involved in a clear conflict of interest and refused to pay the Dixon-Yates group for its expenses while the contract had been in force.

Hell's Canyon is a deep chasm along the Snake River between Oregon and Idaho. The Truman administration had proposed building a high dam there, one of the last good sites for a multipurpose dam in the nation still unexploited. The Idaho Power Company had submitted a scheme for three smaller dams. The issue was unresolved when Eisenhower took office. The new administration came forth with what it called its "partnership" principle on such matters, and the Federal Power Commission gave permission to private utilities to build the three small dams. The fight became hot indeed in the West. When public power advocates concentrated their fight in Congress with a measure to substitute the federal high dam, the White House rallied its strength on Capitol Hill and defeated them. Then the high dam supporters took their case to the courts.

The Federal Power Commission was the focus of another battle royal in the 1956 proposal to exempt natural gas in interstate pipelines from FPC regulation. Oil Democrats and southern states-righters joined most Republicans in support of the measure which would have become law but for the sensational revelation of Republican Senator Francis P. Case of South Dakota. Case said that an oil company had donated $2,500 to his campaign fund without his asking for it and that the company expected him to vote for the natural gas exemption. Case sent the money back and voted against his would-be briber's wishes, but the measure passed Congress anyway. The uproar, however, was too much for an administration that had come to office partly because of its promise to "clean up the mess in Washington." Eisenhower vetoed it. He said he favored the purpose of the bill but that the oil company methods left him no alternative but to reject the measure.

The Republican party was a bit embarrassed by its inability to solve the problem of agricultural surpluses. They had criticized the Democrats for their failure with the problem, but internal pressures and indecision worked as much against Republican as against Democratic success. Republicans were further embarrassed by their large government spending for surplus commodities, a policy that was inconsistent with the ideology of many party members.

During the campaign of 1952, Eisenhower had spoken of "full parity," but Secretary Benson appeared to regard government price supports as at best a temporarily necessary evil. The Agricultural Act of 1949 had established a plan for changing from rigid to flexible—that is, lower—supports, but throughout the rest of the Truman administration and for the first two years of Eisenhower's term, farm pressure had actually been sufficient to keep supports at a 90 per cent parity level. Stocks of government-owned commodities became mountainous; the government spent billions each year in purchasing cotton, wheat, corn, tobacco, and peanuts that no one would buy at a price sufficiently high to keep farm prices in line with other costs. Benson insisted upon lower supports, and Eisenhower backed him. Although the congressional fight was hot, the administration got through the Agricultural Act of 1954, which authorized the Secretary of Agriculture to cut supports on basic commodities to 82.5 per cent in 1955 and 75 per cent in 1956, authorized him to sell government-owned surpluses abroad at low prices, and arranged for part of the surplus to be used in school lunch programs.

Farm prices fell, and Secretary Benson was a highly unpopular man in many agricultural communities. Hoping to benefit from this criticism and with an eye cocked on the 1956 elections, congressional Democrats in early 1956 put through a bill restoring mandatory 90 per cent of parity supports. Eisenhower vetoed it. But he adopted one feature of the Democratic measure, the so-called soil bank idea, and Congress in May appropriated funds for this scheme of taking acres out of farm production. Actually, however, efforts to restrict production by restricting acreage in production were less than successful. The newly developed nitrogen fertilizers made it possible for a wheat farmer, for example, to get, within limits, about any yield per acre he desired. The farmer, then, took his check for his soil bank acreage and grew as much as ever on fewer acres.

The administration supported some extensions of general welfare principles commonly associated with the New Deal. A 1954 law extended Social Security Act coverage to self-employed people. Two years later a Democratic Congress (the Democrats after the 1954 elections had a forty-nine to forty-seven margin in the Senate and a 232 to 203 advantage in the House, less than the usual off-year comeback of the "out" party) further amended the Social Security Act to allow women to retire and receive pensions at age sixty-two and disabled workers to do so at age fifty. In 1956, Eisenhower also asked Congress to raise the minimum wage from seventy-five to ninety cents an hour; Congress raised it to $1.00 an hour.

Government spending for general welfare did not get far under the Eisenhower administration when the proposed spending was in areas which were conventionally in the private sector of the economy. The Housing Act of 1955 provided for only 45,000 new public housing units a year for four years. Eisenhower's proposal for a $25 million program to provide government support to private health insurance schemes so as to enable them to give broader and less expensive coverage received censure from two sides, from some who said the proposal was woefully timid and inadequate and from the American Medical Association who said that it was too close to "socialized medicine." Congress dropped the proposal. Federal aid to states for education similarly came to nothing. Many Republicans opposed the idea on principle, and southern Democrats prevented its passage after Democratic Representative Adam Clayton Powell, Jr., a Negro from New York City, attached a proviso that federal aid could not go to school districts that segregated children by race.

In areas that were traditionally in the public sector of the economy, the administration and the Congress further extended federal spending. For a generation the St. Lawrence Seaway had sporadically become an issue, with the Midwest supporting the idea and the railroads and the eastern states opposing it. When it became clear that Canada would go ahead and construct the Seaway on her own, the United States at last acted. In May, 1954, the President signed a bill that provided for joint Canadian-American construction. Spending for highways was also safe politically. In 1956, Congress and the White House got together on a vast superhighway construction program, the federal government to assume 90 per cent of the costs and the states to do the actual building from federal minimum specifications. Under the law, states were allowed to charge the traveler for use of the roads, and most of them did so.

By far the most spectacular political story of the first Eisenhower term was the further rise and then the rapid fall of Senator Joseph R. McCarthy. In the 1952 campaign, many anti-McCarthy Republicans argued that only with a Republican president could the obstreperous Wisconsinite be calmed down and satisfied. But, if anything, McCarthy's charges became more sensational after Eisenhower's inauguration. McCarthy became the chairman of the Senate Government Operations Committee and its Permanent Subcommittee on Investigations. He used the post to establish himself as his party's official anti-Communist, despite the President's obvious anti-Communism revealed by his administration's further prosecution of Communist party leaders under the Smith Act and by his order imposing a "blank wall" between J. Robert Oppenheimer and government nuclear secrets. (Oppenheimer had been the director of the Los Alamos operation during the war, and many scientists were incensed by the decision.) Although the President made occasional public statements that could be interpreted as critical of McCarthy, he refrained from outright public opposition.

Matters came to a head soon after McCarthy began to attack the army. McCarthy discovered a New York dentist, called to army duty in 1952, who had been a Communist. The army found the dentist's Communist connection and took the easy way out by releasing him with an honorable discharge. McCarthy charged that someone in the army was either a Communist or "soft on Communism" for taking such action. He called General Ralph Zwicker before his subcommittee, but Zwicker was under orders not to reveal who in the service had been responsible for the handling of the dentist's discharge. McCarthy called the general "a disgrace to the uniform." The army soon counterattacked. It charged that McCarthy and his assistant Roy Cohn had sought to get preferential treatment in the army for Private G. David Schine, a former McCarthy committee staff member and a friend of Cohn's. The upshot was a nationally televised hearing by McCarthy's own committee with Senator Karl Mundt of South Dakota presiding.

The televised hearings were intensely dramatic. For their first few days, no television drama was their equal for theatrical thrill. Before long, the public began strongly to turn against McCarthy, whose manners in front of the camera were crude and who, before the whole nation's eyes, revealed the methods that had brought him to national prominence. Soon comedians began to imitate the Senator's rasping refrain, "Point of order, Mr. Chairman, point of order," and other obstructing tactics he frequently used.

Republican Senator Ralph Flanders of Vermont, Democratic Senator William Fulbright of Arkansas, and independent Senator Wayne Morse of Oregon introduced resolutions of censure against McCarthy, and the Senate appointed a committee of three Democratic and three Republican members, headed by former federal judge Arthur Watkins, Republican from Utah, to conduct hearings on the charges. The Watkins committee maintained an especially judicious air. It finally recommended to the Senate that Senator McCarthy be condemned on two counts: for refusing to give the committee information about his finances that the committee held to be relevant to his fitness as a Senator and for contempt of the Senate for his remarks about his colleagues. In December, 1954, the Senate by a sixty-seven to twenty-two vote condemned the junior Senator from Wisconsin. Eisenhower publicly complimented Senator Watkins. McCarthy faded fast, perhaps more because of adverse public opinion after the army-McCarthy hearings than because of the Senate's action. When he died in May, 1957, he was a bitter and largely forgotten man.

McCarthyism subsided almost as rapidly as McCarthy. Undoubtedly, the Korean armistice in July, 1953 (see p. 555) relaxed tensions and set the stage for McCarthy's personal downfall. The nation's attitude became no less opposed to either foreign or domestic Communism. Indeed, in 1954, congressional Democrats, in an effort to defend themselves against Republican charges of softness, instigated the Communist Control Act which for all practical purposes made the Communist party illegal. The Justice Department has not used the law. But irrational suspicion on the whole declined, and political candidates far less frequently tried to demonstrate their fitness for office by appearing to be more intensely anti-Communist than their opponents. In 1956 and 1957, the Supreme Court inhibited the power of congressional committees to demand answers from witnesses to questions not directly relevant and provided better guarantees of constitutional rights to those charged with having Communist sympathies. What little was left of the Communist party engaged in a fierce internal controversy prompted by Premier Nikita Khrushchev's revelations of Stalin's repressions which resulted in many resignations.

We Like Ike, Part II

On September 24, 1955, while on a vacation in Denver, President Eisenhower suffered a heart attack. At first it appeared that a second Eisenhower candidacy was out of the question, but slowly the President resumed his executive activities. In early 1956, when the President's press secretary staged a conference between a group of Eisenhower's physicians and reporters in which the doctors reported that their patient's heart had healed, it became obvious that Eisenhower again would run. His subsequent announcement was

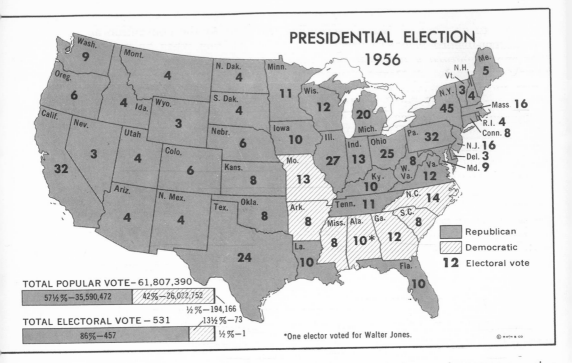

PRESIDENTIAL ELECTION 1956

Republican
Democratic
12 Electoral vote

TOTAL POPULAR VOTE— 61,807,390
57½%—35,590,472   42%—26,022,752
½%—194,166
TOTAL ELECTORAL VOTE — 531   13½%—73
86%—457   ½%—1

*One elector voted for Walter Jones.

an anticlimax. Then in June, 1956, the President had to undergo an operation for ileitis. Partisan Republicans read the newspaper medical reports with more than detached interest.

Contrary to custom, the Democrats held their convention first. The main contenders in the preconvention struggle for the nomination were Stevenson, Governor Averell Harriman of New York, and Senator Kefauver of Tennessee. Kefauver withdrew from consideration just before the convention. Although former President Truman supported Harriman, the convention nominated Stevenson on the first ballot. The real excitement came with the vice-presidential nomination. Stevenson declined to express a preference for a running mate, and the delegates at Chicago settled down to a dogfight such as Democratic conventions seem to enjoy. The battle was between Kefauver and Senator John F. Kennedy of Massachusetts. Although Kefauver was from the South and Kennedy was a Roman Catholic, most southern delegates voted for Kennedy. Kefauver won by a hair. The party platform criticized the Republican agricultural record, called for 90 per cent of parity supports, and condemned their opponents for their electric power policies. Fear of southern disaffection prompted the convention to adopt a weaseling plank on civil rights.

Eisenhower's nomination at the San Francisco convention in August was a foregone conclusion despite his health. Political parties are seldom favored with such popular figures. The only stir about the ticket came from an undercurrent of dissatisfaction with Vice-President Nixon. Harold Stassen, who had moved from the presidency of the University of Pennsylvania to become Eisenhower's adviser on disarmament, announced that Governor Christian Herter of Massachusetts would give the ticket better drawing power than would Nixon. But before the convention opened he backed down and consented to give one of Nixon's seconding speeches. At the convention an independent-minded Nebraska delegate created a sensation when he got the floor and nominated a mythical "Joe Smith" for the second place on the ticket. Chairman Joseph Martin silenced the audacious Nebraskan. Both Eisenhower and Nixon received their nominations by acclamation. The platform was an expression of "modern Republicanism"; it put the GOP on record as opposed to racial segregation in the schools.

The campaign was dull. Stevenson failed to show the sparkle of 1952, and the Republicans lacked a Truman scapegoat. One campaign development was interesting for the future. Stevenson urged an international agreement banning the testing of nuclear weapons on the grounds that radioactive fallout was dangerous to the health and safety of the entire world. Eisenhower declared that the proposal was dangerous unless an international agency had the power to inspect anywhere in the world to see if any nation infringed the agreement. Before Eisenhower left the White House in 1961, he agreed to the kind of proposal Stevenson had made.

A tense international situation developed just before election day. In October, Hungarian nationalists revolted against the Russians only to be ruthlessly suppressed. Then, in the week before the polling, Israel invaded Egyptian territory. France and Great Britain joined with Israel, and full war was a real possibility. These international tensions probably helped Eisenhower because he was experienced in the White House and had military knowledge.

Eisenhower's margin of victory was even greater than in 1952. He received 35,585,316 popular votes to 26,031,322 for Stevenson. In the electoral college Eisenhower's victory was 457 to 73. One Alabama elector cast his vote for an obscure state judge rather than for Stevenson. Stevenson carried only southern states plus Missouri, and Eisenhower won such traditionally Democratic strongholds as Texas, Louisiana, Florida, Tennessee, and Virginia. The congressional elections again showed that Eisenhower was far more popular than his party. Democrats held their previous margin of two seats in the Senate and won 235 of the House positions. Once again different parties controlled Capitol Hill and the White House.

Two Texas moderate Democrats, Speaker of the House Sam Rayburn and Senate Majority Leader Lyndon Johnson, cooperated with Eisenhower. Indeed, Eisenhower had to rely upon their congressional leadership. In general, they supported the President's position with only the modification necessary to mollify dissident sections of their own party. Inevitably, such bipartisan moderation produced no important new departures. Perhaps as great an event with a long-run impact as the Eisenhower-moderate Democratic leadership provided was the admission of Alaska and Hawaii to statehood, the former in January, 1959, and the latter in August of the same year.

At the very beginning of his second term Eisenhower encountered more difficulty with his own party, even his own cabinet, than he did with the Democrats. In January, 1957, he presented Congress with a budget totalling $71.8 billion, the largest any president had ever offered in peacetime. Very quickly, Secretary of the Treasury Humphrey at a press conference, when a reporter asked if there was any hope that the defense budget could be cut, replied: "I think there is, yes, I do. I would certainly deplore the day that we thought we couldn't ever reduce expenditures of this terrific amount, the terrific tax take we are taking out of this country. If we don't, over a long period of time, I will predict that you will have a depression that will curl your hair." When he resigned about a year later Eisenhower replaced him with Robert B. Anderson of Texas, who went on record for deficit financing during a depression although he never actually supported such fiscal policies when a minor recession came. Congress was slow to act, but finally, despite Secretary Humphrey, it cut the budget only about $4 billion.

Congress did not cut taxes and no hair-curling depression developed, but in the last quarter of 1957 and through 1958 the economy did undergo one of its major postwar recessions. Instead of arising from government spending, it probably resulted from a shift in government spending. Less of the budget went for military aircraft, and the recession apparently started when aircraft workers in southern California found themselves on reduced hours or no work at all. The 1957–1958 recession was an odd one. Gross national product continued to grow—from $419.2 billion in 1956 to $442.8 billion in 1957 to $444.2 billion in 1958—but not as fast as the population growth would warrant. Unemployment increased significantly. In July, 1957, just over three million workers were unemployed. The figure rose to about 4,500,000 in January, 1958, and to almost 5,300,000 in July. To carry the story of the national economy on to the end of the Eisenhower administration, recovery in the last half of 1958 and the first half of 1959 was strong. Increased government spending, mostly on defense matters in response to the Soviet Union's successful launching of Sputnik I, the first man-made satellite, in October, 1957, was a factor in the recovery. In the second half of 1959 a long steel strike slowed the economy again. Expectations in early 1960 were high, but in the second quarter of the year the economy's rate of growth slowed again. Unemployment statistics fluctuated but stayed close to four million throughout this period. Another oddity of the economy in Eisenhower's second term was that the cost-of-living index continued to rise gradually despite other economic fluctuation. In summary, one might say that after the 1957–1958 recession the country enjoyed prosperity but not as much economic growth as desirable and that the chronically unemployed in the chronically depressed "sick-industry" areas found small comfort from the happier national picture.

Democrats in 1958 looked forward eagerly to the fall elections because of the recession and because they saw a chance to pin the corruption label on the Republicans that their opponents had pinned on them in 1952. Several GOP officials had resigned under charges of improperly using their office to further their personal finances, including a chairman of the Republican national committee, a Secretary of the Air Force, an Assistant Secretary of Defense, and an Eisenhower-appointed Democrat on the Federal Communications Commission. Then in the spring of 1958 a House subcommittee hit political pay dirt. It alleged that Sherman Adams, Eisenhower's "Assistant President," had interceded with federal agencies in behalf of a friend, Bernard Goldfine, a New England textile manufacturer. Adams, the House group charged, had in return received lavish Christmas presents. The industrialist had given Adams a topcoat made of vicuña, a wool taken from South American goats, and Republican vicuña coats became almost as notorious as Democratic mink ones. President Eisenhower, when warned that keeping Adams as his assistant might

552

be political dynamite, replied, "I need him." Nevertheless, in the late summer of 1958 enough prominent Republicans put pressure on the White House for Adams to leave office; the accused resigned on September 22.

It would be a mistake to ascribe the recession and the Adams case as the only reasons for Democratic victory in November, 1958. As in all elections, local and state issues were important. In 1958, "right-to-work" laws were an issue in several states. ("Right-to-work" laws were a euphemism for prohibitions of the union shop.) When some employers persuaded a few candidates, mostly Republicans, to support such legislation, labor only became more determined to help the Democrats win. The labor vote, plus a division within the Republican organization, was clearly influential in the defeat of Senate Republican leader William F. Knowland for governor of California. Democrats ended up with larger majorities in each house of Congress than they had enjoyed since the Congress elected in 1936: 64 Democrats in the Senate and 283 in the House. Furthermore, Democrats elected governors in usually Republican states such as Iowa, Wisconsin, and Ohio. In both parties, the more progressive candidates fared better than the more conservative members of the same party. In New York, the Republican gubernatorial candidate, Nelson Rockefeller, who seemed as progressive as his Democratic opponent, Averell Harriman, won by an overwhelming majority, while conservative John Bricker lost in Ohio.

It would not have been unreasonable in the winter of 1958–1959 to predict that the new Congress would pass a series of progressive bills. But such was not to be the case. The moderation of the congressional Democratic leadership and the constant threat of a veto prevented the Eighty-sixth Congress from being substantially different from its predecessor. It failed to enact any increased public housing program. Debates over including a medical care program for the aged under the Social Security Act of 1935 were long and well publicized, but Congress made no real change. One generous aged medical care plan passed the House, but the Senate, where presidential aspirant John F. Kennedy supported it, voted it down fifty-one to forty-four. Only one Republican Senator voted for the measure; thirty-two Republicans and nineteen Democrats voted against it. In April, 1960, when the approaching elections were very much on congressional minds, Congress passed a new Civil Rights Act to be described in Chapter 28. Although southern Congressmen opposed the law, they were able to water it down so much that Negro leaders said it made little difference.

Labor unions received much attention from Congress. In 1957, a Senate committee headed by Senator John L. McClellan of Arkansas and assisted by its counsel, Robert Kennedy, Senator Kennedy's brother, began investigating racketeering in labor unions. McClellan and Kennedy concentrated on the Teamsters Union, perhaps the nation's least democratic major union. The Committee alleged that Teamster president David Beck of Seattle had used union funds for his own use. Beck subsequently was indicted and convicted for income tax evasion. When he declined to run for re-election, the Teamster convention elected James Hoffa of Detroit, whose reputation was less savory even than Beck's. While holding no brief for Beck and Hoffa, many friends of labor argued that the Senate committee actually was spotlighting the worst characters in the labor movement so as to discredit all unions, honest and

553

democratic as well as crooked and high-handed. Public opinion polls showed a growing disapproval of the whole labor movement. The investigation resulted in the Labor Reform Act of 1959. This law guaranteed union members secret elections of officers and provided for government supervision of union funds, including welfare funds, which had grown tremendously since the end of the war. It also expanded the Taft-Hartley Act's inhibitions on boycotts and restricted union activities in jurisdictional disputes.

Asia and Brinkmanship

The Republican party divided sharply over Asian policy. A considerable group in the party, usually quite conservative in domestic policies, were commonly called "Asia firsters." That is, they valued American supremacy in Asia and defeat of the Chinese and other Asian Communists more highly than Communist containment in Europe. Eisenhower clearly was not in sympathy with the views of this wing of his party, but he had to yield to it occasionally.

Eisenhower began his administration by seeming to throw support behind the "Asia first," "total victory" in Korea point of view. Followers of the MacArthur line had long been critical of Truman's ordering the Seventh Fleet to neutralize Formosa, charging that the fleet was "shielding" Communist China. Eisenhower announced he would "unleash Chiang Kai-shek." The unleashed Chiang, however, remained quietly on Formosa, undertaking no more than an occasional minor raid of the Chinese mainland which he had been doing even before he was "unleashed."

The Korean truce talks at Panmunjom had been stalled for months over the issue of the return of prisoners. The talks had been suspended altogether since September, 1952. Whether or not Stalin's death on March 5, 1953, was a factor in the resumption of truce negotiations was not known, but at any rate before the end of the month North Korean and Chinese army commanders accepted an American proposal for the exchange of invalid prisoners of war that they had earlier rejected and suggested resumption of negotiations.

Negotiations began again in April. The problem of what to do with the prisoners who did not want to return to their homes remained the main obstacle. In June, both sides agreed to a plan, to be administered by a commission of neutral nations, under which each side would have three months to explain to its prisoner compatriots why they should return. Then Syngman Rhee, president of South Korea, all but wrecked everything by secretly ordering the immediate release of all the North Korean and Chinese prisoners who did not want to return. He also threatened to resume the war unless his terms were met—reunification of all Korea under the South Korean government. Hard pressure from Washington persuaded Rhee to back down, but he won the promise of American military assistance if North Korea should attack again. The United States and South Korea signed a mutual defense treaty in August. Obviously, the major obligation fell upon the United States.

When Rhee released the prisoners, the Communists at first demanded that all twenty-seven thousand of them be rounded up, which would have been extremely difficult if not impossible, but they seemed determined to bring the conflict to an end and on July 27, 1953, signed an armistice. The truce line ran from about thirty miles north of the thirty-eighth parallel at its east end to a little south of the line at its west end. A demilitarized area four kilometers wide ran the length of the line. Repatriation of prisoners was complete by September. Although nearly one-fourth of the North Korean and Chinese prisoners declined to go home, American attention focused on the twenty-two Americans who elected to stay with the Communists.

The war that had never officially been more than a "police action" was over at last. Americans killed in action totalled 33,237, along with an estimated 50,000 South Koreans and 3,124 other UN troops. Estimates of Communist losses ranged from 1,500,000 to 2,000,000.

The end of the Korean war by no means ended America's problems with Asian Communism. The year 1954 saw crises in Southeast Asia and in the Formosan Straits. In Southeast Asia, French Indo-China to be specific, the United States came perilously close to war. Secretary of State John Foster Dulles, upon whom the President leaned heavily, himself gave the term which characterized American policy: *brinkmanship*. *Life* magazine in early 1956 quoted Dulles from an interview:

> The ability to get to the verge without getting into war is the necessary art. If you cannot master it, you inevitably get into war. If you try to run away from it, if you are scared to go to the brink, you are lost. We've had to look it square in the face—on the question of enlarging the Korean War, on the question of getting into the Indochina war, on the question of Formosa. We walked to the brink and we looked it in the face. We took strong action.[1]

Many people were alarmed for fear that in going to the brink the nation might get shoved over it by accident or fail to realize where the precise edge was because of the fast movement of events. Although the entire story is not yet known, it appears that congressional caution and the opposition of Great Britain had more to do with keeping on the peace side of the brink in Indo-China than did State Department calculation.

Since the end of the war, the French had been on the defensive in Indo-China. They declined to make any firm commitments about independence and maintained a reactionary puppet, Bao Dai, over the country. Their position in the guerilla warfare against the Communists, led by Ho Chi Minh, steadily deteriorated, and despite the aid they received from the United States for the Indo-Chinese war (which amounted to about 70 per cent of their costs), French domestic sentiment opposed the financial drain. The French secretly notified Washington in March, 1954, that, unless the United States intervened, Indo-China was lost. French forces were under siege at Dienbienphu, and the situation was hopeless without a great deal of additional force.

On April 7, President Eisenhower told a press conference that if Indo-China fell to the Communists the situation would be analogous to pushing over the first in a row of dominoes. The rest of Southeast Asia, perhaps more, would quickly be led into Communist hands. Although a general conference

---

[1] James Shepley, "How Dulles Averted War," *Life* (January 16, 1956), 78.

SOUTHEAST ASIA

—·—·— Present international boundaries

———— Division between North and South
Vietnam near 17th parallel

------ Borders of Burmese states

············ Borders of old divisions of Vietnam

Areas annexed by Thailand
during World War II

Provinces in Laos occupied by
Communist forces

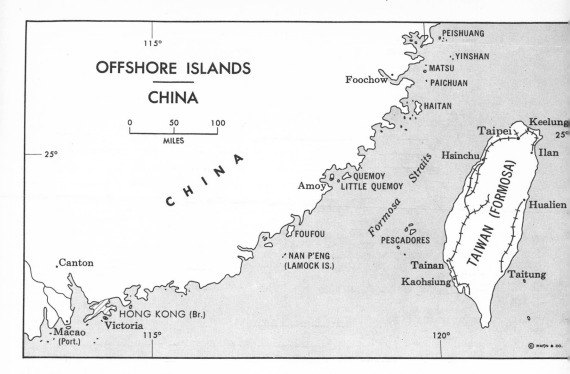

OFFSHORE ISLANDS
—
CHINA

0   50   100
MILES

for discussion of Indo-Chinese matters had already been scheduled to be held in Geneva, Dulles and the chairman of the joint chiefs of staff, Admiral Arthur W. Radford, proposed that the United States send carriers and planes to Indo-China to relieve the French. Congressional leaders warned Dulles that such action would very probably mean full war and urged him to line up support from America's allies. The British government, then under the Conservative party, flatly refused to support the idea. The United States stepped back from the brink. On April 26, the day the Geneva conference opened, President Eisenhower announced that what was sought was a *modus vivendi* with the Chinese Communists. Dienbienphu fell on May 7, 1954. In July, the Geneva conference ended with an armistice and the partition of Indo-China. The states of Cambodia and Laos were to be independent. Vietnam was to be divided, as was Korea, along the seventeenth parallel, Communist to the north and anti-Communist to the south. The United States gave military and economic aid to the anti-Communists; Communist China aided the Indo-Chinese Communists. Continuing Communist penetrations of Loas and South Vietnam created constant tensions.

After the Geneva conference of 1954, Dulles brought about the formation of a Southeast Asian counterpart of NATO, the Southeast Asia Treaty Organization (SEATO). Signers of the treaty in September, 1954, were the United States, France, Great Britain, Australia, New Zealand, the Philippines, Thailand, and Pakistan. The treaty declared that an attack upon any of the signatory powers—and a separate agreement included an attack on Laos, Cambodia, and South Vietnam—would be regarded as a threat to all of them. It did not precisely commit the signatory nations to war; it required each nation

557

"to act to meet the common danger in accordance with its constitutional processes." Actually, SEATO, in comparison to NATO, has been little more than a paper organization.

The United States did not go as close to the brink in the conflict between the Nationalist and Communist Chinese over the islands in the Formosan Strait. When the Nationalists were forced to flee the mainland and go to Formosa, they had left garrisons on several tiny islands in the Formosan Strait and just north of it: Quemoy and Matsu just off the coast; the Tachen Islands near the coast and to the north; and the Pescadore Islands off the coast of Formosa. In September, 1954, the Chinese Communists began artillery bombardment of Quemoy, only five miles off the coast. An invasion of the island appeared likely. That the United States would help defend Formosa from attack was clear, but what would it do if the offshore islands, which had little or no strategic importance, should be attacked? Admiral Radford advocated aerial bombardment of mainland Communist bases. Other military leaders objected, arguing that the risk of general war over islands whose only importance was psychological was useless. The President refused to support Radford's position. There was no invasion.

The mutual defense treaty signed on December 1, 1954, between Nationalist China and the United States did not entirely clarify just what the United States would help defend. The United States made clear it would regard an attack on Formosa or the Pescadores as a provocation of war, but the treaty said nothing about the islands just off the mainland coast. At the time of the treaty's signing, the State Department received a promise from Chiang Kai-shek that he would not attack the mainland without clearing the action with Washington. He was thus "leashed" again. Congress passed the buck back to the President in its resolution of January 28, 1955, which authorized the President to order American forces to the defense of Formosa and the Pescadores but left the status of the "related positions" up in the air.

Two subsequent developments failed to clarify the American position. In January, 1955, the Communists began to move into the Tachen Islands. Eisenhower's party leader in the Senate, William S. Knowland, demanded full support for Chiang, but in the end Eisenhower agreed only to help Chiang retreat from the Tachens. Again in 1958 the offshore islands were in the news when the Communists began heavy shelling of Quemoy. Secretary Dulles at first implied that the United States would defend the island but later indicated that, if the bombardment stopped, Chiang might demilitarize it and perhaps abandon it. The Chinese Communists let up on the shelling, but Chiang kept his troops on Quemoy.

At this point the Chinese Communists inadvertently strengthened the American position in India by blundering in Tibet. After suppressing a Tibetan revolt, Chinese armed forces moved across a vague boundary into territory claimed by India. That vast country had since its independence studiously maintained a neutralist or "third camp" position in the cold war, and it had been anxious about American military aid to its hostile neighbor, Pakistan. Chinese occupation of Indian territory by no means made India bellicose, but her neutralism became considerably less rigid as she moved closer to the West.

Eisenhower and Khrushchev

The Eisenhower administration's view of the proper nature of the American military establishment was at least partly the result of traditional Republican opposition to massive government spending. A military establishment capable of coping successfully with any situation that might develop would be terribly expensive, more expensive than Republican budgeters wanted. The administration compromised by keeping conventional armed forces down as much as it dared and concentrated on nuclear weapons and the instruments for delivering them. As Secretary Dulles put it in a January, 1954, speech, Communist armies were too powerful to match and the United States must rely on the "deterrent of massive retaliatory power." In other words, Communist fear of being exterminated by nuclear weapons would deter them from aggressions.

President Truman had given the green light to the development of the hydrogen fusion bomb, and the United States first successfully tested the new weapon in November, 1952. In August, 1953, Russia tested her first H-bomb. The arms race continued. Each side increased its arsenal of this most devastating weapon and improved its means of sending the weapon to its target. In 1957, the Communists seemed to be at least temporarily ahead in the matter of delivery when they successfully tested intercontinental ballistic missiles and demonstrated by putting Sputnik I into orbit that they had rockets of enormous thrust.

West Europeans were torn between desire to increase their armed strength through NATO and fear of recreating a powerful and possibly dangerous German armed force. The French government, which until 1958 underwent constantly recurring constitutional crises, put forward the idea of the European Defense Community (EDC). EDC would be an international army, composed of troops from West Germany, France, Britain, and the Benelux countries. The United States vigorously encouraged the proposal, and in May, 1952, the European nations signed the EDC treaty. But the French then drew back out of fear of Germany's military potential under the scheme. Dulles' statement that French failure to ratify the EDC treaty would cause the United States to undertake an "agonizing reappraisal" of its policies —an implied threat to cut off military aid to France—did not prevent the French from rejecting the treaty. But the idea was not dead. The British allayed French fears by promising to keep four divisions and an air force in Europe to be used against any aggressor, and Washington said it would also keep troops in Europe, at least for the moment. In the fall of 1954, West Germany, Italy, France, and the Benelux countries formed the Western European Union (WEU). In this arrangement Germany would furnish up to twelve divisions but forbore having nuclear, chemical, or biological weapons. France consented. However, in 1957, West German Chancellor Konrad Adenauer asked for tactical atomic weapons, and the United States granted them. West Germany, however, did not obtain independent control of the weapons.

For a time in the middle years of the Eisenhower era it appeared that some kind of more or less permanent relaxation of cold war tensions might be effected. Stalin's death quite obviously changed the situation within the Soviet Union, although one cannot say yet what the end of the changes will be. Georgi Malenkov succeeded Stalin. In February, 1955, he resigned under pressure to be succeeded by Nikolai Bulganin. However, the new secretary of the Soviet Communist party, Nikita Khrushchev, was the actual force. In March, 1958, Khrushchev himself became the premier, holding the government office as well as the party office, as had Stalin. Whatever Khrushchev was, however (and there was little agreement in the West about this bustling figure), it was clear that he was not a carbon copy of Stalin. He was more flexible, both in internal and external policies, perhaps more of a realist and less doctrinaire, although, clearly, firmly committed to the Communist viewpoint.

Encouraged by Soviet developments and alarmed by the United States and Russia having hydrogen weapons capable of hideous destruction, the people of western Europe yearned for some kind of *rapprochement* between East and West. The aged prime minister of Britain, Winston Churchill, who retired in the spring of 1955, urged a conference of world leaders "at the summit." In the 1955 British elections the Conservatives promised to seek a summit meeting, and the idea was popular in internally torn France. Such a meeting was the hope of probably a majority of Americans. At first scornful of a summit conference, President Eisenhower was impressed by the force of opinion and by Russian willingness to negotiate about an Austrian peace treaty. (On May 15, 1955, the World War II allies signed a peace treaty with Austria which in effect made that country a neutral zone in the cold war.) Just five days before the Austrian treaty's signing, Great Britain, France, and the United States invited Russia to a meeting of the four chiefs of state. Russia accepted.

Eisenhower, Bulganin, the current French premier, Edgar Faure, and the new British prime minister, Sir Anthony Eden, met at Geneva in July. No meeting of heads of state ever received greater publicity. But, even though the meeting was to be only exploratory and was to be followed by subsequent meetings of the foreign ministers, it actually came to no important agreement. At this first meeting of Big Four chief executives since Potsdam ten years earlier, the Russians refused to consider German reunification on the basis of popular elections until they had first, in effect, an American commitment to withdraw from Europe. Eisenhower made his "open skies" proposal: the two sides to exchange maps of their military establishments and to allow one another aerial inspection so as to prevent secret arms concentration. The Russians insisted upon a prior ban on nuclear weapons before they would consider any kind of inspection, a position they clung to tenaciously.

Neither the 1955 summit conference nor the Big Four foreign ministers' meeting made any advance on the critical German and disarmament questions, but there were some less important improvements. In September, 1955, Russia announced it was ready to withdraw from Finland's Porkkala peninsula where it had a naval base, and in 1956 actually did so. East and West began a cultural interchange program that obviously enriched at least the musical experience of both camps. Russia began to admit tourists from the United

States and other NATO countries. The Soviets and the Americans initiated a student exchange program on a small scale.

At the Twentieth Congress of the Soviet Communist party in February, 1956, Khrushchev made statements that were startling indeed. First, he indicated a new Russian position when he said that ultimate war between Communist and capitalist nations was not inevitable. He maintained that the people of the world would sooner or later come to believe that Communism offered them more than capitalism, that Communists would inevitably win the struggle but that the struggle would be peaceful. "Peaceful co-existence" was Khrushchev's phrase. He recognized that really neither side could win a full war in the traditional sense of victory: ". . . there are only two ways: either peaceful co-existence or the most devastating war in history. There is no third alternative."

Then in a "secret" speech before the Congress Khrushchev was highly critical of Stalin. He reported that Stalin had been insanely suspicious, cruel, and unnecessarily dictatorial. He confirmed almost everything that western critics for years had said of the dead Soviet dictator. Needless to say, this kind of speech from the world's number one Communist about the man who had stood in his place only three years earlier shook the Communist movement throughout the world to its very foundations. One result was to stimulate revolts among the more nationalistic satellites.

The Poles, long fierce nationalists, elected Wladyslaw Gomulka, only recently released from a Soviet prison, to their party secretaryship. Gomulka refused to join the government unless a Russian general were dismissed as defense minister. Khrushchev objected, but the Poles dismissed the Russian general, installed Gomulka, and, to the world's surprise, got away with it. The Poles were hardly in a position to break entirely from the Russian orbit, but they did achieve a measure of independence and used it to allow a freer internal atmosphere. Although the Polish government was still undeniably Communist, the United States offered Poland limited economic aid to encourage its "Titoist" policies.

Encouraged by the Polish example, the Hungarians also rebelled against Russia, but their rebellion was against Communism as well as against Russian control of their Communist state. "Titoism" the Russians had demonstrated they would tolerate, even if they did not like it; but anti-Communism they would not tolerate. In early November, 1956, the Russians unleashed a strong military offensive against the Hungarian revolution. Tanks rolled through Budapest. The Hungarians fought back, but they were no match. Nearly two hundred thousand Hungarians fled to the West over the Austrian border.

Neither the United States nor any other power offered to come to the military aid of the Hungarian revolutionists. To have done so almost certainly would have meant full war with the Soviet Union. Secretary Dulles had been critical of the containment policy, arguing that liberation rather than containment was the proper goal. But his argument was apparently intended for domestic political advantage. When the chips were down in the fall of 1956, he and the Eisenhower administration refrained from any more than containment.

The anticolonial peoples of Asia, the Middle East, and Africa, naturally horrified by the Russian suppression of Hungarian self-determination, could

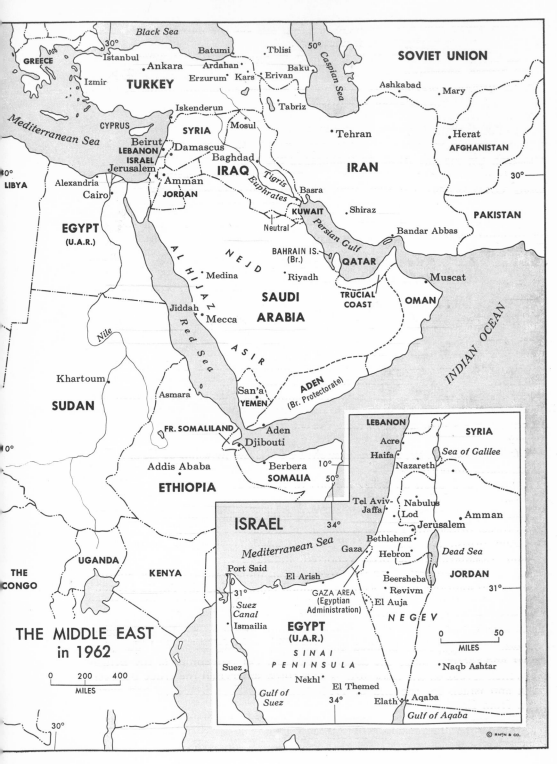

THE MIDDLE EAST
in 1962

have been drawn closer to the western camp but for the almost simultaneous Suez fiasco. Some background is necessary.

In 1952, a nationalist military group in Egypt, led by Colonel Abdel Gamal Nasser, overthrew King Farouk. Nasser became premier of Egypt in 1954. He proposed not only to improve the internal conditions of his country but to unite the various Arab countries into one nation. Secretary Dulles was hopeful of making Nasser an anti-Communist friend and was ever mindful of the vast American investment in Middle Eastern petroleum which had become of much greater importance in the previous fifteen years. But he was not consistent. On the one hand, he encouraged the formation in 1955 of the so-called Baghdad Pact or Middle East Treaty Organization, a defensive alliance among Great Britain, Pakistan, Iraq, Iran, and Turkey, which Nasser vigorously opposed. Nasser's opposition to the Baghdad Pact prompted the Communist camp to try to get Middle Eastern allies. Egypt and Czechoslovakia got together on a cotton-weapons exchange. On the other hand, Dulles cut off arms aid to Nasser's Israeli enemies, hastened British withdrawal of troops from Suez, and in December, 1955, together with Great Britain, offered Egypt $70 million for the construction of the Aswan Dam, a proposed hydro-electric installation on the Nile. A World Bank loan for the dam was contingent upon British and American help.

But Nasser increased his economic ties with the Soviet camp, much to Dulles' disappointment, and on July 19, 1956, Dulles withdrew the offer of help for the Aswan Dam. Nasser replied quickly. Seven days later he nationalized the Suez Canal. Revenues from canal operation would go for the dam's construction. Western European nations, dependent upon the canal and the Middle East for its oil products, were anxious lest Nasser cut off their use of the canal. With Dulles' help, they made several proposals for international control of the canal, all of which Nasser rejected. Then the real trouble erupted.

On October 19, 1956, Israel launched a full-scale invasion of Egypt. The United States supported a UN Security Council resolution calling upon Israel to withdraw and upon all other nations to refrain from using force. Britain and France vetoed the resolution, and the next day, October 31, they began bombing Egypt. On November 5, the day after Russian tanks entered Budapest in force, British and French troops invaded Nasser's territory.

The British and French had not consulted Washington before their invasion. Eisenhower, the press reported, indulged in "barracks room language." The United States and the Soviet Union independently of one another introduced resolutions in the Security Council condemning the Anglo-French-Israeli invasion; Britain and France vetoed. But the UN Assembly, where there is no veto, passed an American-sponsored resolution calling for a cease-fire and withdrawal of armies. The invaders of Egypt first ignored the UN resolution, but the Egyptians blocked the canal by sinking ships and dumping bridges and thereby made the invasion fruitless. On November 6, the British and French agreed to the cease-fire. A UN force supervised the truce between Egypt and Israel. By the end of 1956 British and French troops had withdrawn from Egypt.

The Suez fiasco had a sequel. With France and Britain no longer a major influence and with the Soviets eager to cement their relations with

Nasser and other Middle Eastern leaders, Eisenhower, in a message to Congress on January 5, 1957, asked for authority to grant military and economic aid to any Middle Eastern country that asked for it to preserve those nations' territorial integrity from the Communists. Many Congressmen believed that this Eisenhower Doctrine, as it came to be called, was a kind of buck passing to Capitol Hill. Congress passed the buck back to the White House. It authorized the President to use American forces in the Middle East but left it to him to say when and where they were required. It also appropriated $200 million for military and economic aid.

The administration invoked the Eisenhower Doctrine in July, 1958, in Lebanon. Early in 1958 Nasser had taken a big step toward Arab unification by getting Syria to agree to come into a newly created United Arab Republic with Nasser as its president. Fearful of the potential power of the UAR and distrusting its dealings with the Russians, the administration was sympathetic to Lebanon's request for help in quelling a UAR uprising. Eisenhower dispatched marines to the little country at the east end of the Mediterranean; they withdrew in the fall. The real trouble at the time was in Iraq, where a rebellion in July, 1958, overthrew the pro-Western government. The new government withdrew from the Baghdad Pact but failed to join the UAR, as it was expected to do. The United States was the prime mover in 1959 in remodeling the Baghdad Pact into the Central Treaty Organization (CENTO), composed of the former Baghdad Pact members, excepting Iraq and including the United States.

The Eisenhower administration was unable to do more than maintain the American foothold in the Middle East and failed to resolve the basic conflicts, but perhaps the situation was too complex to permit a more permanent solution to the problems. The Israeli-Arab conflict, the ambitions of the Soviet Union and the Egyptian nationalists, the economic interests of American and other western oil companies, semifeudal governments and land systems, and some of the world's worst mass poverty still combine to make the Middle East a powder keg. A further difficulty was sharply divided opinion within the United States about Israel and the Arab nations. American oil companies with Middle Eastern investments wanted to maintain harmony with the Arabs; American Zionists, concentrated in states with big electoral college votes, strongly resented pro-Arab policies.

During Eisenhower's second term, Russian-American relations continued to stumble along from crisis to crisis, neither side retreating significantly from any of its positions but neither side willing to take a major risk that might set off a mutually destructive war. A "balance of terror" kept the peace, or at least the absence of war, but nothing changed fundamentally.

Clearly, the United States gained a new measure of respect for Soviet technology after the Russians put Sputnik I into the skies. The complacent assumption that American science and technology were and always would be the best in the world all but disappeared; indeed, many Americans became frantic in their talk of "crash programs" for science education. As a practical and immediate countermeasure to Soviet intercontinental rockets, Eisenhower persuaded the heads of the NATO powers at the December, 1957, meeting in Paris to agree to an arrangement whereby the United States would give intermediate range missiles to any NATO country that asked for them. (Eisenhower had suffered a mild stroke on November 25, 1957, but recovered sufficiently to attend the Paris meeting the next month.) At the same time, however, America's allies urged continued negotiation with the Russians to prevent the arms race from going on indefinitely.

Also in December, 1957, Bulganin and Eisenhower began an exchange of letters in which the Russian urged a nonaggression pact between East and West, a prohibition of nuclear testing, an agreement not to use nuclear weapons, and the establishment of a zone in central Europe in which nuclear weapons would be banned. But neither side would give an inch, and the correspondence ended with no result. Independently, however, both sides ended nuclear testing, which had produced enough radioactive fallout in the world to cause justifiable anxiety about health and genetic mutation. Khrushchev announced in the spring of 1958, after Russian scientists had apparently decided that further testing was at least for the moment of no great advantage, that his nation was stopping further bomb tests. Eisenhower announced that American tests would end for a year on October 31. Thereafter, Eisenhower extended the test ban annually. Meanwhile, Russian and American negotiators met in Switzerland for years of fruitless efforts to arrive at a mutually agreeable treaty to prohibit nuclear testing.

Khrushchev dropped a bomb shell at a press conference in Moscow in November, 1958, when he announced that the status of Berlin was out of date. He soon thereafter announced a six-month deadline, after which West Berlin would become a "free city." He would negotiate a separate peace treaty with East Germany and turn over to the East Germans control of East Berlin and access to West Berlin. This threat had the effect of more tightly uniting the West rather than dividing it, as Khrushchev had hoped, and Khrushchev became more conciliatory. He began to urge another summit meeting. Eisenhower consented at first only to a meeting of foreign ministers at Geneva. Secretary of State Christian Herter, who succeeded Dulles when the older man resigned in April, 1959, because he was fatally ill, was unable to achieve anything concrete at the Geneva meetings, but still pressure for a summit meeting grew.

Soviet Deputy Premier Anastas Mikoyan visited the United States in January, 1959; Vice-President Richard Nixon reciprocated with a visit to the Soviet Union in July. While conducting Khrushchev through the American industrial exhibit at Moscow, Nixon engaged the premier in a hot debate over the merits of communism or capitalism. In August, Eisenhower and Khrushchev announced plans for an exchange of visits, Khrushchev to visit America the following month and Eisenhower to visit Russia in 1960.

Khrushchev's thirteen-day American visit was a mixture of earnest but unsuccessful personal diplomacy, incredible press coverage, and low comedy. The visit ended with Khrushchev's staying for two days with Eisenhower at the President's retreat near Washington, Camp David. They discussed disarmament and Berlin but came to no agreements. Khrushchev dismissed any deadline for a Berlin settlement but asserted that the problem could not be left as it was indefinitely.

The face-to-face meeting of the President and the premier eased the way to another summit meeting which Prime Minister Harold Macmillan of Great Britain had long been urging. (Macmillan had succeeded Eden who

EAST.
GERMANY

retired in disgrace soon after the Suez affair.) President De Gaulle of France resisted a summit conference, but after many preliminary talks among the Western powers, the diplomats arranged for a conference at Paris in mid-May, 1960. Meanwhile, both Eisenhower and Khrushchev tried to advance their nations' interests in Asia by personal visits. Khrushchev visited India and Indonesia. Eisenhower had tremendous receptions in the Middle East and India.

Although both Khrushchev and Eisenhower went to Paris, the summit meeting never actually took place. On May 1, 1960, the Russians downed an American reconnaisance plane, the U-2, about a thousand miles within the Soviet border and captured the pilot alive. The resulting confusion would have been humorous if it had not been so dangerous. Khrushchev made the first announcement on May 5 and offered no details. Washington announced that a weather plane was missing and that it might have strayed over the Soviet border. Two days later Khrushchev told more: the pilot, Francis Gary Powers, was alive, had confessed to espionage, and had related that he began his flight in Pakistan and planned to end it in Norway. The State Department, seeing that its first story's falsity was transparent, announced that American planes had been flying over Russia but that Washington had not authorized this particular flight. Western capitals wanted to know what kind of government the United States had if the President was not aware of such a flight only days before a scheduled summit conference. Washington changed its story again. Now it reported to the press that Eisenhower had known of the Powers flight. Such fumbling did not reassure America's allies, and the flight itself was poor preparation for an international conference intended to relax cold war tensions.

At the opening meeting of the conference on May 16, Khrushchev ranted against the United States and the U-2 flight, demanded that the American government punish those responsible for the flight, rescinded the invitation for Eisenhower to visit his country, and demanded that Eisenhower apologize for the "deliberate violation of the Soviet Union." Eisenhower refused to apologize. Khrushchev refused to attend further conference meetings. The conference broke up without achieving anything but bad feelings. On his way home, Khrushchev in an East German speech seemed to retreat when he said that he believed Eisenhower still wanted peace. Perhaps Khrushchev belatedly recognized that he had overplayed his hand at Paris. When the conference began, Eisenhower had been the object of European criticism because of the U-2 flight; when it ended, the Russian premier's bumptious rudeness had turned sentiment against him.

A few weeks later the Soviets tried and convicted Pilot Powers of espionage. He served almost two years in a Russian prison. In February, 1962, to the world's surprise, Moscow and Washington traded spy prisoners, the Russians returning Powers and the Americans returning Colonel Rudolf Abel, who had been convicted of conventional espionage in New York in 1957.

After the Paris fiasco Eisenhower resumed his world travels. He visited the Philippines and South Korea, where Syngman Rhee had recently been overthrown. His visit to Japan, however, had to be canceled because of intense anti-American demonstrations instigated by Communists against the new Japanese-American security treaty to replace the one signed in 1951.

While Americans were warming up to another presidential election in the fall of 1960, the United Nations was the scene of a sort of informal summit meeting. The heads of state of many of the world's powers attended the opening of the Fifteenth General Assembly. Again Khrushchev's exuberant bad manners served to strengthen the United States, at least among its allies. He heckled other speakers and at one point even took off a shoe and used it to pound on his desk. His attacks on UN Secretary General Dag Hammarskjold attracted no new supporters. Quite obviously, whatever his vagaries, Khrushchev realized that the United States had in effect a lame duck administration and that he must await the new administration before beginning a new tack in the cold war.

CHAPTER TWENTY-SEVEN

Troubled Affluence

IF A PROPHET IN THE GRIMMEST YEARS OF THE GREAT DEPRESSION HAD predicted that within a generation the United States would be enjoying the greatest prosperity it had ever known and still be concerned about its economy, he would have been called mad. However, since the war the United States has basked in its greatest and most sustained period of prosperity; yet all has not been perfect in the economy. Economic problems since the war have been different from prewar economic problems, but they have been no less real.

The New Prosperity: How Affluent, How Stable?

In 1940, the population of the United States was about 136,500,000 and the gross national product, measured in 1959 dollars, was about $229 billion; in 1960, the population was about 180,000,000 and the gross national product, measured by the same standard, was about $500 billion. The increase in the GNP was considerably greater than the population increases. In other words, many more goods and services were available to the mythical average person in 1960 than there were in 1940. The pie had more than doubled in size while the number of people to share it had increased by only a little less than one-third. Further, as Table 11 indicates, the growth of the GNP had been fairly stable; when there was a downswing a good surge upward followed.

Statistics can become puzzling, but they are necessary in any discussion of economic matters. The statistics of prosperity were impressive. In 1940, the United States produced just under 67,000,000 tons of steel; in 1959, the figure was 93,446,000. During the same period, primary aluminum production grew

TABLE 11

	GNP in Billions of 1959 Dollars	Output per Man-Hour 1947=100
1940	229	82
1944	353	101
1945	349	105
1946	314	100
1947	314	100
1948	326	103
1949	325	108
1950	353	116
1951	380	119
1952	393	121
1953	410	126
1954	403	129
1955	436	134
1956	447	134
1957	453	138
1958	437	141
1959	480	146
1960	500	150

from 206,280 to 1,953,017 tons. Oil production almost doubled. Passenger car production in 1940 had been 3,700,000; it was 5,900,000 in 1959. In the peak auto year of 1955 it had been 7,920,186. In 1956, there were 315 passenger cars in the United States for every thousand people. Literally, the whole nation could get into its cars at one time, and in some traffic jams a reasonable man might be persuaded that it had. By the end of the 1950's, roughly one-fifth of all American families owned more than one car; at the beginning of the decade about one-tenth had. People spent more for housing and house furnishings. In 1940, they spent $51 billion and in 1959, $83.8 billion (both figures are in 1959 dollars).

Prosperity was the subjective impression as well. Foreign visitors remarked that the United States seemed more prosperous each time they came to its shores. They saw more cars on the road, people better dressed, and families better housed. Most families could look back upon the immediate pre-war or immediate postwar years and feel that they had improved themselves materially. And they had. Most of them had money in their pockets and a full stomach. Indeed, overweight was a common problem. It is valid to generalize that never before had such a large part of a national society been blessed with such an abundance of material things.

However, prosperity had not created a heaven on earth or in the United States—not even an economic one. Two basic problems persisted: distribution of income and stability of the economy. Some distribution figures illustrate what is meant. In 1935–1936 the average income of the bottom one-fifth of the families was only $607, measured in 1950 dollars. By 1950 the average family income of this group had risen to $1,080, an increase of 78 per cent. The next-to-bottom one-fifth had bettered themselves by 81 per cent, from $1,349 to $2,444. This was an obvious and most welcome improvement. Yet anyone who tried to maintain a family in 1950 on $1,080 or even $2,444 knew that it was extremely difficult to do. The Bureau of Labor Statistics in 1950 calculated that a family income of $3,717 was necessary to maintain a family of four on a "modest but adequate" budget.

In 1935–1936, this poorest one-fifth of the families had received just 4.1 per cent of the total family income, and the richest one-fifth had received 51.7 per cent. In 1950, the percentages stood at 4.8 and 45.7 respectively, and by 1958 they were 4.7 and 45.5. The distribution of personal income had actually changed very little. In other words, the improvement in the living standard of the poorest one-fifth came about because total income increased tremendously rather than because they got a significantly larger share of this total.

If figures were available to show the distribution of wages and salaries, they would show a more equitable distribution than do personal income figures. This is because stock and bond ownership was concentrated in the upper income group. A survey by the National Bureau of Economic Research, based upon an examination of estate tax returns, showed that the richest 1.6 per cent of the nation's population which held 30 per cent of the personal wealth, "owned at least 80 per cent of the corporate stock held in the personal sector, virtually all of the state and local government bonds and between 10 and 35 per cent of each other type of property."

Furthermore, personal income was not regionally well distributed. In 1959, the per capita personal income of the entire United States (total of personal income divided by population) was $2,166. In other words, the mythical average American family received that amount for each family member. State figures showed a great diversity: Connecticut, $2,817; California, $2,661; New York, $2,736; South Dakota, $1,476; Mississippi, $1,162. Examination of a time series of these statistics shows that, although the South was behind the rest of the country, its rate of growth was faster than elsewhere. But then the South had farther to go.

A breakdown of per capita personal income by counties would show considerably greater divergence than the state figures. Poor rural areas were a persistent problem. In 1960, more than 60 per cent of the rural families in the Mississippi clay hills received less than $2,000. The situation was also bad in northeast Texas, the Missouri Ozarks, and north central New Mexico. Certain industrial areas were plagued with persistent depression, all the more frustrating with the industrial prosperity so much in evidence elsewhere. The coal industry was even more depressed after 1945 than it had been in the period between the wars, and since so much coal production was in one-commodity communities unemployed miners had little opportunity at home to find work. Coal communities in Pennsylvania and West Virginia were on every dreary list of depressed areas. Towns heavily dependent upon railroading were similarly in a bad way as airplanes, cars, and trucks increasingly took business away from the once high and mighty rail companies. New England textile communities suffered as the long-term movement of the industry to the South continued.

Even when the economy as a whole boomed it seemed unable to provide full employment. In July, 1961, a time when the economy was booming and expanding, 5,140,000 American workers were unemployed. They constituted 6.9 per cent of the labor force, a staggering percentage for a prospering economy. In 1929 the unemployed had constituted only 3.1 per cent of the working force. The nature of unemployment was particularly disturbing. Labor shortages existed in many skilled occupations. The unemployed were, for the most part, the unskilled and untrained. Unskilled workers constituted only 6 per cent of the labor force, but they accounted for one-fifth of the 1,026,000 workers who had been out of work for six or more months in July, 1961. Nonwhites constituted 11 per cent of the total number of workers, but they were 25 per cent of the long-term unemployed. One-fifth of those out of work for six or more months were under twenty-five years old—mostly people who had dropped out of school and were unprepared for any kind of skilled labor. The future for these young people was not encouraging.

Yet, despite persistent unemployment, the postwar years saw a change in the composition of the American poor. Families headed by a person sixty-five years old or older in 1954 accounted for 64 per cent of all the families with incomes of less than $2,000. Most of the aged had low incomes: in 1960, 67.8 per cent of the individuals over sixty-five had incomes of less than $1,000 and 94.3 per cent of them received less than $3,000. Since the number of aged was expected to increase, there was a cause for concern. True, the aged usually had smaller family units, had double personal income tax exemptions, and frequently had savings in the form of paid-for housing and furnishings. But they also had relatively inflexible incomes in the face of steadily increasing living costs, and they generally had higher medical bills than younger adults.

Nor was the economy as stable as one would wish. There was no postwar depression approaching anything like the magnitude of the ones in 1893, 1907, or 1929 and after, but there were three disturbing recessions: 1948–1949, 1953–1954, and 1957–1958. Furthermore, the economic cycles were becoming shorter but no less severe. Although economic growth over periods as long as a decade was heartening, still individuals made most economic decisions in the short run.

Thinking people of all ideological persuasions were also concerned by the degree to which prosperity depended upon government spending or the nature of that spending. Since the war, the federal, state, and local governments have purchased roughly one-fifth of the gross national product each year. Roughly one-tenth of the national product has been armament. What if real peace and disarmament should come? In the highly unlikely event that the federal government would cut back its defense spending to zero within a year, the effect upon the economy would be cataclysmic, just as it would be if any other one-tenth of total spending should suddenly cease. Of course, if the federal government compensated for a reduction of payments for armament by an increase in spending for other purposes there would be only a temporary readjustment. But the political possibilities of spending $55 million more a year for roads, hospitals, schools, and other conventional areas of public spending is a moot point. Furthermore, schools do not become obsolete as quickly as rockets.

Despite sticky economic problems, the national mood was optimistic. Professional economists in general shared the optimism, although they pro-

571

tected themselves with guarded statements. Their argument was that economists and politicians had learned enough about how a capitalist economy functions to take effective compensatory counter action to prevent violent fluctuations of the business cycle. They also emphasized the "built-in stabilizers," such as unemployment compensation. Indeed, unemployment compensation plus privately negotiated arrangements between employers and unions had made a considerable difference.

President Walter Reuther of the United Auto Workers in the early 1950's began to demand a "guaranteed annual wage" from the auto companies. They did not consent, but the 1955 contract between the UAW and the Ford Motor Company broke new ground with supplementary unemployment benefits (SUB). The company agreed to put five cents an hour into a trust fund for each worker to be used to supplement state unemployment benefits during layoffs. Several other labor contracts adopted the Ford-UAW scheme. The 1957–1958 recession first put the SUB scheme to work on a significant scale. Donora, Pennsylvania, an industrial town of a little over twelve thousand population, had a zinc plant operated by the United States Steel Company that closed during the recession throwing 460 wage employees completely out of work. Others were on short hours. Such a percentage of idle workers normally would badly depress a town's economy, but Donora bankers reported that mortgage payments continued to be met and merchants disclosed that installment purchase loans were paid. SUB provided the unemployed from $15 to $25 a week on top of the state unemployment compensation checks which averaged $30 a week. The unemployed worker's income was nothing spectacular, but it was enough to keep him going temporarily and to keep the town's whole economy from the danger of collapse. SUB and state unemployment compensation had put a significant brake on the downward spiral that characterized the early years of the Great Depression.

Whether there were enough such stabilizers and whether government action would be compensatory enough in a severe recession was uncertain. All that was certain in the 1950's was that people did not want to think of the possibility of a depression. When Senator Homer Capehart, conservative Republican of Indiana, proposed to give the president "stand-by" controls to combat recessions, he aroused little enthusiasm in Congress, particularly in his own party. If the economists were right, a severe depression *could* be prevented; the question remained whether one *would* be.

The Supercorporations

Consternation was the general reaction when J. P. Morgan founded the United States Steel Company in 1901, the first American corporation with a capitalization of as much as $1 billion. In the 1950's, billion-dollar corporations became commonplace. The number of corporations with assets of $1 billion or more increased from twelve to twenty-seven during the decade. To become one of the hundred largest American corporations in 1949, a company had to have assets of $141 million. By 1960 such assets would place a firm only among secondary big businesses: the hundredth largest had assets of $378 million. Indeed, in 1955, the General Motors Corporation made a profit of over $1 billion on sales amounting to about $12.5 billion. The early United States Steel Company was a dwarf by comparison. In 1959, the American Telephone and Telegraph Company joined the select circle of firms who made more than $1 billion in a single year.

In the 1950's, huge corporate giants dominated almost every area of business. There were 325,000 manufacturing companies in the United States in 1955, but the fifty largest ones accounted for 27 per cent of all manufacturers' sales. The fifty biggest corporations in all fields that year had sales of $86 billion, more than one-fourth of the gross national product. General Motors alone had sales equal to 3 per cent of the GNP. The fifty largest insurance companies had 90 per cent of the assets of all insurance companies. The "Money Trust" exposed by the Pujo Committee was poverty stricken compared to some banks in the late 1950's. In 1956, there were about 14,000 banks in the country, but the real banking power lay with the 24 banks that had assets of more than $1 billion. The Bank of America in California had resources of over $9 billion and was becoming bigger all the time.

Concentration was the general rule and it was increasing. The Federal Trade Commission reported 617 mergers in 1954, 846 in 1955, and 905 in 1956. In 1958, 812 companies absorbed 1,116 other business units, and the next year 985 firms acquired 1,480 other business entities. In New York and California bank mergers were spectacular. In 1950, California had 149 separate banking firms (as compared with over 600 in economically less important Kansas), but by the end of 1955 mergers and consolidations had removed all but 63 of them. More than 60 per cent of the California banks lost their identity. It became almost routine for big companies to buy up smaller ones. In 1959 alone, 42 per cent of all American corporations in the $100 million class absorbed at least one other corporation.

Holding company pyramids came back into style. They were not as top heavy as the Insull and Van Sweringen empires of the 1920's, but they were wider in their diversity of interests. For example, a former investment banker named Gurdon W. Wattles was the key figure in building a holding company pyramid that skipped across industries. His top firms, Century Investors and Webster Investors, originally in the aircraft and cigar business respectively, controlled American Manufacturing Co., Inc., which in turn controlled the Mergenthaler Linotype Company by owning 25.5 per cent of its stock, which in turn controlled the Electric Auto-Lite Company by owning 11.2 per cent of its stock, which in turn controlled a plumbing supplies firm, the Crane Company, by owning 9.5 per cent of its stock. Every dollar invested in the two top holding companies controlled $26 to $53 in assets in the two lowest companies of the pyramid. Another pyramid, headed by the New York Dock Company, controlled firms in the cosmetics, tobacco, engraving, and sports equipment fields. Pyramids like these hardly integrated production and distribution.

But if the public was aware of the merger trend and the increased strength of the largest corporations, it did not seem to care. News on the financial page did not create more than a ripple of interest unless it concerned a company with which the public had a first-hand acquaintance (e.g., the merger of the Packard and Studebaker automobile companies in 1954 and the decision four years later to stop producing the Packard and the proposed merger of the two largest eastern railroads, the New York Central and the Pennsylvania). Bigness as such in American business aroused practically no popular opposition.

Only when the power of large corporations or combinations of them appeared to be used brazenly against the public interest did the citizen seem concerned. And then the abuse of power had to be dramatic. Senator Estes Kefauver, chairman of the Senate Judiciary Committee's Subcommittee on Antitrust and Monopoly, brought forth hundreds of pages of testimony that pointed up the degree to which price competition was a thing of the past. Kefauver was particularly concerned about the distribution of gains from increased productivity of labor. He pointed out that in the steel industry, for example, there was an average annual increase in productivity of from 3.5 to 4 per cent. Ten years ago the amount of steel it took a hundred men to produce could now be made by only sixty-eight workers. To whom should the benefits accrue? Kefauver argued that the consumer should receive part of the advantages through lower prices, that the benefits should not be divided only between management and labor through their own private haggling. But only when the Senator brought forth evidence of fantastic profits in the drug industry, ranging to as high as 1,000 per cent on a few items, did he attract much attention.

Perhaps it was indicative of the postwar American mood that sociological criticisms of the big business community evoked much more public interest than did the economic activities of corporations. One of the best sellers of the 1950's was William H. Whyte's *The Organization Man*. Whyte, a staff man on *Fortune* magazine, was highly critical of big business bureaucracy not on economic grounds but because it smothered individuality by benevolently demanding and getting a kind of conformity of individuals that he and others found debasing. Whyte's "solution" was one for individuals: they should resist The Organization from within its own confines. His book even included an appendix entitled "How to Cheat on Personality Tests." His most radical advice was that bureaucracies should try not to act like bureaucracies, a far cry from early twentieth-century demands that huge aggregations of capital and power be shattered.

Postwar Business and Government

Despite public sentiment, the antitrust laws were still on the books, and the postwar years saw two spectacular government antitrust actions: one against the DuPont Company's link with General Motors and the other against a conspiracy in restraint of trade by a group of electrical equipment manufacturers.

In 1949, the Truman administration began a suit to force a DuPont–General Motors divorce. DuPont owned 63,000,000 shares of General Motors stock, about 23 per cent of the total. In 1957, the Supreme Court ruled that the effect of this stock ownership could be "substantially to lessen competition or to tend to create a monopoly." The stock ownership, therefore, constituted a violation of the Clayton Act. The question remained, however, of how to separate the two. DuPont lawyers argued that it would be sufficient if DuPont merely denied itself the right to vote the stock. A Chicago federal district judge ruled that the law would be satisfied if DuPont kept the stock and allowed DuPont stockholders to vote it individually. The Department of Justice objected, and in May, 1960, the Supreme Court accepted the case. A year later the Court ruled that within sixty days DuPont would have to submit a plan to get rid of its General Motors stock, that the plan must be put into operation within ninety days, and that within ten years all connection must be dissolved. The problem then was how to put about $3 billion worth of General Motors stock onto the market without depressing its price and harming other investors.

In February, 1960, the Department of Justice obtained a criminal indictment from a Philadelphia grand jury against General Electric, Westinghouse, Allis-Chalmers, and some smaller electrical companies. The indictment charged the companies with conspiring to rig secret bidding. Company executives, said the indictment, met periodically to divide the market, to determine who would bid low on a given invitation for bids, and to raise prices simultaneously. On sales to privately owned utilities and to manufacturers, the government charged the defendants with working under a formula under which the corporations took turns in submitting the low bids according to "the phase of the moon." The companies subsequently pleaded *nolo contendere* which meant that they did not admit guilt but would accept the court's punishment as if they were guilty. A few corporation executives actually served short jail sentences, and the judge levied stiff fines against the offenders. Furthermore, the companies were liable to further suits from buyers who had been the victims of bidding conspiracy.

Antitrust suits, however, were out of the ordinary. Far more common were government actions to stimulate business, even to stimulate mergers. Corporation tax laws directly encouraged financially successful corporations to acquire less fortunate firms. If Corporation A had a large bill it would look favorably upon uniting with Corporation B which had a large tax credit. Many corporations with large tax credits among their assets actually went looking for companies seeking to reduce their tax bills. What business writers called "the urge to merge" was in no small part prompted by tax considerations.

Department of Defense contracts were a mighty boon to businesses, particularly to big ones who received the lion's share of defense largesse. And the Department of Defense spent the lion's share of federal expenditures. Of a total of $77,230,000,000 for government expenditures for fiscal 1960 (ending June 30, 1960), the Department of Defense accounted for $43.7 billion. Over $14 billion of this defense expenditure went for procurement of military and naval hardware; this was a market that American corporations were eager to tap.

The Pentagon was a vast bureaucracy with complicated procedures that puzzled ordinary businessmen, but knowledge of these procedures was a great advantage in getting defense contracts. Consequently, manufacturers of products that the Pentagon was likely to want hired people with experience in the Department of Defense. Many of these people were retired generals and admirals. Negotiated contracts for orders were a target of economy-minded congressional committees. Time and again committees found that the price for some small item in a negotiated contract could have been significantly lower if it had been purchased through a system of multiple bids. A few firms were almost fully dependent upon defense contracts for their livelihood. The importance of one of these, the General Dynamics Corporation, was well illustrated in a *Fortune* magazine article appropriately entitled, "General Dynamics vs. the U.S.S.R."

During the 1950's several federal regulatory agencies displayed a most sympathetic attitude toward the companies they were established to regulate. In early 1960, the House Special Subcommittee on Legislative Oversight looked into the operations of the Federal Power Commission. In questioning the chairman of the FPC, the committee's counsel elicited the information that the FPC had granted "temporary" increases in gas rates amounting to $506 million. If after investigation the FPC found that the increase in rates was not justified, the utility was to reimburse its customers, but the utility was not required to segregate the revenues gained by the "temporary" increase. Sometimes as long as six years expired before the FPC made a permanent decision. In one case, that of the Colorado Interstate Gas Company, the FPC ruled that the utility should refund $50 million to its customers, but when the company argued that to do so would mean financial disaster, the FPC lowered the refund by $12 million. (Among the witnesses, incidentally, was a figure from the past, the New Dealer Thomas G. "Tommy the Cork" Corcoran, who was then an attorney representing utilities before the FPC.)

The Eisenhower administration seemed to support the FPC's generous policies when the President refused to reappoint William R. Connole to the commission. Connole had won the reputation as the FPC's chief defender of consumer interests; Eisenhower replaced him with a man who confessed to reporters, "I've never had anything to do with utilities outside of paying my gas bill." The President's press secretary announced that Connole's release was part of a new administration policy. It had been the practice to appoint FPC members who represented different interests. Connole had favored the consumer, and three others were considered sympathetic to the utilities. Under the new policy, appointments would be made on the basis of ability rather than on interest or sympathy. *Time* magazine, which was certainly not antagonistic to business, commented, "Presumably, to make everything fair and square, the holdovers . . . are expected to forget the grounds on which they were appointed."

One of the greatest of the federal government's services to business—and one that had enormous implications for the nation's foreign relations—was the help it gave business in overseas operations and investments. The 1950's saw the greatest growth in history in American industry's investment abroad. Industry's direct investment abroad in 1950 was about $10 billion; in 1960 it was about $30 billion. Furthermore, in the last years of the 1950's, overseas investment grew at a rate of $2 billion annually. In 1960, roughly 2,800 American firms reported to the Department of Commerce that they had direct investments abroad in more than ten thousand different enterprises. Forty-five companies, about a third of them in oil, had more than half of their assets invested abroad.

How these industrial foreign investments were distributed was of more than passing interest. The largest investments in 1960, were in Canada, amounting to $10.2 billion. Next was Latin America with $8.2 billion. Venezuela was the scene of half of all American industrial investment in Latin America, mostly in oil. European investments amounted to $5.3 billion and were fairly well diversified. Middle Eastern and Asian investments totalled $2.2 billion, again mostly in oil. African investments were relatively small, only $843 million. All other areas accounted for $3 billion.

Federal policies in many ways encouraged industry to invest abroad. Tax laws made foreign investment advantageous. Although earnings by American-owned corporations abroad were liable to taxation by the host country, they were not taxable by the United States unless and until the earnings were brought home. Some countries were virtual tax havens; many of them had lower corporate income tax rates than the United States. A corporation, furthermore, could take its earnings in one foreign nation and either use them for further expansion in that country or use them in still another foreign country. If the American parent company needed to bring the money home, it had the alternative of folding up the foreign operation and paying the lower capital gains tax rather than the corporate income tax.

Some American corporations were anxious about investing in nations with an unstable political situation for fear that their investment might be expropriated or that their assets might be frozen and thereby become unavailable to the parent firm. In 1948, the new International Cooperation Administration quietly began to allay American investors' fears by offering insurance against such possibilities. The cost to the companies was one-half of 1 per cent of the amount of protection stated in the contract. For example, in 1956, the Ford Motor Company arranged to purchase 222,269 shares of stock in a French automobile firm, Simca. It also took an insurance policy with ICA under which, if the French government refused to allow Ford to convert its Simca assets, Ford could recover from ICA up to $6,987,310. The policy also guaranteed Ford up to almost $3.5 million against expropriation. Among the holders of the biggest policies against expropriation was Edwin W. Pauley, for oil exploration in Jordan. It was Pauley's proposed appointment as Undersecretary of the Navy in 1946 that had prompted Harold Ickes' resignation from the cabinet.

The Export-Import Bank increased the sales of American products abroad by lending foreign nations funds to purchase American products. Ex-Im's lending capacity increased from its original $11 million to $7 billion by 1960. Early in the Eisenhower administration, Secretary of the Treasury George Humphrey tried to shut down Ex-Im, arguing that the government should not be in the banking business. But when he came to see that Ex-Im loans were a considerable aid to American industry and that the default rate on the loans was less than 1 per cent, Humphrey helped Ex-Im to expand its operations. In 1959 alone, Ex-Im lent $535.9 million. It became the primary United States lending institution to Latin America.

In 1959 and 1960, the federal government began to become concerned about its deteriorating position in the international balance of payments. For years and years American exports had been greater than imports, but throughout the 1950's American payments abroad exceeded foreign payments in the

United States. The United States advantage of exports over imports was more than lost by foreign aid programs, maintenance of American troops abroad, American tourist spending abroad, and corporate foreign investments. Foreign nations took part of their net gain in gold and a larger part in the form of dollar deposits in New York banks. By 1960 those dollar deposits had reached the point where they almost equalled the remaining United States gold supply.

The United States had several alternatives or combinations of alternatives. What it did was to cut back dollar spending abroad by cutting the duty-free imports that American tourists could bring into the country and reduce the number of families allowed to be with their overseas servicemen husband-fathers. Reducing the dollar gap by separating servicemen's families produced a great political outcry, and one of the first actions in the administration of President John F. Kennedy was to rescind the order. The government also made an effort to increase foreign spending in the United States by a campaign to increase the numbers of foreign tourists in this country and, more important, to widen the gap of American exports over imports.

The Departments of State and Commerce announced plans to double the number of their personnel engaged in the promotion of American exports. The State Department would increase to 225 the number of commercial attachés abroad whose function primarily was to develop the United States export business. The Commerce Department would put a greater effort on informing American firms of export possibilities. Ex-Im was authorized to grant short-term loans to exporters. When exporters went to private banks to arrange credit for a foreign sale they frequently found bankers unwilling to run the risk of possible foreign currency revaluation or nationalization. American manufacturers, therefore, urged foreign customers to arrange their own financing. West Germany and Great Britain granted purchasers of their exports better credit terms than the foreign purchaser could get from his bank where he was often forced to go to finance an American purchase. Now the Export-Import Bank would provide short-term financing in order to increase American exports and thereby help correct the international balance of payments.

Through such devices as these the government of the United States stimulated American business abroad. By the end of the 1950's, Americans who went abroad noticed that they could purchase many of the same brands they bought at home. Foreign grocery stores were stocked with American corn flakes and soap, and Coca-Cola was almost as ubiquitous abroad as it was in America. More and more American corporations that had traditionally done most of their business at home devoted a greater part of their efforts to foreign operations. In 1949, the foreign subsidiaries of the Colgate Palmolive Company had sales of $86,963,000; the parent company's home sales amounted to $203,996,000. In 1958, the sales of the foreign subsidiaries had gone up to $262,725,000; the domestic sales had increased only to $271,322,000.

The trend to international operations was nothing new; it only became greatly accelerated after World War II. Just as the period after the Civil War had been one in which American business became national in scope, in the mid-twentieth century business was becoming increasingly international—and bigger.

Unions in Postwar America

In the 1930's and early 1940's, trade unionism in the United States came into its own. It was a period of unparalleled union growth both in numbers and in economic and political strength. It was also, however, a fighting time and a lean time. Unions became strong through almost constant exercise. They won their power; it was not given to them. The life of most labor officials was a hard one. Dedicated to the vision of a labor force that would not have to wear the employer's collar, labor officials often exposed themselves to physical danger, were economically insecure, and had much the same living standard as the shop workers they organized.

A visit to AFL-CIO headquarters in Washington in the late 1950's indicated a fatter, more comfortable labor movement than there had been before the war. There was nothing about the building itself, a sleek, modern affair, to distinguish it from any other office building except the sign over the door. The building's elevators had piped-in music. Nor was there much to distinguish the offices and their inhabitants from any other business office. The personnel could as well have been selling soap or editing a magazine. If the accepted symbols of power and affluence were a valid guide, the American labor movement had fully arrived.

But there was a paradox: without shifting its goals or its methods, American unionism had both become important and begun to stagnate. It was stable and comfortable in the industries it had organized in the earlier era, but it did not expand into other fields.

Most of American union growth had come about while the AFL and the CIO were at one another's throats. By a few years after the war, the issues that had once divided the two big labor groups had largely disappeared. The birth of the CIO had ended the supine complacency that had once characterized the AFL; industrial unionism versus craft organization had become an outdated issue; most of the leadership in both camps had come around to the dominant CIO view that labor's political fortunes resided with the Democratic party. The deaths of Philip Murray and William Green in November, 1952, removed a great deal of the personality conflict that had brought about the division, and the two houses of labor began to come together.

The new head of the CIO, Walter Reuther of the United Auto Workers, and the new head of the AFL, George Meany of the plumber's union, began to work to bring about a reunion. They set up committees to work out differences. The toughest problem was raiding of one another's membership. A joint AFL and CIO committee recommended approval of a no-raiding pact which forbade attempts to sign up workers in a shop already in a union that was recognized or certified as the bargaining agent. Where disputes arose, both unions would agree to accept the decision of an impartial umpire. In the fall of 1953, the AFL and CIO conventions ratified the no-raiding agreement; it became effective in mid-1954.

Almost immediately Reuther and Meany moved on toward full reunion. In February, 1955, a joint committee agreed upon terms of a merger. At the end of the year both conventions voted for merger by overwhelming votes, and in December the American Federation of Labor–Congress of Industrial Organizations was born. The new organization had about 15,000,000 members, two-thirds of them from former AFL organizations.

Ever since World War II the ratio of union members to the total civilian labor force has remained about the same, about one to three. That is, roughly one-fourth of American workers have belonged to trade unions. In view of organized labor's unity, its bigger bank balances, and its general acceptance by employers in industries where it was well established, why did it not grow during an era of prosperity? The question involves most aspects of recent American labor history.

TABLE 12

UNION MEMBERSHIP, 1945–1958

Year	Union Membership	Civilian Labor Force	Percentage of Unionized Civilian Labor Force
1945	13,379,000	53,860,000	24.8
1946	13,648,000	57,520,000	23.7
1947	14,845,000	60,128,000	24.7
1948	14,916,000	61,442,000	24.3
1949	14,960,000	62,105,000	24.1
1950	14,751,000	63,099,000	23.4
1951	16,211,000	62,884,000	25.8
1952	16,730,000	62,966,000	26.6
1953	17,884,000	63,815,000	28.0
1954	17,757,000	64,468,000	25.7
1955	17,749,000	65,847,000	27.0
1956	18,477,000	67,530,000	27.4
1957	18,430,000	67,946,000	27.1
1958	18,081,000	68,647,000	26.3

From Irving Bernstein, "The Growth of American Unions, 1945–1960," Labor History, II (Spring, 1961). 135.

First, it is clear that organized labor's failure to grow significantly and relatively was not due to declining power in its established areas. Whatever employers wished (most of them were fairly well satisfied with unionized shops after they got used to them) union members were determined that their organizations would not be blasted to bits after World War II as they had been in the early 1920's. In the first four years of the Taft-Hartley Act, 1947–1951, unions won 97 per cent of the NLRB elections over the right to sign a union shop agreement. In the few cases (usually less than twenty a year and involving only small numbers of employees) over the issue of abolishing an already existing union shop, the unions won about one-third of the elections.

However, in many of the traditionally unionized industries, automation or further mechanization significantly reduced the total number of employees and thereby reduced trade union membership. Between 1940 and 1957 the percentage of the labor force in all manufacturing in the United States actually engaged in production dropped from 78.5 to 71.7. Due to increased productivity per man-hour, fewer and fewer Americans were engaged in actual production of any kind—manufacturing, mining, or agriculture. Unionism traditionally was for employees who worked with their hands, and the number of such people declined. In 1919, 61 per cent of all employees in nonagricultural employment were manual workers; in 1930 manual workers constituted 52 per cent, in 1950 the figure had fallen to 49 per cent and in 1959 to 45 per cent. In other words, blue collars were becoming increasingly scarce. The statistics in certain strongly unionized industries reveal the effects of increased productivity through technological advancement. From 1937 through 1960, steel production rose 171.7 per cent, but the number of steel workers engaged in production and maintenance declined 10 per cent. In 1937, 421,788 coal miners produced 445,000,000 tons; in 1960, 197,000 miners produced 410,000,000 tons. Daily output per miner increased from 4.69 tons in 1937 to almost 13 in 1961. Production of electrical machinery increased 21 per cent from 1953 to 1956, but the number of production workers in the industry declined from 925,000 to 836,000. The implications for trade unionism in these fields were obvious. Less obvious but no less real and prickly were the implications for full employment and a level of mass purchasing power consistent with economic health.

Political barriers were a handicap to labor's efforts to expand. Nineteen states, most of them primarily agricultural and without an important labor movement, adopted "right to work" laws barring union shops and prohibiting union membership as a requirement for employment. Other states so restricted picketing as to make successful striking difficult if the employer tried to run in strikebreakers. The Taft-Hartley Act and interpretations of it hampered union activity more than state law. The Wagner Act had prohibited employers from any kind of coercion of employees to keep them from joining a union or voting against a union in a National Labor Relations Board election, and the NLRB had interpreted the law quite strictly. The Taft-Hartley Act removed many of these restrictions, and the NLRB, particularly the members appointed by President Eisenhower, approved employer antiunion activities that would never have been sanctioned by the old board. The Eisenhower-appointed NLRB, for example, ruled that it was legal procedure for management to announce that if the union won an election the plant would be closed. Well-established unions suffered little from Taft-Hartley and NLRB decisions, but gaining a foothold in shops against the employers' wishes became extremely difficult.

Certainly a shift in public opinion about labor unions handicapped their continued growth. During the depression and the war, majority public opinion had been behind labor organization. Antiunion sentiment was based to a considerable extent on the belief that unions were too radical, too socialist or Communist. In 1949 and 1950 the CIO effectively removed Communist leadership from its unions, and ideological antiunion sentiment declined. But soon thereafter large parts of the public came to believe that labor organizations should be curbed either because they abused their power or because they were dominated by crooks or both. "Big labor" and "labor racketeers" became stereotypes with which responsible and honest unions had to contend.

Bad actors in the labor movement tarnished labor's general reputation even when the majority of labor, as represented by its national federations, condemned them. For example, in the winter of 1961–1962, the New York City unit of the International Brotherhood of Electrical Workers used its power in that city's construction industry, which was thriving, to wrest from employers a twenty-five hour week. Rather than a genuine demand for a shorter work week, the demand was only a ruse to get more overtime pay. Leaders of the AFL-CIO, powerless to overrule their constituent, publicly stated their opposition, but the newspaper editorials concentrated upon the grab rather than AFL-CIO opposition to it.

Gangsters and other crooks in a few unions gave all labor a black eye. In the early 1950's, the New York Crime Commission exposed the International Longshoremen's Association as dominated by racketeers who ruled the waterfront by terror. The AFL expelled the ILA and set up a new union for dockworkers, but in NLRB elections the workers three times rejected the new AFL unit in favor of the ILA. The International Brotherhood of Teamsters was a bigger headache. This huge union, the nation's biggest, dominated first by Dave Beck and then by Jimmy Hoffa, was atypical of the vast majority of American unions in its lack of internal democracy, its ties with disreputable figures from the underworld, and its leadership's affiliation with the Republican party. In February, 1957, the AFL-CIO adopted a code of ethical practices aimed largely at the Teamsters and in December of that year expelled them. But the public still seemed to think of all labor leaders as corrupt.

Agricultural Plenty and Farm Troubles

Bryanite agrarian orators used to make much of the argument that the cities were dependent upon agriculture for their well being, that the farmer could live without his urban cousin but the city-dweller could not live without the farmer. But by mid-century the story was different. The situation had not exactly reversed itself, but most urban food consumers were doing very well and most farmers were in trouble.

Prices in grocery stores shot up spectacularly with the end of price controls after the war, but the price curve began to level off in late 1947. After that, consumer food prices rose less than most other items in the cost-of-living index. Americans spent less of their income for food than ever before in their history. In 1959, they spent 21 per cent of their income on food, while the rest of the world spent approximately half of its income for its daily bread. And the people of the United States were eating better too— perhaps too much better judging from the number of "reducing studios" that dotted the country. In 1935, the per capita consumption of meat was 127 pounds, of poultry 16 pounds, and of dairy products 393 pounds; in 1959 the figures were 160, 35, and 428 pounds respectively. In 1959, an hour's work would buy seventeen pints of milk as compared to eight in 1929, three dozen oranges as opposed to fifteen, and a little over two pounds of round steak as compared with one pound four ounces.

But most of the farmers who kept this cornucopia filled to overflowing did not fare very well after the war. In 1959, the farm population's per capita income was only $965; nonfarm per capita income that year was $2,216. In 1945, farm mortgages totalled $4,940,915,000; the mortgage total in 1960 stood at $12,288,759,000. A special farm census in 1959 counted 3,700,000 farms in the United States. On an estimated 1,600,000 of them, gross sales were less than $10,000 a year, not enough to provide a net family income of $2,500.

With farm prices what they were, only very efficient farm units could return enough profit over the year to support a family adequately, and only big farm units were really efficient. In other words, the optimum farm unit's capital, both in land and in equipment, became steadily bigger. Barring a reversal of the long-term trend, over the long run those farmers whose production units were too far below the optimum size and capitalization to make ends meet had no alternative but to get out of agriculture. The flight from the farm, which had been going on for a long time, became almost a mass migration in the 1950's. The number of farms declined by a million from 1954 to 1959. An average of eight hundred thousand people a year left the farm in the 1950's. Total population during that decade increased by a fifth, but the farm population decreased by a fifth. In the three decades preceding 1959, more people left the farm than remained on the land. The greatest number of those leaving were young people who figured that their chances of economic comfort were better in the cities and towns than they were on the farm. The amount of capital necessary to begin farming was too great for young men who did not inherit already profitable farms. Even those who stayed on the land increasingly supplemented their farm incomes with nonfarm work. In 1959, 30 per cent of all farm operators worked off the farm for one hundred days or more.

The central fact of the problem was the technological revolution on the farm. Consumers bought more food and fiber than they had only a few years previously and with a smaller fraction of their whole income, but these commodities had been produced by fewer farmers. Each farmer could feed more consumers. From 1937 to 1941, the average yield of wheat per acre was 14.5 bushels. In 1955 it was 19.8 bushels. In 1958, due mostly to the "nitrogen revolution" in fertilizing, yield per acre of wheat averaged 27 bushels nationally.

Society, as represented by the federal government, had two choices with the farm problem. In order not to subsidize inefficient production it could, at one extreme, leave agriculture to the vicissitudes of an absolutely free market and let the farm population shake itself down until only the large and efficient producers were left. The costs of the shaking-down process to those who would be omitted would be considerable. Or, if society sufficiently valued the continued existence of the family farm, it could vastly increase its agricultural subsidies and more intelligently direct them toward the family farm unit. The government's actual program involved spending billions of dollars (in 1960 about $9 billion), but is was not saving the family farm.

The government's wheat program, which took about a third of all agricultural subsidies, illustrated the problem. In 1954, the government set a maximum of 55,000,000 acres in wheat production, and wheat farmers voted to accept the government's program. But production increased because of the increased yields per acre, and the government each year bought an increased amount of wheat. Despite the Agricultural Domestic Trade and Development Assisstance Act of 1954, which provided for sales of wheat abroad in foreign currencies (many of which could not be converted to dollars) and for foreign gifts of wheat, the amount of government-owned wheat in storage grew steadily. The wheat was sealed in grain elevators and mothballed ships all over the country. In 1960, the government had 1,379,000,000 bushels of wheat in storage. The storage costs alone were about $1.5 million a day. (In 1960, one storage company, the C-F-G Grain Company, received government payments of $23,470,634.) The wheat surplus in 1960, if converted into bread, would have provided 450 one-pound loaves for every person in the nation. Yet thousands of wheat farmers were marginal and thousands of others left the farm altogether. Wheat subsidies saved many farmers from ruin, but they also helped many large and efficient producers.

Such large subsidies offered ripe opportunity for graft, and in 1962 the case of Billie Sol Estes, a west Texas agricultural plunger, focused national attention on the farm subsidy issue. Estes made his original big capital in the surplus wheat storage business and built a huge but flimsily constructed agricultural empire. His business fell to pieces when some of his creditors discovered that the liquid fertilizer tanks that he had put up as collateral for loans were mostly fictional. Investigations by a congressional committee and the Department of Agriculture revealed that Estes had bribed farmers to acquire their acreage allotments and had unethically influenced regional cotton allotment committee members for the same purpose. Estes went bankrupt and faced a series of criminal indictments. But the public, for the most part, saw the case only as an example of personal evil, rather than realizing that the nature of the whole farm subsidy system, given the usual state of mankind's morals, made such a case almost inevitable. With this general public view, the nature of the dominant farm organizations (which reflect the attitudes of the big and successful producers), and the political influence of the farm vote, a wise political solution of the farm problem seemed unlikely.

CHAPTER TWENTY-EIGHT

The American People and Their Culture

PERHAPS THE MOST SPECTACULAR ASPECT OF THE AMERICAN PEOPLE in the middle years of the century was their great and growing number. The 1940 census counted 131,669,275 people in the United States. The count in 1950 was 151,325,798, an increase of 14.5 per cent. The census of 1960 showed a population of 179,323,175, an increase of 18.5 per cent in the decade. (Many demographers, incidentally, calculate that census figures should be increased about 3 per cent.) The population increase between 1940 and 1960 was about equal to the total population of 1880.

Predictions about population often have been inaccurate, but experts predicted the population of the United States would continue to increase at a faster rate, topping two hundred million in 1970 and perhaps three hundred million by the beginning of the twenty-first century. Population prophets, who assumed continued prosperity, based their expectations upon the strong tendency of couples to marry younger than was usual before World War II, upon the trend toward more children in families in middle-income brackets, and upon a longer life expectancy.

As remarkable as the increased number of Americans was the mobility of all these people. In the late 1950's, according to some surveys, one-fifth of the population changed address each year. Quite obviously, some of the moves were long ones. Between 1950 and 1960 the population of the Pacific states increased 40.2 per cent and the Mountain states 35.1 per cent. Florida's growth was the greatest by percentage, 78.7, but California with an almost 50 per cent increase and a growth of over five million had the largest absolute population increase.

Census figures amply illustrated that the United States was an overwhelmingly urban nation. In 1960, about 111,700,000 Americans lived in areas

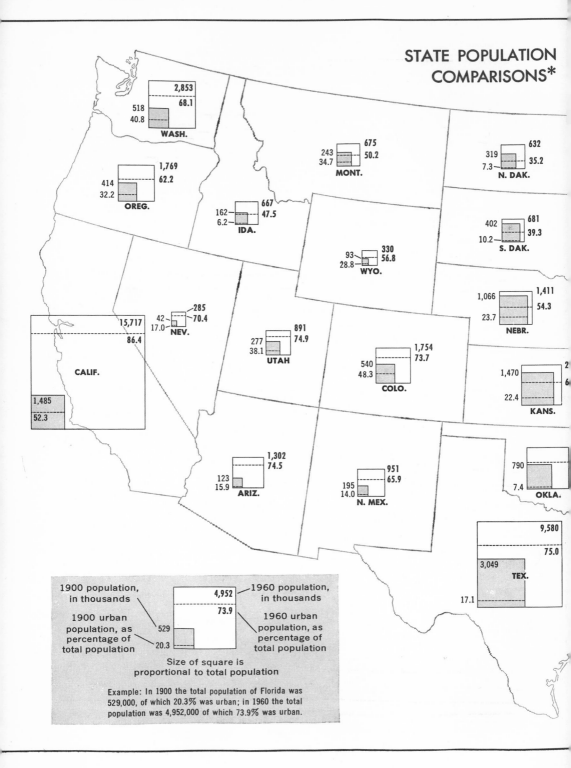

STATE POPULATION COMPARISONS*

WASH.
2,853
68.1
518
40.8

OREG.
1,769
62.2
414
32.2

MONT.
675
50.2
243
34.7

N. DAK.
632
35.2
319
7.3

IDA.
667
47.5
162
6.2

S. DAK.
681
39.3
402
10.2

WYO.
330
56.8
93
28.8

NEBR.
1,411
54.3
1,066
23.7

NEV.
285
70.4
42
17.0

UTAH
891
74.9
277
38.1

COLO.
1,754
73.7
540
48.3

KANS.
2
6
1,470
22.4

CALIF.
15,717
86.4
1,485
52.3

ARIZ.
1,302
74.5
123
15.9

N. MEX.
951
65.9
195
14.0

OKLA.
790
7.4

TEX.
9,580
75.0
3,049
17.1

1900 population, in thousands
1960 population, in thousands
1900 urban population, as percentage of total population
1960 urban population, as percentage of total population
4,952
73.9
529
20.3
Size of square is proportional to total population

Example: In 1900 the total population of Florida was 529,000, of which 20.3% was urban; in 1960 the total population was 4,952,000 of which 73.9% was urban.

Urban, Rural, and Totals
1900 and 1960

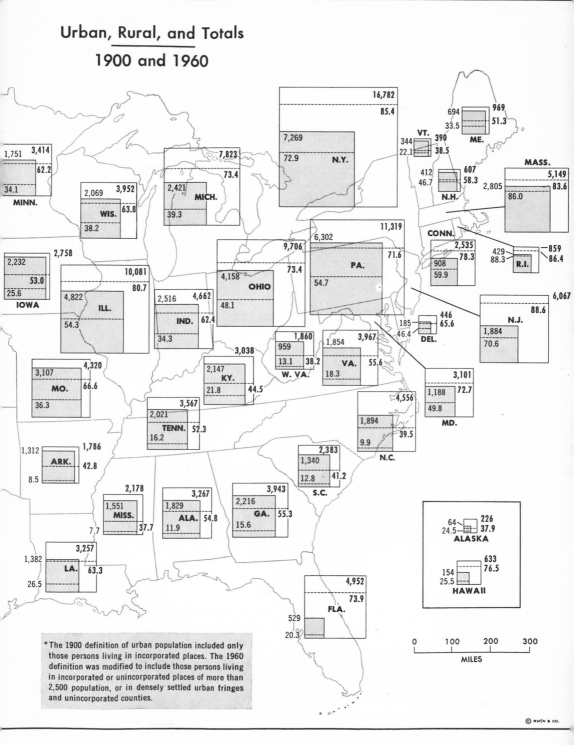

MINN. 1,751 3,414 / 62.2 / 34.1

WIS. 2,069 3,952 / 63.8 / 38.2

MICH. 2,421 7,823 / 73.4 / 39.3

N.Y. 16,782 / 85.4 / 7,269 72.9

VT. 344 390 / 38.5 / 22.1

ME. 694 969 / 51.3 / 33.5

N.H. 412 607 / 58.3 / 46.7

MASS. 2,805 5,149 / 83.6 / 86.0

CONN. 2,535 / 78.3 / 908 59.9

R.I. 429 859 / 86.4 / 88.3

IOWA 2,232 2,758 / 53.0 / 25.6

ILL. 4,822 10,081 / 80.7 / 54.3

OHIO 4,158 9,706 / 73.4 / 48.1

PA. 6,302 11,319 / 71.6 / 54.7

N.J. 1,884 6,067 / 88.6 / 70.6

DEL. 185 446 / 65.6 / 46.4

IND. 2,516 4,662 / 62.4 / 34.3

W. VA. 959 1,860 / 38.2 / 13.1

VA. 1,854 3,967 / 55.6 / 18.3

MD. 1,188 3,101 / 72.7 / 49.8

MO. 3,107 4,320 / 66.6 / 36.3

KY. 2,147 3,038 / 44.5 / 21.8

TENN. 2,021 3,567 / 52.3 / 16.2

N.C. 1,894 4,556 / 39.5 / 9.9

ARK. 1,312 1,786 / 42.8 / 8.5

MISS. 1,551 2,178 / 37.7 / 7.7

ALA. 1,829 3,267 / 54.8 / 11.9

GA. 2,216 3,943 / 55.3 / 15.6

S.C. 1,340 2,383 / 41.2 / 12.8

LA. 1,382 3,257 / 63.3 / 26.5

FLA. 529 4,952 / 73.9 / 20.3

ALASKA 64 226 / 37.9 / 24.5

HAWAII 154 633 / 76.5 / 25.5

0 100 200 300
MILES

*The 1900 definition of urban population included only those persons living in incorporated places. The 1960 definition was modified to include those persons living in incorporated or unincorporated places of more than 2,500 population, or in densely settled urban fringes and unincorporated counties.

© RM̥N & CO.

587

of over 50,000 people. Indeed, nearly half of the population lived in ten great population clusters. The biggest of these was one supercity that extended from the New Hampshire–Massachusetts border south to the metropolitan Washington area of Virginia. More than 31,000,000 people lived in this contiguous belt of cities and suburbs, 17.5 per cent of the national total. The nine other huge clusters were from Albany to Syracuse, New York; Pittsburgh to Youngstown, Ohio; Detroit and environs; Chicago and other cities near Lake Michigan in Indiana and Wisconsin as well as Illinois; the Miami area; Houston east to the Gulf of Mexico; the Dallas–Fort Worth district; the San Francisco Bay area; and greater Los Angeles. Add to these metropolitan clusters such relatively isolated cities as Cleveland, St. Louis, New Orleans, San Antonio, Seattle, San Diego, Buffalo, Cincinnati, Memphis, Denver, Atlanta, and Minneapolis–St. Paul and it will be seen that the average American of 1960 lived in or near a city of over five hundred thousand.

Simultaneous with the urban movement was a sharp increase in the number and population of suburbs. Some large cities—New York, Chicago, Philadelphia, and Cleveland, for example—actually lost population in the 1950's. But their suburban growth was tremendous. In the 211 American urban areas of over fifty thousand population, which had 85 per cent of the national population increase in the 1950's, the growth of the central cities was only 9 per cent between 1950 and 1960. Population growth in the suburbs within these areas was about 48 per cent.

The Negro's Battle: Against Segregation, for Equal Opportunity

About 1940 the American Negro began a militant campaign for equal rights that has not yet diminished and seems likely to continue until the battle is won. One of the most dramatic chapters of recent social history has been the Negro community's determined drive to achieve full first-class citizenship.

The advances toward equality that Negroes won during and after World War II can be attributed to many causes. Clearly, one of the most important was the improved, but by no means rosy, economic condition of the Negroes. With migration out of the South, better chances for employment whether in the South or elsewhere, and better wages, the Negro to a greater degree than ever before freed himself from the direct economic dependence on others that had long kept him from asserting himself. But there were many other factors. Although measuring prejudice is at best an elusive task, it seems highly likely that color prejudice has been in retreat ever since about World War I. As fewer and fewer Caucasians, both North and South, believed that Negroes because they were Negroes should be denied equal opportunity, the resistance to the Negro's march became weaker and his march accelerated. Undoubtedly, the cold war had something to do with the lesser resistance of the whites. If America's democracy were to be its chief social advantage over its ideological enemies, and if it were to gain the respect and cooperation of the newly politically important colored peoples of the world, then the colored people of the United States would have to share in American democracy to a greater extent than ever they had before.

Desegregation of the armed forces was one of the quickest and quietest revolutions in racial matters the United States ever experienced. As late as December 8, 1941, the War Department notified a conference of Negroes at Washington that the army would take no step to alter its racial practices. It would practice the segregation of American civilian society. "The Army is not a sociological laboratory; to be effective it must be organized and trained according to principles which will insure success. . . ." In the postwar decade, however, largely in the pursuit of effectiveness, the army in fact became a sociological laboratory.

In November, 1945, a special army board submitted a report on the Negro in the army that urged the abolition of separate Negro divisions but called for continued segregation at company and battalion levels. But the board, for the first time, also recommended that in the event of another war personnel assignments should be made only on the basis of qualification and merit and that race should be ignored. A second special committee on racial matters in the armed forces reported in the fall of 1948 that the services would be strengthened by the adoption of a "policy of equality of treatment and opportunity," and soon before the election President Truman ordered that such a policy "shall be put into effect as rapidly as possible, having due regard to the time required to effectuate any necessary changes without impairing efficiency or morale." Except for the air force, desegregation proceeded slowly. The target date for desegregation in the armed forces was June 30, 1954, but the Korean conflict hastened the process. Base commanders, confronted with the task of training thousands of draftees, decided their task would be simplified if they disregarded race, and most training camps desegregated, even in the South. In Korea, army officers began to put Negro replacements into all-white units and found that the Negro soldier fought better when he was not segregated. Behind the lines, demand for technical specialists required that the best available man be used regardless of his color. By the end of the Korean War little segregation remained in the armed forces.

Perhaps the most remarkable aspect of military desegregation was that there were very few incidents of racial conflict. Even southern rural white draftees took close order drill from Negro training sergeants without violent objection. There were apparently two reasons for the quick acceptance of military desegregation: military discipline required obedience to orders and whites who otherwise would have strongly resisted eating at the same mess table with a Negro found that, when ordered to do so, the world did not come to an end; and white soldiers accepted desegregation as part of the "army way," not dissimilar to the practice of tucking one's necktie into the shirt between the second and third buttons.

Desegregation in schools, however, was the hottest racial issue in postwar America. As early as 1938, the Supreme Court began to define equality under the 1896 Plessy v. Ferguson doctrine of "separate but equal" facilities in such a way as to pave the way for the reversal of the doctrine. In that year the Court ruled that Missouri, because it provided a state law school for whites, must provide legal education for Negroes as well. In 1950, in Sweatt v. Painter the Court gave the opinion that the law school of the University of Texas, a state institution, must admit a Negro because the state law school for Negroes that Texas provided was not substantially equal in quality. As postwar prosperity made greater public instruction expenditures easier and as it became apparent that the courts were beginning to enforce the "equal" part of the "separate but equal" doctrine, many segregated school districts tried to close the quality gap between their white and Negro schools. In 1940, the capital outlay per Negro pupil in eight southern states was only 23 per cent as much as that for whites; by 1952 the amount had increased to 82 per cent. In the wealthier southern communities with relatively small Negro populations, the quality of education in white and Negro public schools became as nearly equal as money in a brief time could make it, but in less fortunate school districts it was a cruel joke to speak of racial parity in education. A number of southern state universities abolished segregation in their graduate schools, but educational deficiencies earlier in life prevented most Negroes from having the qualifications necessary for graduate study.

In its historic decision of May 17, 1954, the Supreme Court overturned the Plessy v. Ferguson precedent. The Court considered several suits together so as to cover all constitutional aspects of school segregation; the most important of them was Brown v. Board of Education of Topeka. Earl Warren, former governor of California and Thomas E. Dewey's running mate in 1948 who had been appointed Chief Justice in 1953 when Fred M. Vinson died, spoke for the unanimous Court: "We conclude that in the field of public education the doctrine of 'separate but equal' has no place. Separate educational facilities are inherently unequal. Therefore, we hold that the plaintiffs . . . are, by reason of the segregation complained of, deprived of the equal protection of the laws guaranteed by the Fourteenth Amendment." In other words, the laws of the seventeen states that required public school segregation and of the four states that permitted local school districts to segregate were unconstitutional. On May 31, 1955, the Court, again unanimously, ruled further that federal courts "will require that the defendants make a prompt and reasonable start toward full compliance with our May 17, 1954, ruling." If local school boards thought additional time necessary before beginning desegregation, the burden of proof lay upon them; it was the responsibility of the school boards "to establish that such time is necessary in the public interest and is consistent with good faith compliance at the earliest practicable date."

Resistance to the Court's decision was considerable. Delaware and the District of Columbia integrated their schools promptly. The former border states began the gradual desegregation the Court had recommended. The former Confederate states were slower. In the 1960–1961 school year, 3,500 of the 288,900 Negro pupils in Texas were in integrated public schools; Oklahoma had 10,520 out of 40,900; Virginia had 170 out of 211,000; North Carolina had 50 out of 319,000; and Florida had 755 out of 201,100. Only four of the 287,000 Negro public school students in Louisiana were in mixed classes, and Mississippi, Alabama, Georgia, and South Carolina had not integrated at all.

Resistance to desegregation took many forms. Some state legislatures passed resolutions declaring that the Court's decision itself was unconstitutional, and, reviving the thought of John C. Calhoun, raised the constitutional theory of "interposition." What, if anything, this theory meant in practice remained to be seen. Other states authorized local school boards, if ordered by a court to desegregate, to close up shop and use public funds for segregated private schools, an action that surely would meet with constitutional disapproval. In March, 1956, a group of southern members of Congress—nineteen Senators and eighty-one Representatives—issued the "Southern Manifesto" to state their intent to reverse the Court's decision. Most of the headlines, however, went to the extralegal and illegal and sometimes violent actions of rabidly segregationist organizations and their members. White supremacists in some communities revived the Ku Klux Klan, but far more common were the White Citizens Councils. Almost each September as schools opened there was some kind of mass demonstration and violence over a school recently desegregated by court order. The most spectacular conflict was at Little Rock, Arkansas.

Some school districts in northern Arkansas had already desegregated when the trouble began in Little Rock, the state capital. In 1955, Little Rock's school board set up a desegregation schedule that called for registration of Negro students in previously all-white high schools in September, 1957. The federal court approved the plan. School administrators carefully selected a handful of Negro youngsters to be the first to attend Central High School. A group of white segregationists obtained from a state court an injunction to prevent the high school's integration, and during the court proceedings Governor Orval Faubus testified that the admittance of Negro students into mixed classes in Little Rock would bring about mob violence. The federal district court overruled the state court and issued injunctions to prevent any hampering of the already approved desegregation plan.

Apparently sensing political advantage among the white voters of Arkansas, Governor Faubus ordered national guard units to surround Central High School ostensibly to "maintain order." When the Negro pupils who were to register at the school approached the building, the national guardsmen turned them away. The school board asked the presiding judge of the federal district court for a delay, but the judge refused. When the troops continued to prevent the Negroes' entrance, the judge summoned the governor to appear before his court ten days later. Governor Faubus conferred with President Eisenhower at Newport, Rhode Island, where Eisenhower was on vacation. Just what happened at their conference was not made public, but Faubus backed down part way. He did not appear in court, but he complied with the court's injunction to remove the national guardsmen. On the first school day after the withdrawal of the state troops, Little Rock police surrounded the building. Nine Negro students were slipped into the building via a back door, and the fireworks began. An angry mob, upon hearing the news, rushed the building and were only barely turned back by police. The mob beat some Negro newspaper reporters. Photographs of the mob appeared in newspapers all over the world.

Long under fire for not taking action to ensure the edicts of the federal court, President Eisenhower at last acted after the mob scene of September 23, 1957. He issued a proclamation ordering all obstruction to the court order to stop at once, nationalized the state troopers to take them out of the Governor's control, and dispatched a thousand officers and men of an airborne division to Little Rock. On September 25, the Negro students went to school

591

in army vehicles. A mob formed again around the school, but the paratroopers kept it under control. Slowly the hatreds and passions of Little Rock subsided, and as they cooled the soldiers were withdrawn slowly. Early in December, the last soldiers were ordered away. The nine children attended desegregated classes without further important incident. Two years later, four other senior high schools in Little Rock desegregated without trouble.

The sharpest conflict between the federal government and a state since Appomattox erupted in the fall of 1962 when James Meredith, a twenty-nine-year-old Negro air force veteran of Mississippi, endeavored to enroll at the University of Mississippi, to which he contributed in taxes as a citizen of the state. After having exhausted all legal delays, the administration of Governor Ross Barnett, which had taken over the conduct of the matter from University officials, refused Meredith entrance to the campus when he arrived with federal marshals bearing a court order for Meredith's University registration. The federal Court of Appeals at New Orleans found Barnett in contempt and granted him four days to purge himself by permitting Meredith's registration and maintaining law and order so that the new student could remain at the University. Failure to comply before the deadline would cost Barnett $10,000 a day besides arrest.

The Governor backed down part way, and early on Sunday evening, September 30, federal marshals slipped Meredith into the campus and into a dormitory room. The next morning Meredith registered; he began to attend classes following his registration. But on the critical Sunday night, while President Kennedy was addressing the nation on television, an angry mob of students and white segregationists, who had converged from all over the South, indulged themselves in an ugly riot against the federal marshals and the federalized national guard. The mob employed "Molotov cocktails," bricks, and a few conventional arms. A French journalist and a townsman who was merely observing the riot were killed. Edwin A. Walker, a former army major general and a right-wing extremist who had resigned from the army after the Pentagon reprimanded him for his troop indoctrination program and who had run badly in the Texas gubernatorial primary a few months before, was a leader of the mob. He and twenty-three others were arrested. Regular army troops dispatched by Washington soon brought an end to the violence in the once-sleepy town of Oxford that had been William Faulkner's home.

In any showdown of strength between the states and the federal judiciary and executive, the states are almost always the loser, and the kind of defiance that Faubus and then Barnett displayed can only further complicate and trouble an already complex and emotional issue. Increasing numbers of white southerners, especially after Mississippi began token integration with Meredith, hoped that the process of integration would continue to be slow but accepted it as inevitable.

No school board outside the former slave areas segregated Negroes as Negroes after the May 17, 1954, Court decision. Some of them, however, gerrymandered school attendance districts so as to segregate Negro students in actual fact. The problem was a difficult one since it was held generally desirable for students, particularly in elementary school, to attend schools near their homes and since in many northern cities Negro neighborhoods were large. New York and Chicago Negroes charged their school boards with

NON-WHITE POPULATION BY STATES

1910 and 1960

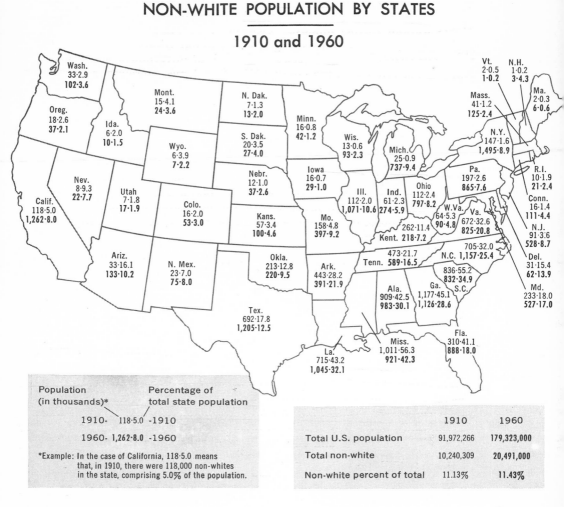

		1910	1960
Total U.S. population		91,972,266	179,323,000
Total non-white		10,240,309	20,491,000
Non-white percent of total		11.13%	11.43%

Population (in thousands)* Percentage of total state population

1910- 118·5.0 -1910
1960- 1,262·8.0 -1960

*Example: In the case of California, 118·5.0 means that, in 1910, there were 118,000 non-whites in the state, comprising 5.0% of the population.

© RAND & CO.

---

pursuing segregationist policies, demonstrated against school actions, and took political action to amend the policies. Here was a case where Negro voting pressure influenced action.

The right of Negroes to vote, supposedly guaranteed by the Fifteenth Amendment, was the subject of much congressional maneuvering. In 1956, President Eisenhower put forward a moderate civil rights program that had been drawn by Attorney General Herbert Brownell. He called for a special commission to study civil rights, a special assistant attorney general for civil rights matters, and authority for the Attorney General to seek injunctions in the federal courts to protect citizens' right to vote. The program passed the House; the Senate bottled it up, however. In 1957, Republican leadership in the Senate managed to keep the bill out of the Judiciary Committee, whose chairman was James O. Eastland of Mississippi, and the Democratic Senate leader, Lyndon Johnson of Texas, dissuaded his colleagues from filibustering. The measure came to a vote. But the final bill was so diluted that it amounted to little, although white supremacists declared that it meant the end of their "way of life" and northern Republicans, before Negro audiences, compared themselves to the Great Emancipator. The Civil Rights Act of 1957 did establish the study commission and the special assistant attorney general, but, instead of the Department of Justice receiving the power to apply for court injunctions on any civil rights issue, it was empowered to seek an injunction only when a citizen had been denied the right to vote and had exhausted other remedies.

The Civil Rights Act of 1960 was another relatively sterile piece of legislation. In the fall of 1959, the civil rights commission established by the 1957 act recommended that wherever the presence of electoral racial discrimination had been established, special electoral registrars appointed by the president be empowered to register all qualified Negroes as voters. For four months after the commission reported the President was silent. In January, 1960, he stated that the proposal might be unconstitutional. The administration bill did not include this voter registration plan, and thus the bill was a compromise even before Congress modified it further. The Senate debated ten weeks and finally let through a complex "voter referee" scheme. The law provided that, if the Department of Justice won a suit seeking an order to require local registrars to register Negroes, it could ask the federal judge to make a further finding that Negroes had been prevented from voting because of a "pattern or practice" of discrimination. If the judge so found, he would appoint referees, who if they found that voting discrimination persisted, would be empowered to put qualified Negro citizens upon the voting rolls. The act also made it a federal offense to transport explosives across state lines to be used illegally, a provision designed to bring the Federal Bureau of Investigation into school and church bombings. The Civil Rights Act of 1960 was no victory for the Negro; Senator John Sparkman of Alabama, who boasted that he held the floor against the bill for twenty hours, said, "The effects of the legislation will be negligible. . . ."

In the fall of 1960 most southern Negroes could not vote. Of the estimated 5,900,000 Negroes of voting age in the eleven former Confederate states, just 1,500,000, slightly more than one-fourth, were registered to vote. Variations among the states were great: 52 per cent in Tennessee, 31 per cent in Texas and Arkansas, and 5 per cent in Mississippi. Still fewer, of course, actually voted.

Heartened by the May, 1954, Supreme Court decision, American Negroes began a new crusade against segregation, often at the local level and often by-passing the traditional national Negro leadership. Late in 1954, a middle-aged Negro woman of Montgomery, Alabama, the Confederacy's first capital, refused to obey a white bus driver's order to sit in the back of the bus. A local magistrate fined her $14. Montgomery Negroes, led by the Reverend Dr. Martin Luther King, a southern Negro who had earned his Ph.D. in philosophy at Boston University, organized a "stride toward freedom" movement, a boycott against public buses. Very quickly, Dr. King became nationally prominent, and his philosophy or strategy of racial relations gained wide acceptance. As a deeply religious man, he put his emphasis upon brotherly love; he added to Christian values the tactics of Indian massive but passive resistance as developed by Mahatma Ghandi in the struggle against British rule. Christian nonviolence was the watchword, and Negro ministers were the leaders. The National Association for the Advancement of Colored People, which was entirely secular and legalistic in its approach, continued to be vigorous, but the new Negro movement around Dr. King captured the imagination. For one thing, the South was less of a secular society than the urban parts of the North and West, and appeals for fairness and decency dressed in religious terminology were effective. For another, the emphasis upon nonviolence made the sporadic violence of the ultrasegregationists appear the more reprehensible.

The great wave of "sit-ins" that began early in 1960 were in the Martin Luther King tradition. Ezell Blair, Jr., a lifelong resident of Greensboro, North Carolina, and three other freshmen at the Negro Agricultural and Technical College at Greensboro, late in the afternoon of February 1, went into a Woolworth store and purchased some small items. Then they sat down at the segregated lunch counter and asked for coffee. They were not served. They would not move. Policemen came in the store and watched them but took no action. The four freshmen sat quietly at the counter until the store closed. Soon Negro students all over the South began sit-ins at lunch counters, and the police retaliated with arrests. Approximately 1,500 Bible-carrying, hymn-singing Negro students were arrested before the end of the school year. White students elsewhere in the nation raised money to pay their bails and fines and picketed chain stores whose national management refused to desegregate lunch counters. What violence there was came almost altogether from the police and white mobs, frequently led by the black jacket and curled forelock type of teenager. Quietly, usually without public announcement at all, restaurants and lunch counters began to serve Negroes.

The next major wave of Negro action came in the spring of 1961 when young Negro "Freedom Riders" began a bus tour of the South to test the Interstate Commerce Commission's 1955 ruling against segregation in trains, buses, and terminals involved in interstate commerce. Most southern bus terminals continued to have segregated waiting rooms. The Freedom Riders were assaulted by mobs in Anniston and Birmingham, Alabama, and all were arrested in Jackson, Mississippi. Jackson quickly became the focus of the Freedom Riders, and throughout the college summer vacation of 1961, white and colored Freedom Riders went to Jackson to violate the local segregation laws and be put in jail.

Quite obviously, in the early 1960's, the older Negro organizations such as the NAACP and the Urban League, while still vigorous, failed to satisfy the new Negro emotionally. A cluster of new organizations took the limelight: the Southern Christian Leadership Conference, headed by Dr. King; the Congress for Racial Equality; and the Negro Labor Council, headed by the aged A. Philip Randolph and designed to eliminate Jim Crow in labor unions. Quite alarming to responsible Negro leaders was the rapid growth of racist and extremist movements among northern urban Negroes. In New York the United African Nationalist Movement, headed by a Negro public relations specialist, James Lawson, preached black supremacy, and in both New York and Chicago the Black Muslim movement gained support. Officially named the Muslim Brotherhood, U.S.A., this throwback to Garveyism of the 1920's was violently opposed to the NAACP, charging that its leaders were "Uncle Toms" selected for leadership by whites. Its two main leaders, who called themselves Elijah Muhammad and Malcolm X, even rejected their former family names as "slave-master" names. In Chicago the Muslim movement was strong enough to maintain a parochial grade school called the University of Islam.

The new Negro did not achieve the goal of his slogan "Completely free by '63," the centennial of the Emancipation Proclamation, but he moved a long way during World War II and afterward. He had momentum and determination, and he had taken matters into his own hands. That he would have further success was almost universally predicted, even by white suprema-cists to whom the outlook was discouraging.

Education in Crisis

From colonial times forward, Americans had great concern for public educa-tion, but perhaps never before was there such widespread interest in and worrying about the education of the young as there was after World War II. Dozens of books written for the layman about the problems of public educa-tion became big sellers, and national magazines of wide circulation carried serious educational articles. The heightened interest in education partly re-flected the increase in the size of the middle class and people's higher aspira-tions for both themselves and their children. It reflected also the unusual, complicated, and expensive problems that American education faced.

The schools had major problems of both quantity and quality. The postwar baby boom enormously increased the number of youngsters society was obligated to educate, and the increasingly complex and technical world required that these students receive a better education than their parents had. Rather than the other-worldly and irrelevant people they had often been stereotyped as being, the nation's teachers at all levels actually stood at a most critical position in society; the future of that society appallingly depended upon the quality of the teachers' work and the support they received.

In 1940, there were 29,805,259 youngsters in the United States between the ages of five and seventeen, and total public school enrollment of this age group was 25,433,542. By 1959, the numbers had climbed to 41,728,400 and 34-758,000, respectively. Enrollments in almost every school district grew, but the real problems were in the cities of rapid growth. In the 1950's, the school boards of Greater Los Angeles had to provide the equivalent of new school facilities for two hundred additional children every Monday just to keep even. The nation needed thousands of new teachers each academic year. The best way to attract people to the profession and to attract better people to it was to increase teacher salaries. Society fell short of the goal, but it did make a tremendous effort. In 1940, the average salary of public school teachers, in-cluding principals and supervisors, was $1,441; in 1959 it was $4,940. Much of the increase came in the 1950's after inflation slowed down from its immediate postwar rate. In 1948 the nation's expenditures for all kinds of education (not including school construction) amounted to 2.4 per cent of gross national product; in 1957 it had grown to 3.1 per cent of GNP, about $14 billion. In 1950, school construction took about $2.2 billion; by the end of the decade it was taking over $3.5 billion annually and was still increasing.

TABLE 13

ELEMENTARY AND SECONDARY PUBLIC SCHOOL
ENROLLMENTS, 1940–1960

	Kindergarten through Grade 8	Grades 9–12
Fall, 1940	18,832,098	6,601,444
Fall, 1946	17,677,744	5,622,197
Fall, 1950	19,386,806	5,724,621
Fall, 1956	24,290,257	6,872,586
Fall, 1960	24,457,321[1]	11,847,783[2]

[1] Kindergarten through grade 6
[2] Grades 7–12

Society demanded that the schools provide the flood of students with a higher quality of education than they had before the war. On the whole, the schools did improve. One of the educational issues debated in America in the 1950's was over the curriculum and teaching methods. The nation's intellectuals, who had been at the forefront of the progressive education movement earlier in the century, reacted rather violently against what progressive education had come to be in thousands of schools. Curriculum specialists in the professional schools of education had in the 1940's come largely to support what they called "life adjustment education" and called upon the schools to provide instruction in whatever were the "felt needs" of the students, whether they related to geometry or improving one's appearance. Critics of "life adjustment" pointed out that the school was the only social institution equipped to provide intellectual training, that other institutions such as the family, the churches, the press, and the youth organizations existed to provide the nonintellectual parts of education, and that the school dissipated its strength at the expense of the intellect if it assumed responsibility for these other functions. These critics did not entirely carry the day, but "life adjustment" proponents, on the whole, were in retreat.

Those demanding intellectual rigor in the schools received a boost for their argument when the Russians put the first earth satellite into orbit in the fall of 1957. The post-Sputnik reaction was more than a little hysterical and some of the new educational suggestions were ridiculous, but nevertheless many schools began to put a greater emphasis upon science and foreign languages and less upon "effective living" and "adolescent problems."

The federal government increased its aid to education in various ways, but Congress failed to pass a general aid program. Washington continued to provide partial support for home economics and vocational instruction which it had done since the Wilson administration, and through loans for dormitories and research contracts it enormously increased its subsidies for higher education. The heterogeneity of the people handicapped a federal aid program more than did abstract attachment to locally financed schools. Representative Adam Clayton Powell, Jr., a member of the House education committee and a Negro, consistently attached a provision to federal aid bills that would withhold subsidies to segregated schools and the bills thereby lost the support of southern Congressmen. Roman Catholics worked against bills that would give financial aid to public but not to parochial schools.

Colleges and universities faced the same problems of quantity and quality. College enrollments climbed quickly after the war (due largely to veterans going to school under the GI Bill of Rights), fell off slightly during the Korean War, and then zoomed after the cease-fire. Private colleges and universities that limited their registration had no problem of quality; they were able through more rigorous student selection to improve impressively the quality of their student bodies. At the other end of the scale, many small institutions of no particular merit quickly doubled and tripled in size. They succeeded in bringing education to a larger percentage of the college-age population, but too often the standards were such as to fail to work the good students to their potential. The state colleges and universities of quality that could not restrict their enrollments became crowded places indeed. The numbers of good students attending state universities increased, but the increased numbers of poor prospects in the freshman class, from which many never emerged, taxed the universities' resources.

TABLE 14

ENROLLMENTS IN INSTITUTIONS OF HIGHER
EDUCATION, 1940–1960

1940	1,494,000	1954	2,200,000
1946	1,677,000	1956	2,637,000
1948	2,616,000	1958	2,909,096
1950	2,659,000	1960	3,582,726
1952	2,302,000		

The increase in college enrollments was due both to a growth of the college-age population and a higher percentage of that population going to college. In 1920, only slightly more than 8 per cent of the population between the ages of eighteen and twenty-one was enrolled in institutions of higher education; in 1940 the percentage was about 15 and in 1960 it was about 30. By the end of the 1960's, the millions of people born in the postwar fertility binge would be college age and, presumably, the trend toward increasing percentage of college attendance would continue. The great range in the quality of American colleges and universities, which has long existed, is likely to

Herbert Hoover in early 1928   UNITED PRESS INTERNATIONAL

Hoover near the end of his ordeal, 1933
UNITED PRESS INTERNATIONAL

Unemployed men, 1930
LEWIS W. HINE FROM THE GEORGE EASTMAN HOUSE COLLECTION

A bonus army group from Cleveland, June, 1932   UNITED PRESS INTERNATIONAL

Hoover and Roosevelt on the way to the inauguration, March 4, 1933

Harold Ickes,
the "Old Curmudgeon"
BROWN BROTHERS

Harry Hopkins
BROWN BROTHERS

The farm holiday idea. Wisconsin farmers dumping milk, January, 1934
STATE HISTORICAL SOCIETY WISCONSIN

An example of depression painting. *"Dockworkers,"* by Moses Soyer
COLLECTION OF MR. AND MRS. HERBERT A. GOLDSTONE. COURTESY ACA GALLERY, NEW YORK

A relief station distributing rough fish, February, 1935
STATE HISTORICAL SOCIETY WISCONSIN

"Okies" on the way west. U.S. Highway 70 in Arizona, 1937
CULVER PICTURES, INC.

A West Virginia coal mining town
LEWIS W. HINE FROM THE GEORGE EASTMAN HOUSE COLLECTION

Wendell Willkie campaigning in Times Square, New York City, 1940

American troops hit the beach of Wadke, Dutch New Guinea
STATE HISTORICAL SOCIETY WISCONSIN

A Normandy beachhead on D-Day plus two   U.S. ARMY PHOTOGRAPH

Harry S. Truman, November 4, 1948   WIDE WORLD PHOTO

American riflemen in the intense cold of Korea   U.S. ARMY PHOTOGRAPH

"Woman I,"
by Willem DeKooning
(1950–1952)
COLLECTION, THE MUSEUM
OF MODERN ART, NEW YORK

The clean lines of
mid-century architecture.
ever House, New York City
LEVER BROTHERS COMPANY

Dwight D. Eisenhower and Nikita S. Khrushchev, 1959
NEW YORK TIMES PHOTO

Rush hour in Brooklyn, 1957   WIDE WORLD PHOTO

increase. The number of properly qualified college teachers has not been increasing enough to keep up with growing undergraduate enrollments. Although undergraduate enrollments increased by approximately two million from 1940 to 1960, the number of doctoral degrees awarded increased by only about six thousand.

The Recognition of "Mass Culture"

From the time most of its people became literate and publishers began to turn out "trash" to sell in the general market, the United States, like other western nations, has suffered some of the problems of "mass culture." Almost from the beginning of mass-cultural trash, intellectuals and artists with higher standards were aware of a possible thorough debasement of the intellectual and artistic coin. The advent of television in the late 1940's and early 1950's brought the problem to general attention as it had never been before.

Television shows were expensive to produce. The hucksters who used television programs to attract an audience for their sales pitches made a heavy investment, and they wanted a maximum audience. No society anywhere at any time has had a majority of highly cultured people. Television producers and sponsors were aware of this fact of cultural life and aimed their product at the lowest common denominator which, in the opinion of the more sophisticated sections of the population, was a very low and very common denominator indeed.

Television programing dominated discussions of the problems of mass culture because it was a new phenomenon, was so widely distributed, and was such a time consumer for millions of people. In 1960, the Census Bureau reported that 88 per cent of the nation's fifty-three million households had a television set. There were more homes with television sets than there were with telephones, refrigerators, bathtubs, or indoor toilets. Estimates of the number of hours per week that the populace watched what intellectuals contemptuously called the "idiot box" varied widely, but huge numbers of people watched it for most of their leisure hours.

Early in 1960, the television industry underwent a crisis when a New York grand jury and a congressional committee turned up evidence that a popular quiz program had been rigged, that contestants whose appearance increased the program's audience rating were supplied with the answers to questions. The personality and position of one of the fraudulent contestants, Charles Van Doren, gave the revelations a special poignancy, irony, and symbolism. Van Doren, an assistant professor of English at Columbia University and a member of a distinguished intellectual family, came to symbolize both the eroding effects upon American culture of commercial enterprise and the lax morality and soft integrity that some people thought were on the increase in the nation. In early 1962, Van Doren, who had retreated from the headlines into obscurity, was found guilty of perjury before the grand jury and received a suspended sentence.

But even as the sordid details of the Van Doren disclosures came forth, there were two reasons for optimism: first, the public, especially the public with a modicum of taste, was recognizing the problems of mass culture; and, second, as the size of the well-educated population grew and increasingly clustered into a few metropolitan areas, it created a new and better than average cultural market. Books and magazine articles about the intellectual and artistic sterility of the culture aimed at the masses of people became prevalent in the 1950's and 1960's. Indeed, looking down one's nose at the effluvium coming from the television networks became so widespread that many confident intellectuals came to regard conspicuous nose holding as a pose adopted by *nouveaux intellectuels* to establish themselves as superior to the herd. But there was also genuine concern about the quality of mass culture, and concern was necessary before any action. When Newton Minow, the new chairman of the Federal Communications Commission, in a widely publicized 1961 speech characterized television programing as "a vast wasteland," he evoked a great deal of sympathetic comment. Television network executives and advertising men expressed consternation and said that Minow threatened censorship. That he had not done, but he had reminded radio and television station license holders that they used the public airways with the permission of society as expressed through the FCC and that the law did not give them automatic renewal of their franchises.

Perhaps television programing with its peculiar economics will be a long time in reaching a general level of quality tolerable to sophisticated or even middlebrow minds. But by the 1960's, there was cause for hope in other cultural media with more flexible economic foundations. In the population centers of a million or more, and to a lesser extent in smaller cities, there were enough people with taste of quality to constitute an audience or a patronage for worthwhile cultural activities. By 1961, there were 1,142 symphony orchestras in the nation, more than half of the world's total. Most of them were predominantly amateur, but that fact did not reflect upon the taste of their communities; and many of them were professional and of world-renowned quality. Many cities boasted an art museum with at least a few good works. Most newspapers did not appreciably improve, but a handful of good metropolitan papers became truly regional and the New York *Times*, as postwar improvement in air transportation made it possible, quickly moved toward becoming a national newspaper. It achieved this status in 1962 when, by the use of facsimile transmission, the paper was printed simultaneously in New York and California. The circulation of the quality magazines increased sufficiently to attract national advertisers. The American people in 1960 spent more money for concert tickets than they did for admission to baseball games and more for records and phonographic equipment than for all spectator sports. More people went to the New York Metropolitan Museum of Art than to Yankee Stadium. Paperbound books sold at the rate of a million copies a day, and, although most of these were not works calculated to raise the level of taste and culture, an increasing number of titles available in inexpensive editions were excellent. Clearly, there were more homes in 1960 with good personal libraries than there had been in 1940. (Americans, however, did not read as much as did some other peoples. A survey in 1960 indicated that only 17 per cent of the population was currently reading a book; the figure for Great Britain was 55 per cent.)

Creating a mass culture of quality was one of the most subtle and complex problems that ever faced American society. The American people organized themselves satisfactorily into a political democracy, although not without some defects, and more painfully and less thoroughly they achieved a good measure of economic democracy. Now, in the last half of the twentieth century, they had to achieve cultural democracy, both for the majority and the minorities of varying tastes. The range of cultural choice available had to be widened and enriched so that there would be something exciting and satisfying for all. The mass of cultural consumers needed to reach the point where they demanded products of such a quality as to make leisure a fulfilling part of life rather than a mere time-killing device. With the almost sure increase in leisure time that was coming with automation and further mechanization, these questions acquired a new importance and urgency.

American Literature at Midcentury

The categories of novelists this book established in Chapter 20 on the culture of the Great Depression (social novelists and "America Singers") might be extended into the postwar era. Some of the giants and well-established novelists of the prewar era continued to be active. Ernest Hemingway, William Faulkner, James T. Farrell, John Dos Passos, John O'Hara, and James Gould Cozzens continued to write and be read. Indeed, some of them produced novels of major importance after World War II. Yet, as great as these writers were, one could reasonably say that their postwar work broke few new trails, that they had said substantially what they had to say before the war, and that they only sometimes improved their technique as they grew older. Other novelists, not well known before the war but active nevertheless, continued the older between-the-wars literary traditions. Conrad Richter's trilogy about Ohio's development from frontier to urban civilization was clearly in the "America Singer" tradition, and much of the work of Wallace Stegner, especially *The Preacher and the Slave*, was of the social novel genre.

But a large group of younger novelists was fundamentally reshaping the American novel. The generations that came to maturity in the 1920's and 1930's found it difficult to realize that young people did not mean Wolfe, Hemingway, Faulkner, and Dos Passos when they spoke of modern novelists. A new generation of novelists had come into prominence, a generation fully as innovating and experimental as their immediate predecessors who had revolted against the Edwardian genteel tradition. The gap that separated the American novel of the 1950's from that of the 1920's and 1930's was as wide as the gulf between the interwar novel and 1910. The little attention the reading public of middle age or more devoted to these highly talented newcomers was amazing. Nor did the new wave receive as large a share of awards as its merits warranted.

The new novelists' work defied pigeonholing in conventional categories. They certainly were not "America Singers," and few of them wrote explicitly social novels. They were experimental but not self-consciously so, as one senses that many of the innovators of the period after World War I were.

If any theme was consistent in their novels, it was that of the search for identity or sense of placement and relationship within the complex modern society and its values. If any mood or attitude permeated their work, it was compassion. Yet they avoided being explicit the way Sinclair Lewis was, for example. They were not naturalistic; nor were they romantic. Subtle and complex, they might be compared to impressionist painters, whereas the preceding generation could be compared to satirically realistic artists. Their styles and techniques varied widely, but many of them departed from the conventional structure of the novel. Instead of a formal sequential structure—beginning, middle, and end—they often wrote a series of incidents, perhaps chronological in order but not necessarily directly related to one another. Nor did they end their books with a note of finality. Instead of a happy ending or a tragic one, many of their novels seemed to have no ending at all.

With the short perspective we have on this generation of novelists one cannot say which ones will live. But certainly some of them will leave a mark upon American letters. Among the most popular were J. D. Salinger, especially for *Catcher in the Rye*, and Norman Mailer whose war novel, *The Naked and the Dead*, had a wide audience. Saul Bellow's *Henderson the Rain King*, the short and powerful *Dangling Man*, and *The Adventures of Augie March* received critical acclaim. A group of novelists from the South, Truman Capote, William Styron, and Carson McCullers, continued that region's remarkable literary tradition. Wright Morris' novels were among the most perceptive works written about American culture. Ralph Ellison, Herbert Gold, Bernard Malamud, Harvey Swados, and Willard Motley were other significant figures in the new wave of novelists.

The American theater, on the whole, did not have the vitality and originality of the novel. Broadway producers, faced with high costs, increasingly turned to the expense-account trade and produced machine-tooled, tried-in-the-marketplace formula shows. Musicals, of which some were charming but most were routine vehicles for popular stars, had the highest costs but yielded the greatest profits. Both the costs of Broadway tickets and the trend toward convention of the main stream of the theater encouraged what came to be known as off-Broadway theater. These small, inexpensive productions, which began in lower Manhattan and spread into other major cities, were frankly experimental. Some of the experiments were without value, but they did provide ferment and an opportunity for unknown playwrights to get their work before the public. Off-Broadway added some excitement to what seemed to be a commercially stultifying cultural institution. After a decade, however, off-Broadway was vulnerable to the criticism that it too was becoming conventional in its off-beat way—it was beginning to develop its own peculiar clichés.

Broadway and the commercial theater generally did not entirely reject serious and troubling playwrights. The commercial success of such writers as Tennessee Williams, Arthur Miller, William Inge, and Paddy Chayevsky was testimony of a survival of serious big-time theater. And the fact that all these men successfully wrote for Hollywood or television or both indicated that a significant market for serious drama truly existed.

Poetry continued to be the most respected and the least read kind of literature in America. Poets of the stature of Marianne Moore, Wallace Stevens, William Carlos Williams, and Archibald MacLeish went on receiving critical plaudits, but their readers outside of college literature courses were small indeed. The vast public, if it paid any attention to poetry at all, preferred the light verse of the clever Phyllis McGinley or the homey rhymes of Robert Frost. "Beatnik" poets such as Alan Ginsberg and Kenneth Rexroth attracted attention with their "readings" (recitations of their poetry against a modern jazz background), but they had little real impact. They were so "far out" in terms of popular taste and understanding that they were understood and appreciated only by one another. To most people they were odd curiosities and vaguely unsavory.

But for all the unevenness of American literature—indeed, of American culture generally—those who observed it from the vantage point of the Old World were impressed. There was a time when whatever cultural influence the United States had on Europe was either restricted to a few intellectuals or, at the other extreme, was mass audience and Hollywoodish. In the generation since World War II, the British and the Europeans came to regard American contemporary culture as worthwhile. American books were translated, read, and taken seriously. The libraries maintained by the United States Information Agency, although the object of attack and ridicule during the height of McCarthyism, were very popular places in European cities, particularly among young people. It is significant that in the 1950's *The Times Literary Supplement* of London, certainly no fly-by-night or capricious publication, twice devoted special editions to American writing. Its second treatment of the subject, in 1959, went so far as to conclude that "the flowering of the American imagination has been the chief event in the sphere of living art since the end of the First World War."

Postwar Art, Architecture, and Music

Perhaps the most important basic development in the arts in America after 1945 was an economic one. The steady growth of the size of the well-educated public created a potential market for the arts that was vastly larger than had ever before existed. Millions of American families wanted a well-designed home with good art and music within it, and postwar affluence enabled more of them than ever before to fulfill their desires at least partially. Architects were busy. Recordings of serious music made new sales records. The established art galleries in the nation's large cities increased their sales volume, and small galleries, even in fairly small communities if there was a university or some other intellectual center nearby, sold enough works to keep going. With more artists of all kinds better supported economically than ever before in American history, it was inevitable that the arts would be an exciting field.

American painters after the war had a greater diversity of styles and subjects. Almost all painters strived to develop a distinctive style, and the mark of a good painter was to a considerable extent the degree to which he was successful in his quest. Truly, it was an age of individualism in the arts. Superrealistic *trompe-l'oeil* (trick the eye) painters, impressionists, expressionists, surrealists, abstractionists, and various unclassifiable artists had their devoted followers.

Yet, certain trends in American painting could be discerned. One was a shift away from art with a social purpose. The word *depression* came to have a psychological rather than an economic meaning. Jacob Lawrence, who had learned to paint in a Harlem settlement house and had been on WPA art projects in the 1930's, entitled one of his 1950 paintings "Depression." It showed what appeared to be a corridor in a mental hospital. Three men in the foreground, dressed in sagging clothes and with heads hung low and faces of blank misery, shuffled about dejectedly. Indeed, psychological themes became very common after the war. In art as well as in other forms of expression, it was an age of Freud rather than of social protest. Hardly a show that represented several painters failed to have some pictures that portrayed the subconscious or projected a feeling of loneliness, personal frustration, or emotional disturbance.

About 1947, it became apparent that abstract art was the dominant form of modernism, both in the United States and in Europe. Abstract expressionist painters made no effort to portray an object realistically, and many of them were not representational at all. Those who did put a recognizable form into their works distorted the form considerably and entangled it in a mass of nonobjective blobs and slashes. Most of these abstractionists used bright and lively colors, but some turned out somber things in black, gray, and white. Some of these works were severely geometric after the manner of Piet Mondrian, some were more softly and naturally geometric, and some were strikingly amorphous. Yet, no matter what their style, abstractionists agreed that the function of the painter was to create a mood or feeling. Viewers were to look at pictures and undergo an emotional experience. Both painting and viewing, these artists believed, was intuitive rather than intellectual or even rational. Many abstractionists compared their work to music and deplored efforts to translate the natural scenes of the earth onto canvas.

Nonobjective painting in the United States was, of course, not an entirely new phenomenon. It merely came to dominate the art world after World War II. The Museum of Modern Art in New York had exhibited abstractionists throughout the 1930's, although more European work than American was on view. The Whitney Museum of American Art had a major exhibition of abstractions in 1935, a group of artists founded the Society of American Abstract Artists in 1936, and the Museum of Non-Objective Painting in New York opened in 1937. Some of the prominent abstractionists of the postwar period already had established reputations in the 1930's: Mark Tobey, of the Pacific Northwest, and Bradley Walker Tomlin, who was well known when he taught at Sarah Lawrence College from 1932 to 1941.

Certainly one of the most talented and powerful of the postwar abstractionists and probably one who will live after lesser figures have been forgotten was Willem de Kooning. Twenty-two years old when he came to the United States from his native Holland in 1926, de Kooning was best known for a series he did in the early 1950's entitled "Woman." In these only semiabstract paintings the distorted forms made a strong impression upon the viewer. Because there was a recognizable form in most of de Kooning's works, he made more of an impact on the consciousness of the average viewer than did, for example, the absolutely nonobjective Mark Rothko who was also considered a giant among the abstractionists. The viewer could admire Rothko's subtle colors, but he felt more relationship to de Kooning because as a viewer he at least thought he had a better idea of what the artist was trying to do.

Easily the best publicized and the most extreme of the prominent non-objective painters was Jackson Pollock, born in Cody, Wyoming, in 1912 and killed in an automobile accident on Long Island in 1956. Pollock was the dean of what came to be known as the "action painters," or "drip school," or *schmierkunst* practitioners. He did his huge canvases on the floor, dripping ordinary house paints on them directly from the can, splashing color everywhere, and even sloshing about on them in rubber boots. Easily burlesqued and ridiculed, Pollock, in the opinion of most art critics, really had something to offer. Despite his wildly unconventional techniques, his finished works did not seem to be accidents. On the other hand, those who asserted that Pollock and other extreme abstractionists were at best only decorative and that a society that honored an artist only because he was exuberantly innovative was a sterile one indeed had a point that could not be ignored.

Some art historians have made a category of painters of fantasies. Some of the fantasies were semiabstract, others were microscopically realistic; yet both kinds could be haunting, disturbing, illusive, and phantasmal. The sickly birds in Morris Graves's semiabstractions evoked this feeling as did the technically realistic (but quite unrealistic in content) work of Alton Pickens, a highly talented teacher of art at Indiana University. Even Andrew Wyeth, who steadfastly called himself a "realist," whose works were photographically precise, and whose technique and use of light and shadow was reminiscent of the old masters, projected this haunting quality.

Realist painting by no means stopped even if the museums often excluded it from their contemporary shows. In 1953, a group of forty-seven realistic artists, most of whom were older than the new wave of abstractionists, began a magazine called *Reality*. Its purpose was to fight for adequate exhibition in museums and to save American art from the "smothering extremes of the abstract and non-objective school." The magazine folded after a few issues, and the movement collapsed. In the early 1960's, however, the realists, still very much alive and still highly critical of abstraction, seemed to be making some headway. In April, 1960, a group of realist painters issued a manifesto which criticized the Museum of Modern Art for developing "the public image of the painter as a madly inspired child, rather than an adult human being." They even picketed the Museum briefly. Straws in the wind indicated that the great vogue of the abstractionists, at least of the absolutely nonrepresentational ones, was beginning to wane. More painters than before, even if abstract in style, began to include representational forms in their works. Art buffs who took their interest seriously, including those whose taste went beyond saccharine treatments of puppies and kittens and nostalgic, primitive snowscapes, increasingly expressed the thought that absolute abstraction was near the end of its inventiveness and that it was becoming empty and cliché ridden.

European visitors to America in the late 1950's who had not been in the country since before the war noted that the greatest change in the appearance of the nation, other than the greater number of cars on the road, was the unusual amount of building construction and of "modern" architecture. The postwar moves to the big cities and the suburbs made an unprecedented increase in new construction necessary. The growth in both size and movement of the population required new hospitals, schools, office buildings, and churches as well as residences. Architects who designed the public buildings almost universally scorned "traditional" forms and the designers of residences, inhibited by the buyers' fears about resale market, made as many "modernistic" innovations of their exteriors as they could.

Actually, "modern" architecture is too loose a term to be very useful, despite its widespread familiarity. At least two main streams were discernible. One was an evolution of the international style: clean, sweeping, geometric lines; new building materials such as stainless steel, aluminum, and vast amounts of glass; alike and anonymous in basic form even though distinctive in superficial details. The other was the continuing tradition of romantic preoccupation with experimental striving for the unique, even the eccentric, in design.

Ludwig Mies van der Rohe may fairly be said to have been the leader of the postwar international school. His Seagram Building in New York, designed with Philip Johnson, was a good example of the international style in office buildings. Another was Lever House on Fifth Avenue, designed by the firm of Skidmore, Owings, and Merrill. This style clearly predominated in the design of big public buildings. Manhattan, Pittsburgh's Golden Triangle, and Chicago's Lake Shore Drive abounded with it. Frank Lloyd Wright was the best example of the more experimental tradition. The Solomon R. Guggenheim Museum in New York, Wright's last major completed project, indicated his emphasis upon the unique. A great, squat, white cylinder, it had a spiral ramp from top to bottom along which were hung the paintings on exhibit.

Either tradition, most critics agreed, could be good in the sense of providing livable, usable, attractive structures. Either could provide drama and interest that would not wear thin with time. But either could be bad, ill-fitted to human use, not designed with its users and inhabitants in mind, forgetful of the human scale. When one looked at some of the sleek business warrens of the international school one thought with a chill of Le Corbusier's famous comment that buildings should be "machines for living." One could sympathize with some of the artists exhibited at the Guggenheim who complained that Wright had overpowered their work and distracted the visitor. In 1960, the Guggenheim's curator, James Johnson Sweeney, left in protest against the new building.

The American public, quite obviously, was much more inclined to accept experiment and innovation in painting and architecture than in music. Relatively few music lovers followed contemporary American composers. For the most part, American composers had to look abroad for audiences, and even there they usually found them only at annual contemporary music festivals.

Americans, however, reacted with warmth and enthusiasm to the performing artist. When the versatile Leonard Bernstein, who had filmed television programs about music of various kinds, became conductor of the New York Philharmonic Orchestra, the story was front-page news. Van Cliburn became a national hero when he won a piano competition in the Soviet Union. Gossip columnists wrote about the affairs of the more celebrated opera stars as well as about Hollywood stars. Record sales reached over $500 million in 1960, and a considerable part of these were recordings of serious music.

Most people of any musical taste, no matter what their age, agreed that popular music went into a quality tailspin after the war, especially in the 1950's. The distinction between jazz and popular music widened as "rock 'n roll" and pseudo-folk music gained in popularity. Jazz remained popular on the campus, and summer jazz festivals attracted huge crowds. But it became difficult to find jazz on the radio, and television almost ignored it. The emptiness, shallowness, and puerility of most popular songs and recordings was difficult to exaggerate. The popular music industry displayed its lack of originality and musical range with gimmicks, such as recording echo chambers, and continual revival of popular songs of a generation or more in the past dressed up in the midcentury popular idiom. In 1959 and 1960, "payola," the industry's euphemism for bribery, gained public attention. Some disc jockeys accepted inducements to play certain records on the air regardless of their quality and thereby gave them an entirely spurious popularity. In the wave of resentment over "payola" there were some dismissals and even a few indictments, but the practice did not disappear.

But for better or worse—and there was some of both—American jazz and popular music had acquired a worldwide following. Students in Stockholm and Paris were avid jazz enthusiasts. One could hear Dixieland in India. King Phumiphon of Thailand played his saxophone with American jazz musicians when he visited the United States in 1960. Jazz became very popular in Poland after the 1956 upheaval, and old American records were available on the Russian black market. "Rock 'n roll" shook British music halls and blared from juke boxes in Teheran. Some people interpreted this phenomenon as testimony to American vitality; to others it was evidence that the whole world was sick, sick, sick.

CHAPTER TWENTY-NINE

The Democrats Again

IN THE CONGRESSIONAL ELECTIONS OF 1958 AND THE PRESIDENTIAL election of 1960 the Democrats clearly demonstrated that they were the majority party. The voters again returned a Democrat, John Fitzgerald Kennedy, to the White House. The Democratic candidates for the presidency had won six of the eight elections from 1932 through 1960. In the generation after the Great Crash of 1929, the Republican party had been able to win only two congressional elections, in 1946 and in 1952. Eisenhower had a Republican majority in Congress for only his first two years.

But, despite the fears of the most orthodox Republicans, Democratic dominance had not produced fundamental alterations of the basic economic fabric. Since the elections of 1938, the nation had for all practical purposes been governed by a conservative coalition of Democrats and Republicans in Congress. And no matter what they wanted to do, which was never anything drastic in domestic affairs, the presidents of both parties were faced with Congresses that had a strong attachment to the middle of the road. American national politics was not absolutely stuck on dead center, but the moderate political center of gravity kept the balance from swinging very far either to left or right.

Many Democrats hoped and many Republicans feared that President Kennedy would bring about a revival of the spirit of the Second New Deal. But before he had been in office more than a few months, some dissident Democrats gnashed their bits and made remarks about the "third Eisenhower administration." Others, remembering the events of 1945 to 1953, replied that it was the fifth Truman administration. And others, still more historically minded, declared that, so far as domestic policies were concerned, the era had begun about 1939.

608

The Election of 1960

Encouraged by their success in the 1958 elections, Democrats looked hopefully toward winning the presidency in 1960. They calculated that they had an excellent chance to win the big contest since the Twenty-second Amendment to the Constitution, pushed through by Republicans still fretful about Roosevelt's four electoral successes, prevented the popular Eisenhower from running for a third term. This being the prospect, Democratic maneuvering for the nomination was more than usually intense.

The Democratic camp had a plenitude of presidential hopefuls: Adlai Stevenson, who had the backing of many Democratic intellectuals; Senator Hubert H. Humphrey of Minnesota, strong with labor; Senate Majority Leader Lyndon B. Johnson of Texas, whose efforts to project himself as a westerner rather than a southerner during the preconvention period were transparent to political observers; Senator Stuart Symington of Missouri, whose backing by ex-President Truman was not an unmixed blessing; and Senator John F. Kennedy of Massachusetts, who had the best-financed and organized personal organization.

Kennedy's main handicaps were his comparative youth (he was born May 29, 1917) and his Roman Catholicism. His youth handicap faded because Richard M. Nixon, the likely Republican candidate, was only four years older; his religious affiliation proved to be no unsuperable obstacle when he entered the primaries. In April, he defeated Humphrey in Wisconsin, and the next month he won over Humphrey again in strongly Protestant and economically depressed West Virginia where he had expected to lose. Humphrey removed himself as a candidate after the West Virginia primary. The Democrats held their national convention in Los Angeles in July, two weeks before the GOP meeting in Chicago. Kennedy won fairly easily on the first ballot. Needing 761 votes for the nomination, Kennedy received 806. His only serious opposition came from Senator Johnson who received 409 votes, most of them from southern delegations. The new nominee surprised the nation and grievously disappointed many of his northern and western supporters when he announced at a press conference that Senator Johnson was his choice for the vice-presidential nomination. Johnson accepted the place on the ticket, although he had said repeatedly that he would rather continue as Senate Majority Leader than be vice-president. Under Texas law, Johnson was permitted to run both for vice-president and for re-election to his Senate seat. Kennedy had named Johnson primarily to keep the South, which was disgruntled with the strong Democratic civil rights plank, from leaving the Democratic camp.

Republican nomination of Vice-President Richard M. Nixon was a foregone conclusion. His desire for the office was clear, as was Eisenhower's support for him. The President had given Nixon the opportunity to play a larger role than most vice-presidents, and the voters knew the forty-seven-year-old Californian well.

Nothing unexpected happened at the Republican convention in Chicago. Governor Nelson Rockefeller of New York, Nixon's only real potential opponent for the nomination, met with Nixon secretly two days before the convention opened. Nixon agreed to Rockefeller's demands for the Republican platform; Rockefeller withdrew from consideration, both for the first and second places on the ticket, and endorsed Nixon. Only one other person besides Nixon was placed in nomination, Senator Barry Goldwater, a self-pronounced conservative from Arizona. Goldwater addressed the convention, withdrew his nomination, and urged all right-wingers to work for Nixon's election. Nevertheless, ten delegates from Louisiana cast ballots for the Arizona Senator. The convention named Henry Cabot Lodge of Massachusetts as the vice-presidential candidate. Lodge, grandson of the Senator Lodge of the Theodore Roosevelt–Wilson era, had been a Senator, had been defeated for re-election in 1952 by John F. Kennedy although Eisenhower carried Massachusetts, and was currently the United States ambassador to the United Nations. The Republican platform, which also had a strong civil rights plank, was mostly a song of praise for the Eisenhower administration and an effort to identify Nixon with the popular President.

The campaign was largely a contest of personality. The substantive differences between the candidates' positions were matters of degree and emphasis. In September and October, the two candidates met in a series of four nationally televised "debates," the first time presidential candidates had tried such a device. Polls indicated that Kennedy gained strength from these television shows, especially from the first one. The main reason was that the "debates," which had an artificial format that prevented them from being very enlightening, made Kennedy nationally known; Nixon, as Vice-President for eight years, had already had a great deal of what the entertainment industry called "public exposure."

The question of Kennedy's religion could have become a nasty issue in the campaign, but the threat never materialized. The Democratic candidate was on record as a supporter of separation of church and state, and during the campaign he reiterated that if elected president he would never accept church authority when he thought that to do so would violate his presidential oath to support the Constitution. Nevertheless, some Protestants, mainly from the more fundamentalist denominations, circulated scurrilous anti-Catholic material, although not to the extent they had in 1928. Kennedy suffered a handicap late in the campaign when the three Roman Catholic bishops of Puerto Rico instructed their parishioners not to vote for Governor Luis Munoz Marin. Munoz Marin won anyway.

Kennedy eked out a narrow victory on election day. His election was indicated within a few hours after the returns began to come in, but the margin of victory was so close in some states that there was some doubt about its certainty for several days. Kennedy received 34,226,925 popular votes to Nixon's 34,108,662. The total vote was 68,412,709. The minor-party vote kept either major candidate from winning a popular majority. Kennedy had 303 electoral votes to Nixon's 219. One Nixon elector in Oklahoma, eight unpledged Democratic electors in Mississippi and six unpledged Democrats in Alabama cast their electoral college ballots for Senator Harry F. Byrd of Virginia. Nixon carried more states than Kennedy, but Kennedy carried most of the states with the big electoral votes: New York, Illinois, Michigan, Pennsylvania, and Texas. Kennedy also came close to winning the thirty-two electoral votes of Nixon's

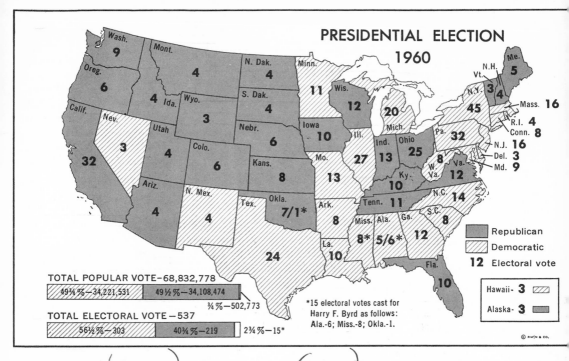

PRESIDENTIAL ELECTION 1960

Republican
Democratic
12 Electoral vote

TOTAL POPULAR VOTE—68,832,778
49¾%—34,221,531   49½%—34,108,474
¾%—502,773

TOTAL ELECTORAL VOTE—537
56½%—303   40¾%—219   2¾%—15*

*15 electoral votes cast for
Harry F. Byrd as follows:
Ala.-6; Miss.-8; Okla.-1.

Hawaii- 3
Alaska- 3

home state. The Democrats retained control of Congress, about holding their own in the Senate and picking up twenty-two new House seats. They also won fifteen gubernatorial races to the Republicans' twelve.

Students of politics expended great effort in analyzing the election results. As had been the situation since 1928, Democratic strength, other than in the South, was concentrated in the big cities. Kennedy would have lost New York, Pennsylvania, Michigan, and Illinois if it had not been for his big pluralities in New York City, Philadelphia, Pittsburgh, Detroit, and Chicago. He also carried Los Angeles and San Francisco. Kennedy's religion was undoubtedly a factor in the voting. Kennedy received the votes of some normally Republican or independent Catholics, but he apparently lost a greater number of normally Democratic Protestants who would not vote for a Catholic. Some experts estimated that he had a net loss of 2 or 3 per cent of the total popular vote because of his Catholicism. The election certainly proved false the political adage, widely believed after Al Smith's defeat, that no Catholic could move into the White House; and judging from public opinion polls a few months after Kennedy's inauguration, the Catholic-Protestant issue in presidential politics had been laid to rest.

About all that Kennedy and Al Smith had in common was that they were both Democrats and Roman Catholics. Kennedy was from a wealthy background. His father, Joseph P. Kennedy, had made millions in banking, real estate, and other investments and had served under FDR as chairman of the Securities Exchange Commission and as ambassador to Great Britain. He had settled $1 million upon each of his children when they were born. The new President attended private elementary and preparatory schools and graduated *cum laude* from Harvard. He later expanded his senior honors thesis and had it published as *Why England Slept*. A naval lieutenant during the war, he was seriously injured in the Solomons when a Japanese craft rammed his torpedo boat. He entered politics soon after the war, serving three terms in the House of Representatives before winning election to the Senate in 1952. His book *Profiles in Courage* won the Pulitzer prize for biography in 1957. Vigorous, intelligent, efficient, and pragmatic, Kennedy during his campaign repeatedly talked of "moving forward" and of "New Frontiers." Large numbers of his supporters expected a new departure.

Some of Kennedy's early appointments strengthened expectations for change, and others indicated a continuation of Eisenhower and Truman policies. The appointment of Arthur J. Goldberg, general counsel of the AFL-CIO, as Secretary of Labor, of ex-Governor of Minnesota Orville Freeman as Secretary of Agriculture; and ex-Governor Abraham A. Ribicoff of Connecticut as Secretary of Health, Education, and Welfare indicated an infusion of militant liberalism into government, as did the naming of Arthur M. Schlesinger, Jr., Professor of History at Harvard University as a presidential assistant. But the appointment of Dean Rusk as Secretary of State, who came to the cabinet from a post in one of the large philanthropic foundations; of Robert S. McNamara, a top official of the Ford Motor Company, as Secretary of Defense; and of C. Douglas Dillon, a Wall Street figure who had served under Eisenhower, as Secretary of the Treasury, reassured those who were generally satisfied with the previous administration. Stewart L. Udall, a Mormon from Arizona, became Secretary of the Interior; J. Edward Day of California became Postmaster General, and ex-Governor of North Carolina Luther H. Hodges became Secretary of Commerce. The naming of the President's younger brother and campaign manager, Robert F. Kennedy, as the Attorney General raised more than a few eyebrows. In 1962 when Justice Frankfurter retired, Kennedy appointed Goldberg to the Supreme Court. Earlier he had elevated Byron White to the Court.

Latin American Chickens Come Home To Roost

President Kennedy had little more than settled into the White House when in April, 1961, he became deeply involved in a Latin American crisis of major proportions. The unsuccessful armed attempt to overthrow the regime of Fidel Castro in Cuba requires some background knowledge of Latin American policy after World War II.

Three basic goals preoccupied most of Latin America after the war, and it was clear that the will to achieve these goals could not be deflected; Latin America was on the move. First, and basic to all else, was a demand for better economic conditions. Latin America was hit hard by the "Revolution of Rising Expectations" that swept over Asia and Africa. Second was a strong movement toward political freedom. Dictator after dictator toppled in South and Central America in the late 1950's. Third was a strong desire for independence. Free from Spain and Portugal for over a century, Latin Americans believed firmly that they had later fallen under the might of the Colossus of the North.

Preoccupied with the Cold War and concerned primarily with events in Europe and Asia, the United States after World War II largely ignored the developing social revolutions and rising expectations south of the border. In the first five years after the war, Latin America received only 1.8 per cent of the total of United States foreign aid. Tiny Taiwan received more than all of Latin America, as did West Germany. Above all else, the State Department wanted two things in Latin America: the prevention of Communist penetration and a favorable climate for investment by United States citizens. American investments constituted four-fifths of all the foreign capital in Latin America. More often than not, United States policy to attain these ends ran against the Latin American tide.

Continued United States participation in inter-American organizations was by no means contrary to its general goals. At the Chapultepec Conference in early 1945, the various American nations agreed that they would insist upon the preservation of their regional organizations in the writing of the United Nations Charter at San Francisco. In 1947, at the Rio Conference and the following year at Bogotá, the United States became a charter member of the Organization of American States (OAS). The treaties signed at these conferences provided for the peaceful handling of disputes among the American nations, and the OAS provided the machinery.

The United States suffered its first postwar Latin American setback in early 1946. Before and during the war, Argentina had been a center of German activity, and despite great pressure it remained neutral in the war until March, 1945, when it too declared war on the Axis. Having been neutral for most of the conflict, Argentina had a large backlog of foreign exchange which the United States ambassador, Spruille Braden, and Secretary of State James F. Byrnes hoped would be used for internal investments to stimulate the growth of the Argentine economy. In the March, 1946, Argentine elections, United States support went to the opponent of Colonel Juan D. Perón who had been a strong man in the preceding dictatorial and Axis-oriented regime of Edelmiro J. Farrell. Perón, a high-handed demagogue, had popular support because he proposed to use the backlog of foreign exchange for wage increases. Perón won the election handily. After the backlog was exhausted, the Argentine dictator pauperized his nation's agriculture to distribute benefits to his followers in the city masses. Perón was not popular elsewhere in Latin America, but neither was United States opposition to him which Latin Americans, extremely sensitive on this issue, regarded as meddling in the internal affairs of a foreign power. A revolt by the army and civilians from the interior overthrew Perón and sent him into exile in September, 1956. In the elections of March, 1960, Perónista candidates received one-fourth of the vote, and in the March, 1962, elections for the provincial governorships, Perónistas won most of the offices. After the 1962 elections, an anti-Perón military group, fearful of rising Perónista strength, overthrew the president, Arturo Frondizi, on the grounds that he would not be sufficiently anti-Perón.

The United States gained its immediate end, the prevention of Communist penetration, but lost respect and prestige in Latin America by its indirect intervention in Guatemala in June, 1954. Guatemalans had overthrown the corrupt and dictatorial regime of Jorge Ubico in 1944. The new government foundered, and in time the Communists worked their way into positions of power in the administration of President Jacabo Arbenz Guzmán. In March, 1954, at the meeting of the OAS at Caracas, Secretary of State Dulles introduced and strongly pushed a resolution that called for "a meeting of consultation to consider the adoption of appropriate action in accordance with existing treaties" should a Communist regime "constitute a threat to the sovereignty and political independence of the American states. . . ." The resolution passed seventeen to one, Guatemala opposing and Mexico and Argentina abstaining. After having set the stage for collective action through the OAS, the United States, only three months later, moved almost unilaterally to overthrow the Arbenz regime. A cargo of Czech arms arrived at a Guatemalan port, and the Central Intelligence Agency went to work quickly. The CIA armed and supported an invasion of Guatemala led by Colonel Carlos Castillo Armas, a Guatemalan anti-Communist rebel, from Nicaragua and Honduras. Together with the army within Guatemala, the Armas invading column overthrew Arbenz and installed Armas as provisional president. The Communists were stopped, but the social and economic conditions that had produced the unrest upon which the Communists could grow were not improved.

After the Guatemalan counterrevolution, Latin Americans began to talk of the Dulles Doctrine, defining it as United States assumption of the right to overthrow Latin American governments of which it disapproved. Even staunchly anti-Communist Latin Americans, who hailed the toppling of Arbenz, condemned the North American action. After the revolution of 1944, the United States had an opportunity to support a genuine social revolution and help to improve Guatemalan conditions. Instead, the United States government under Truman and Eisenhower backed up the refusal of the United Fruit Company, a North American corporation, to countenance any significant change in the *status quo*. In time, the Communists moved in, and the United States supported their removal by force. The cartoon of the British satirist David Low depicting the Statue of Liberty holding aloft a stalk of bananas was a sharp comment on the Guatemalan situation.

The United States was neglectful of Latin America except in crises such as occurred in Argentina and Guatemala, and American popularity south of the border sunk to lows unprecedented since the inauguration of the Good Neighbor policy. Mobs in Lima and Caracas dramatized the situation when they roughed up Vice-President Nixon when he visited there on a "good-will" tour in May, 1958. Thereafter, the United States tried to mend its Latin fences. It helped the coffee-producing nations to negotiate export quota agreements to stabilize the world price and viewed sympathetically the development of a Latin American common market scheme similar to the one being developed in Europe. In March, 1960, at Montevideo, Argentina, Brazil, Chile, Mexico, Peru, Uruguay, and Paraguay signed a free-trade treaty. But the legacy of implicit American support of dictators like Fulgencio Batista in Cuba and Rafael Trujillo Molina in the Dominican Republic, both of whom received their military training from United States officers when they were members of their American-sponsored constabularies, was a very serious handicap to good will.

Trujillo had been dictator of his country since 1930, although he had been forced to yield nominal control to his brothers or others periodically. In 1956, Trujillo's terror figured in the news prominently when Jesus de Galindez, a lecturer at Columbia University and a leader of exiled anti-Trujillo forces,

614

disappeared. It was widely assumed that Trujillo agents had kidnapped and killed him, but conclusive evidence was not discovered. Trujillo was extremely unpopular in the United States, but the government continued to supply him with arms until only a few months before his downfall. In May, 1960, Trujillo followers made an attempt on the life of President Romulo Betancourt of Venezuela, and two months later the OAS met in Costa Rica, condemned the Dominican government for "acts of aggression and intervention" against Venezuela, and called upon member nations to break diplomatic relations with the Caribbean dictatorship. The United States did so. In May, 1961, Trujillo's enemies within his domain assassinated him. His son, who had recently received military training in the United States, became the head of the army in an effort to maintain the family's control, but in the fluid situation the dead dictator's brothers left the country. When they returned in November, apparently to attempt to restore the old regime fully, the United States announced its opposition. Young Trujillo resigned as armed forces chief and left for Europe on his private yacht. United States warships took positions off the coast. Strikes and riots in the capital city broke the back of Trujillo strength. The United States hoped for the emergence of political stability in the little republic under a friendly regime that was tolerant, democratic, anti-Communist, middle-class, and committed to economic growth within a capitalist framework. The United States was in a ticklish position vis-à-vis the Dominican Republic in which it was likely to be damned if it intervened and damned if it did not. But, on the whole, considering the decades it had supported Trujillo and the manner in which it had intervened unsuccessfully in Cuba in April, 1961, against a leftist revolution, its modest intervention against a right-wing regime in the Dominican Republic in the fall of 1961 was a welcome change.

United States relations with Cuba after Fidel Castro came to power on January 1, 1959, were trying to North American patience, were exasperating to most Latin Americans, and were always highly charged with emotion. Castro had begun his revolt against the Batista regime faced with great odds. After successful defense of his troops in the mountains, he rode the storm of a social revolution to power. He was extremely popular in the United States while he was fighting against Batista. Indeed, in the spring vacations of 1958 several college students went to Cuba with the romantic purpose of aiding the Castro cause. As in the case of Trujillo, the United States government did not go along with popular opinion. The government continued to supply arms to Batista, which were used against Castro, until mid-1958 and maintained a military mission with Batista until the day he resigned and fled from the island.

Castro was an unknown quantity when he came to power. He began to lose ground in United States public opinion in early 1959 after his wholesale executions of his former enemies. The United States government protested when in May, 1959, Cuba promulgated the Agrarian Reform Law, which empowered the Castro government to expropriate American-owned property. When the Fidelistas actually began to take the property, the cry went up in the United States that Castro's regime was Communist. That he had strong Communist connections and convictions was clear in 1961, but whether he had at the time that he won power is a matter of debate. It seems probable that he was an anti-American, generally Marxist but not Communist, rebel in early 1959, but that he had Communist lieutenants who had no great difficulty guiding his regime in the direction they wished when it encountered opposition from the United States and encouragement from the Soviet Union and China.

Certainly Castro encountered American opposition. Besides many vigorously worded diplomatic notes and speeches, the United States, under Eisenhower, cut the Cuban sugar import quota, severed diplomatic relations, and pressured the OAS to take a stand against the Cuban regime. The Declaration of San José, adopted by the OAS in August, 1960, condemned "intervention or the threat of intervention in the affairs of the American republics" but did not mention Cuba by name. Pro-Castro political movements had gotten underway all over Latin America. Secretary of State Herter declared that the declaration applied to Cuba and the Communist world, but not all agreed that it did. Mexico issued a special statement denying that the declaration referred specifically to Cuba, "whose aspirations for economic improvement and social justice have the strongest sympathy of the Government and people of Mexico." Mexico's position, plus the further opposition of Venezuela and Peru to the American stance, indicated that United States policy toward Cuba was hardly winning and influencing Latin Americans.

And, just as certainly, Castro received Communist encouragement. Soviet Deputy Premier Anastas I. Mikoyan visited Havana in February, 1960, and signed a trade agreement by which Russia promised to buy five million tons of Cuban sugar over a five-year period. This agreement became the model for subsequent pacts with Poland, Czechoslovakia, East Germany, and China. The Soviet Union also extended Cuba a $12 million credit, payable at 2.5 per cent interest over the next twelve years. Khrushchev obviously welcomed the break in the solidarity of the Western Hemisphere. He embraced the bearded Cuban when they attended the United Nations in New York, but, on the other hand, there was some evidence that Khrushchev basically regarded Castro as a welcome but irregular and untrustworthy thorn in the American side. Clearly, ties between Cuba and the Communist world further strained American-Cuban relations. The presence of a power friendly to China and Russia only ninety miles off the Florida coast was not reassuring, nor was Khrushchev's statement of July 9, 1960: ". . . if need be, Soviet artillerymen can support the Cuban people with their rocket fire, should the aggressive forces in the Pentagon dare to start intervention against Cuba."

The first climax of Cuban-American tension thus came in April, 1961, when an armed force of 1,400 Cuban exiles, armed and trained by the United States Central Intelligence Agency in Florida and then Guatemala, attempted to invade Cuba. The invading force made landings at Bahia de Cochinos (the Bay of Pigs). The exiles expected a sympathetic uprising by the Cubans, but it never developed, and the Castro forces easily captured most of the invaders and repulsed the others. For weeks, the Cuban press had been saying that such an invasion was imminent which only lent weight to its subsequent charges against the United States.

The Cuban invasion was a disaster no matter how considered. If one takes the position that an invasion was justifiable, the invasion was vulnerable because it was thoroughly botched. The CIA did not perform its job effectively. Perhaps the greatest of its mistakes was putting the most reactionary group of the Cuban exiles in charge of the operation, which militated against the possibility of an uprising within Cuba, and preventing participation by most of the

Cuban exiles who had at first supported Castro but later disavowed him as a betrayer of the ideals of the revolution.

But many agreed with Senator J. William Fulbright, chairman of the Senate Foreign Relations Committee, who asserted that the invasion was unjustified and a grievous error. American prestige and reputation suffered badly throughout Europe, Asia, and Latin America. The invasion plan and the training of the exile force, begun under Eisenhower and continued under Kennedy, was in violation of American treaty agreements and even of United States statute. The unsuccessful invasion only strengthened the Cuban government and evoked sympathetic sentiment for it in the rest of the world. Had the invasion actually been a military success, especially given its reactionary leadership, it is quite doubtful that it would have solved the Cuban problem or enhanced the United States position in Latin America.

Yet, apparently, Kennedy's popularity increased within the United States with the Cuban fiasco. He made an impassioned and troubled defense in a televised speech before the nation's editors immediately after the invasion failed and subsequently conferred personally with Truman, Eisenhower, Nixon, MacArthur, Hoover, and Goldwater in an apparent attempt to head off criticism. As much as these conferences dismayed some of the people who had voted for him, public opinion polls indicated that the President had the support of a larger part of the population than he had before the fiasco in the Bay of Pigs.

After the invasion, American activities against Cuba took the form of economic sanctions and work against Castro within the OAS. An embargo of most items but food and medicine undoubtedly hurt Cuba as did the ban, imposed in early 1962, against Cuban imports. At an OAS meeting in Punta del Este, Paraguay, in January, 1962, the United States sought to get the other American republics to break off diplomatic relations and trade with Cuba, as well as to expel Cuba from the organization. The Latin American states refused to break diplomatic and trade relations, and the United States gained Cuban expulsion only at the cost of a split with the principal Latin nations which abstained on the expulsion vote. In the summer of 1962 Cuban-American relations again approached crisis as Moscow sent thousands of military technical specialists to Havana. Domestic political pressure on Kennedy mounted, and the administration attempted to tighten the Cuban nonintercourse policy by putting pressure on the European nations that still shipped to Castro. But yet American opinion did not support another invasion. A poll in early October showed that 63 per cent opposed an invasion at the moment.

The Cuban affair did have the effect of awakening the United States to the problems of Latin America. The Kennedy administration announced a new aid and development plan a month before the Cuban invasion. This too was begun, in a much smaller way, under the Eisenhower administration. At a meeting of the economic policy planning section of the OAS in Bogotá in September, 1960, Under Secretary of State C. Douglas Dillon (later to be Secretary of the Treasury under Kennedy) spoke of a new United States fund of $500 million to be used for social betterment in Latin America. In August, 1961, all the Latin American nations except Cuba approved the Kennedy proposal of an Alliance for Progress. The Alliance would provide over a ten-year period a minimum of $20 billion, half of which would come from the American government and the balance from international financial agencies, European governments, and private capital. To qualify for these funds, which were to be used to stimulate economic growth and improve social conditions, the Latin nations promised to cooperate in introducing necessary reforms. In the first several months of the Alliance's operation, it was not clear that the United States was adamant about the required reforms before granting the funds.

The Continuing Cold War

The United States was not so fortunate as to have an end of the Cold War, or even a relaxation of it, with the change from Republican to Democratic control of the executive branch. The Kennedy administration's foreign policy goals and methods remained substantially as they had been under Truman and Eisenhower: avoidance of war but resistance to communism, both in Asia and the West; strengthening of the armed forces and general military potential, especially in space flights and rocketry; support of the United Nations; and encouragement of American foreign trade. The foreign trade matter will be considered in the next section of this chapter. JFK, as the headlines referred to the President, sometimes showed an original flair and a slight new departure in method, but the general outlines of American policy with the rest of the world remained essentially unchanged.

The abnormal and illogical situation of Berlin remained the most dangerous point of conflict between the United States and the Soviet Union. The Berlin situation, established when America and Russia were still allies in 1945, simply did not fit the new shape of the world but neither East nor West was willing to make concessions. Much more hinged on Berlin than just the settlement of the German question. Most observers held that there could be no real disarmament agreement until the problem of Central Europe was settled and that Central Europe could not be satisfactorily stabilized until the two sides reached a workable and logical arrangement in Berlin.

Russia's objective was to force the British and Americans out of Berlin and incorporate West Berlin into East Germany. The United States and Great Britain were determined to stay in Berlin, as provided for in the 1945 agreement. West Germany was perhaps even more determined to keep West Berlin, and Chancellor Adenauer at least never lost hope for unification of the two Germanies under West German and anti-Communist control. A logical compromise would be to make West Berlin an international city, guaranteeing its freedom and ties with the West and the right of transit through East Germany from Berlin to West Germany, all under the jurisdiction of the United Nations with NATO and Warsaw Pact approval. But the Russians believed that they could not recognize that West Berlin and the corridors to it were not under the sovereignty of East Germany, and the United States believed that it could not explicitly approve the idea of two German states.

Given this impasse, which could not go on forever, the best that could be hoped was that neither side would do anything about Berlin that would bring war and that in time conditions would change sufficiently to arrange a compromise satisfactory to both sides. Apparently, Russia did not want a war over Berlin, and clearly the United States did not either, but it would not back down from conflict if Russia pressed the issue. Khrushchev periodically irritated the Berlin sore, but when the West remained adamant he stopped short of all-out attack.

During the Eisenhower administration Khrushchev had announced that if a Berlin settlement were not reached soon he would sign a separate peace treaty with East Germany and turn control of the Russian sector in East Berlin over to the East German government. Not only did the West expect the East Germans to be more difficult to deal with than the Russians, but they also refused officially to recognize the East German state at all. Khrushchev kept implicitly extending his deadline. When he renewed the threat in the spring of 1961, Kennedy met with him at Vienna for two days, and the Berlin problem simmered down momentarily.

Two of the problems from the Russian and East German governments' point of view were that West Berlin offered too easy an escape route for East Germans wanting to flee to the West and that West Berlin prosperity offered too much of a contrast with the dismal conditions of East Berlin and East Germany. Refugees from East Germany escaped to West Berlin at the rate of 25,000 a day in the summer of 1961. The East met this situation by effectively sealing the East-West border in Berlin, building a high wall at many points so as to make escape very dangerous and almost impossible. Berliners, accustomed to passing back and forth freely to visit friends and family, were furious. Tensions mounted rapidly.

The United States sent more troops to West Berlin, but the troop movement could be no more than a psychological maneuver because the western military position in the city was basically untenable in the event of major attack. Kennedy ordered some national guard divisions to active duty for a year, ostensibly to free other units for other activities but probably actually as another psychological maneuver. The federalized troops were released before the end of a year although international tensions had not significantly abated. The crisis slowly passed without more than incidents and threats back and forth across the wall. In the summer of 1962 Khrushchev again brought the Berlin problem to a boil after letting it simmer for months. The Russians in piecemeal fashion began to pass part of their military functions to the East Germans and to harass transportation from the border to isolated West Berlin. The situation was one that could easily get out of hand.

One of the sillier side effects of the 1961 Berlin crisis was the bomb shelter craze. The President in a loosely worded speech urged citizens to consider constructing family bomb shelters. Soon unscrupulous salesmen combed residential neighborhoods selling shoddily built and quite useless bomb shelters. To build or not to build effective fallout shelters—protection against direct hits was out of the question—was a complex problem. Undoubtedly, an effective system of fallout shelters would save, or at least prolong, lives in the event of full-scale nuclear war. But some people argued that they would as soon die quickly as live in a radioactive world, and many urged that the resources and energy that would go into a crash program of shelters be applied to an effort to bring about less chance of nuclear war. In late November, the President cleared the air by announcing a policy of federal aid for community shelters, although he still urged family ones. The furor subsided, and not very many families went ahead with shelter plans. Nor did the community shelters get far. Kennedy asked Congress for a $400 million program; Congress appropriated only $38 million for research and surveys.

The first two years of Kennedy's administration also saw the Cold War get a little hotter in Southeast Asia. The 1954 settlement by no means brought stability to the once-French area between the Gulf of Siam and the South China Sea. North Vietnamese and Chinese Communists, sometimes advised by Russian specialists, continued to wage guerilla warfare in South Vietnam. The United States was committed to the South Vietnam regime of President Ngo Dinh Diem, although his regime was by no means popular.

When Vice-President Johnson visited South Vietnam in the spring of 1961 and the guerilla warfare was going badly for the anti-Communists, the United States and South Vietnam reached an understanding that America would send combat troops if they were requested. General Maxwell Taylor subsequently visited the area to ascertain the possible effectiveness of greater American military aid. By 1962, about eight thousand American troops were in South Vietnam, as well as about four thousand in pro-western Thailand. These troops' function was not primarily to fight the Vietcong, or Communist guerilas, but to train, advise, and transport the South Vietnamese forces. Inevitably, however, American troops were killed even if they were technically only "advisers." The buildup of American force there did turn the tide of the warfare at least temporarily in the anti-Communists' favor. In July, 1962, a new and perhaps unworkable scheme was arranged for Laos in which both sides agreed that it would be neutral. Its neutrality was to be enforced by an International Control Commission composed of Canadian, Polish, and Indian inspectors.

Southeast Asia was another situation that, like Berlin, could easily blow up into a major conflict. If the South Vietnamese did especially well in their guerilla warfare against the Vietcong, there was a real possibility that North Vietnam and perhaps China as well might launch an all-out attack. At least in the fall of 1962, American public opinion was not ready for another Korea. On the other hand, if the United States withdrew altogether and South Vietnam and Thailand fell to the Communists, besides the loss of the rice lands that supplied much of non-Communist Asia with its staple, the status of Cambodia, Malaya, and Indonesia would at least be seriously threatened. As with Berlin, both sides seemed to be following a strategy of trying to gain advantage without precipitating a full war, hoping that in time conditions would change sufficiently to bring about a more general reapprochement. It was a frustrating strategy to live with, but a full nuclear war would be much worse.

Throughout Kennedy's first two years in office, the likelihood of a real agreement between the United States and the Soviet Union to ban permanently nuclear testing was little more than remote. The nuclear talks in Switzerland droned on, but they came to nothing. The essential difficulty was that both sides wanted to resume nuclear testing, Russia because she thought she was behind America in nuclear technique and America because she wanted to stay ahead. The Russians broke off the talks and resumed testing in the atmosphere in the fall of 1961. The administration, now more anxious than before about maintaining its nuclear lead, consented to further American tests. Many of the

620

new American tests, but not all of them, were below the earth and did not create a fallout problem. One American shot into space created a radiation belt that might hamper future manned space flights. Given each side's understandable anxiety about relative nuclear status, it seemed likely that there would be no agreement on testing until each thought it could learn nothing more from testing in the atmosphere. But meanwhile the "nuclear club" might grow. France had already developed a crude atomic bomb. Russia did not, as far as is known, help China's effort to develop a bomb, but the prospect of China having a strong nuclear force was a frightening possibility.

The rivalry in space continued to be sharp. At the end of 1962 it appeared that Russian scientists were still ahead of the United States in this field but that Americans were doing much better than they had been only recently. In the summer of that year a Russian manned flight made eighteen orbits, which was better than their American counterparts then could accomplish. But the American astronauts were becoming more skilled and professional. The third American manned orbital flight, in early October, 1962, seemed a routine operation, and many Americans were more interested in the sensational National League pennant race. So fast had the technology of flight developed that many people who had been thrilled by Lindbergh's 1927 exploit took little notice of a man hurtling around the earth in a small satellite. But some of the space achievements of both sides were nevertheless amazing. The American Mariner spaceship, an unmanned vehicle that started its months-long journey toward Venus in the summer of 1962, was an engineering feat of major proportions.

The Kennedy administration did not restrict its military buildup to the dramatic fields of nuclear weapons and spaceships. It increased by 50 per cent the number of Strategic Air Command bombers kept on alert, increased the size and efficiency of the ground forces with a special emphasis on preparation for "brush fire" conflict rather than full nuclear war, increased the number of operational intercontinental ballistic missiles, and continued to produce and man nuclear-powered submarines and other naval vessels.

The United Nations became embroiled in unusual expenses and controversy during Kennedy's first half-term, and the new President and his ambassador to the United Nations, Adlai Stevenson, vigorously supported the world organization. When Belgium withdrew from the Congo in 1960, the new central African nation was soon reduced to anarchy. So poorly had the Belgians educated the Congolese that educated native leaders were almost nonexistent. In the incredible confusion and warfare among various Congolese factions, the United Nations, by authority of its legislative bodies, stepped in to restore order. Katanga province, a mineral rich area and the only part of the Congo with appreciable industrial capacity, perhaps under the influence of the western owners of its biggest mining company, announced its secession from the rest of the new nation. Congo without Katanga would be doomed to backwardness and poverty, and the United Nations resisted the Katanga move. UN Secretary General Dag Hammarskjold called for a UN armed force to police the Congo, and soon this force was engaged in sporadic warfare with Katanganese troops, many of whom were professional mercenaries. This military venture cost more than the UN had, and it was forced to ask member nations to buy UN bonds in the amount of $200 million. President Kennedy requested Congress to authorize the purchase of up to one-half the bond issue. After some resistance from those who argued that the UN was actually intervening in the Congo's internal affairs, Congress approved the purchase but qualified it slightly by forbidding the United States to purchase more bonds than the total bought by all other UN member nations.

Hammarskjold was killed in a plane crash in September, 1961, while on a mission to the Congo to arrange a truce. Although the evidence was not conclusive, his Swedish compatriots believed he had been the victim of foul play. His death plunged the UN into a vigorous struggle in which the Soviets and their allies attempted to change the nature of the Secretariat to what they called a "troika," or three-horsed harness arrangement, composed of Communist, western, and neutralist representatives, each to have a veto. Such a scheme would have made the Secretariat powerless in matters affecting the Cold War. Early in November, the UN defeated the "troika" plan, with strong American help, and elected U Thant of Burma as Acting Secretary General.

Aside from a stronger tendency to support foreign democratic movements than with either the Eisenhower or Truman administrations—and this tendency was not consistent, as in South Vietnam, or fully realized, as in the Alliance for Progress—the main change in foreign policy under Kennedy was in better administration and some imaginative new methods. The most original and dramatic new program was the Peace Corps. The idea of sending American specialists to underdeveloped nations as teachers, agricultural specialists, medics, and engineers was not entirely new, but the emphasis on youth in the Peace Corps and the far greater number of such grass roots educational and technical ambassadors were novel. The Peace Corps captured the imagination of young people especially, although middle-aged persons were eligible to join, and thousands of college students enlisted. The Peace Corps insisted that the people it sent to underdeveloped areas, largely to Latin America and Africa, be technically competent in their specialty and able to communicate in the language of the area. The task of language training and teaching Corps members the customs, traditions, and problems of the nation concerned fell largely to American universities, which on the whole did an outstanding job. The degree of success of the Peace Corps remains to be seen and undoubtedly there will be unfortunate situations arising from the program, but if the Corps members are as good in practice as they promise to be they should improve living standards and build a reservoir of American good will.

The primary administrative change under Kennedy was strengthening the quality of many ambassadors and giving them greater control over the various missions at their posts. Two of the outstanding ambassadorial appointments were of Harvard University professors, John Kenneth Galbraith, an economist who became ambassador to India, and Edwin O. Reischauer, a Japanese specialist who became the ambassador at Tokyo. Kennedy made fewer political appointments to embassies abroad, and the percentage of Foreign Service career ambassadors appointed in 1961 was the highest in the nation's history. Nearly all of the ambassadors could speak the official language of the country to which they were assigned, an obvious prerequisite that had too often been ignored.

Clarifying the ambassador's authority and responsibility for all United States programs in his country of assignment was another obvious reform. After 1945, American missions abroad grew rapidly in size and complexity. A major foreign capital might have representatives from the Pentagon, the United States Information Service, and Departments of Labor, Commerce, and the Treasury, as well as regular State Department personnel. Sometimes the work of these representatives was uncoordinated and even at cross purposes. Putting ultimate responsibility on the ambassador made greater efficiency possible.

At a time when either the Communist or western camp could precipitate a total nuclear war with a major effort for "total victory," when political pressures in the United States against any compromise whatsoever were matched only by Communist recalcitrance, when a miscalculation or blunder by either side could trigger world destruction, to conduct foreign policy with wisdom was all the more difficult even if all the more important. To avoid full war, to prevent falling behind in the continuing struggle, and to be prepared to agree to a workable and just world arrangement were legitimate and reasonable aims of American foreign policy in the mid-twentieth century. On the successful attainment of these objectives rested the happiness of the future and perhaps even future civilization itself.

"Moving Forward"—By Short Steps

During the 1960 campaign, Kennedy spoke often of "New Frontiers" and of the need to get the nation "moving forward." With Democratic majorities of 64 to 36 in the Senate and 263 to 174 in the House and with the excitement that accompanied the new chief executive's inauguration, it was not unreasonable in early 1961 to expect an important wave of reform and progressivism. No such wave developed. Despite some executive innovations and some progressive programs and despite a quickening of liberal hopes unequalled since at least 1948 and perhaps since FDR's death, the first half of Kennedy's administration added up to only a slight shift to the left of "moderate Republicanism."

Kennedy certainly presented Congress with legislative programs that were in contrast with presidential messages of the previous eight years. He urged a major revision of the tariff structure to meet new situations and several tax changes. In the area of welfare legislation, he proposed Medicare, federal aid to education, a program to combat unemployment, and a new Department of Urban Affairs. Others, notably Senator Kefauver, urged a law to regulate the drug industry. The President also came forward with a proposed revision of agricultural subsidies. Some passed, some failed utterly, and some passed in watered down form.

Perhaps the most solid achievement of the early Kennedy administration and the Eighty-seventh Congress was the Trade Expansion Act of 1962, a measure that significantly had little to do with domestic progressive versus conservative struggles. The reciprocal trade program inaugurated in 1934 had worked reasonably well at its purpose of increasing American exports, but new conditions in the 1950's required a new policy.

In 1957, France, West Germany, Italy, and the Benelux countries signed the Treaty of Rome creating the European Common Market, often called "The Six" or "The Inner Six." The purpose of the Common Market was gradually to eliminate tariff walls between its members and thereby create a free trade market of 270,000,000 people, even larger than the American free trade market that had much to do with developing American manufacturing capacity. "The Six" also proposed to raise tariff walls around their community of nations. On many large items of American export the new tariff would be higher than the old ones of the individual nations. For example, a tariff on American automobiles and trucks of 27 per cent, effective in 1966, would replace old rates of 16 per cent in Germany, 24 per cent in the Benelux countries, 26 per cent in France, and 33 per cent in Italy. If American trade and tariff policy did not change, not only would American exporters find it more difficult to sell in the Common Market but as American exports were squeezed the French would find it easier to purchase Volkswagens and the Germans would find it easier to buy Renaults. Further, other European countries were likely either to go into the Common Market, as Great Britain was considering doing, or making more effective a parallel organization, "The Outer Seven." United States exports to Europe amounted to over $6 billion a year in the late 1950's, more than half to the Common Market nations, and the loss of this export trade would have harmful effects on the American economy.

In January, 1962, Kennedy requested legislation authorizing the executive for the next five years to negotiate trade agreements in which American duties could be reduced as much as 50 per cent on categories of goods (rather than on individual items as in the existing legislation) and to eliminate tariffs altogether on groups of products for which the United States and the Common Market together accounted for 80 per cent of world trade. For American industries and their workers who would be jeopardized by foreign competition in the domestic market, Kennedy proposed that instead of continuing protection the federal government aid the companies to modernize and diversify their production and finance the retraining of whatever workers might be displaced.

For the last several Congresses, protectionist forces had imperiled renewal of the reciprocal trade laws, and many observers predicted Kennedy's proposal would have a difficult time. A Nation-Wide Committee on Import-Export Policy organized to fight the measure. Charles P. Taft, brother of the late Senator Taft, was the head of a businessmen's organization for the proposal, which also received the support of the AFL-CIO. Within three months it became apparent that the substance of the bill would pass, and opponents concentrated thereafter on getting safeguards for particular industries. The legislation passed by large majorities in September, 1962, substantially as Kennedy requested. Negotiating favorable trade agreements would not be an easy task, but the new legislation made it possible for America to adjust its trade to changing world conditions.

The administration's greatest defeat in the Trade Expansion Act was a House amendment that denied most-favored-nation treatment to any Communist country, not only to nations in the Russian or Chinese bloc as in the previous legislation. Thus Poland and Jugoslavia, "revisionist" Communist states but Communist nevertheless, would be driven away from economic ties to the West and toward closer relations with the Soviets.

Kennedy requested tax revisions designed to stimulate the sluggish but not foundering economy and asked for other measures to give the government more tools to combat economic downswings. Congress either watered down or rejected the whole program. The tax bill the President requested would grant a 7 per cent tax credit to business firms for investment in new equipment, a proposal designed to stimulate economically beneficial new investment. To make up for the revenue loss, he suggested collecting income tax on dividends and interest by the withholding method and tightening up on expense account tax deductions for customer entertainment and similar dodges. Congress granted the tax credit for new investment, a boon to most firms, but did little on the business expense deductions and rejected withholding on dividends and interest altogether. The lobbyists against withholding resorted to deliberate distortion of the truth. Their propaganda made it appear that Kennedy's proposal was for a new tax altogether rather than a changed method of collecting an already taxable source of income. The intensity of the opposition to withholding was due primarily to the fact that tax collection on this kind of income was relatively poor because many taxpayers were dishonest in reporting income from such sources. Congress approved Kennedy's request to eliminate the 10 per cent excise on train, bus, and boat fares and to cut the excise on plane fares to 5 per cent.

Congress passed Kennedy's three-year $435 million program to get unemployed workers in sick industries off the relief rolls by retraining them for new jobs, but it almost completely rejected his three-pronged plan for fighting recessions. The President asked for authority to make personal income tax cuts for up to six months by as much as 5 percentage points. To meet the constitutional provision that only Congress can levy taxes his plan provided that any executive tax cut proposal would have to be submitted to Congress one month in advance for possible veto by joint resolution. The economic effect of a tax cut of this nature could be important in a recession because a five-point drop, from the 20 per cent most people pay to 15 per cent, would create about $5 billion in additional purchasing power. Congress, however, never seriously considered the proposal. Nor did Congress enact his request to amend the Social Security Act's unemployment insurance by bringing more employees into the coverage, enlarging the payments, and extending the number of weeks unemployed workers could collect. Congress enacted the third part of his plan, a scheme for emergency public works in areas that had shown a steady and important rise in unemployment for several months, only after cutting back the size of the program. Kennedy asked for $2 billion; Congress appropriated one-fourth that amount.

Kennedy's proposal for agriculture was relatively modest in that it contained no general solution for the intricate problem. He suggested that the size of the agricultural surplus be reduced by toughening up production controls, making most of them on a basis of actual production rather than acreage allotment. Congress disagreed. The House defeated the measure in June, 1962. Eager for some kind of a new agricultural act, the White House cut back its request considerably and pressed hard for the compromise. In September, Congress barely passed a bill that maintained the existing controls through 1963 but provided for tighter controls on wheat and feed grains beginning in 1964. Republican opposition was nearly unanimous.

Kennedy's welfare legislation proposals got the hardest beating from the Eighty-Seventh Congress. The administration measure that excited the most passion for and against was what the Department of Health, Education, and Welfare called Medicare, a modification of the Forand bill presented to the previous Congress. Medicare would have provided medical insurance under the Social Security Act for retired workers over sixty-five years old, the insurance to be financed by payroll deductions as in the case of other retirement benefits. The plan was extremely popular with the aged, of course, as well as with many younger people who contributed to the support of aged relatives. The primary opposition came from the American Medical Association, which intensified its cry of "socialized medicine," and from health insurance firms. According to the opponents, the existing Kerr-Mills law (which offered limited funds to states for medical care of the indigent aged under certain circumstances) and privately financed medical care were sufficient. They further asserted that bringing medical care for the elderly under Social Security would regiment American medical practice, although the bill in no way limited the patient's choice of medical facilities.

The administration opened all stops for Medicare's passage. The President addressed a Medicare rally of aged people at Madison Square Garden. Health, Education, and Welfare Secretary Ribicoff, who resigned in the summer of 1962 to run for the Senate in Connecticut and was replaced by Mayor Anthony J. Celebrezze of Cleveland, worked almost full time on pressuring for Medicare. But a Senate coalition of Republicans and southern Democrats defeated it fifty-two to forty-eight. When Kennedy proposed to make Medicare a major issue in the 1962 congressional elections, the American Medical Association inaugurated the AMA Political Action Committee to subsidize the campaign expenses of anti-Medicare candidates.

Medicare's defeat came after two previous rejections of White House welfare proposals. In 1961, the President had urged Congress to enact a broad program of federal aid to education in an effort to bring schooling in the poorer states closer to the national standard. Most of Kennedy's fellow Catholics in and out of Congress insisted upon including parochial and private schools under the aid provisions, contrary to the President's wishes, and the Catholic issue prevented passage. It seemed that Catholics would not support a federal aid bill that excluded parochial schools and Protestants would not support one that included them. Opponents of federal aid for ideological reasons—they maintained that local school board authority would give way to Washington control, although the experience of the Wilson administration Smith-Hughes Act and of government research contracts with universities did not seem to support their view—cleverly played off one religious group against the other. In the summer of 1962, the Senate defeated a compromise aid to education bill, one that would have subsidized only college and university building construction. Congress did, however, pass a repealer to the special non-Communist oath that students and faculty members had to take to be eligible to receive National Defense Education Act funds. Thirty-two colleges and universities had refused to participate in NDEA until the oath was repealed, and many others had participated only under protest. The other major welfare defeat was the loss of the proposed Department of Urban Affairs in February, 1962. The new cabinet level department would have incorporated all federal housing activities; after it became known that Kennedy's choice for the new cabinet post would be Federal Housing Administrator Robert A. Weaver, a Negro, the House defeated the measure.

From this account of the Eighty-seventh Congress, one might conclude that it passed nothing. Indeed, a conservative Republican Representative from Iowa called it a "goof-off Congress" and a liberal Democratic Senator from Pennsylvania agreed. But it did enact some measures. It put through a drug safety measure near the end of the second session that did not go nearly as far as the proposal of Senator Kefauver. The new law was more the result of the 1962 thalidomide scandal than Kefauver's investigation. Thalidomide, a European-manufactured tranquilizer, when taken by pregnant women, had caused many babies to be badly malformed at birth. Congress also passed the Twenty-fourth Amendment to the Constitution and sent it to the states for ratification after a ten-day Senate filibuster. The amendment, if ratified, would forbid states to levy poll taxes as a condition for voting.

Congress also enacted the administration's communications satellite or Telstar bill, and thereby hangs a tale that indicated the President's relations with Congress were not simply those of a progressive executive being frustrated by a conservative legislature. The development of man-made satellites made it possible to "bounce" microwaves off them and thus extend microwave communications much beyond the ground-level horizon. Two systems were possible. The American Telephone and Telegraph Company advanced a scheme of several relatively low satellites with ground stations switching to the next one coming up over the horizon as the last one disappeared over the opposite horizon. The Hughes Aircraft Corporation had another system under development. Its scheme would have three equally spaced satellites at 22,300 miles above the equator traveling at a speed synchronized with the rotation of the earth. This system would eliminate the need for ground switching.

The administration proposed that communications satellites using any system be owned by a private corporation, chartered by Congress, with two types of stock in equal amounts. One type would be available for purchase by anyone; the other could be bought only by communications companies. Given the corporate structure of the American communications industry, this meant that the giant in the new corporation would be AT&T. Senators who called themselves "liberals," led by Kefauver and Douglas of Illinois, argued that most of the research funds that had made these electronic wonders possible had come from the federal government and that the federal government should own the satellites. Kennedy firmly rejected their argument. A small group of Senators filibustered to prevent the bill's passage, but they were defeated by a cloture motion and the bill became law.

In late July, 1962, the first fragmentary transatlantic telecasts indicated the vast cultural implications of communications satellites. When Europeans and Americans routinely watch one another's television programs there will be a very strong tendency toward a common western culture. The satellites also will be used for telephonic and radio transmission.

Kennedy's ardent defenders saw him as a progressive hamstrung by a reactionary Congress. His conservative Republican opponents saw him as a wild-eyed radical restrained only by a sensible Congress. There could be little doubt that Kennedy's position on most matters was to the left of a large part of Congress. The national legislature had defeated or watered down all of his proposals that were relevant to the domestic issues that divided Americans into left, center, and right. Despite heavy Democratic majorities, Congress did this with the coalition of Republicans and southern Democrats. For example, on the Medicare vote in the Senate, defeated by four votes, only five of the thirty-six Republicans (Clifford Case of New Jersey, John Sherman Cooper of Kentucky, Jacob Javits and Kenneth Keating of New York, and Thomas Kuchel of California) voted for the bill. Forty-three Democrats voted for Medicare and twenty-one against. Of the twenty-one Democratic opponents, all but three (Robert Kerr and A. S. Mike Monroney of Oklahoma and Jennings Randolph of West Virginia) were from former Confederate states. Of the Senators from the South, only four (Kefauver and Albert Gore of Tennessee, Ralph Yarborough of Texas, and, surprisingly, Olin Johnston of South Carolina) voted for the measure.

Those who saw Kennedy as a progressive or a dangerous radical (depending upon their predilections) cited the President's actions in his April, 1962, battle with Roger Blough, board chairman of United States Steel, over a steel price increase. Since inauguration, the administration had been urging unions to be moderate in their demands so that industry would not increase prices, and only the previous month the steel workers had signed a noninflationary contract. The steel industry had argued during the labor bargaining that a significant increase in costs would jeopardize its competitive position with foreign steel. The administration opposed price increases, particularly in the basic commodities, for two reasons: the cost of living had been slowly rising despite the relatively sluggish economy, and price increases complicated the delicate international balance of payments problem by making it more difficult to sell abroad.

Late in the afternoon of April 10, Blough called at the White House and notified Kennedy that his firm had just raised its prices $6.00 a ton and that the news had been released to the press. The next day five other steel companies likewise increased their prices. Kennedy was furious. After forty-five minutes Blough left the White House visibly shaken. The administration unleashed an attack on the price rise that included Kennedy's denouncing the action at a press conference, maneuvering a break in the industry's united front by getting Kaiser and Bethlehem to decline to raise prices, threatening a Defense Department boycott of steel firms that raised prices, and announcing a grand jury investigation of the increases, which implied a possible antitrust law violation. United States Steel and the other firms that had raised prices capitulated within seventy-two hours after Blough's conference with Kennedy. With the exception of the Cuban invasion, the steel battle was the most dramatic incident of Kennedy's fifteen months in office.

Some political columnists saw the steel episode as a turning point in the Kennedy administration. The belief was widespread that Kennedy was anti-business; some hailed and others deplored this supposed stance. Soon jokes and stories about "That Man in the White House" reminiscent of the ones about FDR circulated at middle-class cocktail parties. The decline of the stock market in May, 1962, was partly attributable to apprehension about a hostile administration, although the softness of the economy in general and the fall of prices on foreign stock exchanges were more important factors.

But it was probable that both those who condemned and those who praised Kennedy's supposed toughness with business were wrong in their fundamental assumption. The evidence that Kennedy was no doctrinaire opponent of the business community nor a typical progressive or liberal was voluminous.

Aware that businessmen since FDR were prone to believe any Democratic administration was hostile, Kennedy had on many occasions asserted "how really untrue" it was that "we are antibusiness." After the steel strike he again went out of his way to improve his reputation with business. He supported AT&T's position on Telstar. The Justice Department approved the merger of Standard Oil of Kentucky with Standard Oil of California. Kennedy's tax reform proposals did not include rescinding the oil industry's 27.5 per cent depletion allowance. The White House dropped Kefauver's drug control bill and supported a less inclusive one. In late July, 1962, Kennedy rejected the AFL-CIO's strong urging to bring about an immediate tax cut to stimulate the economy.

As one examines Kennedy's relations with his balky Congress, one finds other evidence that does not fit the view of the President as antibusiness or as liberal. Kennedy's method to get what he wanted from Congress was primarily to bargain with Congressmen, to entertain them, to implore them, and sometimes to pressure them with harder methods. With but a few exceptions, he refrained from taking his case to the citizens to build a public opinion fire under sluggish and conservative Capitol Hill.

It may be that the President realized that he must work with Congress, that he regarded it as impossible to bring Congress around to a more compatible point of view, and that therefore he felt that he should not antagonize an already uncooperative body. His call for the voters to elect "more Democrats" in the 1962 congressional elections, similar to Wilson's plea in 1918, may have been a compromise with a desire for a "purge" of Democratic conservatives such as FDR tried and failed to achieve in 1938. Perhaps he feared a national swing to the far right, symbolized by the strength of the extremist John Birch Society whose leader asserted that even Eisenhower was a tool of international communism. It might be that the President hoped that the reapportionment of state legislative districts, which in some states were not much different from early nineteenth-century England's "rotten boroughs" and which the Supreme Court had declared unconstitutional in Baker v. Carr in March, 1962, would weaken Democratic conservatives and thereby in time provide him with a more cooperative national party. In sum, he may only have been paying homage to the principle that "politics is the art of the possible." But in any case the practical results of the President's first two years in office had not been to move more than a few short steps away from Eisenhower's "middle of the road."

The Cuban Crisis and Elections of 1962

Kennedy's campaign to persuade the voters to send "more Democrats" to the Eighty-eighth Congress was in full swing when a Cold War crisis erupted that was to be the most serious since the Korean conflict. The manner in which the congressional elections coincided with the crisis was reminiscent of Eisenhower's re-election and the simultaneous Hungary and Suez affairs. The President was campaigning in Chicago on Saturday, October 20, when his press secretary announced that Kennedy was cancelling the balance of his trip and returning to Washington. It soon developed that Cuba was the reason for Kennedy's return. When the crisis eased soon before election day, the Republican cry that the President should "do something about Cuba" would have a hollow ring.

Early in September, Kennedy had ordered regular aerial photography flights over all of Cuba. Many of the flights were made in the U-2 type of plane that had precipitated a crisis in the spring of 1960. Hurricanes over the Caribbean interrupted the flights in early October. When the flights resumed, the cameras showed evidence that the Russians were installing about forty intermediate range missile sites in Cuba which would be capable of hitting targets as far north as northern Georgia and that Russian ships were delivering twin-engine jet bombers to Havana.

On October 18, the President met with Soviet Foreign Minister Andrei Gromyko in a session that had been scheduled long before. Kennedy did not indicate at this meeting that American intelligence services had discovered the presence of Russian offensive weapons in Cuba, and Gromyko told the President that all weapons being delivered to Cuba were purely defensive. Kennedy did not present the Russian minister with the photographic evidence because he and his administration had not yet fully decided what course of action they would pursue. There were several alternatives. At one extreme, Washington could do nothing overt and merely protest to Havana and Moscow. At the other extreme, the United States could launch another invasion of Castro's Cuba, a dangerous recourse because it might ignite a general nuclear war and because in any case it would probably be viewed unfavorably by America's allies. In between the two extremes were several possibilities: bombardment of the missile sites, commando raids at the critical places in Cuba, a blockade of offensive weapons, or a total blockade. Over the weekend, the President and his advisers decided upon a blockade of all offensive weapons destined for Cuba and a demand that the Russians and Cubans remove those weapons which had already been delivered. After alerting United States armed forces the world over, the President issued the blockade proclamation and spoke to the public on television the evening of Monday, October 22.

While the United States—indeed, the world—waited anxiously to see what would happen when an American naval vessel first intercepted a Russian freighter laden with offensive weapons, European and Latin American nations rallied to the defense of the American action. Although they had not been previously consulted, all of the NATO nations expressed their approval of the blockade, as did the Organization of American States by unanimous vote. Before there was any naval conflict, the Russians ordered twelve of their twenty-five ships then bound for Cuba to reverse direction. These ships presumably carried offensive arms. According to the press, an American invasion of Cuba remained a real possibility.

During the weekend of October 27–28 Khrushchev capitulated. Khrushchev and Kennedy had been in frequent communication, and most of the Russian premier's notes had been conciliatory. After Kennedy's refusal to abandon American bases in Turkey in exchange for Russian abandonment of its Cuban bases, Khrushchev agreed to dismantle the Cuban bases in exchange for Kennedy's pledge to lift the blockade and not to stage an invasion. The crisis eased, but the world would not have been surprised by a Russian action elsewhere where she had a military advantage, probably in Berlin. No such action came.

630

The next few weeks were uneasy ones. Kennedy continued to insist upon verification of the withdrawal of the offensive weapons, but Castro consistently refused United Nations inspections that the Russians were willing to grant. The Kennedy administration was firm but at the same time conciliatory, apparently not wishing to embarrass Khrushchev to the point where his position at home and in the Communist world generally might be endangered or where he might fall to a new and harder regime. (The Chinese Communists were openly critical of Khrushchev's capitulation.) Kennedy ordered the blockade lifted in mid-November after seeing photographs of Russian ships carrying missile parts away from Cuba. In early December, Russian ships were seen carrying dismantled twin-engine bombers away. It appeared that the Kennedy administration's victory had been virtually complete.

The Cuban crisis undoubtedly had an effect upon the way citizens voted on November 6, but political observers were not agreed upon just how much of the Democratic victory was attributable to Kennedy's Cuban policies. Clearly, the Cuban crisis did enhance Kennedy's stature in the eyes of most voters and did remove what many Republicans believed was their best issue. For the first time since 1934, the administration party gained seats in both Senate and House in an "off-year" election. In the new House there were 259 Democrats to 176 Republicans, as compared to 263 to 174 in the previous one. (The House had been temporarily increased to 437 seats with the admission of Hawaii and Alaska to statehood, but it reverted to the traditional 435 seats with the Eighty-eighth Congress.) The Democrats gained three seats in the Senate. Actually, they gained four, but the Republican governor of New Mexico, recently defeated for re-election, named himself to fill the unexpired term of the Democratic senator who died soon after election. Former Vice-President Nixon seemed to come to the end of his political career when he was defeated in his bid to become governor of California, but Republicans removed Democrats from governorships in Pennsylvania, Michigan, and Ohio. In general, Republican candidates with a reputation for liberalism fared better than those who avowed conservatism. The voters removed two Republican Congressmen from California who were members of the John Birch Society and rejected the candidacies of two other Birchers.

The public granted the President "more Democrats" in Congress as he had requested, but the Republican-Bourbon coalition that balked much of Kennedy's program remained strong. The new House had the same number of nonsouthern Democrats as before, 164, and southern Democrats continued to be chairmen of important committees because of the seniority rule.

The Last Year of the New Frontier

President Kennedy's hopes for the new Congress proved false. Conservative Democrats on Capitol Hill, many of them in advantageous positions on important House and Senate committees, resisted the administration's programs and succeeded in watering them down or getting them sidetracked in the congressional freight yards. The Eighty-eighth Congress enacted some Kennedy recommendations but not until after the President's assassination on November

22, 1963. Most of Kennedy's domestic program fit into two main classifications: improvement of the plight of the nation's impoverished through federal action; and further legislation to guarantee the Negro his civil rights.

We associate the term War on Poverty with President Lyndon B. Johnson rather than with President Kennedy for it was the former Vice-President who made the term a slogan. (Kennedy had used the term, however. During the 1960 campaign he declared, "The war on poverty and degradation is not yet over," and in his 1963 State of the Union message he had called for an "unconditional war on poverty in America.") But slogan or not, much of JFK's program was designed to diminish the extent of poverty. For example, using legislation already on the books, Kennedy in the spring of 1963 created the Committee on the Appalachian Region, a joint federal-state enterprise, and appointed Under Secretary of Commerce Franklin D. Roosevelt, Jr. as chairman. The committee coordinated special vocational training and public works programs in an effort to lift the economically depressed area.

The country as a whole enjoyed prosperity in early 1963, but there were several anomalies in the economy. Although the GNP was at a new peak—it increased 20 per cent in the almost three years of Kennedy's presidential term—and personal income was at an unprecedented level, unemployment continued to be a major problem. In 1961, 6.7 per cent of the civilian labor force was unemployed, and the figure declined only to 5.6 per cent in early 1963. Kennedy proposed again to give the economy a shot in the arm by reducing taxes and to reform the tax system as well. He called for a reduction of the federal tax rate from 20 to 14 per cent on the first $1,000 of personal income. The principle of stimulating the economy by increasing purchasing power was well established, but Congress was recalcitrant. Most Republicans in Congress and many highly placed Democrats seemed to agree less with Kennedy than with the retired Eisenhower, who write a blast against deficit spending in the *Saturday Evening Post* reminiscent of GOP oratory in the 1920's and 1930's. In the hope of making the package more palatable to congressional conservatives, the administration backed down on closing loopholes that enabled some wealthy people to avoid income taxation in a spectacular way, but the retreat did little to advance the bill. Finally, in late September the House voted a tax bill that reduced personal income taxes less than Kennedy had requested; the Senate withheld action until Johnson was President.

Kennedy's sympathy for the Negro's struggle for rights and respect strengthened black America's attachment to the Democratic party. Although Negro leaders sometimes were impatient with JFK for what seemed to them too much caution in dealing with Congress on Negro matters, Kennedy endeared himself to the Negro rank and file. He rallied to the support of Martin Luther King in Birmingham (Kennedy sent 3,000 troops to the city to keep the peace after the Chief of Police, "Bull" Connor, ordered unusual force used against Negro demonstrators), and he won a showdown with the governor of Alabama, George C. Wallace, over the admission of Negro students to the University of Alabama.

Racial strife came to one of its many climaxes in the spring and summer of 1963. In April and May came the conflict in Birmingham, the following month the Kennedy-Wallace confrontation. Kennedy, after appealing for racial justice on television, sent Congress a civil rights bill calling for the abolition of

632

discrimination in places of public accommodation, in publicly owned facilities, and in employment. The bill also would strengthen Department of Justice powers to speed desegregation of schools and to enforce voting rights. At the end of the summer, A. Philip Randolph, whose threatened march on Washington in 1941 had sandbagged FDR into ordering an end to racial discrimination in hiring workers for defense industries, with the organizing aid of Bayard Rustin staged a demonstration in Washington that dwarfed all previous such affairs. The hope at first was to have a turn-out of 100,000, but the March on Washington of 1963 attracted almost a quarter-million people, most of them Negro, who listened to a speech by Martin Luther King. Speaking from the steps of the Lincoln Memorial, Dr. King moved his audience deeply, especially in his peroration with its repeating refrain, "I have a dream. . . ." But the Civil Rights bill made little progress on Capitol Hill. The Judiciary Committee was unable to report the bill to the House until two days before the President was killed. It did not pass the House until February, and then it faced strong opposition in the Senate.

Although domestic tensions seemed to intensify during the months following the Cuban crisis and elections of 1962, relations between the United States and the Soviet Union improved. It appeared that, having come to the brink of war in the missile crisis, both sides sought accommodation and steps looking toward understanding and peace. In his commencement speech at American University, Kennedy declared it time to concentrate upon Russian–American common interests and to attempt to resolve differences. He announced as an earnest of good will that America would engage in no further nuclear testing in the atmosphere as long as other nations similarly refrained. Premier Khrushchev responded quickly and favorably. By the end of July, American, British, and Russian diplomats, meeting in Moscow, completed the so-called Test Ban Treaty, which bound the signatories not to detonate nuclear explosives in the atmosphere, in outer space, or under water. Underground detonations would be permissible if they released no radioactive debris outside the nation. The powers writing the treaty invited other nations to sign the pact. Most of them did so within a few months, the important exceptions being De Gaulle's France and Mao's China, each of which was working on its own nuclear weapons. The Senate ratified the Test Ban Treaty on September 24, 1963, with only nineteen dissenting votes. One of the votes against it came from Senator Barry Goldwater of Arizona. A few days later President Kennedy approved the sale to the Soviets of 150 million bushels of badly needed wheat.

Expressing sympathy for the Negro cause and relaxing tensions with the Soviet Union were sure-fire methods of inflaming the American right wing. Conservatives reacted to JFK with the kind of passion they once had reserved for FDR. The "Kennedy haters" were similar to the "Roosevelt haters"—shrill, harsh in their accusations, extreme in their derision. For example, there appeared in the *Dallas Morning News* the day of the assassination a full-page advertisement that accused the city's visitor of pursuing policies that could please only Communists.

In June, 1963, Kennedy had agreed with Vice President Johnson and Texas Governor John Connally to visit their state in late November. In the Byzantine politics of that state there had developed serious feuds between Democrats that threatened the party's success in 1964. The purpose of the

President's visit was to promote harmony—or at least the appearance of harmony. Hence, public appearances with leaders of the main factions. Hence, motorcades.

The assassination, the confusion, the grief, the television pictures of Lee Harvey Oswald and of Jack Ruby killing Oswald, the funeral—these are matters all Americans know, that are not likely to be forgotten by people who in 1963 were old enough to be aware of national events. All Americans know, and yet the nagging doubt persists that they do not know. The President's Commission on the Assassination, headed by Chief Justice Warren, made its report in September, 1964, and almost immediately its conclusions were called into doubt and remained subjects of controversy. But whether Lee Harvey Oswald acted alone or whether the President was the victim of a conspiracy, the country soon entered a new political era.

CHAPTER THIRTY

Consensus and Convulsion

ONE WHO LIKES IRONY AND PARADOX CAN FIND MUCH TO SAVOR IN THE direction of national politics during the years Lyndon Baines Johnson was President of the United States. In 1960 LBJ was generally considered the most conservative Democratic contender for the presidential nomination, but as President he vigorously and successfully sponsored a program of domestic legislation reminiscent of the Second New Deal. A man whose nomination for Vice-President had shocked and disappointed liberals in the next election was an ogre to the nation's right wing and the darling of the liberals. A southerner, he signed the strongest civil rights acts the nation had ever adopted. An "accidental" President who had been unable to gain the presidential nomination, he subsequently won re-election by the largest popular majority in the country's history. Like Truman, who also succeeded a man who in death was more loved than he had been in life, LBJ had a "hard act to follow"; but, unlike Truman, his electoral success when he ran on his own far outshined his predecessor.

Perhaps more important, a man whose political style was to seek consensus—and who, even when President, enjoyed some major successes by achieving consensus—spent his last White House years in an exceptionally hostile atmosphere. He brought to the presidential office a vast experience in political persuasion, bargaining, and maneuvering. He could find agreement where others failed. He could minimize conflict. His watchwords were steady progress, stability, harmony; one of his characteristic expressions was, "Come, let us reason together." For the first two or three years Johnson was President his political experience and manner stood him in good stead, but in time the skills of consensus became inadequate and were unable to prevent defeat and frustration. In an era of sharp conflict, of spasmodic social and political convulsion, the LBJ style simply did not go over. And the atmosphere of conflict and convulsion was partly of his own making.

The Politics of Consensus

Lyndon B. Johnson was born August 27, 1908, in Stonewall, Texas, to an agricultural family that had been active in local politics. He graduated from Southwest Texas State College and taught school for a year in Houston, but most of his career was in politics. In 1931 LBJ became secretary to the Congressman from his district and four years later became Texas director of the National Youth Administration. He won a special election to a vacant seat in the House in April, 1937; he won re-election each time thereafter until 1948. In that year he ran for the Senate and squeaked through the Democratic primary by 87 votes. Rising fast in the Senate, he became minority leader in 1952 and majority leader after the Democrats' electoral success in 1954. In this role he acquired a reputation as a thoroughly professional and adroit party leader who could keep harmony within his ranks and deliver the votes. Several Presidents have served in the Congress, but rarely have they been prominent in the official leadership. LBJ's experience as majority leader was to serve him well.

When President Kennedy died most of his domestic program remained unpassed. It is true that JFK had talked of an "eighteen-month delivery" program for his domestic bills, but his successor was able to get through more of Kennedy's program in one year than the Bostonian had been able to in three. Passing some of these measures could be accomplished only with unusual executive effort. Perhaps never before had the White House played such a major role in the legislative process. LBJ not only conferred with his congressional leaders; sometimes he got on the telephone to needle and wheedle obscure Representatives.

Among the more important acts of 1964 were the tax cut, the Urban Mass Transportation Act, the Economic Opportunity Act, and the Civil Rights Act. The tax measure went through by a lopsided majority, each party voting better than two-to-one for it. Of the eleven Democratic Senators who voted against the bill, all but three were from the South. Although the amount of money appropriated for the mass transport measure was small by federal standards—$375 million to be spent over three years, less than the Vietnamese War costs taxpayers each week—this act might well be the beginning of a solution to one of the nation's most important non-ideological problems. Noted for their technological ingenuity and organizational prowess, American city dwellers in the 1960's tolerated transportation problems that would not be acceptable to the citizens of London or Tokyo. The money was used to study ways to improve transport within large cities and in concentrations of large cities, as in the so-called Northeast Corridor. The Economic Opportunity Bill became law in August with easy passage in each house despite overwhelming opposition from the Republicans. (Senate GOP members voted against it 22 to 10, their House colleagues by 145 to 22.) This measure's purpose was to "break the cycle" of poverty among young people by establishing job-training centers and by setting up the Job Corps, a domestic equivalent of the Peace Corps. In October, President Johnson named R. Sargent Shriver, Jr., a brother-in-law of JFK who had been head of the Peace Corps, to head the Office of Economic Opportunity, which the act created within the Executive Office of the President.

Johnson's most dramatic legislative victory in 1964 was passage in June of the Civil Rights Act. Southern Senators delayed and filibustered the bill, but its advocates were ultimately able to invoke the cloture rule. After Dixie delegates were unable to talk the measure to death, passage came fast. A week later the bill passed the Senate with only 188 opposing votes.

Not always, however, was LBJ able to have his way with Congress. His Appalachia Bill, which was to provide a billion dollars for the rehabilitation of poverty-stricken people in eleven states in the eastern mountains, passed the Senate but failed to get through the House machinery. Medicare, long a vigorously contested idea, failed to overcome the opposition of Congressman Wilbur Mills of Arkansas, chairman of the House Ways and Means Committee, and did not pass. Each house had passed a bill increasing Social Security benefits, and the Senate members of the conference committee attached a Medicare rider to the bill. The amended bill passed the Senate, but Representative Mills used his committee chairmanship to bottle it up, thereby killing both Medicare and the benefit increase.

President Johnson enjoyed wide popularity for having carried forward the Kennedy policies. Few political observers could see hope for the Republicans in 1964, and the polls offered the GOP little encouragement. Nevertheless, competition for the Republican nomination was intense. The early favorites were Senator Barry Goldwater of Arizona and Governor Nelson A. Rockefeller of New York. Rockefeller's recent divorce and remarriage were a political liability, and it was difficult for Republican moderates to take the extraordinarily conservative Goldwater very seriously. In the New Hampshire primary, the first of the presidential primaries to be held, Republican voters rejected both the New Yorker and the Arizonan and elected Ambassador to South Vietnam Henry Cabot Lodge, Jr. with a write-in campaign. That was Lodge's high-tide, however; a former Senator from Massachusetts and Nixon's running-mate in 1960, Lodge had little support outside New England. Rockefeller won the Oregon primary in May and Goldwater came in only third, but Goldwater had been getting many commitments from states without primaries. When Goldwater won the California primary—although not by a large margin—his nomination was almost assured. Two weeks before the GOP convention, which met in San Francisco in mid-July, Republican moderates put forward the candidacy of Pennsylvania Governor William Scranton as a stop-Goldwater candidate.

Goldwater's nomination and campaign illustrated powerfully the strength of ideology in American politics. The tenacity with which conservative Republican leaders clung to their doctrines, symbols, and myths was stronger than their capacity to see the political situation objectively and realistically. A week before the Republican convention the newspapers carried the latest Gallup Poll, which showed that Goldwater would get only 18 per cent of the popular vote against Johnson, less than Scranton or former Vice-President Nixon. What was it, then, that led the convention to nominate Goldwater on the first ballot with 883 votes to 214 for Scranton, who came in second? Part of the answer lay in the conservatives' belief that previous Republican candidates would have won if only they had been true-blue conservatives rather than "me too" candidates who minimized their differences with their more liberal Democratic opponents. The argument was that there was a large "silent vote" that would turn out if the party nominated a true believer. Part of the answer lay in Goldwater's personality and background. A clean-cut former fighter pilot with a Hollywood jaw, he was more sincere and outspoken than articulate. It was not difficult to imagine Goldwater as a successful local businessman and social chairman of the country club. But much of the answer lay in Goldwater's unabashed, old-fashioned conservative political stances. Thirty years later, Goldwater still did not accept the New Deal. In a press release in February, 1964, he said, ". . . the federal government should sell or otherwise dispose of TVA in its present form." He argued that Social Security should be put on a voluntary basis. "I am against the progressive features of the income tax. . . . We can't repeal the income tax totally. It's an evil, but we obviously need major sources of tax revenue," he told an interviewer. He said the United States should withdraw from the United Nations and cease to recognize the Soviet Union. He voted against the Nuclear Test Ban Treaty in the Senate and told a *Newsweek* reporter, "I'd drop a low-yield atomic bomb on Chinese supply lines in North Vietnam." While he was an active candidate for the nomination he voted against ending the southern filibuster against the Civil Rights Bill and against the bill itself, being one of the six opposing Republicans. He voted against the Economic Opportunity Act and Medicare. Goldwater selected William Miller, a Representative from western New York, to share the ticket.

The element of suspense was missing in the Democratic convention at Atlantic City in late August. There was some support for nominating Robert F. Kennedy for Vice-President, but Johnson gave the nod to Senator Hubert H. Humphrey of Minnesota. After the emotion of the Republican convention, in which delegates booed Rockefeller so loudly he could not be heard, the Democrats, who in some earlier conventions had engaged in spectacular internal conflicts, were dully harmonious.

The campaign was not very exciting because the outcome was never much in doubt. It is almost a rule of politics, given normal conditions, that a candidate should endeavor to project himself as moderate, sound, and middle-of-the-road. As commanding the high ground is a military axiom, commanding the middle ground is a political one. Thus, if a candidate's appeal is mainly to those right-of-center, he will attempt to identify his opponent as a left extremist. The left-of-center candidate will attempt the reverse. Candidate Goldwater got his campaign off to a disastrous start as far as the middle ground was concerned. In the pre-convention campaign Goldwater opponents had sought to get him to disclaim support from the right-wing John Birch Society, which Goldwater refused to do. Phrases such as "extremists within the party" became a euphemism for the Birchers. In his acceptance speech at the convention Goldwater, before a national television audience, yielded the middle ground. He explicitly welcomed all who would give him sincere support, a bow toward the Birch group, and declared, "I would remind you that extremism in the defense of liberty is no vice. And let me remind you also that moderation in the pursuit of justice is no virtue." Johnson and other Democrats played the situation to advantage, picturing Goldwater as a trigger-happy, shoot-from-the-hip reactionary without the sound judgment necessary to be President. Johnson spoke in generalities about the Great Society in terms that would seem ironic before the next election:

> This nation, this people, this generation, has man's first chance to create a Great Society: a society of success without squalor, beauty without barrenness, works of genius without the wretchedness of poverty. We can open the doors of learning. We can open the doors of fruitful labor and rewarding leisure, of open opportunity and close community—not just to the privileged few, but, thank God, we can open those doors to everyone.

Senator Goldwater led his party to the worst defeat in a presidential election since the development of the present party system and popular suffrage. Goldwater carried six states, better than Landon in 1936, but his popular percentage was a new low. Johnson received 61.3 per cent of the popular vote; FDR had half a percentage point less in 1936. Besides his home state, Goldwater carried only states in deep Dixie: South Carolina, Georgia, Alabama (where Governor George Wallace kept Johnson off the ballot), Mississippi, and Louisiana. With Goldwater heading their ticket, lesser Republicans fell like dominoes. The Democrats' net gain in the Senate was only two, but they had thirty-nine more House seats. Indeed, only in the House elected in 1936 had the Democrats enjoyed a greater majority. The Democratic landslide extended even to state legislatures, the Republicans losing over five hundred seats in the fifty states.

Conservative Republicans now found themselves in a worse position than they had faced for years. Confident of popular support because of the electoral landslide, LBJ faced less conservative opposition in Congress than any Democratic President since the mid-1930's. Several northern and western members of the conservative coalition in Congress had been defeated, and many freshman Democrats in the House realized they were there primarily because Johnson had headed the ticket—or that Goldwater had headed the opposing slate. The President recognized his advantageous position and presented Congress with a long list of requests. In 1965–1966 Congress enacted most of the requested Great Society measures; the Eighty-ninth Congress passed more reform and welfare legislation than any Congress since the New Deal.

The idea of extending Social Security to include medical care for the elderly had been before the people for almost a generation, sometimes a hot issue, sometimes quiescent, but always opposed by the American Medical Association, which lobbied vigorously. Having come close to passage in 1964, Medicare in 1965 sailed through each house with big majorities. A complicated measure, it provided a basic health plan for most people over sixty-five years old and offered a supplementary $50-deductible health insurance plan for which the insured paid a premium of $3 a month. Congress also amended the basic Social Security Act to provide higher retirement benefits and coverage for more people. Another extension of a New Deal law was an amendment in 1966 of the Fair Labor Standards Act of 1938 that increased the minimum legal wage to $1.40 an hour, effective in early 1967, and to $1.60 a year later. The amendment also broadened the law's coverage to include an estimated additional eight million workers.

The much publicized War on Poverty received almost twice as much in appropriations in 1965—$1.5 billion—as the year before. And the new Congress relented and passed the Appalachia Bill it had rejected in 1964. Yet the law and the Public Works and Economic Development Act of August, 1965, an extension of the Appalachia idea to other depressed areas, was more of what a nineteenth-century American would have called an internal improvements act than a direct aid to the poverty-stricken. Most of the $1.1 billion for the Appalachia program was earmarked for highway construction, and most of the subsequent measure was similarly set aside for roads, airports, and parks. Labeling building programs as poverty programs magnified the public's view of the amount of federal money going to the nation's poor.

Similarly, there was more sound than substance in the urban-problems and housing field. At LBJ's insistence, Congress passed a bill creating a new Department of Housing and Urban Development to administer existing public-housing programs, FHA, and all other federal activity in the field. Essentially a matter of administrative reorganization, the President dramatized the new Department by naming Robert C. Weaver to be its Secretary. Weaver, an experienced administrator in the field, became the first Negro Cabinet member. (A similar reorganization was the 1966 creation of the twelfth Cabinet-level agency, the Department of Transportation.) The act creating HUD had an interesting section providing for the possibility of federal grants to poor families of supplementary funds to provide adequate rental housing. Under the rent supplement provision the government would pay the difference between the actual rent charged low-income families by special non-profit housing corporations and what was a reasonable share of the family income for housing, about 25 per cent. The House Appropriations Committee, however, made the provision ineffective by withholding the necessary funds. The Demonstration Cities and Metropolitan Development Act of 1966 provided for federal grants to local units of government of up to 80 per cent of the cost of comprehensively planned "model" neighborhoods in some sixty cities over the country. This scheme, if supported with massive appropriations and intelligently administered, could greatly improve housing in the inner cities. Despite these measures, however, the nation's housing problem became more acute. New housing starts in 1966 fell below the rate of a million a year for the first time in twenty years.

Actual achievement was greater in education. Federal aid to education had existed since the Morrill Act of 1862 provided land-grant colleges, but federal education measures had been disconnected and piecemeal. No comprehensive federal education law existed before 1965, when Congress passed the Elementary and Secondary School Act and the Higher Education Act. The former law provided $1.3 billion for assistance to both public and private (mostly parochial) schools for books and other materials, and it got around the sticky religious issue by granting the funds to state agencies. The Higher Education Act was complex. Among its provisions were funds for scholarships, financial aid to colleges for buying books and laboratory and teaching equipment, and for a National Teacher Corps to train special teachers for substandard schools. Congress, however, failed to provide funds for the Teacher Corps until the next year, and then it cut back LBJ's requested $31.4 million to $7.5 million. Related to education also was the so-called Cold War GI Bill of Rights, which offered educational assistance to veterans of the armed services who had served six months or more since 1955, when the earlier GI Bill expired. Congress also created and modestly funded the National Foundation on the Arts and Humanities, a counterpart to the National Science Foundation.

Congress enacted still another Civil Rights Act in 1965, this one to remove barriers to Negro voting, which were common in the South. Indeed, the central issue in the Alabama demonstrations, to be described later, was the right to vote. The law suspended literacy tests for voting in any state or county where less than half the voting age population was registered or voted in the last election; it further empowered the Attorney General to send federal examiners to counties where he had reason to believe an examiner was necessary to prevent voting discrimination.

The Immigration Act of 1965 reversed the nation's policy in this field by abolishing the national origins and quota system, in effect since the early 1920's. By no means a new idea—every President since Truman had called for an end of the national quota policy—the act of 1965 established a ceiling of 120,000 a year on immigrants from the Western Hemisphere and 170,000 from elsewhere. Aspiring immigrants with the highest priority were immediate relatives of American citizens or alien residents; next highest priority went to people with special professional qualifications or education. Under this arrangement immigration from England, Ireland, and Germany fell off importantly while it increased from Italy, Greece, and Portugal.

Finally, Congress passed a group of measures that had to do with consumer problems and pollution of the environment. A rather weak Truth in Packaging Act passed in 1966, although a Truth in Lending Bill got pigeonholed. After Ralph Nader's book *Unsafe at Any Speed* appeared in late 1965, calling attention to inadequately designed automobiles, public opinion developed to require auto-makers to incorporate more safety features, especially after it became known that a detective agency hired by General Motors had investigated Nader in an attempt to find something embarrassing about him. The Motor Vehicle Safety Act set minimum standards of safety for autos and established a uniform system of grading tires. Highway beautification and stepped-up programs to alleviate water and air pollution also were enacted, but they were no more than a first step.

The legislative achievements of this Congress in domestic affairs were impressive, especially when contrasted with the dead-center politics that had prevailed for a generation. Journalists and Democratic leaders extolled the record and praised the President's ability to achieve a consensus for forward motion; they had some basis for their assertions. On the other hand, it was easy to overstate the case. For all its acts, the Eighty-ninth Congress for the most part only extended New Deal concepts of federal action and filled in some of the gaps. Perhaps only in its greater concern about urban problems did the Congress of 1965–1966 go beyond the thought of 1935.

In any case, the likelihood of further such achievements was fading fast. Two issues were dividing the nation as it had not been torn since the Great Depression, perhaps since the Civil War: the war in Vietnam and racial tensions at home. LBJ's consensus melted away quickly while the Eighty-ninth Congress was in session, and it was to disappear soon thereafter. As FDR's domestic coalition was torn apart by foreign policy issues in the late 1930's, so

LBJ's support divided remarkably sharply over policy in Southeast Asia. The lines of alliance shifted on Capitol Hill and within the political parties. The President struggled to preserve domestic consensus by keeping the Vietnam issue separate. In his 1966 State of the Union Message he declared for guns *and* butter: "This nation is mighty enough ... to pursue our goals in the rest of the world while still building a Great Society here at home." But many who were for the Great Society ideal opposed the President on Vietnam, and many who begrudged every federal welfare dollar and each reform supported his war policies. As the war wore on and dissatisfaction with it increased, the production of Congress declined. Progressive measures in 1966 were fewer than in 1965, and many of them, such as the National Teacher Corps, were done cheaply.

The congressional and state elections of 1966 pointed up the administration's deteriorating strength. Republicans made a strong comeback, gaining forty-seven seats in the House, three in the Senate, and eight governorships. The states were divided exactly evenly between Republican and Democratic governors. No one seriously expected the new Congress to carry forward the direction of its predecessor; they would have been disappointed if it had.

Vietnam: Hawks and Doves

Time and again in the nation's history reasonable predictions about the next three or four years have turned out wildly wrong. The week after Johnson rolled over Goldwater a perceptive analyst might have predicted some of the measures of the new Congress, but he probably would not have foreseen that in less than four years Johnson would be highly unpopular. Public opinion polls in late 1967 revealed that less than a majority of people thought Johnson was doing a good job, an about face from late 1964. Nor would a prophet have predicted that before the 1968 elections there would have been more American servicemen killed in Southeast Asia than had been killed in the Korean War. After all, Johnson had pictured himself as peaceful and prudent and Goldwater as trigger happy. "Which man," LBJ asked a few days before the election, "do you want to have his thumb close to that atomic button?" Goldwater was critical of what he called the "no win" policy in Vietnam— there were about 25,000 Americans there then—but Johnson said the nation should not "get tied down to a land war in Asia." On another occasion the President had said, "I have not thought that we were ready for American boys to do the fighting for Asian boys."

Such are the tides of politics that by the spring of 1968 the landslide winner of 1964 had become so unpopular that he restricted his public appearances in the nation's large cities; his domestic progressive achievements had slowed to a virtual stop; the black revolution had moved so far so fast that a march of poor people, most of them Negro, was about to come to Washington to make demands upon his administration as the Bonus Army had upon Hoover's; and other leaders of his party were threatening to take the 1968 nomination away from him, primarily because of the war in Vietnam. The force of the urban black revolution, which promised to become more acute unless government spent far more on urban problems and the problem of poverty, combined with the Vietnamese war, which cost about $33 million a day in 1967, put enormous pressures upon the government's fiscal position. Unless total spending increased tremendously, it was clear, military spending precluded significant boosts in spending on urban and poverty problems. As a matter of fact, federal spending declined in most non-military fields. The vision of a Great Society had heightened expectations that had no political reality if military spending continued at the 1967 rate.

The war was central to crisis-ridden, rebellious, explosive developments in almost every area of social concern in the later 1960's. One could not understand the black revolution without the Vietnamese context, or the student revolt or the phenomenon of accelerated social change and ferment.

Earlier in this book (see pages 555–558 and 620) we have briefly considered the American situation in Vietnam during the Eisenhower and Kennedy administrations, but it is necessary to review the situation when Johnson became President. Vietnam occupied Kennedy's attention increasingly in 1963, although American involvement there was still relatively small. The regime of Ngo Dien Diem, which began in 1954, was thoroughly undemocratic, protective of the landlords who extracted unconscionable rents from the peasants, ineffective in combating the Vietcong, and repressive toward non-Communist reformers and religious groups such as the Buddhists. Buddhist demonstrations became more frequent in 1963, and South Vietnamese government troops put them down with unnecessary force. Americans became increasingly aware of the strife between the Diem government and the Buddhists after some Buddhist monks publicly burned themselves to death as an indication of protest. Disgusted with Diem, and his brother Nhu and Mme. Nhu, Kennedy publicly criticized the South Vietnamese ruling family, whereupon South Vietnamese generals overthrew the Diem government and killed Diem and Nhu on November 1, 1963. (Succeeding South Vietnamese governments were not significantly more effective until a military junta took over in mid-1965, and all were highly unstable as well; the junta, headed by Air Force Marshal Nguyen Cao Ky, was the eighth government in eighteen months.)

American involvement in Vietnam escalated under Kennedy, but only by a little. American military personnel increased from about 4,000 in early 1962 to about 11,000 in early 1963 and to about 16,500 by November 22, 1963. On the one hand, Kennedy accepted the Southeast Asia Domino Theory of Eisenhower and Dulles, although he rejected their notion that communism was monolithic, a view difficult to defend after Soviet-Chinese conflict became open. On the other, Kennedy was uncomfortable about American presence in the little country. When Kennedy asked Canadian Prime Minister Lester Pearson for his advice about Vietnam and the Canadian replied, "Get out," Kennedy's response was, "That's a stupid answer. Everybody knows that. The question is: How do we get out?"

President Johnson devoted little of his time to Vietnam until the summer of 1964. During these months, however, the Vietcong steadily increased their strength and area of influence, and some of Johnson's advisers in the State and Defense Departments were apprehensive the Vietcong would have overwhelming control before the 1964 elections.

On August 2, 1964, between the Republican and Democratic national conventions, the newspapers reported that three North Vietnamese patrol boats had attacked the American destroyer *Maddox* in the Gulf of Tonkin some thirty miles off the North Vietnamese coast. The United States protested to North Vietnam and warned it would take retaliatory action in the event of another attack. Two days later came reports that the *Maddox* had again been attacked by patrol boats as had another destroyer, the *C. Turner Joy.* There was no damage to the destroyers on either date. The United States retaliated immediately on August 4 with air strikes against the patrol boat base in North Vietnam, destroying about twenty-five of the vessels. On August 5 Johnson sent Congress a message asking for authority "to take all necessary measures to repel any armed attack against the forces of the United States and to prevent further aggression." Johnson told Congress that "hostile nations" must be given to understand that the campaign would not prevent the nation from protecting its interests "and that in these matters there is no division among us." On August 7 the House unanimously passed the administration's resolution, and the Senate passed it with two dissenting votes by Wayne Morse and Ernest Gruening.

Senator Gaylord Nelson of Wisconsin sought to amend the resolution to put Congress on record against "extension of the present conflict," to prevent a substantial change in the nature of American involvement in Vietnam. Foreign Relations Committee Chairman J. William Fulbright talked Nelson out of pushing the amendment, saying that the amendment was not necessary since Nelson's proposal was "an accurate reflection of what I believe is the President's policy." Senator Fulbright would later refer to this action on the Senate floor as his "greatest mistake." The administration subsequently cited the Tonkin Gulf Resolution as a blank-check congressional authorization of its military activities in Vietnam; in 1967 Under Secretary of State Nicholas deB. Katzenbach called the resolution "the functional equivalent" of a declaration of war.

American military forces were involved in one other significant military encounter with Vietnamese Communists before the presidential election. Soon after the Tonkin Gulf incidents, the administration moved some B-57 bombers to an air base at Bien Hoa, South Vietnam, for the specific purpose of impressing North Vietnam with American air power. The Vietcong regarded the bombers as a symbol as well, and in late October eluded the base security guard and destroyed six of the bombers with mortar fire, killing five American servicemen and wounding 76. The ambassador to South Vietnam, General Maxwell Taylor, recommended air attacks on the North as a reprisal, but coming only days before the election it was not surprising that the President rejected his counsel.

During the winter of 1964–1965 United Nations Secretary General U Thant endeavored to bring the United States and North Vietnam together for talks. Nothing came of his effort. Essentially, the administration did not want negotiations but would have to accept them if North Vietnam indicated it wanted them, and the North Vietnamese, feeling that they had been tricked out of their 1954 victory over the French by the negotiations that ended in the Geneva accords and the partition of Vietnam, wanted nothing short of American withdrawal.

The United States sharply escalated the war in February and March, 1965. On February 7, after a Vietcong raid on an installation at Pleiku, which killed eight American soldiers, American bombers flew missions over the southern part of North Vietnam. Three days later came another Vietcong attack on Americans and another retaliatory bombing of the North. This tit-for-tat pattern soon ceased, and the air force began systematic bombing of North Vietnam, at first avoiding Hanoi. The war was on.

"It was almost imperceptible, the way we got in," said an administration official who resisted escalation. "There was no one move that you could call decisive, or irreversible, not even very many actions that you could argue against in isolation. Yet when you put it all together, there we were in a war on the Asian mainland, with nobody really putting up much of a squawk while we were doing it." On February 28 the administration announced a decision to conduct continuous but limited air raids on the North, and a month later the President announced his intention of sending several thousand more troops to Vietnam. In May, Johnson requested a supplementary appropriation for the war and two Marine divisions went to Vietnam. Without much fanfare, the American military's function shifted from training South Vietnamese and protecting American bases to mounting offensives against the Vietnamese Communists. In a guerilla war without conventional battle lines and territorial control, American units, both Marine and Army, engaged in "search and destroy missions" with the purpose of eliminating the guerilla enemy. In many cases an area the South Vietnamese or the Americans controlled during the day was effectively the enemy's during darkness. And as the United States escalated with more troops and more bombing, both in North Vietnam and Communist concentrations in the South, the North Vietnamese escalated by sending more troops to fight alongside the Communists of the South, the Vietcong. Hopeful that strategic bombing of North Vietnamese supply routes would provide

TABLE 15

American Troops in Vietnam	
Nov. 1963	16,500
Nov. 1964	25,000
Dec. 1965	180,000
Dec. 1966	380,000
Dec. 1967	450,000

(The peak during the Korean War was 325,000.)

American Deaths in Vietnam from All Causes	
Jan.-June 1965	385
June-Dec. 1965	1,343
Jan.-June 1966	1,926
June-Dec. 1966	4,127
Jan.-June 1967	5,603
June-Dec. 1967	5,445
Jan.-June 1968	10,503

an easy method to prevent continued North Vietnamese escalation, the American military ordered heavier aerial bombardment. By early 1968 American bombers had dropped more bomb tonnage on Vietnam than they had on Europe in all of World War II, but their efforts simply failed to be effective. Despite the bombing of supply routes and other strategic targets, there were more Communist guerillas in South Vietnam and they were better supplied than they had been before. As Senate Majority Leader Mike Mansfield put it, the war had become "open-ended": each side's enlargement of it met reciprocal escalation by the other.

As the war escalated, so did the conflict between critics and supporters of the war at home, between the Doves and Hawks as they soon came to be called. Americans were deeply and passionately divided over the war; in earlier internal divisions over foreign policy, only the Versailles issue and the "isolationist-interventionist" scrap of 1938–1941 approached the pervasiveness and intensity of differences over Vietnam. Forthright opposition to American policy in Vietnam developed almost immediately after initiation of bombing the North in February, 1965. At first only a minority (largely on the campuses, where there were several anti-war "teach-ins" in the spring of 1965), critics of the war in time became a majority. The Dove population increased and the Hawk decreased as it became increasingly apparent that from the beginning the military establishment had grossly underestimated the Vietcong and the North Vietnamese and that a victory in the sense of V-E Day probably could not be achieved without destroying the country the war was intended to save and without incurring a grave risk of World War III. By late 1967 or early the next year, a majority of Americans considered it a mistake to have got into Vietnam; the question then became what Kennedy had asked the Canadian Prime Minister: "How do we get out?"

Dove arguments ranged from objections based upon abstract ethical principles to practical balancing of probable gains and costs. Pacifist arguments, both religious and secular, were prevalent; church action groups and the clergy—Protestant, Catholic, and Jewish—were prominent in the anti-war movement. Humane considerations played a large part in many people's thinking. Extraordinary numbers of noncombatant Vietnamese, both North and South, were killed or wounded by American bombing; civilian casualties may even have been larger than military ones. Large numbers of South Vietnamese peasants became refugees, shunted about from one military zone to another. And people felt an immediacy about the bloodshed because they frequently saw newsreel clips of military action on television; never before had Americans had a war brought into their living rooms.

Philosophical political principles about democracy and the propriety of being involved in what was at least partly a Vietnamese civil war were part of Dove thinking. Anti-communists who had no sympathy for North Vietnam found it difficult to be enthusiastic about South Vietnam. Its governments were spectacularly unstable until Ky came to power, and while the Ky government provided continuity, it was by no means democratic. Ky, from the North before the 1954 partition, had been a cadet in the French air force while his countrymen were fighting French colonialism, and the General lost American support when he publicly voiced his admiration for Adolf Hitler. Lagging in the land reforms that American advisers urged and corrupt or ineffective in policing corruptionists, the various Saigon governments appealed little to most Americans. The military government that came to power in 1965 won an election, however suspect, in 1967, in which Ky was demoted to Vice-President, and the former second man, General Nguyen Van Thieu, moved up; but making its power legitimate failed to change American opinion.

Principled objections to the war lent passion to the Doves, but practical considerations were extremely important. First was the question of whether or not any military solution to the problem of South Vietnam was possible or whether only political means could bring about an acceptable solution. Certainly, the South Vietnamese army was hampered by the government's lack of real political popularity. Its soldiers did not have the determination and zeal the enemy had. Secondly, if there was a military solution, was it one that Americans with their western industrialized, military traditions and abilities could bring about? A mechanically sophisticated force built upon the world's most industrialized economy, the American army had won most of its victories because of overwhelming firepower, both on the ground and in the air. Superior firepower was an advantage even in guerilla warfare, obviously, but it was not as advantageous against a concealed enemy as it was against one who openly concentrated his strength to defend territory.

The war's effect on other foreign relations caused concern. After the Cuban crisis there seemed to develop a movement toward détente with the Soviet Union, but such a relaxation of tensions was unlikely to continue while the United States remained involved in the Vietnamese war. (That détente was a popular idea among Americans was clear from the warm response to the surprise conference with the Russian premier, Alexei Kosygin, at Glassboro, New Jersey, in June, 1967. Nothing visible or essential came from the conference.) Détente or not, the nations the United States regarded as its friends and allies had little taste for the war in Vietnam. In Europe America's role in Vietnam was highly unpopular. Another basic and practical matter, apart from considerations of principle, was the question of costs and priorities among needs, such as aid to education and the war on poverty. Problems at home and other problems abroad, all of which cost money, suffered from financial neglect.

The most common Hawk argument used an historical analogy: North Vietnamese or Chinese designs on their neighbors were latter-day parallels of Nazi expansion, and the Vietcong were the analogues of the Sudeten Germans. Munich, the symbol of British and French appeasement of Hitler, had lessons to teach: Stop the aggressors where they were or be faced with a more powerful enemy later. Sometimes explicit and sometimes not, this reasoning was common in the top echelons of the Department of State.

Another point the Hawks stressed was that anti-war marches, demonstrations, and other manifestations of opposition strengthened the Vietcong and North Vietnamese and postponed a settlement of the war because outward dissent made it appear that America might eventually abandon the war effort. Sometimes pro-war right-wingers equated opposition to the war with outright treason. Even President Johnson, who while raising the stakes in the war kept saying that he sought an honorable peace, came close to an endorsement of suppression. He told a Chicago audience in May, 1966, "There will be some

Nervous Nellies and some who will become frustrated and bothered and break ranks under the strain. And some will turn on their leaders and their country and on our own fighting men."

Hawk arguments made less of an impact after mid-1967, largely because of a serious suspicion that the administration was not candid with the nation—the "credibility gap"—and because of the course of events in Vietnam. Whether because of naïve optimism or dissimulation, American military commanders issued overconfident statements about the war's progress that made subsequent setbacks the more disappointing and undermined belief in the necessity of their calls for more troops. Johnson, off to a bad start on the credibility matter with the contrast between his campaign and subsequent positions, lost further credibility in 1967 when the Senate Foreign Relations Committee investigated the Tonkin Gulf incidents and concluded that the administration's evidence when it ordered retaliation had been extremely scanty. The destroyers' crews had not actually seen the patrol boats but had only observed blips on the radar screen.

The attitude of disbelief and feeling of futility became stronger with the success of the Vietcong's Tet offensive that began January 31, 1968. In surprise strikes on Saigon and Hué, carefully prepared by infiltration of troops and supplies into the cities, the Vietcong thoroughly disrupted American plans. The Vietcong in Hué controlled a section of the city for several days. When American troops rushed to the cities, Vietcong forces extended their influence in the countryside. The nation was incredulous when the American commander in Vietnam, General William C. Westmoreland, characterized the Vietcong's action as a loser's "last gasp." If it was a last-gasp effort of a defeated foe, critics wondered, why then did the General ask for 206,000 more American troops? How was it that hundreds, perhaps thousands, of Vietcong infiltrated Saigon and Hué under the noses of American intelligence? Why had not non-Communist Vietnamese informed American commanders? If they had been informed, why were the Vietcong so successful?

The Tet Offensive had brought the Vietnamese issue to a head. In the next few weeks there would be dramatic political developments and a change of direction.

The Black Revolt

The momentum the Negro movement developed in the mid-1950's continued for several years before it began to shift direction and mood in the mid-1960's. Forward motion toward its conventional goals was impressive. Indications of advance were particularly plentiful in political matters. Between 1957 and 1968, Congress passed five Civil Rights Acts. The Acts of 1957 and 1960 (see pages 593–594) were weak, but there was greater substance in the latter three. Under the laws of 1964 and 1965 Negroes registered and voted in significant numbers in states where their right to vote had by some device or another been denied. By 1966 in most southern states—perhaps only Mississippi was a real exception—a candidate for statewide office had to reckon seriously with the Negro vote. However, because of northward and westward black migration, there was

TABLE 16

PERCENTAGES OF NEGROES REGISTERED TO VOTE

	1960	1966
Texas	35	80
Arkansas	37	54
Louisiana	30	42
Tennessee	52	72
Mississippi	5	28
Alabama	15	49
Virginia	24	44
North Carolina	31	46
South Carolina	16	45
Georgia	29	43
Florida	35	62

relatively less Negro vote potential in the South than before Pearl Harbor. In the 1966 Democratic primary in Alabama, for example, Negroes went all out to defeat Mrs. Lurleen Wallace. (Mrs. Wallace was a stand-in candidate for her husband, George Wallace, who was unable to succeed himself under the state constitution.) The favorite of the Negro voters received an estimated 90 per cent of the Negro vote, but Mrs. Wallace won. Outside the South where voter discrimination had not been important in this century, Negroes concentrated their efforts and in 1968 there were Negro mayors in Cleveland, Gary, and Washington. In addition, there were Negro members of the Supreme Court, the Cabinet, and the Federal Reserve Board. In 1966 the Republican Attorney General of Massachusetts, Edward W. Brooke, was elected to the Senate, where he was the first Negro to serve since Reconstruction.

Another indication of growing black political force was the 1964 cloture vote to cut off a southern filibuster against the Civil Rights Bill. For three months Dixie Democrats succeeded in stopping the Bill, but finally, for the first time in history on a civil rights matter, the Senate invoked the cloture rule, with four votes to spare beyond the required two-thirds. The voting pattern revealed sensitivity, or lack of it, to the Negro votes in the states. Every Senator from the historic Civil War border states, irrespective of party, voted for cloture. However, Robert C. Byrd of West Virginia, which had separated from Virginia during the Civil War, voted with the Confederate Senators, all of whom but Ralph Yarborough of Texas were against cloture. Six Republican Senators voted with the Dixie group; all of them were from the Rocky Mountain or Great Plains states, an area with a small Negro population. (Senator Goldwater was one of the six.)

The 1968 Civil Rights Act concerned housing primarily. The law prohibited discrimination in selling, renting, advertising, and financing most classifications of housing, an estimated 80 per cent of the country's housing units. Preceding this law several states and local governments had enacted open-housing laws of some sort. Soon after the 1968 Act, the Supreme Court in a surprise decision declared discrimination in the transfer of real estate and other property was contrary to a Reconstruction measure still on the books.

There were some economic gains—and some economic losses. Some big employers had made a strong effort to upgrade Negro employees, and several excellent colleges and universities had systematically scoured the country for promising Negro freshmen. With changed personnel policies and wider educational opportunities there was little question that the caliber of jobs held by Negroes improved in the 1960's; the number of Negroes who were middle class in income and job status was growing. In other respects, however, there were serious problems. Unemployment and underemployment among Negroes were tragically high. The situation was worst among two groups of Negroes: those in the agricultural areas of the South, largely in the Mississippi River delta, where technological innovation sharply reduced the number of farm jobs; those in the northern big city ghettos—and this was the more explosive situation—where unemployment in 1967 was 9.3 per cent as compared with the national white rate of 3.3 per cent. Furthermore, more than a third of the employed black workers in the eight largest cities earned less than $3,000 a year, as compared with about 4 per cent for whites. There was strong statistical evidence that in the ghettos there was forming a class of more or less permanently poor, an "underclass" that perpetuated itself from generation to generation. The poorest one-fifth of the black citizens of America were worse off in real earnings in 1967 than they had been ten years earlier.

There was some impressive evidence of Negro unity and white solidarity with the Negro cause. The March on Washington of 1963, described briefly in the previous chapter, was a case in point. In the spring of 1965 came another massive march, this one in Alabama. In January, Dr. Martin Luther King called for street demonstrations in Selma, Alabama, a symbol of resistance to Negro demands, if voter registration did not quicken. Matters came to a head in February and March. Dr. King and hundreds of Negro pickets were arrested on February 1, and two days later a thousand Negro children were arrested in a nearby town when they started a march on the county courthouse. A week later Sheriff James G. Clark and his deputies drove 165 black children and adolescents on a forced march, using clubs and electric cattle prods on them when they faltered. A white minister from Boston died of a beating, and a young Alabama Negro died in a clash between police and demonstrators. Dr. King was determined to organize a march from Selma to Montgomery, fifty-four miles away, as a symbolic gesture. Governor Wallace tried to prevent the march, but a federal court upheld the right to hold it and President Johnson called units of the Alabama National Guard to federal duty to protect the marchers. In late March thousands walked from Selma to Montgomery, and for the final entry into the Confederacy's first capital there were about 25,000 participants on the road. One striking aspect of the Montgomery march was the commitment of white liberals and of clergymen of all faiths and both races.

But if one looked more deeply into the Negro movement in the mid-1960's and into white attitudes one noticed that the Negro movement and expressions of it were changing in important ways. The movement was entering

650

a new stage, and the newer developments were widening the gulf with a majority of whites.

Just as rivers have a way of overflowing their banks and cutting new channels so did the stream of revolt of American Negroes; the movement that had gained unprecedented momentum since the mid-1950's experienced basic changes in the years Johnson was President. Where the main focus of black struggle had been in the South, the center of primary attention was shifting to northern and western cities. (By the late 1960's, only a minority of Negroes lived in the former Confederate states, and most of the northern and western majority lived in big cities.) Where the main thrust of the movement had been for voting and other political rights, it was beginning to veer off in other directions, largely economic. Where the movement had once been almost unanimously behind the goal of racial integration, there were increasing doubts about the possibility and even the desirability of integration and an increasing interest in black separatism. Where the main effort of the movement, unconsciously or not, had been to gain access to white-dominated traditional institutions (in the pattern of earlier groups, both economic and ethnic who strived to gain a place at the nation's table) there now was a growing tendency to say that institutions such as government, unions, and schools were hopeless even if Negroes shared their direction and that what really was needed was a fundamental economic and social reconstruction. Where only a few had dissented from the view that only non-violent tactics should be used, now there were increasing numbers who rejected non-violence as a philosophy, at least doubted its effectiveness as a tactic, or who advocated violence, or the threat of it, as a means toward the goal. There was rapidly developing a new mood, more impatient, angrier, more desperate.

The new mood and attitudes could be seen in what was happening in the main Negro organizations. The biggest and oldest of them, the NAACP and the Urban League, continued to grow, but whites became less prominent in them, there was more internal bickering, and they became generally more militant and radical. Established leaders had to run fast to stay ahead of their followers. In 1968 the remarks to a group of young black militants by the highly able but unmistakably middle class director of the Urban League, Whitney M. Young, Jr., were applauded and welcomed with shouts of "Amen, the brother has returned." CORE (Congress of Racial Equality), which was predominantly white from its founding in 1942 until the mid-1960's, suffered a split in 1968. The large Brooklyn and Bronx chapters announced their departure, charging CORE leadership was a "civil rights aristocracy" and asserting it was not working hard enough for "the destruction of white capitalism in black communities." The Student Nonviolent Coordinating Committee (SNCC, "Snick") underwent an upheaval in the summer of 1966 when non-students who were not advocates of non-violence gained control. The Southern Christian Leadership Conference seemed to flounder after the death of its leader, Dr. King, in April, 1968.

Behind these developments in the main Negro organizations were several matters that were bringing about a shift in the whole movement. One clear factor was the "generation gap." Most of the leaders had been in their forties or older—as are the leaders in most stable institutions—and the young people, those who were most active in demonstrations and most likely to be beaten or jailed or both, were impatient and rebellious. Many of the young militants had been in the movement from childhood, and they could not see that their activities had got the results they wanted. Another factor was that the frustrations of the black militants were real ones: gains in civil rights as such, in the right to vote primarily, had not significantly improved their lives. Perhaps even there had been a retrogression. In any case, expectations had exceeded reality, and disappointment and disillusion triggered bitter impulses of retribution. Still another factor were outbreaks of violent rioting in the Negro quarters of large cities, especially in 1965 and thereafter. In sum, the Negro temper was changing from a demand for full political participation in a democracy, irrespective of region but with a primarily southern focus, to a bristling, short-tempered revolt against conditions in the ghettos. The movement was becoming increasingly involved in old-fashioned class conflict, such as had existed in densely populated cities in America and abroad since the seventeenth and eighteenth centuries. It was class conflict, but it had the significant difference of race.

The slogan of "black power," which became popular in 1966, both excited and confused the Negro movement. The slogan symbolized different things to different people, both black and white. To some it meant simply immediate victory or fight; a resort to violence. This was the way frightened whites frequently understood it. To others it meant Negro control of the ghetto and the various institutions there, with whites being completely out of policy matters. To still others it meant what could be called black capitalism: Negro businesses of all kinds, with Negro capital, workers, managers, and customers. Late in the decade there seemed to be a sketchy consensus developing toward the latter two positions, but there was little agreement about how it could be reached. One matter on which there was a wide consensus was Negro "cultural nationalism": black art, "soul" music, Negro literature, "black is beautiful."

Many ghetto problems, it was clear, would remain if there were no racial prejudice and if political democracy were perfect, even though in fact they were enormously complicated by prejudice and democratic imperfections. The black ghetto's problems were similar in many ways to those of white slums, particularly in an earlier day. Rural people without urban and industrial skills, ill-prepared for the complexities of densely populated society, present special problems, and government generally failed to meet them satisfactorily. Housing in ghettos was deplorable beyond the imagination of more fortunate people. Lack of adequate sanitation facilities and insufficient public sanitation, combined with poverty and inadequate private health services, created and perpetuated fearful health problems. (Nationally, the Negro infant mortality rate was twice as high as the white.) Poor public education reduced the chances of children to break out of the ghetto or gain the powers and skills to improve it. Crime (and fear of crime among the law-abiding) was worse in the slums than elsewhere. Transportation was poor, which made it difficult to get to jobs far from home. Because of poor education, formal and informal, slum-dwellers were vulnerable to sharp business practices and other ways of exploiting the ignorant and socially weak.

Situations like this were not new in America. They had existed, for example, in Irish slums in Boston and in Italian and Jewish poor neighborhoods in New York recently enough to be remembered by thousands. But this is not to say that the black ghetto was just a latter-day version of the immigrant slum. Color identified the black ghetto inhabitant more immediately and permanently than those who lived in South Boston or the Lower East Side. European immigrants had no background of slavery. And while there certainly was prejudice against the Irish, Italians, and Jews, it was not so virulent or pervasive as anti-black feelings. America would be foolish to look to the historical record of immigrant slum-dwellers and their rise in a few generations and assume that the future holds a parallel development for the residents of black ghettos. There are many differences other than race and a background of severe oppression. The number of unskilled workers needed is smaller today. The pattern of inner-city ghetto surrounded by white suburbs—a white doughnut surrounding a black hole—is different from the nineteenth- and early twentieth-century pattern, where industry and other employment existed close to the slums. Historical analogies are tricky; the history of the European migrants may or may not be repeated by the migrants from the rural South. Historical situations may recur, but history does not necessarily repeat itself.

There had been many uprisings in nineteenth-century America, particularly where the Irish were the largest immigrant group, but they had not attracted as much attention nationally as the Negro ghetto riots of the 1960's. The first really big black riot, the first one to shake the nation deeply, was in the Watts section of Los Angeles in 1965, although there had been lesser disturbances the two previous years in several other cities. In 1966 there were more riots than ever before, but none was as serious as the Watts upheaval. Then in 1967 came worse ones; the biggest riots were in Newark and Detroit, but matters were serious in Tampa, Cincinnati, Atlanta, and several cities near Newark. In the spring of 1968 there was much looting and burning in the nation's capital. The usual pattern was an "incident" between young men of the ghetto and white policemen, followed by angry reaction to the real or imagined injustice, bricks through store windows, looting, arson, police reinforcement with national guardsmen, and the gradual restoration of order. Particularly in 1967, the police and guardsmen behaved with a disdain for law and prudence that rivalled the rioters'. President Johnson in 1967 appointed a special panel on riots with Governor Otto Kerner of Illinois as chairman, and this group's *Report of the National Advisory Commission on Civil Disorders* described the disturbances and analyzed their causes cogently.

The evidence does not suggest that the riots were started by black militant organizations—although some of the farthest-out leaders tried to exploit them for ideological advantage—or that the rioting was other than spontaneous. But the riots had a profound effect upon Negro organizations even though they did not arise directly from the movement. Black revolutionists could point to the outbreaks as evidence of a revolutionary spirit in the ghetto, or at least a violent one in some circumstances, and they could argue that the excessively violent reaction of the police and guardsmen indicated that "whitey" was not susceptible to reasoned appeal and would not consent peacefully to a basic change in racial matters. The riots also appeared to move Negro moderate leaders to a more militant position.

Quite clearly, the riots polarized black and white attitudes. The "white backlash" was strong, and there were conservative demagogues ready to take advantage of it. White liberals, sensitive to being cursed with that label because they had thought it an honorable one, rarely defended the riots; they only urged that such violence be understood and that the roots of it be attacked. Those whose sense of justice and morality had been outraged by Alabama police chiefs, Mississippi sheriffs and Ku Klux murderers were less prone to give aid and sympathy. Among both Negroes and whites was a growing tendency to lump together all in the other population except for the people one knew personally. Few who yearned for justice, harmony, and peaceful relations could see grounds for optimism.

Some 1968 glimpses into the detail of American life, as revealed in newspaper stories, told a great deal about the Negro past and present. The first story, an obituary of Hartman H. Brown, born a slave in Louisiana in 1844, reminded readers not how far American Negroes had come but how recently they had been chattel slaves. The other reminded perceptive readers of the glaring inequality between Negroes and whites. The women's page of the *Washington Post* on the hundredth anniversary of the first Memorial Day, a day of mourning for those who died in the Civil War, carried a story about Mrs. Roena Rand, a Negro activist, and an illustration of Mrs. Rand distributing rubber boots to Negro children in the sticky mud of Resurrection City, site of the encampment of the Poor People's March sponsored by the Southern Christian Leadership Conference. Elsewhere on the page, in the regular "society column," were two items that contrasted with the little children in the mud. Charles Engelhard, described in the column as a "platinum king" and a "good friend" of President Johnson, had beeen unable to attend a pre-Kentucky-Derby party in Lexington, Kentucky, and, to make amends, had sent "the world's most expensive 50-pound can of caviar" by his own jet plane. The other item began with the observation, "The rich have such fun with their money." The story continued: "Mrs. Clint Murchison, Jr. of Texas was at the White House earlier this week, fluttering a life-size jeweled butterfly on her index finger. The exotic coloration on the wings was achieved . . . with diamonds and emeralds and rubies and sapphires. Mrs. Murchison has two other rings to match—one for the big toe of each foot."

The Winds of Change Blow Harder

Hard and abundant evidence that social change in America accelerated its pace in the 1960's is difficult to find, statistics in such matters being what they are. And there is a tendency for each generation—an admittedly imprecise term in the social sense—to magnify the differences between it and succeeding ones. Nevertheless, in the 1960's there was overwhelming agreement that social evolution was speeding up; that change was coming more rapidly than ever before in this century seemed clearly to be the case.

The pervasiveness of important and more rapid change was striking. Even from our too close vantage point it appears that in the 1960's more people changed their attitudes—their assumptions about society and their role in it, their "mind set," their tastes, and their style of life, affecting a range of activities from politics to fashion—than in most earlier comparable periods and changed them more. The "Age of Conformity," a term often used during the 1950's to

describe that decade's flavor, shifted to an age of rebelliousness and nonconformity. With hindsight one can see foreshadowings between the war and the
election of President Kennedy of some of these later developments, but few, if
any, foresaw them. Who would have thought in the era of Joseph R. McCarthy
that the Communist party in the next few years would be regarded as stodgy
and old-hat by many of the New Left? Or have even foreseen the coming of
the New Left? When Francis Cardinal Spellman broke a strike of New York
gravediggers in the early 1950's, would one have anticipated that in the next
decade Catholic clergymen would lead Negro marches or that Jesuit the-
ologians would publicly criticize a papal letter against birth control? The contrast between the Berkeley campus in 1949 when the Regents imposed a faculty
loyalty oath and the student upheaval of 1964, or of Columbia University when
Dwight D. Eisenhower was its president and 1968 when there were police-
student battles, illuminated the changed values and behavior of university
students. It was beyond imagination during the Korean War that there could
be a protest march on the Pentagon such as occurred in October, 1967, against
the war in Vietnam. Edmund Wilson, whose *Memoirs of Hecate County*
aroused indignation soon after the war because of its treatment of sex, must
have been bemused upon reading through some publishers' lists twenty years
later.

Many who disapproved of the new political style—demonstrations against
the war in Vietnam, civil rights marches, or campus political rebellions—saw it
as part and parcel of new tastes, fashions, and ways of living which they
equally, perhaps more vigorously, disapproved. Those who deplored the new
developments tended to assume that any young man with long hair was a
New Leftist, a marijuana-smoker, a devotee of avant garde art and music, and
sexually promiscuous. They were wrong, of course; there was no necessary
relationship between fashion and personal behavior and politics. Yet the political
activist, whether a student rebel or a black militant or something much milder,
and the cultural avant gardist and even in a way the hippie, although different
in basic and important ways, had some characteristics in common; and these
characteristics were more prevalent than they had been in the 1950's. First was
a deep dissatisfaction with American life and society or some part of it. This
dissatisfaction frequently amounted to complete rejection and refusal to compromise. Second, there was a willingness (sometimes even eagerness) to assault
in a drastic, overt way what was rejected. Rebels did not express their rejection
mildly or patiently, whether they were in art or politics, and if they were in
politics they had a special affinity for direct rather than parliamentary action.
They were ready to make strong commitments and to demonstrate their commitment with some kind of overt act, often a romantic and symbolic one. Even
the hippie expressed his rejection of the mainstream of American life overtly
and dramatically when he "dropped out" of it.

How does one explain this seemingly sudden burst of rejection and rebelliousness?

Part of the answer lies in certain liberating social conditions, and one of
the important ones was the degree of affluence among middle class people.
Poverty was a serious problem, to be sure, but it was largely in a few depressed
rural areas and in inner-city ghettos; those fortunate enough to escape poverty
had it economically better than ever before. Poverty breeds discontent, cer-

tainly, but affluence affords opportunity and security to rebel. With a good income, one can take a few days off to participate in a march or demonstration in a distant city. When the Bonus Marchers of 1932 went to Washington they rode freight cars; in the "petitions in boots" of the 1960's the participants went in chartered buses, passenger trains, and planes. Since 1941 the nation had enjoyed prosperity, and in 1967, when the nation's population reached 200 million, the median age was 27.7. That is to say, half the population was younger than that, half older. Half the population, in other words, had been born later than 1940 and could have had no personal memory of the Great Depression. Unemployment, real poverty, were no longer specters that inhibited nonconformity or rebellion. If one's act of defiance, whether it be storming the Pentagon or merely growing hair to the shoulders, should cost him his job, there was usually another if he wanted it. This was a new economic condition in industrial America. There had been nothing quite comparable since the disappearance of free or cheap land in the nineteenth century, and it is significant that the typical political protestor of the 1960's (if one excludes Negro activists and to a degree it was true among them too) was middle class and young.

Another new condition that tended to take off the brakes on dissent and protest was the thaw in the Cold War, which in several ways, some of them subtle, had inhibited and restricted political nonconformity at home. Even the vigorous battlers against McCarthy and McCarthyism, doubly scarred as they were by the Depression, were more repressed by what they fought than they realized. There was no declared armistice in the Cold War of course, and cold warriors still existed. But they were not taken so seriously as they had been even in 1960.

Thus in the next decade the lid was off for dissent and nonconformity as it had not been since the 1920's. The Depression, the all but unanimous nation during the war, and the Cold War were of a unity when viewed in this manner. There were even some similarities between the rebels of the 1960's and what Professor Henry May has called the Innocent Rebellion of the years immediately preceding World War I.

The rapid urbanization of America and the blanketing of the nation's

TABLE 17

GROSS NATIONAL PRODUCT

Year	Billions of Current Dollars
1961	520.2
1962	560.3
1963	590.5
1964	631.7
1965	681.2
1966	739.6
1967	791.2
1968 (est.)	857.0

population with television probably contributed to the new spirit as well. Cultural isolation still existed in the 1960's, of course, but a smaller part of the population lived in isolated backwaters than ever before in the nation's history. The urban drift partially drained the backwaters of people, and mass communications shrank their size. Not to suggest that the rebelliousness of the 1960's was only a fad, but it is revealing how much quicker fads spread, flourished, and died away under the saturation of the country with mass communications.

But a mere lessening of restraints would not alone bring about an unrest as wide and deep as existed in 1968. In the summer of that year a political novelist, Fletcher Knebel, wrote in a mass circulation magazine that "social revolution in this country is no longer a probability. It is a fact. Like it or not, our society and our values are being battered by a storm of dissent." He wrote that it was entirely possible there would be "a convulsion to rival the excesses of the French Revolution." There had to be powerful engines impelling people toward such a level of dissent and rebelliousness. The main force was moral indignation, and the targets of it were injustice and inequality for the Negro and the war in Vietnam. Concern about the impersonality and anonymity of inhumanly scaled institutions such as government bureaus, corporations, and universities abounded. Indeed, cliché collectors noted the prevalence of *faceless* and *alienation*. But it was the plight of black Americans and the war that provided the main impulse.

Facing the 1970's

In some years the maneuvering for presidential nominations, the campaigns, and the elections become the vital focus of many public questions more important than the ever present personal struggles for political power. Such a year was 1968, when, particularly in the early stages of the complicated process of presidential selection, excitement surrounded the election as it had not since 1948, perhaps 1912.

In November, 1967, Senator Eugene McCarthy of Minnesota—not related either by family or principle to the late Senator Joseph R. McCarthy of Wisconsin—announced he would seek the presidential nomination of the Democratic party. McCarthy, a soft-spoken and rather self-effacing former instructor of sociology and economics at St. Thomas College in Minnesota, had been elected to the House in 1948, where he remained until elected to the Senate ten years later. A Dove, McCarthy made the war in Vietnam his main issue, at first hardly considering other issues except to point out that war spending precluded a real attack on matters such as the urban crisis and the black revolt. When he announced his candidacy, he vowed to stay in the nomination fight until the end. The first reaction to his candidacy—he was not widely known nationally—was that the Minnesota Senator was an admirable person but a kind of Don Quixote who had no chance of dislodging Lyndon Johnson.

The first of the presidential primaries, New Hampshire's, was on March 12, about five weeks after the vexing news of the Tet offensive. McCarthy surprised the country by receiving 42 per cent of the vote and winning a majority of the state's delegates to the Democratic national convention. He looked less like Don Quixote when the votes were counted; it was clear that Dove sentiment was a political force of major dimensions. Until the New Hampshire primary Robert F. Kennedy of New York (he had moved from Massachusetts and been elected to the Senate in 1964) had hung back from an electoral challenge of Johnson. Kennedy's presidential aspirations were evident, and it appeared until New Hampshire that to challenge Johnson for the nomination was a sure way to block the road to the White House forever. McCarthy, on the other hand, was not taken seriously as a presidential prospect—he was a protest, anti-Johnson, anti-Vietnam candidate—until New Hampshire and later primaries. Senator Kennedy declared himself a contender for the nomination on March 16, and the contest for the nomination took on a different character.

Robert F. Kennedy, eight years the junior of the late President, was not a man who evoked a mild or neutral response; people either liked him or disliked him immensely. Kennedy and McCarthy did not disagree in any important particular in their Dove positions, and they were in general agreement on domestic issues as well, although Kennedy had greater sensitivity for and familiarity with the problems of cities and the Negro. Certainly he was far more popular than McCarthy in the ghetto. Some who liked Kennedy better than McCarthy, or thought he had a better chance of getting the nomination, switched from McCarthy to Kennedy, but probably most of the Kennedy support came from elsewhere. Kennedy's disadvantages were his reputation for political ruthlessness and the fact that he had not challenged Johnson until McCarthy had shown a challenger had a chance. But it appeared to be only a chance. On March 24, a week after Kennedy's announcement, the *New York Times* published a survey which indicated that Johnson would have the support of 1,725 convention delegates; to win the nomination one needed 1,312.

President Johnson thoroughly surprised the world and changed the entire nature of the contest when on March 31 he told a national television audience that he would not seek renomination, that he was restricting bombing of North Vietnam to an area slightly north of the seventeenth parallel that excluded Hanoi, and that he hoped this action would result in peace talks with North Vietnam. (Exploratory talks, which gave every indication of becoming long and difficult, began at Paris in May.) Weeks after Johnson's withdrawal it became known that he had considered removing himself from the race as early as January, but the timing of his announcement in the spring radically altered the political outlook. The Vietnam issue became less important, at least in the short run, for it seemed that the Doves had won their point. On the other hand, it opened up the possibility of Republican Hawks' making the charge that the administration had "lost" the war. And the President's withdrawal temporarily took a lot of wind out of McCarthy's and Kennedy's sails.

Then, on the Thursday night following Johnson's Sunday night withdrawal, Dr. Martin Luther King, Jr. was killed by an assassin in Memphis. Weeks later the suspected killer was apprehended in London. King's murder brought about a crisis in the civil rights movement—the Washington riots followed almost immediately—and strengthened the position of black militants who rejected non-violence. Dr. King was the main advocate and symbol of non-violence, and he had been killed by a violent white man. The assassination also lent the civil rights issue an unusual political immediacy.

After the funeral of King and too late to enter any presidential primaries, Vice-President Hurbert H. Humphrey made his anticipated declaration of candidacy. A liberal hero until he became Vice-President, Humphrey's political base had shifted a great deal in four years; by 1968 he had gained support from party conservatives north and south, while holding the affection of the AFL-CIO hierarchy. Both his main strength and his main problem was his strong identification with Johnson, whose policies he had defended loyally. According to Humphrey's and Johnson's opponents in the party, he had gone beyond the call of duty in the vigor of his support. Humphrey efficiently went about the task of collecting convention delegates, getting most of the former Johnson people, while McCarthy and Kennedy slugged it out in the primaries. Kennedy won all of them he entered against McCarthy except Oregon.

On June 4 Kennedy was shot just after he had addressed campaign workers celebrating his victory in the important California primary at an election-night affair in a Los Angeles hotel. He died the next day. A young Jordanian immigrant who had been a resident of the Los Angeles area for several years was arrested immediately and subsequently indicted. The nation was in shock. Doubly disturbed because of his brother's murder in 1963 and by the King assassination just two months before, the nation suffered, besides the personal bereavement, from a sense of shame and loss of confidence in its political stability and health.

In due time, Kennedy's supporters apparently went mostly to McCarthy although some of the more prominent people in the Kennedy camp announced for Humphrey. Some urged the candidacy of the Dove Senator from South Dakota, George McGovern, a former professor of history who announced his availability in August. McCarthy supporters proved themselves a majority in the New York primaries on June 18.

The national political climate in late spring of 1968 was not quite like any there had been before. In less than three months, a relatively obscure Senator had demonstrated that what Johnson had contemptuously called "Nervous Nellies" were strong in the party, the President had appeared to admit defeat and reversed himself on the Vietnam issue, and two prominent and widely-loved political figures had been killed. Contemporaneously, Columbia University students turned a campus into a battlefield, other American universities had student upheavals not so serious, and French students triggered an abortive revolution. President Johnson's consensus of 1964–1965 had frayed out to a national convulsion.

The Republicans' story had little of the Democrats' drama. Richard M. Nixon, who had appeared at the end of his political career when he lost the 1962 gubernatorial election and had moved to New York, began his drive for the nomination early, and quickly became the front-runner. Governor George Romney of Michigan, after an intense but unsuccessful effort in early 1968, withdrew his candidacy. Governor Nelson A. Rockefeller of New York called a press conference in March, presumably to throw his hat in the ring, changed his mind at the last minute and announced he was not a candidate, and then changed his mind again and made a tremendous bid for the nomination in the late spring and summer. Governor Ronald Reagan of California, the favorite of the Goldwater wing, continued to woo delegates while he professed not to be an aspirant. Going into the convention in early August, Nixon had a plurality of delegates, but Rockefeller was ahead in the public opinion polls. The Republican national convention, meeting in Miami Beach, after adopting a platform that attempted to straddle controversy—one commentator said, "Lincoln or Hitler could both have run on it"—nominated Nixon on the first ballot. Rockefeller was a poor second and Reagan was third. Nixon, after in effect giving southern party leaders a veto in the matter, chose Maryland Governor Spiro T. Agnew as his running-mate.

One of the unusual features of the political struggle was the third-party candidacy of former Governor George C. Wallace. The Alabaman took a frankly right-wing position, promising that if he were President he would shoot looters in ghetto riots and "crease the skulls" of student rebels. A clever demagogue, he demonstrated surprising strength in northern states in the polls, and many observers conceded him several southern electoral votes. His strategy was to win enough electoral votes to prevent either major party nominee from gaining a majority, thereby throwing the election into the House of Representatives (as provided by Article II, Section 1 and Amendment XII of the Constitution) as had been the case in 1824. Governor Wallace did not have a national convention for his American Independent party, and he waited until late in the campaign before he named Curtis E. LeMay, a retired Hawkish Air Force general from Ohio, to the second place on the ticket.

The Democratic convention at Chicago in late August embittered an already badly divided party. Vice President Humphrey won the nomination on the first ballot, but other events at Chicago left such a bad taste with many normally Democratic voters that his victory seemed Pyrrhic. Millions of television viewers saw the Democrats berate each other on the war, on procedures within the convention, and, most of all, on the subject of the extraordinary display of force which Chicago police, with the approval of Mayor Richard J. Daley, used against the young antiwar and anti-Humphrey protesters who thronged the city's streets and parks. Humphrey began his campaign with the double disadvantage of identification with LBJ and Mayor Daley.

The hopes, enthusiasm, and excitement which had characterized the presidential contest until Kennedy's murder was sadly lacking in the campaign except among Wallace partisans, whose emotionalism ran wild when Wallace, in what came to be known as "the speech," lashed out at radical youths, "pseudo-intellectuals," and "pointy-heads." Many citizens, perhaps most, chose the man they regarded as the least objectionable candidate from an unattractive lot. Of the major party candidates, only Humphrey's running mate, Senator Edmund S. Muskie of Maine, appeared to grow in national reputation and popularity. The polls showed Nixon and Agnew comfortably ahead until the closing days of the campaign, when they indicated Humphrey was gaining rapidly. The President's announcement, a week before election day, of a halt in the bombing of North Vietnam and widened peace talks at Paris did not appear to have much to do with Humphrey's late rally because by then every presidential candidate had tried to identify himself with peace.

The presidential vote was unusually close. Nixon polled only about a third of a million plurality over Humphrey in a total vote of over 71 million. Humphrey conceded defeat about noon of the day after election, but the final count, even in the electoral college, remained in doubt for several days. No one received a clear mandate. Nixon received slightly over 43 per cent, Humphrey slightly under 43 per cent, and Wallace about 13.5 per cent of the popular vote. Nixon failed to get a majority of the popular vote by the largest margin since the last major three-cornered race when Wilson won in 1912. (However, there had been three subsequent Presidents who failed to receive a majority: Wilson again in 1916, Truman in 1948, and Kennedy in 1960, all of whom polled a shade less than 50 per cent of the popular vote.) Nixon's party also failed to win a majority of seats in either house of Congress, although the likelihood of continued regional and ideological divisions among its congressional Democratic opponents gave Republicans some hope for reasonable relations between White House and Capitol Hill.

SUGGESTIONS FOR
ADDITIONAL READING

This list of titles is not comprehensive. It is designed for the student and teacher in planning a program of "outside reading." For the historical researcher it is no more than a place to begin. I have tried to include titles my students have found useful over the years and upon which I relied in the preparation of this volume. For more extensive bibliographies the student should consult Oscar Handlin *et al.*, *Harvard Guide to American History* (1955) and bibliographies and footnotes in the books cited here.

When a title is available in a paperback edition it is followed by an asterisk (*). However, new paperback editions appear constantly and old ones become difficult to find.

CHAPTER 21. DEPRESSION DIPLOMACY, 1929–1938

For foreign affairs in the Hoover administration, particularly the Manchurian affair, see Sara Smith, *The Manchurian Crisis, 1931–1932* (1948); Reginald Bassett, *Democracy and Foreign Policy: The Sino-Japanese Dispute, 1931–1933* (1952); Robert Langer, *Seizure of Territory: The Stimson Doctrine* (1947); Henry Stimson and McGeorge Bundy, *On Active Service in Peace and War* (1948); Richard N. Current, *Secretary Stimson* (1954), critical of Stimson; Elting E. Morison, *Turmoil and Tradition: A Study of the Life and Times of Henry L. Stimson* (1960), a defense of Stimson; Armin Rappaport, *Henry L. Stimson and Japan, 1931–1933* (1963); Robert Ferrell, *American Diplomacy in the Great Depression* (1957); Alexander De Conde, *Herbert Hoover's Latin American Policy* (1951); and W. S. Myers, *The Foreign Policies of Herbert Hoover* (1940).

On foreign economic policy under FDR, see Lloyd C. Gardner, *Economic Aspects of New Deal Diplomacy* (1964); Seymour Harris, *The Economics of Social Security* (1941); Herbert Feis, *The Changing Pattern of International Economic Affairs* (1940); Raymond L. Buell, *The Hull Trade Program* (1938); and Jeannette P. Nichols, "Roosevelt's Monetary Diplomacy in 1933," *American Historical Review*, LVI (1951).

Allan Nevins, *The New Deal and World Affairs* (1950) provides a quick survey. Herbert Feis, *The Spanish Story: Franco and the Nations at War* (1948) and F. Jay Taylor, *The United States and the Spanish Civil War, 1936–1939* (1956); Grayson L. Kirk, *Philippine Independence* (1936) for that subject and Edward O. Guerrant, *Roosevelt's Good Neighbor Policy* (1950); Bryce Wood, *The Making of the Good Neighbor Policy* (1961); Howard F. Cline, *United States and Mexico* (1953); and E. David Cronon, *Josephus Daniels in Mexico* (1960) for New Deal

Latin American policy. For the recognition of Russia, see William Appleman Williams, *American-Russian Relations, 1781–1947* (1952) and Robert P. Browder, *Origins of Soviet-American Diplomacy* (1953). See also Manny T. Koginos, *The Panay Incident* (1967).

For neutrality legislation, see Edwin Borchard and William P. Lage, *Neutrality for the United States* (1937) and James M. Seavy, *Neutrality Legislation* (1939). Thomas A. Bailey, *The Man in the Street* (1948), a study of public opinion and foreign policy, treats the neutrality sentiment. See, also, Elton Atwater, *American Regulation of Arms Exports* (1941). William E. Dodd, Jr. and Martha Dodd, eds., *Ambassador Dodd's Diary, 1933–1938* (1941) is the document of the American ambassador to Berlin in the early Hitler days.

CHAPTER 22. AND THE WAR CAME

The most comprehensive general works on United States involvement in World War II are William L. Langer and S. Everett Gleason, *The Challenge to Isolation, 1937–1940* (1952) and *The Undeclared War, 1940–1941* (1953). Langer and Gleason generally support FDR's policies but are critical at times. Other general works are Department of State, *Peace and War: United States Foreign Policy, 1931–1941* (1943); Forrest Davis and Ernest K. Lindley, *How War Came, an American White Paper: From the Fall of France to Pearl Harbor* (1942); Selig Adler, *The Isolationist Impulse* (1957)*; and Alexander De Conde, ed., *Isolation and Security: Ideas and Interests in Twentieth-Century American Foreign Policy* (1957). Wayne S. Cole, *America First, The Battle against Intervention, 1940–1941* (1951) and Walter Johnson, *The Battle against Isolation* (1944), on the Committee to Defend America by Aiding the Allies, provide good accounts of the great foreign policy debate. Hans L. Trefousse, *Germany and American Neutrality, 1939–1941* (1951) is a worthwhile special study.

For relations with Japan before the war, see P. W. Schroeder, *The Axis Alliance and Japanese-American Relations, 1941* (1958); Harold S. Quigley, *Far Eastern War, 1937–1941* (1942); Herbert Feis. *The Road to Pearl Harbor* (1950); W. C. Johnstone, *The United States and Japan's New Order* (1941); and C. A. Buss, *War and Diplomacy in Eastern Asia* (1941). For the attack on Pearl Harbor, see Walter Millis, *This Is Pearl!* (1947) and Walter Lord, *Day of Infamy* (1957),* a popular account.

There is a considerable body of historical literature critical of American entry into the war; its writers are usually called "revisionists." Basic to an understanding of some of the revisionists is Charles A. Beard, *The Open Door at Home* (1935). Beard also wrote the best of the revisionist histories, *American Foreign Policy in the Making, 1932–1940* (1946), and *President Roosevelt and the Coming of the War, 1941* (1948). Basil Rauch prepared a reply to Beard in *Roosevelt, from Munich to Pearl Harbor* (1950). Less judicious than Beard are these revisionists volumes: Frederick R. Sanborn, *Design for War: A Study of Secret Power Politics, 1937–1941* (1951); Charles C. Tansill, *Backdoor to War* (1952); and George E. Morgenstern, *Pearl Harbor: The Secret History of the War* (1947). Harry Elmer Barnes, ed., *Perpetual War for Perpetual Peace* (1953) contains some shrill criticisms.

Among the relevant memoirs are Cordell Hull, *Memoirs* (2 vols., 1948); Joseph E. Davies, *Mission to Moscow* (1941); Joseph C. Grew, *Ten Years in Japan* (1944) and *Turbulent Era, A Diplomatic Record of Forty Years* (2 vols., 1952).

CHAPTER 23. MOBILIZING FOR VICTORY

Historians have not made as much effort to write of events at home during World War II as of the conflict itself, and, therefore, the bibliography is not satisfactory. No single satisfactory book on World War II America exists. However, see Jack Goodman, ed., *While You Were Gone: A Report on Wartime Life in the United States* (1946), which has some good chapters, and William Kenney, *The Crucial Years, 1940–1945* (1962),* sometimes entertaining but superficial.

On industrial mobilization, see Eliot Janeway, *The Struggle for Survival* (1951); Bruce Catton, *The War Lords of Washington* (1951), critical of the role of big business; Donald M. Nelson, *Arsenal of Democracy* (1946), the story as the WPB administrator saw it; Edward R. Stettinius, Jr., *Lend-Lease, Weapon of Victory* (1944); Civilian Production Administration, *Industrial Mobilization for War, 1940–1945* (1947); R. H. Connery, *The Navy and Industrial Mobilization in World War II* (1951); Frederic C. Lane *et al., Ships for Victory* (1951); and Henry A. Toulmin, Jr., *Diary of Democracy: The Senate War Investigating Committee* (1947). On other aspects of the wartime economy, see Seymour E. Harris, *Economics of America at War* (1943); Randolph E. Paul, *Taxation for Prosperity* (1947); W. A. Nielander, *Wartime Food Rationing in the United States* (1947); Marshall Clinard, *Black Market* (1952); John K. Galbraith, *Theory of Price Control* (1952); Harvey C. Mansfield *et al., A Short History of OPA* (1948); Seymour E. Harris, *Inflation and the American Economy* (1945); and L. V. Chandler, *Inflation in the United States* (1950).

Roland Young, *Congressional Politics in the Second World War* (1955); Jonathan Daniels, *Frontier on the Potomac* (1946); and Joseph Gaer, *First Round: The CIO Political Action Committee* (1944) are useful for wartime politics. For sociological studies, see William F. Ogburn, ed., *American Society in Wartime* (1943); Reuben Hill, *Families under Stress* (1949); and Francis E. Merrill, *Social Problems on the Home Front* (1948). For the war's effects on farmers, laborers, and scientists, see Walter W. Wilcox, *The Farmer in the Second World War* (1947); Joel Seidman, *American Labor from Defense to Reconversion* (1953); Fred Witney, *Wartime Experiences of the National Labor Relations Board* (1949); and James P. Baxter, III, *Scientists against Time* (1946).

On civil liberties during World War II, see Edward S. Corwin, *Total War and the Constitution* (1947); Carey McWilliams, *Prejudice: Japanese-Americans, Symbol of Racial Intolerance* (1944); Dorothy S. Thomas and R. S. Nichimoto, *The Spoilage* (1946) and Thomas *et al., The Salvage* (1952); Morton Grodzins, *Americans Betrayed* (1949); Jacobus ten Broek *et al., Prejudice, War and the Constitution: Japanese-American Evacuation and Resettlement* (1958); Mulford Q. Sibley and P. E. Jacob, *Conscription of Conscience: The Conscientious Objector, 1940–1947* (1952); and David R. Manwaring, *Render unto Caesar: The Flag-Salute Controversy* (1962).

CHAPTER 24. FIGHTING FOR VICTORY

The problem for the general reader about World War II is one of selection. The reader only casually interested in military history may be satisfied with the appropriate chapters of a military history of the United States such as R. Ernest Dupuy and Trevor N. Dupuy, *Military Heritage of America* (1956). The informed citizen should be familiar with the history of military policy. Walter Millis, *Arms and Men* (1956)* is a provocative essay on the subject. Millis extends his range much wider than World War II. Roger W. Shugg and Harvey A. DeWeerd, *World War II* (1946) and Fletcher Pratt, *War for the World* (1950) are brief histories of the war, the latter popularly written. *General Marshall's Report: The Winning of the War in Europe and the Pacific* (1945) is useful. Winston S. Churchill's blend of memoir and history in his several volumes are informative and superbly written: *The Grand Alliance* (1950)*; *The Hinge of Fate* (1950)*; *Closing the Ring* (1951)*; and *Triumph and Tragedy* (1953).* A. Russell Buchanan, *The United States and World War II* (2 vols., 1964)* is a first-rate work.

There is an abundance of more specialized works. The Office of the Chief of Military History, United States Army, has brought forth a huge list of books, of which Louis Morton, *The Fall of the Philippines* (1953), a model of military history, indicates the scale of the series' volumes. Samuel Eliot Morison has produced fourteen volumes about the *History of United States Naval Operations in World War II* (1947–1961). Wesley F. Craven and James L. Cate, eds., *The Army Air Forces in World War II* (6 vols., 1948–1955) is an official publication. Among the other worthwhile military studies are Chester Wilmot, *The Struggle for Europe* (1952); Walter Millis, ed., *The War Reports* (1947); Jeter A. Isley and Philip A. Crowl, *The U.S. Marines and Amphibious War* (1951); Hanson W. Baldwin, *Great Mistakes of the War* (1950); S. L. A. Marshall, *Bastogne: The First Eight Days* (1946); Charles A. Willoughby and John Chamberlain, *MacArthur, 1941–1951* (1954); S. McKee Rosen, *Combined Boards of the Second World War* (1951); Samuel A. Stouffer *et al.*, *The American Soldier* (2 vol., 1949), a sociological study of the fighting man; James A. Field, *The Japanese at Leyte Gulf* (1947); and Ken Hechler, *The Bridge at Remagen* (1957).*

Among the more important memoirs are Dwight D. Eisenhower, *Crusade in Europe* (1948); William F. Halsey, *Admiral Halsey's Story* (1947); George S. Patton, *War As I Knew It* (1947); Jonathan M. Wainwright, *General Wainwright's Story* (1946); Harry C. Butcher, *My Three Years with Eisenhower* (1949); Theodore H. White, ed., *The Stilwell Papers* (1948); Henry Stimson and McGeorge Bundy, *On Active Service in Peace and War* (1948); Clair L. Chennault, *Way of a Fighter* (1949); H. H. Arnold, *Global Mission* (1949); Mark W. Clark, *Calculated Risk* (1952); William D. Leahy, *I Was There* (1950); Toshikazu Kase, *Journey to the Missouri* (1950); Omar N. Bradley, *A Soldier's Story* (1951); and Robert L. Eichelberger and M. Mackaye, *Our Jungle Road to Tokyo* (1950).

On wartime diplomacy, see Robert E. Sherwood, *Roosevelt and Hopkins* (1948);* Herbert Feis, *Churchill, Roosevelt, and Stalin* (1957) and *Japan Subdued* (1961); William L. Langer, *Our Vichy Gamble* (1957); Robert J. C. Butow, *Japan's Decision to Surrender* (1954); R. F. Fenno, Jr., ed., *The Yalta Conference* (1953); John L. Snell, ed., *The Meaning of Yalta* (1956); Felix Winner, *The Yalta Betrayal* (1953); Edward R. Stettinius, *Roosevelt and the Russians: The Yalta Conference* (1949); Sumner Welles, *Seven Decisions that Shaped History* (1951); and Carlton J. H. Hayes, *Wartime Mission to Spain, 1942–1945* (1945). Gar Alperovitz, *Atomic Diplomacy: Hiroshima and Potsdam* (1965) is provocative and important.

CHAPTER 25. THE TRUMAN ERA: FOREIGN AND DOMESTIC COLD WAR

Scholarly historical studies of postwar America are still relatively scarce, and the student is forced to resort to memoirs and contemporary journalistic accounts. Eric F. Goldman, *The Crucial Decade—and After: America, 1945–1960* (1960)* and Herbert Agar, *The Price of Power: America since 1945* (1957)* are two early efforts to write a general history of postwar America. Goldman's is far better than Agar's. Frederick Lewis Allen in *The Big Change: America Transforms Itself, 1900–1950* (1952) contrasts conditions at the beginning and the middle of the century.

On the Truman administration, see Truman's memoirs, *Year of Decisions* (1955) and *Years of Trial and Hope* (1956); Morris B. Schnapper, ed., *The Truman Program* (1949), a collection of the President's speeches; Louis W. Koenig, ed., *The Truman Administration* (1956); Jonathan Daniels, *The Man of Independence* (1950), not satisfactory but the best Truman biography published thus far; Walter Millis, ed., *The Forrestal Diaries* (1951); Arthur E. Vandenberg, Jr., ed., *The Private Papers of Senator Vandenberg* (1952); William S. White, *The Taft Story* (1954), a rudimentary book on the Ohio Senator who deserves better treatment; Robert S. Allen and William V. Shannon, *The Truman Merry-Go-Round* (1950), a critical journalistic treatment; and C. Herman Pritchett, *Civil Liberties and the Vinson Court* (1954), a scholarly work. Samuel Lubell, *The Future of American Politics* (1952)* is useful for postwar politics, but at many points the reader would do well to keep his critical powers sharp. See also, Samuel Lubell, *The Revolt of the Moderates* (1956). For the 1948 election, see Lindsay Rogers, *The Pollsters* (1949), an acid comment on the subject, and for the Wallace movement, see Karl M. Schmidt, *Henry A. Wallace: Quixotic Crusade, 1948* (1960) and David A. Shannon, *The Decline of American Communism: A History of the Communist Party of the United States since 1945* (1959). On corruption and political pressure, see Paul H. Douglas, *Ethics in Government* (1952); Blair Bolles, *How To Get Rich in Washington* (1952); H. Hubert Wilson, *Congress: Corruption and Compromise* (1951); and Karl Schriftgiesser, *The Lobbyists* (1951).

Many writers have examined aspects of the postwar red scare and its relationship to civil liberties. See C. Herman Pritchett, *Civil Liberties and the Vinson Court* (1954); Robert K. Carr, *The House Committee on Un-American Activities, 1945–1950* (1952), a careful and scholarly study; Clair Wilcox, ed., *Civil Liberties under Attack* (1951); Alan Barth, *The Loyalty of Free Men* (1951); Max Lowenthal, *The Federal Bureau of Investigation* (1950), critical; Donald S. Whitehead, *The FBI Story: A Report to the People* (1956),* quite favorable; Walter Gellhorn, *Security, Loyalty, and Science* (1950) and *The States and Subversion* (1952); John W. Caughey, *In Clear and Present Danger* (1958); and James A. Wechsler, *The Age of Suspicion* (1953). On the Hiss case, see Allistair Cooke, *A Generation on Trial* (1950); William A. J. Jowitt, *The Strange Case of Alger Hiss* (1953); Whittaker Chambers, *Witness* (1952); and Alger Hiss, *In the Court of Public Opinion* (1957). On McCarthy, see Richard H. Rovere, *Senator Joe McCarthy* (1959); Wisconsin Citizens Committee, *The McCarthy Record* (1952); Jack Anderson and R. W. May, *McCarthy, The Man and the Ism* (1952); Joseph R. McCarthy, *McCarthyism, The Fight for America* (1952); William F. Buckley, Jr., and L. Brent, *McCarthy and his Enemies* (1954); and Michael Straight, *Trial by Television* (1954). Michael

SUGGESTIONS FOR ADDITIONAL READING

Rogin, *McCarthy and the Intellectuals* (1967) is an important argument against the theory that McCarthyism was Populism and progressivism turned sour.

There is no end to the writing of books about foreign policy. For a concise general history of world affairs since World War II, see Hans W. Gatzke, *The Present in Perspective: A Look at the World since 1945* (1961).* Three brief general accounts of American policy are William G. Carleton, *The Revolution in American Foreign Policy* (1957)*; John W. Spanier, *American Foreign Policy since World War II* (1960)*; and Norman A. Graebner, *Cold War Diplomacy, 1945–1960* (1962).* which contains documents. See, also, Graebner, *The New Isolationism* (1956). Denna F. Fleming, *The Cold War and Its Origins, 1917–1960* (1961) is a huge, thorough, and critical work.

Among the special studies are Leften S. Stavrianos, *Greece: American Dilemma and Opportunity* (1952); Seymour E. Harris, *The European Recovery Program* (1954); Theodore H. White, *Fire in the Ashes* (1953); Robert E. Osgood, *NATO: The Entangling Alliance* (1962); Klaus Knorr, ed., *NATO and American Security* (1959); Drew Middleton, *Defense of Western Europe* (1952); and L. V. Thomas and R. N. Frye, *The United States and Turkey and Iran* (1951).

For Far Eastern relations, see Kenneth S. Latourette, *The American Record in the Far East, 1945–1951* (1953); Department of State, *United States Relations with China* (1949); Herbert Feis, *The China Tangle* (1953); Tang Tsou, *America's Failure in China, 1941–1950* (1963); Edwin O. Reischauer, *Wanted: An Asian Policy* (1955). For the Korean conflict, see Carl Barger, *The Korean Knot, A Military-Political History* (1957); John W. Spanier, *The Truman-MacArthur Controversy and the Korean War* (1959); Richard Rovere and Arthur M. Schlesinger, Jr., *The General and the President* (1951); S. L. A. Marshall, *The River and the Gauntlet* (1953); Courtney Whitney, *MacArthur: His Rendezvous with History* (1956), highly favorable; and Department of the Army, *Korea—1950* (1952).

Raymond F. Mikesell, *United States Economic Policy and International Relations* (1952); Brian Tew, *International Monetary Cooperation, 1945–1952* (1952); and Samuel Lubell. *The Revolution in World Trade and American Economic Policy* (1955) are useful places to start on the complex problems of foreign economic policy.

CHAPTER 26. THE EISENHOWER ERA: MODERATION AND BRINKMANSHIP

General histories of the Eisenhower administrations have yet to be written. For journalistic accounts, see Merlo J. Pusey, *Eisenhower the President* (1956), quite favorable; Robert J. Donovan, *Eisenhower: The Inside Story* (1956); Richard H. Rovere, *Affairs of State: The Eisenhower Years* (1956); and Marquis Childs, *Eisenhower: Captive Hero* (1958), quite critical. Arthur Larson in *A Republican Looks at his Party* (1956) has made the clearest statement of "modern Republicanism." Relevant memoirs are Richard Nixon, *Six Decisions* (1962); Lewis L. Strauss, *Men and Decisions* (1962); and Sherman Adams, *Firsthand Report: The Story of the Eisenhower Administration* (1961). See John Lord O'Brian, *National Security and Individual Freedom* (1955) and C. P. Curtis, *The Oppenheimer Case* (1955) for conflicting views of the Eisenhower policies on internal security. Walter F. Murphy, *Congress and the Court* (1962) and Carl B. Swisher, *The Supreme Court in Modern Role* (1958) deal with the Warren Court.

On the election of 1952, see Kevin McCann, *Man from Abilene* (1952), an Eisenhower campaign biography; Adlai Stevenson, *Major Campaign Speeches, 1952* (1953); Samuel Lubell, "Who Elected Eisenhower," *Saturday Evening Post*, CCXXV (January 10, 1953); and a compilation of voting statistics, Richard Scammon, *America Votes* (1956). Stevenson's *Call to Greatness* (1954) and *What I Think* (1956) are useful for the Democratic opposition and the 1956 campaign.

For foreign policy in the Eisenhower years, see the appropriate titles listed for the previous chapter and John R. Beal, *John Foster Dulles* (1956); the chapter on Dulles by Hans J. Morgenthau in Norman A. Graebner, ed., *An Uncertain Tradition: American Secretaries of State in the Twentieth Century* (1961); Roscoe Drummond and Gaston Coblenz, *Duel at the Brink* (1960); and David Wise and Thomas Ross, *The U-2 Affair* (1962), a journalistic account.

CHAPTER 27. TROUBLED AFFLUENCE

Among the worthwhile general books on America's postwar economy are George A. Steiner, *The Government's Role in Economic Life* (1953); Wassily W. Leontief, *Studies in the Structure of the American Economy* (1953); Alvin Hansen, *Economic Policy and Full Employment* (1947), *The American Economy* (1957), and *Economic Issues of the 1960's* (1960); John Kenneth Galbraith, *American Capitalism* (1952)* and *The Affluent Society* (1958), each of which excited a great deal of thought and comment. Robert Lampman, *The Share of Top Wealth-Holders in National Wealth, 1922–1956* (1962), an important work of economic analysis, demonstrates that wealth distribution is still far from equitable. The Editors of *Fortune* in *The Permanent Revolution* (1951),* *The Changing American Market* (1955),* and *America in the Sixties* (1960)* present an optimistic point of view.

On the concentration of economic power, see Federal Trade Commission, *The Merger Movement* (1948), *Interlocking Directorates* (1951), and *The Concentration of Productive Facilities* (1949); Corwin D. Edwards, *Maintaining Competition* (1949); and John Herling, *The Great Price Conspiracy: The Story of the Antitrust Violations in the Electrical Industry* (1962). David Lilienthal in *Big Business: A New Era* (1953) and Adolph A. Berle, Jr., in *The 20th Century Capitalist Revolution* (1954) present the midcentury revision of progressive ideas about economic power. Ferdinand Lundberg, *The Rich and the Super-Rich* (1968) represents the older view. Expressions of concern for the sociological and psychological effects of concentration, rather than economic effects, are William H. Whyte, *The Organization Man* (1956).* David Riesman *et al., The Lonely Crowd* (1950),* and C. Wright Mills, *White Collar* (1951).*

On labor in the postwar era, see Jack Barbash, *The Practice of Unionism* (1956); C. Wright Mills, *The New Men of Power* (1948); Harry A. Millis and Emily C. Brown, *From the Wagner Act to Taft-Hartley* (1950); Alan K. McAdams, *Power and Politics in Labor Legislation* (1960); and Clark Mollenhoff, *Tentacles of Terror: The Teamsters Defy the Government* (1959). On agriculture, see Murray Benedict and O. C. Stine, *The Agricultural Commodity Programs: Two Decades of Experience* (1956) and C. C. Taylor *et. al., Rural Life in the United States* (1949).

CHAPTER 28. THE AMERICAN PEOPLE AND THEIR CULTURE

There are many books about the Negro in postwar America. See Arnold M. Rose, *The Negro in Postwar America* (1950); Harry S. Ashmore, *The Negro and the Schools* (1954); Bucklin Moon, *The High Cost of Prejudice* (1947) and *Balance of Power, The Negro Vote* (1948); J. Saunders Redding, *On Being Negro in America* (1951); Carl T. Rowan, *South of Freedom* (1952); President's Committee on Civil Rights, *To Secure These Rights* (1947); Milton R. Konvitz, *The Constitution and Civil Rights* (1947); Robert K. Carr, *Federal Protection of Civil Rights* (1947); and C. Eric Lincoln, *The Black Muslims in America* (1962) and E. U. Essien-Udom, *Black Nationalism: A Search for Identity in America* (1962) on the Black Muslim movement. Thomas D. Clark, *The Emerging South* (1961) is a thoughtful book on the Negro as well as the South generally. Louis E. Lomax, *The Negro Revolt* (1962) is the best survey of Negro struggles from 1955 to 1962.

On postwar education, see Lawrence A. Cremin, *The Transformation of the School: Progressivism in American Education 1876–1957* (1961); James B. Conant, *Education in a Divided World* (1948) and *The American High School Today* (1959); Eli Ginzburg and Douglas W. Bray, *The Uneducated* (1953); Robert M. MacIver, *Academic Freedom in Our Time* (1955); Benjamin Fine, *Our Children Are Cheated: The Crisis in American Education* (1947); Ernest O. Melby, *American Education under Fire* (1951); Arthur E. Bestor, Jr., *Educational Wastelands* (1953); and Christopher Jencks and David Riesman, *The Academic Revolution* (1968).

On literature, see Ihab Hassan, *Radical Innocence: The Contemporary American Novel* (1961), one of the few books on really contemporary American literature; Russel B. Nye, "The Modern Quest," *The Progressive* (October, 1960); and Lionel Trilling, *The Liberal Imagination* (1953),* perhaps the most influential postwar work of literary criticism. On religion, see Ralph L. Roy, *Apostles of Discord* (1953); Conrad H. Moehlman, *The Wall of Separation between Church and State* (1951); Paul Blanshard, *American Freedom and Catholic Power* (1949); a reply to Blanshard, James M. O'Neill, *Catholicism and American Freedom* (1952); and Will Herberg, *Protestant, Catholic, Jew: An Essay in American Religious Sociology* (1955). On art, see Sam Hunter, *Modern American Painting and Sculpture* (1959); John H. Baur, ed., *New Art in America* (1957); and John Canaday, *Embattled Critic* (1962).*

CHAPTER 29. THE DEMOCRATS AGAIN

Almost all the works suggested for this and the next chapter are the products of journalists. Some of them are perceptive and reasonably objective, and some are not; they all necessarily suffer from the lack of enough time-perspective and from insufficient research in the best primary sources. James M. Burns, *John Kennedy: A Political Profile* (1960), is an unusually detached biography for a campaign year, and Earl Mazo was fair in his *Richard Nixon: A Political and Personal Portrait* (1959). Theodore H. White, *The Making of the President 1960* (1961) inaugurated his series of journalistic election histories. Helen Fuller in *Year of Trial: Kennedy's Crucial Decisions* (1962) treats JFK's first year as President. Aida DiPace Donald, ed., *John F. Kennedy and the New Frontier* (1966) is a useful collection. Arthur M. Schlesinger, Jr., *A Thousand Days: John F. Kennedy in the White House* (1965) is a comprehensive and perceptive combination of memoir and history by an adviser to Kennedy, as is Theodore Sorensen, *Kennedy* (1965). For the assassination see *Report of the President's Commission on the Assassination of President John F. Kennedy* (1964).

CHAPTER 30. CONSENSUS AND CONVULSION

Journalists were quick to write books about President Johnson. See Hugh Sidey, *A Very Personal Presidency: Lyndon Johnson in the White House* (1968); Roland Evans and Robert Novak, *Lyndon B. Johnson: The Exercise of Power* (1966); Tom Wicker, *JFK and LBJ* (1968), a perceptive comparison of the men; Alfred Steinberg, *Sam Johnson's Boy: A Close-up of the President* (1968), which is good for the Texan's earlier years; and Robert Sherrill, *The Accidental President* (1967)*, a shrill indictment. Special studies are James Deakin, *Lyndon Johnson's Credibility Gap* (1968); William McGaffin and Erwin Knoll, *Anything but the Truth* (1968); and Bruce Ladd, *Crisis in Credibility* (1968). Marvin E. Gettleman and David Mermelstein, eds., *The Great Society Reader: The Failure of American Liberalism* (1967)* is a collection of quite critical articles. For the Johnson foreign policies see Philip Geyelin, *Lyndon Johnson and the World* (1967). See also Bill Boyarsky, *The Rise of Ronald Reagan* (1968); Theodore H. White, *The Making of the President 1964* (1965); and Marshall Frady, *Wallace* (1968).

Books on the Vietnamese war abound. For the background, see Joseph Buttinger, *Vietnam: A Dragon Embattled* (2 vols., 1967), which carries the story down through France's 1954 defeat; Jules Roy, *The Battle of Dienbienphu* (1965); and Bernard B. Fall, *The Two Vietnams* (rev. ed., 1967). Frank N. Trager, *Why Vietnam?* (1966) defends the Johnson policies; there are both pro and con articles in Wesley R. Fishel, ed., *Vietnam: Anatomy of a Conflict* (1968). See also Roger Hilsman, *To Move a Nation* (1967) and Franz Schurmann, *et al*, *The Politics of Escalation in Vietnam* (1966).*

For the hippie phenomenon see Nicholas von Hoffman, *We are the People Our Parents Warned Us Against* (1968) and the title essay of Joan Didion, *Slouching Toward Bethlehem* (1968).

For the black revolt see, besides Meier and Rudwick, *From Plantation to Ghetto*, John Hope Franklin and Isidore Starr, eds., *The Negro in 20th Century America* (1967)*. The *Report of the National Advisory Commission on Civil Disorders* (1968)* is invaluable for the ghetto riots, and see John Hersey, *The Algiers Hotel Incident* (1968)*. *The Autobiography of Malcom X* (1964) is a powerful book by the late leader of the Black Muslim movement. See also C. Eric Lincoln, *The Black Muslims in America* (1961) and E. U. Essien-Udom, *Black Nationalism: A Search for Identity in America* (1962). Charles E. Silberman, *Crisis in Black and White* (1962) is a perceptive book by a first-rate magazine journalist. Talcott Parsons and Kenneth B. Clark, eds., *The Negro American* (1966) contains several important chapters. This volume appears also in the journal *Daedalus*, XCIV (fall, 1965) and XCV (winter, 1966). Dr. Martin Luther King's works include *Stride Toward Freedom* (1958) and *Why We Can't Wait* (1964). For CORE in its earlier days, see James Peck, *Freedom Ride* (1962); for SNCC, Howard Zinn, *SNCC: The New Abolitionists* (1964). Gary T. Marks, *Protest and Prejudice: A Study of Negro Attitudes* (1968) is an important book that shows the popular support for black militancy.

INDEX

689